Brother Swaggart, How Can I Understand The Bible?

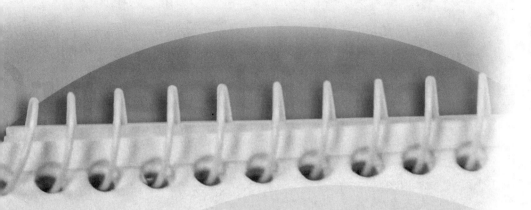

Brother Swaggart, How Can I Understand The Bible?

By Jimmy Swaggart

Jimmy Swaggart Ministries
P.O. Box 262550 • Baton Rouge, Louisiana 70826-2550
Website: www.jsm.org • Email: info@jsm.org
(225) 768-7000

TABLE OF CONTENTS

INTRODUCTION

The Word of God, the Bible, is the only revealed Truth in the world today and, in fact, ever has been. Because it is the Word of God that means it is also, by far, the most important Book, or rather a collection of Books in existence.

MAN IS INTENDED TO LIVE BY
THE WORD OF GOD

Jesus said, (Mat. 4:4). That being the case, every Believer should make the Bible a lifelong study. Inasmuch as it is the Word of God, it is absolutely inexhaustible, irrespective as to how many times one would peruse its contents.

THE MAJOR DOCTRINES
OF THE WORD OF GOD

In order to help one understand the Word of God hopefully a little better, we have addressed ourselves in this Volume to the major Doctrines of the Bible. I speak of etc. I personally believe the information given will make these Doctrines more understandable and, thereby, beneficial as the Holy Spirit desires.

In effect, the Holy Spirit is the Author of the Word of God. The Scripture says concerning this:

"**Knowing this first** *(harks back, as stated, to the Old Testament, which, in effect, was the Bible of Peter's day)*, **that no Prophecy of the Scripture is of any private interpretation.** *(This refers to the fact that the Word of God did not originate in the human mind.)*

"**For the Prophecy** *(the word 'Prophecy' is used here in a general sense, covering the entirety of the Word of God, which means it's not limited merely to predictions regarding the future)* **came not in old time by the will of man** *(did not originate with man)*: **but Holy men of God spoke** *as* *they were* **moved by the Holy Spirit.** *(This proclaims the manner in which the Word of God was written and, thereby, given unto us)*" **(II Pet. 1:20-21).**

THE EXPOSITOR'S STUDY BIBLE

In the explanations given concerning the various Doctrines addressed, we have freely used **THE EXPOSITOR'S STUDY BIBLE,** along with its notes. Of necessity, there will be some repetition.

As it regards the Bible student, I personally believe that this Volume carries the potential of adding to your knowledge of the Word of God. And, if that is the case, your study of its contents will be well worth the time spent.

PERSONAL

I gave my heart to Christ when I was 8 years of age. The Lord baptized me with the Holy Spirit a few weeks later. I began studying the Word of God at that early age, actually carrying a very small print Bible with me everywhere I went. I love the Word of God. It means more to me today than ever.

Approximately 3,000 years ago the Psalmist wrote:

"**O how I love Your Law! it is My Meditation all the day.** *(Even though all the Passages in this Psalm refer to the Messiah and His Love for God's Word, still, the Holy Spirit lifts the greater Son of David to a higher exclamation in this thirteenth chorus than all previously given. Once again, we are drawn to His constant 'Meditation.')*

"**You through Your Commandments have made Me wiser than My enemies: for they are ever with Me.** *(The pronoun 'they' refers to the 'Commandments.')*

"**I have more understanding than all My Teachers: for Your Testimonies are My Meditation.** *(Even as a young boy, Jesus knew more about the Word of God than*

His Teachers [Lk. 2:40-49].)

"I understand more than the ancients, because I keep Your Precepts. *(The claim is made, accurately so, that Christ understood more about God and His Word than even the great Patriarchs and Prophets of the past — all because of the knowledge of and the keeping of 'Your Precepts.')*

"I have refrained My Feet from every evil way, that I might keep Your Word. *(Only Christ can make such a statement!)*

"I have not departed from Your Judgments: for You have taught Me. *(In previous choruses of this One Hundred and Nineteenth Psalm, we have witnessed the petition of the Holy Spirit to serve as Teacher. We have here the exclamation that the petition was heard and granted.)*

"How sweet are Your Words unto My Taste! Yes, sweeter than honey to My Mouth! *(As in the previous Stanza, the Messiah sang of the strength of God's Word, so here he sings of its sweetness.)*

"Through your precepts I get understanding: therefore I hate every false way. *(This Stanza closes with a statement that the wisdom which flows from the Scriptures destroys all desire for false teaching.)*

"Your Word is a Lamp unto My Feet, and a Light unto My Path. *(The only 'Lamp' in the world that produces 'True Spiritual Light' is the Bible)*" **(Ps. 119:97-105).**

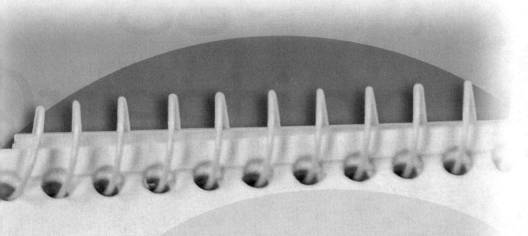

CHAPTER 1

The Doctrine Of The Bible

THE DOCTRINE OF THE BIBLE

The Bible does not merely contain the Word of God; it is, in fact, the very Word of God.

Of the translations, there are none that can equal the King James. As one of the most noted Greek Scholars of the Twentieth Century stated, *"When you hold the King James Bible in your hands, you can be certain that you are holding the very Word of God."*

But yet, we must remember, while the Word of God is inspired by the Holy Spirit, meaning that it is error-free, that does not include the translations. The King James Translation was finished in 1611; the men who did the work were some of the most able scholars in the world of that day. As many people may not know, some of them did not even claim to be Born-Again. But yet, the Lord turned this to His Favor.

These men were not trying to favor any particular interpretation of the Word, their only ambition was to get the Hebrew of the Old Testament translated into English as perfect as possible, and the same with the Greek as it regards the New Testament. And yet, the King James Translation has been revised several times since it was originally written, and rightly so.

I have a page from the very first translation of the King James. It is framed and hanging on the wall in our Administration Building. Due to the heavy Elizabethan usage of the language, it would be very difficult for most people to read it at all. So it was good that it was edited, again with the thought in mind of keeping it as close to the original Text as possible.

THE ORIGINAL MANUSCRIPTS

There are no original manuscripts of the Bible, due to antiquity. The first Books were written by Moses (Genesis, Exodus, Leviticus, Numbers, and Deuteronomy). In fact, Moses probably wrote Job before he wrote any of the Books listed above, and did so in collaboration with Job, who was alive the last years of Moses' sojourn in the desert, before leading the Children of Israel out of Egypt. If, in fact, that is the case, then Job is the oldest Book in the world.

Of course, the last Book written, which was approximately 1,600 years after Moses, was the Book of Revelation, written by John the Beloved. Incidentally, he was the last Apostle of the original Twelve to die.

Even though there are none of the original manuscripts left, and that is because of age, Scholarship states, that for any work of antiquity, if there are ten identical copies, the original is judged as genuine. There are over 10,000 copies of the Books of the Bible, or copies of part of the Books. This means that there is greater proof of the authenticity of the Bible, than any other book in the world. Probably the most recent discoveries of copies of particular Books in the Bible are the Dead Sea Scrolls.

THE DEAD SEA SCROLLS

In 1947 three Arab shepherds were tending their sheep and goats along the cliffs on the northwest coast of the Dead Sea. One of them, Juma Muhammed Khalil, threw a stone into a small hole he saw in the cliff and heard a shattering sound that raised his hopes that gold might have been stored within. Muhammad edh-Dhib, a younger companion, later returned and entered the cave. Here he found about ten elongated jars, only two of which contained anything. Three large rolls were removed from one jar and later taken to Bethlehem where the shepherds sought to sell them to antique dealers. The Bedouins found several other Scrolls and fragments there some months later. Four of the manuscripts were sold to the Syrian Orthodox Monastery in Jerusalem, and later three Scrolls were obtained by the Hebrew University. After the discovery of these first Scrolls was publicized in late 1948, a clandestine search in many caves was undertaken by the Ta'amirah Bedouins. The Antiquities Department of the Jordan took charge in 1949 and worked out an arrangement with the Bedouins that encouraged them to offer their discoveries to the officials in charge. Thus began what has proved to be the greatest recent discovery of Biblical and related materials in the Holy Land.

THE PROPHET ISAIAH

From the first cave came the complete Isaiah *"A"* Scroll, which dates from about 100 B.C., the Isaiah *"B"* Scroll, which preserves parts of Chapters 16 through 66, dates from about A.D. 50; an almost complete commentary on Habakkuk 1 and 2, copied about 40 B.C. through A.D. 25; a fragmentary Aramaic interpretation of Genesis, from about A.D. 1 through A.D. 25; and, an important document containing the rules and teachings of the religious community (probably the Essenes) that occupied the settlement of Qumran, about seven and a half miles south of Jericho. The Essenes were a sect of the Jews who believed they had been chosen by God to prepare the way for the new age to come (Isa. 40:3) by living a holy life in the wilderness away from the *"sons of darkness"* dwelling in the cities of Judah.

THE ESSENES

They sought to observe the Old Testament Law perfectly, according to the Apocalyptic interpretations by their *"teacher of righteousness."* They came to Qumran in the late Second Century B.C. and took over the ruins of an ancient fortified settlement built during the Ninth and Eighth Centuries B.C. by the Hebrews and destroyed in the Sixth Century B.C. Here the Essenes lived, farmed, wrote down their beliefs and rules, composed interpretations, and made copies of the Old Testament.

In periods of religious and civil tension among the Jews, their adherents apparently grew in number. The group at Qumran was evidently the largest, but the Essenes' followers seem to have been scattered widely. They'd rendered a great service in their devotion to the copying of the Scriptures. During the

First Century A.D. they were victims of the political disorder between the Romans and Jews and were forced to abandon their settlement in A.D. 68 when the Roman army attacked the revolting Jews in Jerusalem. Before leaving, the Essenes hid their sacred documents in tightly sealed jars in the nearby cliffs. Qumran was occupied by the tenth legion of the Roman army for a few years and again during the Bar Kokhba rebellion of A.D. 132 through A.D. 135. Evidently some of the caves had been entered, jars broken, the contents scattered, and some manuscripts removed during the centuries since. From 1951 through 1958 the site was excavated, and its complex of buildings proved to be an Essene settlement.

MANUSCRIPTS

From 1952 through 1956 ten other caves with related materials were discovered. In addition, five caves in Wadi Murrabbaat produced materials from the revolt of A.D. 132. The latter was twelve miles south of Qumran. More than 250 caves in the area have been carefully examined by archaeologists. In the nearby caves IV and XI, more than 40,000 fragments of manuscripts have been found. Almost 400 manuscripts of varying sizes from Qumran cave IV alone have been identified since 1956. Of a total of almost 600 manuscripts from the eleven Qumran caves about 125 are Biblical. Every Book of the Old Testament is represented except Esther, but only Isaiah *"A"* is complete.

In cave XI a manuscript, copied about A.D. 50, containing 37 Psalms was found and has since been translated and published. Included in this collection is the 151st Psalm, previously known only from the Greek. A Scroll of Ezekiel from cave XI was so disintegrated that it is a complete loss. In the same cave a copy of the Targum of Job was found (paraphrased in Aramaic), two-fifths of which is readable. It was translated in 1962; scholars set its date as A.D. 50. Also during 1962, in a monastery in Spain, a copy of the Palestinian Targum was recovered and it is believed to date from as early as A.D. 50.

These discoveries have reopened the study of the history of the Targums, indicating an earlier origin than was previously thought. Thus, the study of the Essene writings found in the various caves not only greatly expands our knowledge of sectarian Judaism in the New Testament period, but also verifies the historical accounts left by Philo and Josephus concerning the Essenes, their practices, history, and doctrines.

(Incidentally, a *"Targum"* was an Aramaic paraphrase of the Old Testament, which in later Judaism was often used to accompany the reading of the Hebrew original in the Synagogues. In fact, it was probably similar to *"THE EXPOSITOR'S STUDY BIBLE"*.)

WORD-FOR-WORD TRANSLATION

Our present society is being flooded with so-called translations which are really interpretations or thought for thought translations, such as the Message Bible. Actually, these types of efforts cannot even be construed as Bibles. At best they are religious books.

The only translation that can be concluded as the Word of God is a word-for-word translation, such as the King James. There are one or two other word-for-word translations; however, with these I am not familiar. But yet there are several other things that need to be said about the King James Translation.

THE KING JAMES TRANSLATION

As we have already mentioned, the King James Translation, despite being edited several times, still contains a fairly liberal usage of Elizabethan English. To all King James devotees, and I am one, it must be understood, that the Prophets and the Apostles who were used by the Spirit of God to write the Sacred Text, did not speak Elizabethan English. As well, when Matthew, Mark, Luke, and John, were originally written, the Words of Christ were not in red. These particular words in red are actually a marketing tool that was not used until the Twentieth Century. And again we emphasize, while the original manuscripts were most definitely inspired by the Holy Spirit and, thereby, error-free, doesn't mean that the translation is error-free. No translation was inspired by the Holy Spirit, and none to my knowledge were claimed to be.

A CHRONOLOGY OF BIBLE TRANSLATION

The following chronology includes events of major importance in the long and dramatic story of Bible translation. The list is necessarily selective and places special emphasis on the background of the English Bible, providing information basic to further study of a fascinating field.

1500 B.C. through 500? B.C. — The Old Testament is put into writing.

250 B.C. through 100 B.C. — The Septuagint, a translation of the Old Testament into Greek, according to tradition, by 72 Hebrew scholars, was completed in Alexandria, Egypt. This version contains 45 Books, the Alexandrian Canon, used by the Early Church, and continues to be the Old Testament Canon of the Latin and Greek Church.

A.D. 52? through A.D. 100? — The New Testament is written, coming to us in Koine (common) Greek, the common language of the time, although some portions may have been first set down in Aramaic, the language spoken by Christ.

A.D. 100? — Formulation of Palestinian Canon of Hebrew Bible at Synod of Jamnia.

350 through 400 — First stabilization of New Testament Canon of 27 Books.

About 400 — Jerome completes his final translation of the Bible, the Latin Vulgate, based on the Septuagint and translated from the Hebrew, and other ancient versions.

About 600 through 900 — The Masoretic Text in Hebrew is developed by the Masoretes, a school of Jewish textual critics. The Masoretic Text, used in the Jewish Bible, has been an important reference in preparing translations into other languages.

1382 — John Wycliffe completes his translation, the first complete Bible in English.

1456 — The Gutenberg Bible, a folio edition of the Latin Vulgate, is printed from moveable type, an epochal event that inaugurated the era of printing.

1516 — Erasmus completes his translation in Greek.

1522 — Martin Luther translates the Bible into German.

1535 — William Tyndale issues his English translation, which powerfully influenced all of the English versions that followed.

1535 — Miles Coverdale issues his translation dedicated to King Henry VIII.

1537 — Coverdale's Bible becomes the first Bible to be printed in England.

1537 — Matthew's Bible is produced, based primarily on the Tyndale and Coverdale Bibles.

1539 — Coverdale issues the Great Bible, essentially a combination of his own earlier work and Tyndale's Bible. This work was authorized by Henry VIII.

1560 — The Geneva Bible, produced by Coverdale, William Whittingham, John Knox, and others in Geneva after Mary became queen. It is the first English Bible to divide the Chapters into Verses.

1582 through 1610 — Douay-Rheims (Catholic) Bible appears, a direct translation into English from the Vulgate by the Catholic College; the New Testament issued at Rheims, the Old Testament in 1609 and 1610 at Douay, France.

1611 — The great King James (or Authorized) Version. Completed by the group of *"learned men,"* all renowned scholars, appointed by King James.

While there have been other translations from then until now, the King James is concluded by many scholars to be closer to the original text than any other effort. Down through the last several centuries, it, by far, has been the most widely used and widely known.

THE CANON OF SCRIPTURE

At the end of the First Christian Century, the Jewish Rabbis, at the Counsel of Gamnia, closed the Canon of Hebrew Books — these Books considered as authoritative by the Jews. Their decision resulted from:

• The multiplication and popularity of sectarian apocryphal writings.

• The fall of Jerusalem (A.D. 70), which created a threat to the religious tradition of the Jews.

• The disputes with Christians over their interpretation of Jewish Scriptures in preaching and writing.

• There never was any doubt about the five Books of the Law — the Pentateuch — but, beyond that various sects of Judaism disagree. The prophetic collection was generally agreed upon by 200 B.C., but the major problem concerned the other writings. Four criteria operated in deciding what Books should occupy a place in the authoritative Old Testament Scriptures:

1. The content of each Book had to harmonize with the Law.

2. Since Prophetic inspiration was believed to have begun with Moses (1450 B.C.) and ended with Ezra (450 B.C.), to qualify for the Canon and to be considered inspired, a Book had to have been written within that time frame.

3. The language of the original manuscript had to be Hebrew.

4. The Book had to have been written within the geographical boundaries of Palestine, with the exception of Daniel and possibly Esther.

WHAT IS MEANT BY THE TERM *"APOCRYPHA"*?

On the basis given above, the thirty-nine Books of the Old Testament were selected for the Palestinian Canon of Scriptures. Failing these criteria, the rest of the ancient Jewish writings came to be classified as *"Apocrypha"* or *"Pseudepigrapha"* literally, *"false writings."*

A number of Christian writings, other than those that came to be accepted from the New Testament, appeared early and were considered by some authorities to be worthy of Canonical status. The Didache, the Epistle of Barnabas, I and II Clement, the Shepherd of Hermas, the Apocalypse of Peter, and the Acts of Paul were some of the more popular ones. By the beginning of the Third Century, twenty-two of the Books comprising our present New Testament had become widely accepted. Four principles or considerations operated in determining which Books should occupy a place in the authoritative New Testament Scriptures:

1. Was the Book written by an Apostle?
2. Was the Book's content of a Spiritual nature?
3. Was the Book widely received by the Churches?
4. Was evidence in the Book of Divine Inspiration?

As far as is known, it was the Easter letter of Archbishop Athanasius of Alexandria in A.D. 367 that first listed the 27 Books of the New Testament as authoritative. Jerome, by his Latin translation of these same twenty-seven Books (A.D. 382), further established this list as Canonical for the Churches.

The group of Books, which numbered about 14, and referred to as the *"Apocrypha"* is believed to be spurious, or at least non-Canonical. This in no way implies that the Books in question do not contain some good things, nor does it mean they were written by evil men. It simply means they were believed not to be inspired; consequently, they were not placed in the Canon of Scripture.

Eleven of these Apocryphal Books have been accepted by the Catholic Church, included in the Roman Catholic Canon and placed in the *"Douay Version"* of the Bible.

Why were these Books not considered inspired or Canonical by the rest of the Church? Some of the reasons relate specifically to the Old Testament, some to the New Testament.

THE REASONS

• As far as the Old Testament was concerned, these

particular Books were not included in the Hebrew Canon of Scripture.

• The Lord Jesus Christ, the Apostle Paul, nor any other writer in the New Testament ever quoted from these writings. Yet they quoted frequently in the New Testament from the Books that were included in the Hebrew Canon of Scripture.

• Josephus, the Hebrew historian, expressly excluded these as *"false writings."*

• None of the Apocryphal books claimed Divine Inspiration.

• The Apocryphal have historical, geographical, and chronological errors.

• As literature, they are considered to be myth and legend.

• Their spiritual and even moral stance is generally far below both the Old and the New Testaments.

• Most of these books were written much later than the Books that were considered to be authoritative and inspired.

DIVINE INSPIRATION

Satan has done everything within his power to hinder, destroy, dilute, and outright do away with the Word of Almighty God. But through the Power of God, the Bible as we have it today — all 66 Books, both Old and New Testaments, from Genesis to Revelation — is the Word of God. Nothing else can be added to it.

When any person or any Church claims that other writings, other books, other so-called inspirations should be included in the Canon of Scripture, we can be sure that the Evil One has been at work. Paul put it aptly when he said,

"Though we, or an Angel from Heaven, preach any other gospel unto you than that which we have preached unto you, let him be accursed. As we said before, so say I now again, If any man preach any other gospel unto you than that you have received, let him be accursed" (Gal. 1:8-9).

Some so-called scholars have said that the Bible is filled with historical, chronological, and doctrinal contradictions. But a close examination of their objections reveals that the problem lies, not with the Bible, but with our limited perspective.

CONTRADICTORY PASSAGES EXPLAINED

For instance, there are several seemingly contradictory Passages about what happens when men gaze upon the Face of God, etc. St. John 1:18 says, *"No man has seen God at any time"* and Exodus 33:20 says, *"And God said, You cannot see My Face: for there shall no man see Me, and live."* Yet, in Genesis 32:30 it says, *"And Jacob called the name of the place Peniel: for I have seen God face to face."* Further, Exodus 33:11 says, *"And the LORD spoke unto Moses face to face, as a man speaks unto his friend."* Which is correct?

What most of us fail to realize is that the word *"seen"* or *"see"* also means *"to comprehend"* or *"to understand."* So, the Verse in St. John does not contradict the Verses in Genesis and Exodus at all. What John was saying was that no man has ever comprehended or understood everything about God — not at any time. We use the same kind of terminology in our conversations today. For instance, we will explain something to someone and then say, *"Do you see?"* But we don't really mean *"see,"* as to look with the natural eye. We simply mean, *"Do you understand? Do you comprehend?"* So there is clearly no contradiction here.

Another quote of inconsistency, so-called, along this line appears in Exodus 3:20 where God says *"No man can see My Face and live."* Yet Genesis 32:30 says that Jacob saw God face-to-face. Again what must be understood is that God was not talking about appearance only. He was not talking about Moses looking upon His Face, as we would look upon someone's face. The word, *"see"* in Exodus 3:20 pertains to more than outward features. Here God was talking about His Glory, because He said in Exodus 33:22, *"And it shall come to pass while My Glory passes by, that I . . . will cover you with My Hand."* Moses wanted not just to see God's Face, but to see it in His usual Glory — in the Light in which He dwelt — which no man has seen or can see (I Tim. 6:16). Actually, God has appeared a number of times, according to the Word of God, and they did look upon His Face. They did not, however, behold His Glory.

ANOTHER WORD EXPLAINED

Another apparent contradiction that scholars wrestle over concerns Jesus' warning against calling anyone a fool. In Matthew 5:22, Jesus said that if a person called another a fool, he would be in danger of Hellfire. Yet, Jesus Himself repeatedly called people fools in Matthew and in Luke. In Matthew, Chapter 5, where Jesus forbade the use of that kind of accusation, the Greek word translated fool is *"moros,"* which means a wicked reprobate, destitute of all spirituality. This, in effect, consigned a person to Hell. No one but God has the right to pass that kind of judgment. But, in Luke, Chapter 11, as well as in Matthew, Chapter 23, the word *"fool"* in the Greek is a totally different word — *"aphron"* — which means *"senseless ones without reason; foolish; stupid; acting without intelligence,"* so I think it's fairly obvious that Jesus was not saying the same in Matthew, Chapter 5 as He was in Matthew, Chapter 23 and Luke, Chapter 11.

Our English word *"fool"* was used in each instance, but it meant two different things altogether in the Greek. The problem then comes with the translation from one language to another. Often the only way to resolve these complex difficulties is to study the Text of Scripture in the original Greek and Hebrew languages. We may have trouble understanding the context of a Passage or a translator may have been imperfect in his choice of words, but the Bible itself is error-free.

THREE SUCCESSIVE STEPS AS IT REGARDS PROPERLY UNDERSTANDING THE WORD OF GOD

They are:
1. Revelation;

2. Inspiration; and,
3. Illumination.
We'll look at *"revelation"* first of all!

REVELATION

"But as it is written (Isa. 64:4), *Eye has not seen, nor ear heard, neither have entered into the heart of man, the things which God has prepared for them who love Him"* (I Cor. 2:9).

The first step in the transmission of Truth from the Heart of God to the heart of the Believer is *"Revelation,"* the Act of God the Holy Spirit uncovering the things in the Heart of God to the Bible writers, thus imparting the Truth of Scripture to them.

Paul explains that the Bible did not come by way of scientific investigation and human reason, because it could not come that way, but that it came in another way, by Revelation. He further said,

"But God has revealed them unto us by His Spirit: for the Spirit searches all things, yes, the deep things of God" (I Cor. 2:10).

The word *"revealed"* is the translation of a Greek word which means *"to uncover, to lay open what has been veiled or covered up."*

The word *"us"* in Verse 10 pertains to both the writers of Holy Scripture, and, as well, to whom they were writing.

The Apostle continues by saying, *"For what man knows the things of a man, save the spirit of man which is in him? even so the things of God knows no man, but the Spirit of God"* (I Cor. 2:11).

Paul is actually saying in his explanation that while it may be possible for us as human beings to know and understand some things about our fellowman, and even that is very limited, by that same means we cannot know nor understand God in any manner. What we are to know about God and His Word can only be revealed to us by the Holy Spirit. In fact, it can come no other way, even as the Holy Spirit here through Paul tells us. So, to attempt to understand God by natural means, simply cannot be done; however, when we come to *"illumination"* the Holy Spirit will then inform us through the Word as to how the Lord actually does reveal Himself to us.

INSPIRATION

The Apostle now says, *"Which things also we speak, not in the words which man's wisdom teaches, but which the Holy Spirit teaches; comparing spiritual things with spiritual"* (I Cor. 2:13).

Paul now tells us exactly as to how the Word of God was given by God to man, how it was received, and how it was written down.

The Apostle tells us that the Word of God, as it was given to the writers who served as instruments, was what they were given and what they wrote down and not words taught by human wisdom. That is, the words which the Bible writers used were not dictated by their human reason or wisdom. In other words, none of the Bible writers embellished at all what God gave them to give to the world.

Paul plainly tells us that the way the Word of God was given was *"but in words taught by the Spirit."* He says that the words which the Bible writers used were taught them by the Holy Spirit.

It means that the Holy Spirit searched through the vocabulary of the writer, choosing the correct word, which content of meaning will give to the Believer the exact Truth God desires us to have. This, however, does not imply mechanical dictation or something different from the writer's own personality. The idea is, the Holy Spirit took the writers as He found them and used them infallibly.

That's the reason that every single Word of God is important, meaning as we have related in this article, that a word-for-word translation of the Bible is an absolute necessity. These books that claim to be Bibles, which give a thought for thought translation, which fill the land presently, are not Bibles at all, but only religious books and, in fact, will do no one any good whatsoever, but rather great harm.

When Paul used the phrase, *"comparing spiritual things with spiritual,"* this tells us as to exactly how the Holy Spirit gave the Divine Text, and how it was inspired. The word *"comparing"* means *"to judge,"* or better yet, *"to judge with."* It speaks of the action of judging something with something else.

In other words, somewhat like a computer that would search for the word, the Holy Spirit would search for the right word to be used in every sentence, which came from the writer's vocabulary. Thus, the Holy Spirit allowed the writers the free play of their personalities, vocabulary, and training, while at the same time guiding them to make an infallible record of truth infallibly revealed.

ILLUMINATION

We now come to this part, which is also very important, namely the Act of God, the Holy Spirit, enabling the Believer to understand the Truth written down given by *"Revelation"* and by *"Inspiration."* Paul says, *"But the natural man receives not the things of the Spirit of God: for they are foolishness unto him: neither can he know them, because they are spiritually discerned"* (I Cor. 2:14).

The word *"natural"* as the Holy Spirit used it through Paul, describes the unregenerate man at his best, meaning very educated. No matter, as to how educated he might be, he simply by that means cannot understand the Word of God. So, the natural man here spoken of is the educated man at the height of his intellectual powers, but devoid of the Spirit of God. Actually, the things of the Lord are but *"foolishness"* unto such a man, Paul says!

"But he who is Spiritual judges all things, yet he himself is judged of no man" (I Cor. 2:15).

The word *"judgeth"* is the translation of a Greek word rendered *"discerns."*

Continuing with our explanation of *"Illumination,"* we

understand from the Word of God that it was to Paul that the Revelation, i.e., the meaning of the New Covenant was given. In fact, the entirety of the New Covenant is wrapped up in the Cross of Christ (I Cor. 1:17-18, 23; 2:2). If we study Paul at all, we have to come to the conclusion that the Jew from Tarsus preached the Cross. Understanding this, we must come to the conclusion that unless one properly understands the Cross of Christ as it regards both Salvation and Sanctification, then one cannot truly understand the Word of God as one should. Considering that the Cross of Christ is the foundation of all that we know and understand as it regards the Plan of God, then we find that this is the key that unlocks the door.

THE CROSS OF CHRIST

I think one could probably say, and without fear of Scriptural contradiction, that all error, all false doctrine, stems from an improper understanding, or an ignoring, or an outright denial of the Message of the Cross.

MATURITY AND THE CROSS OF CHRIST

Maturity in the Lord, in His Word, is dependent solely on a proper understanding of the Cross of Christ. That's the reason that Paul further said:

"And I, Brethren, when I came to you, came not with excellency of speech or of wisdom *(means that he depended not on oratorical abilities, nor did he delve into philosophy, which was all the rage of that particular day)*, declaring unto you the Testimony of God *(which is Christ and Him Crucified)*.

"For I determined not to know any thing among you *(with purpose and design, Paul did not resort to the knowledge or philosophy of the world regarding the Preaching of the Gospel)*, save Jesus Christ, and Him Crucified *(that and that alone is the Message which will save the sinner, set the captive free, and give the Believer perpetual victory)"* **(I Cor. 2:1-2).**

We must understand that the Lord desires, and does so strongly, that we understand His Word. He hasn't made it hard or difficult; however, if we ignore His Way, which is the Way of the Cross, our understanding will be most unfruitful, or even harmful!

"For the preaching *(Word)* of the Cross is to them who perish foolishness; but unto us who are Saved it is the Power of God" (I Cor. 1:18).

"Your Word is a Lamp unto my feet, and a Light unto my path" **(Ps. 119:105).**

The only *"Lamp"* in the world that produces *"true Spiritual Light"* is the Bible. It is the road map for life, and the blueprint for eternity, and it is the only road map for life and the only blueprint for eternity.

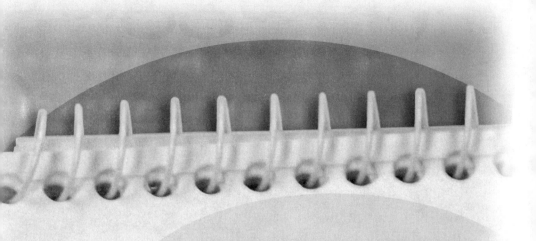

CHAPTER 2

The Doctrine Of Angels

THE DOCTRINE OF ANGELS

The Hebrew word for *"Angels"* as used in the Old Testament, is *"malak,"* and means *"messenger."* The New Testament word used for *"Angels,"* is *"angelos,"* and also means *"messenger."*

The word *"Angel,"* is at times used interchangeably for the Lord of Glory, for men, and for the beings we commonly refer to as Angels. Examples are:

• The Scripture says, *"And the Angel of the Lord appeared unto him in a flame of fire out of the midst of a bush."* In fact, this was a preincarnate appearance of Christ to Moses. We know it was the Lord of Glory because He said, *"I am the God of your father, the God of Abraham, the God of Isaac, and the God of Jacob. And Moses hid his face; for he was afraid to look upon God"* (Ex. 3:2, 6).

• As it regards men, the Scripture says, *"Unto the Angel of the Church of Ephesus write; These things says He Who holds the Seven Stars in His Right Hand, Who walks in the midst of the Seven Golden Candlesticks"* (Rev. 2:1). The *"Angel"* addressed in this Scripture and, as well, six other times in Chapters 2 and 3 of Revelation, actually refers to the Pastors of these respective Churches.

• Concerning the beings we commonly refer to as *"Angels,"* the Scripture says, *"And the Seventh Angel sounded; and there were great voices in Heaven saying, The kingdoms of this world are become the Kingdoms of our Lord, and of His Christ; and He shall reign forever and ever"* (Rev. 11:15).

From the associating Text, the reader can ascertain as to who is our Lord, or man, or an Angel as we think of such.

THE ROLE OF ANGELS

Basically, Angels function in three basic categories. They are:

1. At times they carry or bring a message. Concerning the conception of Christ, the Scripture says:

"Now the Birth of Jesus Christ was on this wise: When as His Mother Mary was espoused *(engaged)* to Joseph, before they came together *(before they were married)*, she was found with Child of the Holy Spirit *(by decree of the Holy Spirit)*.

"Then Joseph her husband, being a just *man*, not willing to make her a public example, was minded to put her away privily *(to quietly break the engagement)*.

"But while he thought on these things, behold, the Angel of the Lord appeared unto him in a dream, saying, Joseph, you son of David, fear not to take unto you Mary your wife; for that which is conceived in her is of the Holy Spirit.

"And she shall bring forth a Son, and you shall call His Name JESUS *(Saviour)*: for He shall save His People from their sins" (Mat. 1:18-21).

2. To fulfill a special, specific commission. Concerning this, the Scripture says:

"And in the sixth month *(refers to six months after Elisabeth had conceived; consequently, John was six months older than Jesus)* the Angel Gabriel was sent from God unto a city of Galilee, named Nazareth *(strangely enough, Nazareth was held in scorn by Israel at that time)*,

THE VIRGIN MARY

"To a virgin *(in the Greek Text is 'parthenos,' which refers to a pure virgin who has never known a man, and never experienced a marriage relationship; in the Hebrew, the word is "Ha-alma," which means, 'the Virgin — the only one who ever was, or ever will be a mother in this way')* espoused *(engaged)* to a man whose name was Joseph, of the house of David *(he was in the direct lineage of David through Solomon)*; and the Virgin's name *was* Mary

(Mary went back to David through another of David's sons, Nathan; so their lineage was perfect as it regards the Prophecies that the Messiah would come from the House of David [II Sam., Chpt. 7]).

"And the Angel came in unto her, and said *(presents the greatest moment in human history, the announcement of the coming birth of the Lord of Glory in the Incarnation, i.e., 'God becoming man')*, Hail, *you that are* highly favoured *(means 'much engraced,' not 'full of grace,' as the Catholic Church teaches, but one who, herself meritless, had received signal Grace from God)*, the Lord *is* with you *(signals her position of humility)*: blessed *are* you among women *(does not say 'above women,' as the Catholics teach; however, she definitely was much blessed)*.

"And when she saw *him,* she was troubled at his saying *(a total disturbance; not a partial, or light agitation),* and cast in her mind what manner of salutation this should be *(she in no way understood the reason that he addressed her as he did).*

"And the Angel said unto her, Fear not, Mary: for you have found favour with God *(should have been translated, 'you have received Grace from God').*

CALL HIS NAME JESUS

"And, behold, you shall conceive in your womb *(should have been translated, 'You shall forthwith conceive in your womb,' meaning immediately)*, and bring forth a Son *(proclaims the Incarnation, 'God manifest in the flesh, God with us, Immanuel' [Isa. 7:14; 9:6])*, and shall call His name JESUS *(the Greek version of the Hebrew, 'Joshua'; it means 'Saviour,' or 'The Salvation of Jehovah').*

"He shall be great, and shall be called the Son of the Highest *(actually means 'The Most High,' and refers to 'Jehovah')*: and the Lord God shall give unto Him the throne of His father David *(II Sam., Chpt. 7):*

"And He shall reign over the house of Jacob for ever; and of His Kingdom there shall be no end *(this will begin at the Second Coming, and will last forever; it could have begun at the beginning of His Ministry, but He was rejected by Israel; but at the Second Coming, they will accept Him as their Saviour, Messiah, and King [Zech., Chpts. 12-14]).*

THE ANGEL GABRIEL AND THE HOLY SPIRIT

"Then said Mary unto the Angel, How shall this be, seeing I know not a man? *(She was probably in her late teens.)*

"And the Angel answered and said unto her, The Holy Spirit shall come upon you *(has the same connotation as, 'the Spirit of God moved upon the face of the waters' [Gen. 1:2]),* **and the power of the Highest shall overshadow you** *(has the same reference as, 'And God said, let there be light: and there was light' [Gen. 1:3])*: **therefore also that holy thing which shall be born of you shall be called the Son of God** *(constitutes the Incarnation, 'God becoming Man'; He would be Very God and Very Man)"* **(Lk. 1:26-35).**

3. Angels at times represent the Lord, Who sends them. The Scripture says, *"And it came to pass, when I, even I Daniel, had seen the Vision, and sought for the meaning, then, behold, there stood before me as the appearance of a man.*

"And I heard a man's voice between the banks of Ulai, which called, and said, Gabriel, make this man to understand the Vision" **(Dan. 8:15-16).**

THE CREATION OF ANGELS

As to exactly when the Lord created the Angelic Host, of that, the Scripture is silent. It is obvious that it happened in eternity past.

Every evidence is that the Lord created all Angels at the same time. This means that there is no such thing as a baby Angel. This means also that all Angels are of the same age, having been created perfectly mature. While Angels can do many things that humans cannot do and, as well, these beings have unlimited lifetimes and unusual powers, yet the writer to the Hebrews points out, even in awed tones, that *"it is not to Angels that He* (God) *has subjected the world to come"* (Heb. 2:5). It is not really the Angels for which our Lord has done great things, but rather *"Abraham's descendants"* (Heb. 2:16). Because of the Lord Jesus Christ and what He has done for humanity, we will be brought to glory and lifted far above the Angels.

Richards says, *"Angels, then are not only God's Ministers, assigned to serve the heirs of Salvation; they are also eager witnesses to all that God is doing in this world"* (Lk. 15:10; I Cor. 11:10; I Tim. 3:16). Ultimately, human beings will be called on to judge the Angels (I Cor. 6:3).

Everything the Bible says about Angels is exciting to say the least; however, the thrust of the Old Testament and the New Testament is clear. Human beings, not Angels, are the focus of God's concern. As the result of such, we are directed by God to fix our thoughts and our Faith on the Lord Jesus Christ — not on Angels.

DIFFERENT TYPES OF ANGELIC BEINGS

Actually there are different ranks among Angels, and there are different types of Angels, that is, if we are allowed to use the word *"Angel"* in a generic sense.

As it regards rank, only one Angel in the Bible is referred to as an *"Archangel."* That is Michael (Jude 9). And yet, the Angel Gabriel, although not referred to by rank, still is spoken of as, *"Gabriel who stands in the Presence of God"* (Lk. 1:19). That just might be the highest rank of all.

As it regards the Angels who threw in their lot with Lucifer, thereby rebelling against the Lord, the Apostle Paul referred to them according to the following:

• **Principalities:** (Rulers or beings of the highest rank and order in Satan's kingdom).

• **Powers:** (The rank immediately below the *"Principalities"*).

• **Rulers of the darkness of this world:** (Those who carry out the instructions of the *"Powers"*).

• **Spiritual wickedness in high places:** (This refers to demon spirits).

Actually, the Scripture indicates that one third of the Angels threw in their lot with Lucifer when he rebelled against God. John the Beloved gave the account. He said:

SATAN AND HIS ANGELS CAST OUT OF HEAVEN

"**And there appeared another wonder in Heaven** *(should have been translated, 'another sign')*; **and behold a great red dragon** *(denotes Satan and his murderous purpose, typified by the color of 'red')*, **having seven heads** *(refers to Empires that persecuted Israel, even until John's day; those Empires were Egypt, Assyria, Babylon, Medo-Persia, Greece, and Rome)* **and ten horns** *(represents ten nations that will be ruled by the Antichrist in the Last Days, and will greatly persecute Israel; actually, the seventh head is those 'ten horns'; Daniel tells us that these 'ten horns' representing ten nations will be in the old Roman Empire territory, which refers to the Middle East and parts of Europe [Dan. 7:7])*, **and seven crowns upon his heads** *(represents the fact that Satan controlled these particular kingdoms)*.

MANCHILD

"**And his tail drew the third part of the stars of Heaven** *(this goes all the way back to the original rebellion of Lucifer against God; at that time, one-third of the*

Angels threw in their lot with him; we know these 'stars' represent Angels, because Vs. 9 tells us so), **and did cast them to the earth** *(is given to us more clearly in Vss. 7-9)*: **and the dragon stood before the woman who was ready to be delivered** *(does not pertain to the birth of Christ as many claim, but rather the manchild which is the 144,000 Jews who will give their hearts to Christ [Chpt. 7])*, **for to devour her child as soon as it was born.** *(This pertains to the fact that the Antichrist will hate these Jews who have come to Christ. This will take place in the first half of the Great Tribulation, and may well be the primary reason the Antichrist will turn on Israel at that time.)*

144,000 JEWS

"And she *(Israel)* **brought forth a manchild** *(as stated, this is the 144,000 Jews who will come to Christ during the first half of the Great Tribulation [Chpt. 7]; we aren't told exactly how this will be done)*, **who was to rule all nations with a rod of iron** *(Israel, under Christ, will definitely fill this role in the coming Millennial Reign)*: **and her child was caught up unto God, and *to* His Throne.** *(This refers to the Rapture of the 144,000, which will take place at about the midpoint of the Great Tribulation.)*

"And the woman fled into the wilderness *(the 'woman' is National Israel; at the midpoint of the Great Tribulation, the Antichrist will turn on Israel and defeat her, with many thousands of Jews fleeing into the wilderness)*, **where she has a place prepared of God** *(this place is actually ancient Petra, located in Jordan [Isa. 16:1-5])*, **that they should feed her there a thousand two hundred *and* threescore days.** *('They' mentioned here refers oddly enough to the Arabs of Jordan. The 1,260 days constitute almost all of the last half of the Great Tribulation. Incidentally, Petra is now empty of people, awaiting the arrival of Israel.)*

MICHAEL THE ARCHANGEL

"**And there was war in Heaven** *(pertains to the 'Mystery of God' being finished [10:7])*: **Michael and his Angels fought against the dragon; and the dragon fought and his Angels** *(this pertains to Satan and all the Angels who followed him being cast out of Heaven, which will take place at the midpoint of the Great Tribulation; why the Lord has allowed Satan and his minions to remain in Heaven all of this time, we aren't told; it is a 'Mystery,' but it will now be finished)*,

"**And prevailed not** *(Satan will then be defeated; incidentally, it is not Satan who instigates this war, but rather the Archangel Michael at the Command of God)*; **neither was their place found any more in Heaven** *(joins with the close of the Book of Revelation, where the Evil One has no more place on Earth as well, but rather the place of torment forever and ever [Rev. 20:10])*.

"**And the great dragon was cast out, that old serpent, called the Devil, and Satan** *(he is referred to as 'the Great Dragon' because of his propensity to 'steal, kill, and destroy' [Jn. 10:10]; he is the 'old serpent' because in his first appearance in the Bible, he chose to work through a serpent; thereby, he is what the curse caused the serpent to be, wryly subtle, and treacherous)*, **which deceives the whole world** *(deception is his greatest weapon; he deceives, and is himself deceived)*: **he was cast out into the earth, and his Angels were cast out with him** *(pronounces the beginning of the end for this evil monster)*.

OVERCOMERS

"**And I heard a loud voice saying in Heaven** *(presents the white-robe wearers of Rev. 6:10-11)*, **Now is come Salvation, and Strength, and the Kingdom of our God** *(presents the triumph of Christ)*, **and the power of His Christ** *(refers to the fact that Christ will rule this world,* *not Satan)***: for the accuser of our Brethren is cast down, which accused them before our God day and night.** *(This implies that either Satan or one of his fallen Angels is before the Throne of God, accusing the Brethren constantly [Job, Chpts. 1-2].)*

"And they overcame him by the Blood of the Lamb *(the power to overcome and overwhelm the kingdom of Satan is found exclusively in the Blood of the Sacrifice of the Son of God, and our Faith in that Finished Work [Rom. 6:3-5, 11, 14])***, and by the word of their testimony** *(the 'testimony' must pertain to the fact that the Object of our Faith is the Cross, and exclusively the Cross, which then gives the Holy Spirit latitude to work within our lives)***; and they loved not their lives unto the death.** *(This refers to the fact that the Believer must not change his testimony regarding the Cross to something else, even if it means death)***"** **(Rev. 12:3-11).**

WEIRD CREATURES

Inasmuch as we are dealing with Satan and the coming day, when he and his fallen Angels will be dispossessed from Heaven, never again having access to those portals, this may be the place to discuss something of which there aren't many answers.

In the Book of Revelation we are given a glimpse into the spirit world of darkness, which portrays creatures, which are beyond our comprehension. In fact, in the spirit world of Righteousness, we will see the same thing, which we will address momentarily. But first we will look at the creatures of darkness. The Scripture says:

"And the fifth Angel sounded *(presents the fifth Judgment, and as stated the first 'woe')***, and I saw a star fall from Heaven unto the earth** *(actually refers to Satan, as the next phrase proclaims [Lk. 10:18])***: and to him was given the key of the bottomless pit.** *(Christ gives this 'key'* to Satan, although He may use an Angel to hand the key to the Evil One [Rev. 20:1].)

"And he *(Satan)* **opened the bottomless pit; and there arose a smoke out of the pit, as the smoke of a great furnace; and the sun and the air were darkened by reason of the smoke of the pit.** *(This will probably be concentrated in the old Roman Empire territory.)*

"And there came out of the smoke locusts upon the earth *(these are demon locusts, even as the following Verses prove)*: **and unto them was given power, as the scorpions of the earth have power** *(refers to the sting in their tails, and the pain this will cause).*

"And it was commanded them that they should not hurt the grass of the earth, neither any green thing, neither any tree *(normal locusts destroy plant life; but these are not allowed to do so)*; **but only those men who have not the Seal of God in their foreheads** *(refers to the 144,000 Jews who have accepted Christ as their Saviour [Rev. 7:2-8]).*

"And to them it was given that they should not kill them, but that they should be tormented five months *(this will be literal, yet these creatures will be invisible)*: **and their torment** *was* **as the torment of a scorpion, when he strikes a man** *(pain and swelling).*

"And in those days shall men seek death, and shall not find it; and shall desire to die, and death shall flee from them. *(For pain to be so bad that people want to die is bad indeed! Evidently pain-killing drugs will not work. It will be interesting how medical doctors diagnose all of this, to say the least.)*

SHAPED LIKE LOCUSTS, WITH FACES OF MEN

"And the shapes of the locusts *were* **like unto horses prepared unto battle; and on their heads** *were* **as it were crowns like gold, and their faces** *were* **as the faces of men.** *(These are demon spirits, but will be invisible. If they could* *be seen, this is what they would look like. We aren't told their origin in the Bible. We know they were not originally created in this manner, but evidently became this way in the revolution instigated by Lucifer against God [Isa. 14:12-20; Ezek. 28:11-19].)*

"And they had hair as the hair of women, and their teeth were as *the teeth* of lions. *(They were, no doubt, originally created by God to perform a particular function of praise and worship, even as the 'living creatures,' but they have suffered this fate due to rebellion against God.)*

"And they had breastplates, as it were breastplates of iron; and the sound of their wings *was* as the sound of chariots of many horses running to battle. *(We are given a glimpse here into the spirit world. This is the reason such foolish efforts as humanistic psychology are helpless against such foes. The only answer is Christ and the Cross.)*

"And they had tails like unto scorpions, and there were stings in their tails: and their power *was* to hurt men five months. *(This Judgment is limited to five months, which tells us Satan can only do what God allows him to do.)*

THE FALLEN ANGEL, APOLLYON

"And they had a king over them, *who is* the Angel of the bottomless pit *(gives us further insight into the spirit world of darkness)*, **whose name in the Hebrew tongue *is* Abaddon, but in the Greek tongue has *his* name Apollyon** *(this is a powerful fallen Angel, who evidently threw in his lot with Lucifer in the great rebellion against God; only four Angels are named in Scripture, 'Gabriel, Michael, Lucifer, and Apollyon,' the first two being Righteous)*" **(Rev. 9:1-11).**

TYPES OF RIGHTEOUS ANGELS AND THEIR FUNCTIONS

Even though some of the creatures we will address cannot

technically be referred to as an Angel, still, they fall into the same category.

We find in the Word of God that the Ministry of Angels is phenomenal to say the least. We find them active in just about every capacity. We will look first of all at those that we commonly refer to as Angels.

ANGELS

Technically, Angels are Messengers sent by God for a specific purpose, with that purpose revealed to an individual. Examples are: The Angel Gabriel appearing to Zacharias and informing him of the coming birth of John the Baptist (Lk. 1:11-20). As well, Gabriel also appeared to Mary who would be the Mother of our Lord (Lk. 1:26-37).

One of the great Revelations concerns the Angel Gabriel also appearing to Daniel. In fact, this account proclaims to us the fact that powerful fallen Angels oversee certain countries or Empires, so to speak. Even though they are unseen, still, they exert tremendous influence, even though the source is not known by the individuals involved. In the following account, we will see the mighty Angels Gabriel and Michael literally changing out the rulership of certain Empires, in other words, forcing the demise of one Empire, in order that another would take its place. All of this tells us, even as we shall see, that important events on Earth are preceded by events in the spirit world. In this account, we will also see a preincarnate appearance of our Lord.

DANIEL

"In the third year of Cyrus king of Persia a thing was revealed unto Daniel, whose name was called Belteshazzar; and the thing was true, but the time appointed was long: and he understood the thing, and had understanding of the Vision. *('And the thing was true, but the time appointed was long,' has reference to the fulfillment of this*

Vision being in the far distant future, at least from Daniel's day. In fact, some of it has yet to be fulfilled, but will be fulfilled shortly!)

"In those days I Daniel was mourning three full weeks *(it is thought that this Vision was given about five years after the Vision of the seventy weeks of the previous Chapter).*

"I ate no pleasant bread, neither came flesh nor wine in my mouth, and neither did I anoint myself at all, till three whole weeks were fulfilled. *(There are some who argue that Daniel was on a total fast, in other words, abstaining from any food whatsoever; however, the phrase, 'No pleasant bread,' seems to indicate otherwise, meaning that he was on a partial fast, with his diet being vegetables, which is the same thing he ate in Chapter 1 when presented to Melzar [Dan. 1:5, 8, 12-16].)*

"And in the four and twentieth day of the first month, as I was by the side of the great river, which is Hiddekel *(the 'Hiddekel' is the modern Tigris River)***;**

THE VISION OF THE MESSIAH

"Then I lifted up my eyes, and looked, and behold a certain Man clothed in linen, whose loins were girded with fine gold of Uphaz *(the similarity of the apparition in Vss. 5 and 6 and in Rev. 1:13, 16 suggests that it was Immanuel Himself Who appeared to Daniel)***:**

"His Body also was like the beryl, and His Face as the appearance of lightning, and His Eyes as lamps of fire, and His Arms and His Feet like in colour to polished brass, and the Voice of His Words like the voice of a multitude. *(I think there is no doubt that this is a preincarnate appearance of Christ.)*

THE EFFECT OF THE VISION

"And I Daniel alone saw the Vision: for the men who

were with me saw not the Vision; but a great quaking fell upon them, so that they fled to hide themselves. *(Even though these companions 'saw not the Vision,' still they greatly felt the Power of the Presence, for 'a great quaking fell upon them.' This means they were terrified!)*

"Therefore I was left alone, and saw this great Vision, and there remained no strength in me: for my comeliness was turned in me into corruption, and I retained no strength. *(The phrase, 'For my comeliness was turned in me into corruption,' underlies the true meaning of this Passage. When our Righteousness is compared with that of Christ's, there truly is no comparison.)*

"Yet heard I the Voice of His Words: and when I heard the Voice of His Words, then was I in a deep sleep on my face, and my face toward the ground. *(This is the same reaction that Daniel had upon the appearance of Gabriel, concerning the Vision of Chapter 8. The experience of Peter, James, and John on the Mount of Transfiguration was similar.)*

"And, behold, an hand touched me, which set me upon my knees and upon the palms of my hands. *(Even though the Scripture is unclear, it seems that the 'hand' that 'touched' Daniel was not necessarily the Hand of Christ, of Vss. 5 and 6. Every implication is that it is Gabriel's.)*

"And he said unto me, O Daniel, a man greatly beloved, understand the words that I speak unto you, and stand upright: for unto you am I now sent. And when he had spoken this word unto me, I stood trembling. *(The message that Gabriel is about to give Daniel will be the concluding 'Vision,' and will actually tie all the other Visions together.)*

THE DETAINING OF GABRIEL BY SATAN'S FORCES

"Then said he unto me, Fear not, Daniel: for from the first day that you did set your heart to understand,

and to chasten yourself before your God, your words were heard, and I am come for your words. *('For from the first day,' speaks of his petition to God and his effort to understand God's Purpose concerning His People. Then God commissioned Gabriel to come to him.)*

"But the prince of the kingdom of Persia withstood me one and twenty days: but, lo, Michael, one of the Chief Princes, came to help me; and I remained there with the kings of Persia. *('The prince of the kingdom of Persia,' refers to an evil Angel appointed by Satan to control the Persian Government, which, of course, was done without the knowledge of its earthly king. This Passage appears to reveal that Satan places an agent in charge of every nation [fallen Angel]; and, if so, this may explain national hatreds and national movements.*

"Similarly, God has His Angelic Agents operating in opposition to Satan's. The conflict of Eph., Chpt. 6 and the Battle of Rev., Chpt. 12 harmonize with this supposition.)

THE EFFECT OF THE VISION ON DANIEL

"Now I am come to make you understand what shall befall your people in the latter days: for yet the Vision is for many days. *('What shall befall your people,' refers solely to the Jews [9:24; 12:1]. Therefore, the Gentile nations are included, but only as they affect Israel, and only as Israel is ensconced in her land and offering Sacrifices in the Temple; in fact, this Temple will soon be built.)*

"And when he had spoken such words unto me, I set my face toward the ground, and I became dumb. *(Quite possibly, the many times mentioned concerning the Vision being fulfilled in the 'latter days' is because Daniel may have thought that these things would happen shortly with Israel ultimately being restored to her place and position of power and supremacy.)*

"And, behold, one like the similitude of the sons of

men touched my lips, then I opened my mouth, and spoke, and said unto Him Who stood before me, O my Lord, by the Vision my sorrows are turned upon me, and I have retained no strength. *(Quite possibly, this was Christ, because Daniel addressed Him as 'O my Lord!')*

"For how can the servant of this my Lord talk with this my Lord? for as for me, straightway there remained no strength in me, neither is there breath left in me. *(The implication is that it is not the Vision alone causing the physical weakness, but rather the very Presence of Christ.)*

"Then there came again and touched me one like the appearance of a man, and he strengthened me,

"And said, O man greatly beloved, fear not: peace be unto you, be strong, yes, be strong. And when He had spoken unto me, I was strengthened, and said, Let my Lord speak; for You have strengthened me. *(It seems that this is the Lord, in a preincarnate appearance, actually speaking to Daniel.)*

THE PRINCE OF GRECIA

"Then said He, Knowest thou wherefore I come unto you? and now will I return to fight with the prince of Persia: and when I am gone forth, lo, the prince of Grecia shall come. *(It seems that now Gabriel once again picks up the conversation. 'And now will I return to fight with the prince of Persia,' did not mean that he would leave immediately, but, when the Vision was completed, he would resume the conflict with this Satanic prince.*

" 'And when I am gone forth, lo, the prince of Grecia shall come,' refers to Gabriel ultimately being successful in this conflict, allowing the Satanic prince to bring in the Grecian Empire. This would take place less than 200 years in the future.

"The 'prince of Grecia' is not an earthly prince, but instead a fallen Angel working under the direct instructions

of Satan, who would control the Grecian Empire when it did come into being. It was this evil prince which helped Alexander the Great conquer the known world of that day, although without his knowledge. This 'prince' is now confined to the underworld, but will be released in the Last Days in order to help the Antichrist [Rev. 17:8-14].

"It is the same presently, with fallen Angels controlling entire nations [Eph. 6:12]).

MICHAEL AND GABRIEL

"But I will show you that which is noted in the Scripture of Truth: and there is none who holds with me in these things, but Michael your prince. *('The Scripture of Truth' refers to the dream originally given to Nebuchadnezzar [2:39], which showed these Empires, as well as the two Visions already given to Daniel, as noted in Dan. 7:5-6 and 8:3-8. 'And there is none who holds with me in these things, but Michael your prince,' denotes the Truth that as these fallen Angels reigned supreme over certain empires, Michael served in the same position over Israel and, in fact, still does!)"* **(Dan. 10:1-21).**

As is obvious in the Book of Revelation, and due to the fact that this Book opens up the Spirit world as nothing else, we see Angels at work constantly. While their activity may be more pronounced at that coming time, still, if the veil could be pulled back presently, we would see similar activity.

THE CHERUBIMS

In the great Book of Ezekiel we have the account of the Cherubims. The description is given both in Chapter 1 and then in Chapter 10. While Chapter 1 does not list them as *"Cherubim"* but rather *"Living Creatures,"* the designation of Cherubim is given to them in Chapter 10. The account of these powerful creatures is as follows:

"**The Word of the LORD came expressly unto Ezekiel the Priest, the son of Buzi, in the land of the Chaldeans by the river Chebar; and the Hand of the LORD was there upon him.** (*'The Word of the LORD came expressly unto Ezekiel,' means 'in reality' or 'without doubt.' 'In the land of the Chaldeans,' refers to the Divine Truth that wherever a searching heart is, God will be found. Actually, the deeper the darkness, the brighter the Light.*)

"**And I looked, and, behold, a whirlwind came out of the north, a great cloud, and a fire infolding itself, and a brightness was about it, and out of the midst thereof as the colour of amber, out of the midst of the fire.** (*'And I looked, and, behold,' refers to the fact that what was described could be seen. In other words, it was not a figment of Ezekiel's imagination.*

"*The phrase, 'A whirlwind came out of the north,' refers to the Holy Spirit. It was the same 'rushing wind' that came on the Day of Pentecost [Acts 2:2]. Actually, Ezekiel is given a vision of the traveling Throne of God, one might say.*)

THE APPEARANCE OF THE CHERUBIMS

"**Also out of the midst thereof came the likeness of four living creatures. And this was their appearance; they had the likeness of a man.** (*We learn, as stated, from 10:1 that these 'Living Creatures' are Cherubims.*)

"**And every one had four faces, and every one had four wings.** (*Their hands and their wings were in proportion, which means that equal intelligence indwelt their entire being, and the One Spirit energized them all.*)

"**And their feet were straight feet; and the sole of their feet was like the sole of a calf's foot: and they sparkled like the colour of burnished brass.** (*The phrase,*

*'straight feet,' means they were shaped like those of an ox,
which emphasizes the fact that they did not move by walking. Even though like an ox, there their similarity ended.)*

**"And they had the hands of a man under their wings
on their four sides; and they four had their faces and
their wings.** *(The number 'four' is not without intense
meaning. Four refers to fourfold and, therefore, 'completion,' i.e., complete within itself, which can only speak of
the Creator, and not the Creation. These Creatures attend
the Throne of God [Rev. 4:6-8]).*

**"Their wings were joined one to another; they turned
not when they went; they went every one straight forward.**
*(When adding Vss. 11 and 24, two of the wings were always
down, and, when the Living Creatures moved, two were
extended upwards, so that their tips touched, and were in a
sense 'joined.' When at rest, these were let down again.*

*" 'They turned not when they went,' refers to the fact that
the four wings were not in motion as wings normally are
when the Cherubim moved. In other words, their power of
movement was not in the wings.)*

FOUR FACES

**"As for the likeness of their faces, they four had the
face of a man, and the face of a lion, on the right side:
and they four had the face of an ox on the left side; they
four also had the face of an eagle.** *(First of all, it is impossible to exhaust the meaning of the symbolism given here.
One can connect all of this with the human face of the Son
of Man, Who shared in the Glory of the Father: the Ox, with
that of His Sacrifice; the Lion, with that of His Sovereignty,
as the Lion of the Tribe of Judah [Rev. 5:5]; the Eagle, with
that of His bearing His People, as on Eagle's Wings unto
the highest heavens [Ex. 19:4; Deut. 32:11]).*

**"Thus were their faces: and their wings were stretched
upward; two wings of every one were joined one to**

another, and two covered their bodies. *('Thus were their faces,' seems to imply that the Holy Spirit desired for us to understand the symbolism, at least as far as is possible for man to do!)*

THEIR MANNER OF TRAVEL

"And they went every one straight forward: whither the Spirit was to go, they went; and they turned not when they went. *('And they went every one straight forward,' seems to imply that from point to point, they always traveled in a straight line, thereby denoting perfect knowledge of direction and perfect ability to travel the designated course.*

"The phrase, 'Whither the Spirit was to go, they went,' refers to the Holy Spirit giving direction, which the Cherubim instantly obeyed. [The Hebrew word for 'Spirit' is a noun, and should have been translated 'the Spirit,' as in Gen. 1:2.])

THE APPEARANCE OF LAMPS

"As for the likeness of the Living Creatures, their appearance was like burning coals of fire, and like the appearance of lamps: it went up and down among the Living Creatures; and the fire was bright, and out of the fire went forth lightning. *(It seems that these 'Living Creatures' were bathed, as it were, in the fire that played around them, yet were not consumed. 'Fire,' as distinct from 'Light,' seems to be the symbol of the Power of God, as manifested against evil [Deut. 4:24; Heb. 12:29].)*

"And the Living Creatures ran and returned as the appearance of a flash of lightning *(the idea is of speed and incomprehensible to the human mind and overwhelming in brightness; perhaps one can say that they traveled with the 'speed of thought')*" **(Ezek. 1:3-14).**

More descriptions are given in this First Chapter of Ezekiel, but I think it now becomes plain as to the strange appearance of these creatures. There is nothing like them on Earth. But one thing is certain, every Believer, upon going to Heaven, will see these creatures exactly as did Ezekiel that day.

THE ACCOUNT IN THE BOOK OF REVELATION

We will find in this account in Revelation that these creatures are very similar to the ones observed by Ezekiel, but with some differences. For instance, the Cherubims observed by Ezekiel had six wings, and these pictured in Revelation have four wings.

Incidentally, the Greek word translated *"beast"* by the translators, is *"zoon,"* and means *"Living Creatures,"* and should have been translated accordingly.

The account says:

"And before the Throne *there was* a sea of glass like unto crystal *(presents that which is perfectly transparent)*: and in the midst of the Throne, and round about the Throne, *were* four Beasts *(living creatures)* full of eyes before and behind. *(This is introducing creatures we have no knowledge of and which are beyond comprehension, as so much in Heaven actually is.)*

"And the first Beast *(living creature) was* like a lion, and the second Beast like a calf, and the third Beast had a face as a man, and the fourth Beast *was* like a flying eagle. *(These strange creatures are before the Throne constantly.)*

"And the four Beasts *(living creatures)* had each of them six wings about *him;* and *they were* full of eyes within *(signifying the revealing of their innermost nature and being)*: and they rest not day and night *(proclaiming that these beings are 'spirit' and not 'flesh')*, saying, Holy, Holy, Holy, Lord God Almighty, which was, and is, and

is to come *(using the threefold repetition calls attention to the infinite Holiness of God)*" **(Rev. 4:6-8).**

CHERUBIMS AND THE GARDEN OF EDEN

Actually, we find Cherubims mentioned at the very beginning of creation with the Scripture saying the following:

"**Therefore the LORD God sent him forth from the Garden of Eden** *(in effect, this was an act of mercy; man is expelled from the Garden, lest by eating the Tree of Life he should perpetuate his misery; but God's Love for him, though fallen and guilty, is so strong that He accompanies him into exile; as well, through Jesus Christ, God's only Son, Who will be given in Sacrifice, the Lord will show Adam, and all who would follow him, how to come back into Paradise; regrettably, there is no record that Adam and Eve placed any faith in the Lord; unfortunately, untold billions have followed suit)***, to till the ground from whence he was taken** *(refers to a place of toil, not to a place of torment).*

"**So He** *(God)* **drove out the man** *(implies the idea of force and displeasure)***; and He placed at the east of the Garden of Eden Cherubim** *(these Cherubim signified the Holiness of God, which man had now forfeited)***, and a flaming sword which turned every way, to keep the way of the Tree of Life** *(the 'flaming sword' was emblematic of the Divine Glory in its attitude towards sin)*" **(Gen. 3:23-24).**

THE ARK OF THE COVENANT

On the Ark of the Covenant, which was placed in the Holy of Holies in the Tabernacle, all symbolizing Christ, a Cherubim was at either end of the Mercy Seat, which, in effect, was the lid for the Ark. The Scripture says:

"**And you shall make a Mercy Seat of Pure Gold**

(the Mercy Seat formed the covering for the Ark; on it was sprinkled the Atoning Blood, which the High Priest did once a year, on the Great Day of Atonement; it was of this Blood-sprinkled Mercy Seat that God spoke when He said: 'There will I meet with you'; here, in Type, was the only meeting place between God and the sinner; here, Righteousness and Peace kissed each other; it was all gold, signifying the Deity of Christ, signifying also that His Deity was not marred by Him becoming Man; Christ is the Mercy Seat): **two cubits and a half shall be the length thereof** *(3 and 3/4 feet)*, **and a cubit and a half the breadth thereof** *(2 and 1/4 feet)*.

"And you shall make two Cherubims of gold *(they pertained to God's Judicial authority; they seemed to be the highest among the Angelic order, or at least in the capacity in which they function)*, **of beaten work shall you make them, in the two ends of the Mercy Seat.** *(They were not attached to the ends of the Mercy Seat, but were actually a part of the Mercy Seat. In other words, the Mercy Seat and the two Cherubim were all one piece of gold. The two Cherubim looked down on the Mercy Seat.)*

THE FUNCTION OF THE CHERUBIMS

"And make one Cherub on the one end, and the other Cherub on the other end: even of the Mercy Seat shall you make the Cherubims on the two ends thereof.

"And the Cherubims shall stretch forth their wings on high, covering the Mercy Seat with their wings *(stretched above their heads, and pointing forward, with the four wings meeting each other in the middle)*, **and their faces shall look one to another; toward the Mercy Seat shall the faces of the Cherubims be.** *(They looked down upon the blood which was applied to the Mercy Seat once a year, on the Great Day of Atonement.)*

"And you shall put the Mercy Seat above upon the Ark; and in the Ark you shall put the Testimony *(Ten*

Commandments) **that I shall give you.**

"And there I will meet with you, and I will commune with you from above the Mercy Seat, from between the two Cherubims which are upon the Ark of the Testimony, of all things which I will give you in Commandment unto the Children of Israel. *(It is only above the Blood-stained Mercy Seat that God will meet with sinful human beings, because that's the only place that He can meet with sinful human beings, and not malign His Righteousness and Holiness. Concerning this, Mackintosh says: 'Thus it is that the soul of the believing sinner finds peace. He sees that God's Righteousness and His Justification rest upon precisely the same basis, namely Christ's accomplished Work. When man, under the powerful action of the Truth of God, takes his place as a sinner, God can, in the exercise of Grace, take His place as a Saviour, and then every question is settled, for the Cross having answered all the claims of Divine Justice, Mercy's copious streams can flow unhindered. When a Righteous God and a ruined sinner meet on a Blood-sprinkled platform, all is settled forever — settled in such a way as perfectly glorifies God, and eternally saves the sinner')"* **(Ex. 25:17-22).**

SERAPHIMS

These creatures are mentioned only by the Prophet Isaiah. They are very similar to the Cherubim observed by Ezekiel, but yet, it seems that whereas the Cherubim had four faces, the Seraphim had only one.

Concerning these creatures, the Bible says:

"In the year that king Uzziah died I saw also the LORD sitting upon a Throne, high and lifted up, and His train filled the temple. *(That which Isaiah saw, Who is Jehovah, was actually a preincarnate appearance of the Lord Jesus Christ, and is declared so by the Holy Spirit in*

Jn. 12:37-41. It places Jehovah, Jesus the Saviour, in the midst of guilty and lost men, just as He is seen at Golgotha, for there they crucified two thieves with Him, placing Him in their midst.

"It is believed that king Uzziah died in 759 B.C.)

"Above it stood the Seraphims: each one had six wings; with twain he covered his face, and with twain he covered his feet, and with twain he did fly. *(The word 'Seraphim' means 'fiery ones.' This is the only mention of these celestial beings in Scripture. These Seraphim were stationed above the Throne of God and appear to have led in Divine Worship.*

"In the light of the Throne, Isaiah learned that he was a moral leper, that his people were moral lepers, and that they altogether were as vile as king Uzziah.

"If the sinless Seraphim, in the Presence of the thrice-Holy Lord of Hosts, had to veil both their face and their feet, then how hopeless was it for a moral leper such as Isaiah to stand in such a light!)

"And one cried unto another, and said, Holy, holy, holy, is the LORD of Hosts: the whole Earth is full of His glory. *(The phrase, 'one cried,' means 'kept crying.' Day and night they are saying, 'Holy, Holy, Holy.' The triple repetition of 'Holy, Holy, Holy' has been understood in all ages of the Church as connected with the Doctrine of the Trinity.)*

THE FUNCTION OF THE SERAPHIMS

"And the posts of the door moved at the voice of him who cried, and the house was filled with smoke. *(First of all, let us look at the energy of the worship conducted here. So vigorous was this act that the thresholds of the Divine Temple shook, and the Holy Place was filled with smoke.)*

"Then said I, Woe is me! for I am undone; because I am a man of unclean lips, and I dwell in the midst of a

people of unclean lips: for my eyes have seen the King, the LORD of Hosts. *(In Chpt. 5, Isaiah had pronounced six 'Woes!' upon Judah; now he pronounces one on himself!*

"The sinless King of this Verse is to be contrasted with the leprous king of Verse 1.

"The word 'undone' means 'justly doomed to death.' Such thought is the product of true Repentance. What Isaiah saw produced in him a deep feeling of unworthiness.)

"Then flew one of the Seraphims unto me, having a live coal in his hand, which he had taken with the tongs from off the Altar *(Isaiah needed a cleansing and a covering of his sin. The living coal from off the Altar of Burnt Offering, symbolizing the fire of the Wrath of God and the Blood of the Lamb of God, when brought in contact with his 'unclean lips,' removed his iniquity and expiated his sin.*

"The 'Altar' represented Calvary, to which sinful man is exposed before he can be cleansed and Saved. The essence of true conviction is a deep overwhelming concern over what I am, not so much what I have done or not done. It is more important what man is than what he has done, and man is a sinner.

"Genuine moral cleansing must be carried out in the heart of the sinner in order to be Saved, and that can only be accomplished by Faith in the shed Blood of Christ, of which this was a symbol [Rom. 3:24-25; Heb. 9:22; I Pet. 1:18-23; I Jn. 1:7-9]):

"And he laid it upon my mouth, and said, Lo, this has touched your lips; and your iniquity is taken away, and your sin purged. *(There is no other way to be cleansed and expiated than through the Wrath of God and the Atoning Blood of Christ. These are revealed and glorified at Calvary. There, God judged sin infinitely and eternally in the Person of Christ, and His Precious Blood shed there is the one and only and perfect expiation for cleansing of sin)"* **(Isa. 6:1-7).**

THE LORD JESUS CHRIST AND THE ANGELS

Due to God becoming Man, i.e., *"The Lord Jesus Christ,"* the tendency might possibly be there to think of Him as less than the Angels. So, the Holy Spirit through Paul addresses Himself to that. And to be sure, if the danger did not persist the Holy Spirit would not have addressed the subject. Paul said:

"God, Who at sundry times and in divers manners *(refers to the many and varied ways)* spoke in time past unto the fathers by the Prophets *(refers to Old Testament Times)*,

"Has in these Last Days *(the dispensation of Grace, which is the Church Age)* spoken unto us by *His* Son *(speaks of the Incarnation)*, Whom He has appointed Heir of all things *(through the means of the Cross)*, by Whom also He made the worlds *(proclaims His Deity, as the previous phrase of Him being the 'Heir of all things' proclaims His Humanity)*;

"Who being the brightness of *His* Glory *(the radiance of God's Glory)*, and the express Image of His Person *(the exact reproduction)*, and upholding all things by the Word of His Power *(carries the meaning of Jesus not only sustaining the weight of the universe, but also maintaining its coherence and carrying on its development)*, when He had by Himself purged our sins *(which He did at the Cross, dealing with sin regarding its cause, its power, and its guilt)*, sat down on the Right Hand of the Majesty on high *(speaks of the Finished Work of Christ, and that the Sacrifice was accepted by the Father)*;

BETTER THAN ANGELS

"Being made so much better than the Angels *(He was better than the Angels, which refers to the Incarnation, the price paid at Calvary [the reason for the Incarnation], and then His Exaltation as Saviour; as God, Jesus has always been greater than the Angels, but this is speaking of Him here as man)*, **as He has by inheritance obtained a more excellent Name than they.** *(This refers to what Christ did at the Cross, with the present result being that the inheritance is in His permanent Possession.)*

"For unto which of the Angels said He *(God the Father)* **at any time, You are My Son** *(Son of God)*, **this day have I begotten You?** *(This speaks of the Incarnation. God never said such of Angels, only of His Son [Ps. 2:7].)* **And again, I will be to Him a Father, and He shall be to Me a Son?** *(When uttered, referred to the future tense, but now is past tense. All had to do with Redemption, and all for you and me.)*

"And again, when He *(God the Father)* **brought in the Firstbegotten into the world** *(refers to Jesus being born of the Virgin Mary)*, **He said, And let all the Angels of God worship Him.** *(The idea is only Deity can be worshiped. Jesus is God!)*

"And of the Angels He said, Who makes His Angels spirits *(the emphasis upon the variableness of the Angelic nature)*, **and His Ministers a flame of fire.** *(This does not speak of Preachers, as some have suggested, but continues to address itself to Angels)"* **(Heb. 1:1-7).**

And then Paul said:

"But to which of the Angels said He *(God the Father)* **at any time, Sit on My Right Hand** *(Angels stand before God; it is a mark of superior dignity that the Son sits)*, **until I make Your enemies Your footstool?** *(This refers to God rendering all Christ's enemies utterly powerless, which is carried out by the Cross.)*

"Are they not all Ministering spirits *(the function of Angels)*, **sent forth to Minister for them Who shall be heirs of Salvation?** *(This proclaims that they attend only those* who have made Christ their Saviour)" **(Heb. 1:13-14).**

The idea of all of this is, our Lord, although becoming Man in order to redeem mankind, still in no way is lessened by the Incarnation. While He did lay aside the expression of His Deity, He never for a moment laid aside its possession.

ALL THINGS SUBJECT TO CHRIST

And then Paul wrote:

"For unto the Angels has He not put in subjection the world to come, whereof we speak. *(The Lord hasn't given the Angels dominion and rulership as He has Christ.)*
"But one in a certain place testified, saying *(Ps. 8:4-6)*, What is man, that You are mindful of him? *(This delves into the reason God has given man so much notice.)* or the son of man, that You visit him? *(This refers to looking upon in order to help or benefit. This clearly indicates the 'son of man' spoken of here is the human race and not Christ.)*
"You made him a little lower than the Angels *(should have been translated, 'You made him a little lower than the Godhead'; the Hebrew word translated 'Angels' is 'Elohim' which means 'God,' and should have been translated accordingly)*; You crowned him with glory and honour *(proclaims that which was never said of Angels)*, and did set him over the works of Your hands *(some of that dominion is retained despite the Fall; however, as would be obvious, much has been lost; but to be sure, it has all been regained in Christ, and will ultimately be realized in Christ)*:
"You have put all things in subjection under his feet. *(This speaks of Adam before the Fall, but more particularly it speaks of Christ and what He did at the Cross on our behalf.)* For in that He *(God)* put all in subjection under him *(man)*, He *(God)* left nothing *that is* not put under him. *(Once again speaks of the original Adam, but more*

than all speaks of the 'Last Adam,' the Lord Jesus Christ.) **But now we see not yet all things put under him.** *(Due to the Fall, we do not now see what was originally intended for man, but through Christ it will ultimately be seen.)*

"But we see Jesus, Who was made a little lower than the Angels *(the Incarnation)* **for the suffering of death** *(unequivocally proclaims the fact that Jesus came to this world for one specific purpose — to die upon a Cross, which was planned even before the foundation of the world [I Pet. 1:18-20]),* **crowned with glory and honour** *(the mission was accomplished, and now Christ is exalted)*; **that He by the Grace of God should taste death for every man.** *(This proclaims the fact that He needed the Grace of God to accomplish this task, because He was a man, 'the Man, Christ Jesus')*" **(Heb. 2:5-9).**

ANGELS AND BELIEVERS

Jesus said:

"Take heed that you despise not one of these little ones *(one who trusts in Christ and the Cross)*; **for I say unto you, That in Heaven their Angels do always behold the Face of My Father which is in Heaven** *(every true Believer is assigned an Angel, who reports to the Heavenly Father, any and all things pertaining to that Believer)*" **(Mat. 18:10).**

Then Paul wrote:

"Are they not all Ministering spirits *(the function of Angels)*, **sent forth to Minister for them Who shall be heirs of Salvation?** *(This proclaims that they attend only those who have made Christ their Saviour)*" **(Heb. 1:14).**

This Passage does not mean that Believers can order Angels

to do certain things, etc. The Scripture uses the phrase *"sent forth,"* which means they are sent by God, given instructions by the Lord, all on behalf of Saints; however, Believers cannot direct Angels to do anything. The reasons for that should be abundantly obvious.

First of all, only the Lord knows all things about all situations. Our knowledge is very, very limited! So, in regard to that, the Lord always keeps the reins in His Hands so to speak.

A perfect example of this pertains to a heathen king who sent an army to capture the Prophet Elisha. Elisha's servant stepped outside one morning to find the town of Dothan surrounded by an enemy force. He ran in terror to the Prophet. Elisha quieted his fears and then asked God to open the servant's eyes. Suddenly the servant saw *"the hills full of horses and chariots of fire all around Elisha"* (II Ki. 6:17). An Angelic army was present to protect the Lord's Prophet; however, it was the Lord Who did the sending, and the directing, and not Elisha.

IN CONCLUSION

While this simple study about Angels is intriguing and stimulates speculation, still, the thrust, as we've already stated, of both the Old Testament and the New Testament is clear. Human beings, not Angels are the focus of God's concern. So, we are to fix our eyes, our heart, and our attention solely upon our Lord and our Saviour, Jesus Christ, rather than on Angels. To be sure, the Lord can supervise the Universe according to His Will, while we concentrate our attention, our affection, and our deep and abiding love upon the One Who has redeemed us. He is truly the Lord of all!

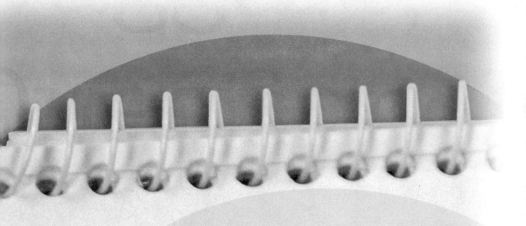

CHAPTER 3

The Doctrine Of Blessings

THE DOCTRINE OF BLESSINGS
(The Prosperity Gospel)

The Gospel of Jesus Christ is the greatest Fount of Blessing and prosperity in the world today and, in fact, ever has been. There is nothing that can remotely come close to the prosperity afforded by Christ; however, the prosperity of the Bible is different than that of the world.

The world looks only at the outward, which speaks of secular education, and money above all. All of this, it is hoped by the world, translates into fame.

The Bible is totally different. It does teach financial prosperity, but, as well, and above all, it teaches Spiritual Prosperity.

The Holy Spirit said it perfectly through John the Beloved:

"Beloved, I wish above all things that you may prosper *(refers to financial prosperity, and should be the case for every Believer)* and be in health *(speaks of physical prosperity)*, even as your soul prospers *(speaks of Spiritual Prosperity; so we have here the whole Gospel for the whole man)*" (III Jn., Vs. 2).

Some claim that this Second Verse given to us by John the Beloved, was meant only as a Salutation and is not a Promise of God. Nothing could be further from the Truth.

Every Word in the Bible is inspired by the Holy Spirit. That's the reason that Jesus said, *"Man shall not live by bread alone, but by every Word that proceeds out of the Mouth of God"* (Mat. 4:4). This means that man is a Spiritual being as well as a physical being; therefore, totally dependent on God (Deut. 8:3).

The Holy Spirit meant exactly what He said as it regards financial prosperity, physical prosperity, and Spiritual Prosperity.

PROVE ME!

Every Believer ought to live in a spirit of expectation, and we speak of expecting God to do great, wonderful, and mighty things for us. In fact, God loves us, and does so supremely. He has purchased us at great Price; consequently, He desires, longingly desires, to give good things to us. He is limited only by our unbelief.

He said to Israel a long, long time ago: *"If you be willing and obedient, you shall eat the good of the land"* (Isa. 1:19).

However, there are conditions, even as there should be conditions. The Lord also said:

> **"But if you refuse and rebel, you shall be devoured with the sword: for the Mouth of the LORD has spoken it.** *(This means, 'If you consent in your wills and are also obedient in your actions.'*
>
> *"The 'eating of the good of the land' refers to blessing and Satan's not devouring the increase.*
>
> *"The idea is that God controls all. If we obey Him, blessing will be ours. If we do not obey Him, He will allow enemies to come in and 'devour with a sword')"* **(Isa. 1:20).**

Financial Blessings from the Lord presents the only occasion in the Bible where we are allowed to prove or test the Lord. He does not take kindly to any other type of proving; however, as it regards this one factor, He challenges us actually to prove Him. The great Prophet Malachi said concerning this:

THE CONDEMNATION

> **"Will a man rob God? Yet you have robbed Me. But you say, Wherein have we robbed You? In tithes and offerings.** *(The question, 'Will a man rob God?' is blunt and to the point. It instantly portrayed Israel's present condition, in that they had, in fact, robbed God! 'Yet you have robbed Me!' proclaims unequivocally that they had robbed God, which is a serious charge indeed!*
>
> *"The question, 'But you say, Wherein have we robbed*

You?' brings back the quick answer through the Prophet, 'In tithes and offerings.' Some claim that 'tithes' are a part of the old Mosaic system and are not applicable under the New Covenant! However, paying tithes was practiced long before the Law [Gen. 14:20; 28:22]; it was also commanded under Grace in the New Testament [Mat. 23:23; Rom. 2:22; I Cor. 9:7-14; 16:2; Gal. 6:6; Heb. 7:1-10].

"*Abraham, a type of all Believers, paid tithe to Melchizedek, a Type of Christ [Gen. 14:20], which sets the standard; inasmuch as we are children of Abraham, we are to continue to pay tithe to the Work of God, which, in effect, is the propagation of the Message of Christ and Him Crucified [Gal. 3:6-7; I Cor. 1:23].)*

THE CURSE

"**You are cursed with a curse: for you have robbed Me, even this whole nation.** *('You are cursed with a curse,' is dire indeed! The effect of this curse was scarcity and barrenness, as we see from Verses 10 through 12. Robbing God of tithes and offerings brings a curse. These belong to God by virtue of Covenant agreements with man; to use them for personal gain is robbery of that which rightly belongs to Him.*

"*The phrase, 'For you have robbed Me, even this whole nation,' proclaims the reason for the poverty, among other things, of the nations of the world)*" **(Mal. 3:8-9).**

THE WINDOWS OF HEAVEN

"**Bring you all the tithes into the storehouse, that there may be meat in My House, and prove Me now herewith, says the LORD of Hosts, if I will not open you the windows of Heaven, and pour you out a Blessing, that there shall not be room enough to receive it.** *('Bring you all the tithes into the storehouse,' referred to the Temple* *and cities of the Levites under the Old Covenant. Under the New Covenant, it refers to the place where one's soul is fed, wherever that might be. Some have claimed that the local Church is the 'storehouse' where all giving is to be brought; however, that is incorrect, inasmuch as those who propose such fail to understand what 'Church' actually is! 'Church' is made up of all members of the Body of Christ, irrespective of who they are or where they are. It has nothing to do with the building, organization, or religious institution. It is the 'Message' which must be supported — not an institution.*

"The phrase, 'That there may be meat in My House,' has reference to the support of the Priesthood in the Temple of old. The Lord has no such 'house' at present, because Jesus fulfilled all that the ancient Temple represented, with Him now residing through the agency of the Holy Spirit in the hearts and lives of all Believers [I Cor. 3:16].

PROVE ME!

" 'And prove Me now herewith, says the LORD of Hosts,' presents a challenge presented by the Lord for men to prove Him regarding the rewards of tithing. 'If I will not open you the windows of Heaven, and pour you out a Blessing, that there shall not be room enough to receive it,' speaks of a superabundant amount. The same phrase, 'Windows of Heaven,' is used in Gen. 7:11 regarding the flood; therefore, we are speaking of Blessings unparalleled!)" **(Mal. 3:10).**

REBUKING THE DEVOURER

"And I will rebuke the devourer for your sakes, and he shall not destroy the fruits of your ground; neither shall your vine cast her fruit before the time in the field, says the LORD of Hosts. *(In the first phrase, the Holy Spirit uses the word 'devourer'; then, He uses the pronoun 'he,' symbolizing a personality behind the destruction, i.e.,*

Satan. *As well, the word 'rebuke' means 'to turn back' or
'keep down.'*

"So, if we fail to give to God, the Lord proclaims that
He will not turn back the 'devourer.' This will result in the
'fruits' of our efforts being destroyed. To give to God means
the opposite. Crops will be abundant, with efforts resulting
in prosperity.*

"The last phrase simply speaks of the harvest being
gathered, and abundantly so, and not being lost.)*

"**And all nations shall call you blessed: for you shall
be a delightsome land, says the LORD of Hosts.** *(The
first phrase speaks of the Blessings of the Lord as being so
abundant that other nations will enquire as to the reason)*"
(**Mal. 3:11-12**).

One of the great reasons for God's Blessings of prosperity
upon America is because our Government allows giving to the
Work of God to be deducted from one's income tax; consequently, this nation is the envy of the world. If looking for the
reason, at least a great part of it is that which we have said. God
always honors His Word, and He said if we would be generous
with Him, He would be overly generous with us, and *"all nations
shall call you blessed: for you shall be a delightsome land."*

So, the Lord says, as it regards giving to the Work of God,
we are allowed to *"prove Him,"* meaning to test Him, to see if
He will hold to His Promise. To be sure, He will hold to every
Word that He has said. Untold millions can testify to the veracity of these great Promises. You can't out give God!

GOD'S ECONOMY

When a person comes to Christ, they literally enter into
God's Economy, which is not tied to the system of this world.
As a result, they have the guarantee of His Blessings, that is, if
we do our best to live a life of obedience, which means to place
our Faith and Trust exclusively in Christ and what He has done

for us at the Cross. In fact, all Blessings are made possible by the Cross of Christ. We had best not forget that! Regarding His Care for us we are given some great instructions, and powerful promises. Our Lord said, and I continue to quote from THE EXPOSITOR'S STUDY BIBLE:

DON'T WORRY

"Therefore I say unto you, Take no thought for your life, what you shall eat, or what you shall drink; nor yet for your body, what you shall put on *(don't worry about these things)*. Is not the life more than meat, and the body than raiment? *(Life is more than things, and the physical body is more than the clothes we wear.)*

"Behold the fowls of the air: for they sow not, neither do they reap, nor gather into barns; yet your Heavenly Father feeds them. Are you not much better than they? *(The fowls of the air are a smaller part of God's great Creation. If the Lord has provided for them, most assuredly, He has provided for His Children.)*

"Which of you by taking thought *(worrying and fretting)* can add one cubit unto his stature? *(Whatever is going to happen cannot be stopped by worry; and if it doesn't happen, there is nothing to worry about. For His Children, the Lord always fills in the bottom line.)*

"And why do you take thought *(worry)* for *(about)* raiment *(clothes)*? Consider the lilies of the field, how they grow; they toil not, neither do they spin *(the man grows the flax [toil] the woman weaves it [spins]; the statement is meant to proclaim the fact that the beauty of the lily has nothing to do with its effort, but is given completely by the Creator)*:

"And yet I say unto you, That even Solomon in all his glory was not arrayed like one of these *(it is said that the lilies of Israel had brilliant coloring, and especially the purple and white Huleh Lily found in Nazareth)*.

THE PROMISE OF GOD

"**Wherefore, if** *(since)* **God so clothed the grass of the field** *(is meant to portray God's guarantee)***, which today is, and tomorrow is cast into the oven** *(portrays how inconsequential is this part of His Creation, and yet, how much care He expends on it)***, shall He not much more clothe you, O you of little faith?** *(We are told here the reason for our lack; it is 'little faith'; because God is Faithful, He can be trusted fully to completely carry out His Commitments to us in Christ [I Cor. 1:9; 10:13; II Cor. 1:18; I Thess. 5:24; II Thess. 3:3; etc.].)*

"**Therefore take no thought** *(don't worry)***, saying, What shall we eat? or, What shall we drink? or, Wherewithal shall we be clothed?** *(The Greek Text actually means that even one anxious thought is forbidden. Such shows a distrust of the Lord.)*

"**(For after all these things do the Gentiles seek:)** *(Gentiles had no part in God's Covenant with Israel; consequently, they had no part in God's economy, and, basically, had to fend for themselves)* **for your Heavenly Father knows that you have need of all these things** *(the phrase is meant to express the contrast between those who do not know the Lord and those who do; if we live for Him, ever seeking His Will, we have the guarantee of His Word, which He will provide for us. Is God's Word good enough? I think it is!)***.**

SEEK FIRST THE KINGDOM OF GOD

"**But seek you first the Kingdom of God, and His Righteousness** *(this gives the 'condition' for God's Blessings; His Interests are to be 'first')***; and all these things shall be added unto you** *(this is the 'guarantee' of God's Provision)***.**

"**Take therefore no thought for the morrow** *(don't worry* *about the future)*: **for the morrow shall take thought for the things of itself** *(this is meant to refer back to Verse 27)*. **Sufficient unto the day** *is* **the evil thereof** *(this means that we should handle daily difficulties in Faith, and have Faith for the future that the present difficulties will not grow into larger ones; we have God's Assurance that they won't, that is, if we will sufficiently believe Him)*" **(Mat. 6:25-34).**

GOD'S ECONOMY IS TOTAL

The economy of our Lord is a *"way of life."* Traveling all over the world preaching the Gospel, I have heard many speak about the culture of particular places. The truth is, when the Believer comes to Christ, as stated, we enter *"God's Culture,"* which means that we enter *"God's Economy,"* which covers every strata of our life and living.

Simon Peter addressed this by saying:

"**According as His Divine Power has given unto us all things** *(the Lord with large-handed generosity has given us all things)* **that** *pertain* **unto life and Godliness** *(pertains to the fact that the Lord Jesus has given us everything we need regarding life and living)*, **through the knowledge of Him Who has called us to Glory and Virtue** *(the 'knowledge' addressed here speaks of what Christ did at the Cross, which alone can provide 'Glory and Virtue')*:

"**Whereby are given unto us exceeding great and Precious Promises** *(pertains to the Word of God, which alone holds the answer to every life problem)*: **that by these** *(Promises)* **you might be partakers of the Divine Nature** *(the Divine Nature implanted in the inner being of the believing sinner becomes the source of our new life and actions; it comes to everyone at the moment of being 'Born-Again')*, **having escaped the corruption that is in the world through lust.** *(This presents the Salvation experience of the sinner, and the Sanctification experience* *of the Saint)"* **(II Pet. 1:3-4).**

DO NOT SEEK RICHES MERELY
FOR THE SAKE OF RICHES

There are times that God will make some of His Children rich. If He does such, it is right and correct, as should be obvious; however, we as Believers are not to set our heart on the fact of riches. While it's perfectly satisfactory to ask God to bless us, and to do so abundantly, as we have been saying over and over again; however, our purpose and reason, in other words our motives should be, as the Lord blesses us, we in turn can bless His Work.

It is said that the Lord said more about money in His Word, than He did anything else. While I haven't counted the times in the Scriptures, I would be surprised if that wasn't true.

Why?

As we've already stated, the Blessings of the Lord as it regards money, is the only thing in the Word of God where we are allowed to prove the Lord, in other words, to test the Lord. That should tell us something!

As someone has well said,

"It's not what you would do with riches should such ere be your lot,

"But what you're doing at present with the dollar and the quarter, you've got."

Unfortunately, the faith of many is judged presently by the make of their automobile, or the price of their suit of clothes. Such must be repugnant in the Eyes of God.

The Holy Spirit said much through Paul as it regards the situation of riches. He said:

WHAT THE HOLY SPIRIT SAID ABOUT RICHES

"Perverse disputings of men of corrupt minds *(should have been translated, 'of men corrupted in mind')***, and**

destitute of the Truth *(refers to the fact that they had once possessed the Truth, which is the Cross, but had turned away to other things)*, **supposing that gain is Godliness** *(should have been translated, 'supposing that Godliness is a way or source of gain')*: **from such withdraw yourself** *(have no dealings with these preachers)*.

"**But Godliness with contentment** *(content with what we have, which means we are thankful to God for what we have)* **is great gain** *(true gain)*.

"**For we brought nothing into *this* world, *and it is* certain we can carry nothing out.** *(This speaks of worldly possessions. The only thing a person can keep is their Faith, that is if it's true Faith, which refers to Faith in Christ and the Cross.)*

"**And having food and raiment let us be therewith content.** *(The Lord can never bless grasping greed.)*

"**But they who will be rich fall into temptation and a snare, and *into* many foolish and hurtful lusts** *(speaks of the sacrifice of principle)*, **which drown men in destruction and perdition.** *(This refers to the wreck and ruin of the mind and body, but more particularly to the awful ruin of the eternal soul.)*

THE LOVE OF MONEY

"**For the love of money is the root of all evil** *(there is no conceivable evil that can happen to the sons and daughters of men, which may not spring from covetousness — the love of gold and wealth)*: **which while some coveted after, they have erred from the Faith** *(speaking of Believers who have lost sight of the True Faith, which is the Cross, and have ventured into a false faith, trying to use it to garner much money)*, **and pierced themselves through with many sorrows** *(the end result of turning in that direction; let all understand that the Word of God is true, and what it says will happen!)*.

"But you, O man of God, flee these things *(the Holy Spirit is unequivocally clear in His Command; we can follow the Lord, or we can follow other things; we can't follow both!)*; and follow after **Righteousness, Godliness, Faith, Love, Patience, Meekness.** *(In a sense, this is Fruit of the Spirit, or at least that which the Spirit Alone can bring about in our lives, which He does by the Cross ever being the Object of our Faith)*" **(I Tim. 6:5-11).**

Let us say it again, it's not a sin to be rich, neither is it a sin to make money, that is if we do it legally and righteously. And, if the Lord does see fit to place a goodly sum of this world's goods into our hands, we should realize the reason that He has done this. It's not just because of our tremendous business acumen. It is that we might further the Work of God.

The Believer must remember, everything that the Lord does with us, and I mean everything, is in one way or the other, a test of Faith. How will we act, how will we react?

WHAT SHOULD THE BELIEVER SUPPORT?

That's an excellent question!

It doesn't matter how much money is given to that which claims to be the Work of God, if it isn't, then our money has been wasted, and worse yet, we can find ourselves actually supporting the work of Satan. Paul had much to say about imposters. Read it carefully:

"For such *are* false apostles, deceitful workers *(they have no rightful claim to the Apostolic Office; they are deceivers)*, transforming themselves into the Apostles of Christ. *(They have called themselves to this Office.)*

"And no marvel *(true Believers should not be surprised)*; for Satan himself is transformed into an Angel of light. *(This means he pretends to be that which he is not.)*

"Therefore *it is* no great thing if his ministers

(Satan's ministers) **also be transformed as the ministers of righteousness** *(despite their claims, they were 'Satan's ministers' because they preached something other than the Cross [I Cor. 1:17-18, 21, 23; 2:2; Gal. 1:8-9])*; **whose end shall be according to their works** *(that 'end' is spiritual destruction [Phil. 3:18-19])*" **(II Cor. 11:13-15).**

If anyone studies Paul very much, it becomes quickly obvious that his greatest opposition came from the Judaisers. Now who were these people?

THE JUDAISERS

They were Jews from Jerusalem or somewhere in Judea, who claimed to believe in Christ, but at the same time claimed that one had to keep the Law of Moses, that is if they were to be Saved, at least to be a complete Christian. Of course, their message was diametrically opposed to that of Paul, who stated that Christ had fulfilled the Law in totality; consequently, everything now was by Faith in Christ and what Christ had done at the Cross (Gal. 1:8-9; I Cor. 1:17-18, 23; 2:2).

After Paul would build Churches, which he did in scores of cities, or else his associates, these Judaisers would come into these Churches and attempt to turn the people toward the Law. They are the ones that Paul was referring to as *"Satan's ministers."*

As well, these Judaisers were getting money from the people — in fact, those who had been Saved under the Ministry of Paul. With their erroneous doctrine, the truth is, they couldn't get anybody Saved, so they had to parasite off of others, and in this case, the Apostle Paul.

Now, does anyone honestly think that giving money to these people was furthering the Cause of Christ? was spreading the Gospel? No, any money given to these people was actually furthering the work of Satan, as he did his best to destroy the great Gospel of Grace which had been given to Paul directly by the Lord Jesus Christ (Gal. 1:12).

Unfortunately, the Judaisers, albeit in another form, did not die out in the First Century. They are still alive and well in the world today, and prospering greatly off of Christians who seemingly do not know better. In fact, I think one could say and not be wrong, that at least 90 percent, and more than likely as high as 99 percent of all money given to that which claims to be the Gospel is, in fact, something else altogether. This means that such money at best is wasted, and at the worst, is furthering the cause of Satan.

Plainly and clearly the Apostle Paul tells us what we should support. We should read it very carefully.

THE CROSS OF CHRIST

When Paul was in prison in Rome, the Church at Philippi, which had been founded on the Message of Grace preached by the Apostle Paul, sent him a very generous offering, which he needed very much. He wrote them back a thank you letter which actually comprises his Epistle to the Philippians. In closing the letter, he said:

> "But I rejoiced in the Lord greatly *(concerning the gift they had sent him)*, that now at the last your care of me has flourished again *(it seems that for a period of time, the Philippians had ceased to help the Apostle)*; wherein you were also careful *(the Church at Philippi had not forgotten Paul, but lacked the means to get the gift to him)*, but you lacked opportunity *(thank the Lord, opportunity had finally presented itself)*.
>
> "Not that I speak in respect of want *(declares his independence from creature comforts)*: for I have learned, in whatsoever state I am, *therewith* to be content *(to be independent of external circumstances)*.
>
> "I know both how to be abased *(to keep rejoicing when there is no money)*, and I know how to abound *(to*

keep rejoicing when there is money): **everywhere and in all things I am instructed both to be full and to be hungry, both to abound and to suffer need.** *(All will come sooner or later, and the negative is not for a lack of Faith, but rather for our instruction in Righteousness.)*

"I can do all things *(be abased or abound)* **through Christ which strengtheneth me** *(from Whom I draw strength).*

"Notwithstanding you have well done *(he is not meaning to disparage the gift of the Philippian Church)*, **that you did communicate with my affliction.** *(They helped Paul with his needs, as it regards the offering they sent him.)*

"Now you Philippians know also, that in the beginning of the Gospel *(refers to the time when Paul first preached the Word to them, about ten years previously)*, **when I departed from Macedonia, no Church communicated with me as concerning giving and receiving, but you only** *(proclaims the fact that the Philippians had always been generous).*

"For even in Thessalonica *(when he was starting the Church there)* **you sent once and again unto my necessity** *(proclaims their faithfulness).*

"Not because I desire a gift *(presents the Apostle defending himself against the slanderous assertion that he is using the Gospel as a means to make money)*: **but I desire fruit that may abound to your account.** *(God keeps a record of everything, even our gifts, whether giving or receiving.)*

"But I have all, and abound: I am full *(proclaims the fact that the Philippian gift must have been generous)*, **having received of Epaphroditus the things *which were sent* from you** *(Epaphroditus had brought the gift from Philippi to Rome)*, **an odour of a sweet smell** *(presents the Old Testament odors of the Levitical Sacrifices, all typifying Christ)*, **a Sacrifice acceptable, well-pleasing to God.** *(For those who gave to Paul, enabling him to take the Message of the Cross to others, their gift, and such gifts presently, are* *looked at by God as a part of the Sacrificial Atoning Work of Christ on the Cross. Nothing could be higher than that!)*

"But my God shall supply all your need *(presents the Apostle assuring the Philippians, and all other Believers as well, that they have not impoverished themselves in giving so liberally to the cause of Christ)* **according to His Riches in Glory** *(the measure of supply will be determined by the wealth of God in Glory)* **by Christ Jesus** *(made possible by the Cross)***" (Phil. 4:10-19).**

GIVING BLESSED BY THE LORD

Pure and simple, the Holy Spirit through the Apostle here tells us, that if the Message or the Work we are supporting is not based upon the Cross of Christ, then whatever it is, it's not the Gospel. First of all, Paul has already told us what the Gospel of Christ actually is. He said, when writing to the Church at Corinth:

"For Christ sent me not to baptize *(presents to us a Cardinal Truth)***, but to preach the Gospel** *(the manner in which one may be Saved from sin)***: not with wisdom of words** *(intellectualism is not the Gospel)***, lest the Cross of Christ should be made of none effect.** *(This tells us in no uncertain terms that the Cross of Christ must always be the emphasis of the Message)***" (I Cor. 1:17).**

WHAT DOES IT MEAN TO PREACH THE CROSS?

The Apostle also said:

"For the preaching *(Word)* **of the Cross is to them who perish foolishness; but unto us who are Saved it is the Power of God" (I Cor. 1:18).**

The word *"preaching"* in the original Greek is *"logos,"* and

should have been translated *"Word,"* or *"Message."* There are some four ways we can look at this question. They are:

OPPOSING THE CROSS

1. A large part of the Charismatic segment of the Church actually repudiates the Cross. I speak of the Word of Faith people so-called. They refer to the Cross as *"past miseries,"* or *"the worst defeat in human history."* They also state if a preacher preaches the Cross, he is preaching death, and the person hearing such a message will lose their way.

That's very strange when we read the statements given by the Apostle Paul, some of which I have just quoted.

These people are somewhat like the Judaisers of old. They cannot get anyone Saved, because their gospel is erroneous, meaning that the Holy Spirit cannot anoint such. So they have to parasite off of Churches that are built by Preachers who do preach the Gospel.

Unfortunately, most of the people in these Churches have been lured in by the doctrine of riches. In other words, they are made to believe by associating themselves with these Churches, and giving heavily of their income, that they are going to get rich. Their emphasis, for the most part, is on money.

So, the idea that the Cross of Christ is repudiated in this doctrine little connects with their thinking. To be frank, they are not that interested in the True Gospel anyway, once again, with money being the object.

UNBELIEF REGARDING THE CROSS

2. These are preachers who claim to believe in the Cross, but never preach the Cross, because they say *"it offends people."* I heard the other day one of their most renowned Pastors whose Church runs twenty to thirty thousand, state, they never preach the Cross. In fact, he went on to say that they will never sing songs about the Blood, etc. Once again, such may

offend people.

The truth is their claims are false as it regards their believing in the Cross. Pure and simple, they don't believe the Cross and, if they did, they would preach it. They don't preach it, because they don't believe it.

THE CROSS AND SALVATION

3. These are preachers, who are sincere, and who preach the Cross as it regards Salvation, but that's as far as they go with the Message, simply because they have no understanding at all as it regards the complete Message of the Cross. In fact, what was given to the Apostle Paul by the Lord Jesus Christ, is what He gave to us. These preachers are preaching the truth as far as they know the truth, and should be supported; however, their gospel is at best an incomplete Gospel, and will show up as such in the lives of their supporters.

PREACHING THE CROSS

4. The Preacher who is proclaiming what the Apostle Paul gave to us, which is the Message of the Cross as it refers to both Salvation and Sanctification, are preaching a complete Message.

As we've already stated, it was to Paul that the meaning of the New Covenant was given, which, in effect, is the meaning of the Cross. It was given to him directly by Christ (Gal. 1:12). The Apostle gave this great Word to us in his fourteen Epistles.

In these fourteen Epistles, 90 percent or more of the instruction given pertains to the manner in which the Believer is to live for God. The sad fact is, in today's modern Gospel, even those who truly love God, most simply do not know how to live for God. It is because they do not understand the Message of the Cross as it refers to our Sanctification, i.e., *"our everyday life and living,"* in other words, how we order our behavior. As a result, there is precious little overcoming victory in such hearts and lives, even though such people truly love the Lord. This is the Message, as should be obvious, that should be supported. It is the Message that will set the captive free. It's not the ways of man; it is the Ways of God. It is God's Prescribed Order of Life and Living. Let us close with the following statements:

• The only way to God is through Jesus Christ (Jn. 14:6).

• The only way to the Lord Jesus Christ is by and through the Cross (I Cor. 1:17; 2:2).

• The only way to the Cross is a denial of self (Lk. 9:23).

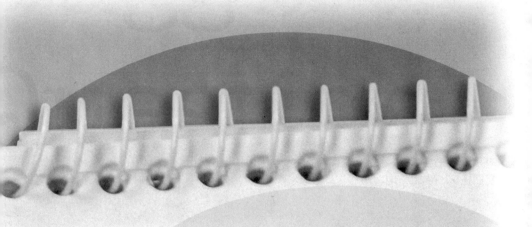

CHAPTER 4

The Doctrine Of Divine Healing

THE DOCTRINE OF DIVINE HEALING

James, our Lord's brother, gave us a clear, concise promise as it regards Divine Healing. And let me quickly add, while there is such a thing as Divine Healing, there is no such thing as divine healers. In other words, man cannot heal anyone. There is only one Divine Healer, and that is the Lord Jesus Christ. James said:

"**Is any among you afflicted? let him pray.** *(Prayer is the recommendation of the Holy Spirit concerning affliction. But how many Christians take advantage of this privilege?)* **Is any merry? let him sing Psalms.** *(In effect, refers to singing as a form of prayer, which it actually is, that is if we sing songs that rightly glorify the Lord.)*

"**Is any sick among you?** *(This refers to physical or emotional illness of any nature.)* **let him call for the Elders (Pastors) of the Church; and let them pray over him** *(refers to asking the Lord for healing regarding the need)*, **anointing him with oil in the Name of the Lord** *(the 'oil' has no medicinal purpose, but is rather meant to symbolize the Holy Spirit, and is used as a point of contact concerning our Faith; prayer is to be offered in the Name of Jesus [Jn. 16:23])*:

"**And the prayer of Faith shall save the sick** *(the 'prayer of Faith' is simply the belief that God hears and answers prayer)*, **and the Lord shall raise him up** *(proclaims the Lord as the Healer, as is obvious, with the Cross being the means of all this; it is the Holy Spirit Who carries it out)*; **and if he have committed sins, they shall be forgiven him.** *(The conditional clause, 'if he has sinned,' makes it clear that not all sickness is the result of sin, but some definitely is. That being the case, the Lord will both heal and forgive upon believing Faith.)*

CONFESSING FAULTS

"**Confess *your* faults one to another** *(refers to being* *quick to admit fault, if such be the case)*, **and pray one for another, that you may be healed.** *(The Holy Spirit, through James, broadens the aspect of prayer for the sick as applicable to any Believer.)* **The effectual fervent prayer of a Righteous man avails much** *(from any 'Righteous man,' Preacher or otherwise; 'Righteousness' pertains to the fact that the Faith of the individual is strictly in Christ and the Cross, and not in other things).*

"Elijah was a man subject to like passions as we are *(is said in this manner because the Holy Spirit wants us to know that what is in the reach of one is as well in the reach of the other)*, **and he prayed earnestly that it might not rain: and it rained not on the earth by the space of three years and six months** *(showing us the power of prayer, that is if we pray in the Will of God).*

"And he prayed again, and the Heaven gave rain, and the earth brought forth her fruit *(refers to the effect of one man's prayers)*" **(James 5:13-18).**

A PERSONAL EXPERIENCE

As I relate my own personal experience of the Power of the Lord to heal, I want to preface it by saying that I'm so very thankful that my parents attended a Church, albeit very small, where the Pastor believed that Jesus Christ still heals the sick. Had that not been the case, I doubt very seriously that I would be here today, for I think Satan was trying to kill me. I was about ten years of age. I had been Saved and baptized with the Holy Spirit with the evidence of speaking with other Tongues at eight years old.

Whatever sickness I had the doctors were not able to ascertain what it really was. I stayed nauseous constantly, and at times would just go unconscious. My parents took me to the doctor, and they ran whatever tests they could run in those days, but found nothing. They ruled out malaria, and whatever else they thought it might have been.

The situation became critical, inasmuch as I would go unconscious while at school. The principal would call my parents, and they would come pick me up. The last time it happened, the principal told my Mother and my Dad, *"If something is not done, you are going to have to take Jimmy out of school."* And then he added, *"We don't want him dying on our hands."*

I believe that the Evil One knew that the Lord would use me in later years, and he set about to try to stop that process. As stated, he was trying to kill me.

PRAYER

Any number of times during this situation, which lasted for several months, the Pastor and others prayed for me, anointed me with oil, invoking the Name of the Lord, asking for healing, but all to no avail.

Looking back, I'm so very, very glad, that they did not get discouraged and quit. After praying for me several times, with seemingly no outward results, but rather me growing worse, it would have been very easy for them to say that it was no use, or that the Lord doesn't heal today, or whatever reason one could think of. But, they didn't do that, they kept praying and kept believing.

THE DAY OF MY HEALING

The way the Lord chose to heal me, carried with it no dramatic occurrences. Actually it was a Sunday, and the Service had just ended. My parents were going to take the Pastor and his wife to lunch, but before we did that, we had to go by the home of a particular parishioner, and pray for him, as he had been ill.

These particular people were faithful to Church, but at the same time, they were very poor. They lived in a little small three room house, and I can still see it in my past recollection.

We prayed for the Brother, and then walked to the front

room and was about to leave. Brother Culbreth, our Pastor was standing by the wall beside my Dad, along with my Mother and the Pastor's wife. The lady of the house was standing there as well.

I was standing near the door that led outside. My Dad turned to the Pastor and said, *"Brother Culbreth, would you anoint Jimmy with oil again and pray for him, because if the Lord doesn't do something, we are going to have to take him out of school."*

I can still see the scene in my mind, as it is forever freeze-framed in my recollection. I can see the Pastor with a bottle of oil in his hand. I can see him smile as he nodded his head in agreement, and walked toward me, putting a little oil on his finger, and touching my head with everyone beginning to pray. It was instant!

The Power of God came down in that room and it settled on me.

A MANIFESTATION

All of a sudden I felt something, which seemed like a ball of fire, about the size of a softball that started at the top of my head, and slowly went down the back of my body, all the way down to my feet. I could distinctly feel the heat from it, and I knew, even though I was only ten years old, that when it reached the bottom of my feet that I was healed. And so I was, never being bothered with that sickness again.

In fact, as I dictate these notes on January 4, 2009, I am 73 years old, and have experienced very little sickness throughout my life. Now there are all type of questions that come to mind as it regards what the Lord did that day. Some of them are:

• Why didn't the Lord heal me when the Pastor and others first prayed for me? I cannot answer that! As stated, I will ever be eternally grateful, however, that my Parents didn't get discouraged and quit praying. Perhaps the Lord conducts Himself in that fashion, in order to test our Faith. Will we quit, or will we persist?

• Why didn't the Lord heal me in Church, when I was prayed for there, instead of healing me in this particular house? Was it something special about this family? About this house?

No! In fact, this man and his wife, although faithful, were not, as I remember, paragons of Spiritual Maturity.

• Is healing always accompanied by a ball of fire being felt in a person's physical body? No! But I have heard of that happening quite a number of times with others also.

• Does one always have to be anointed with oil in order to be healed? Again, no! While being anointed with oil is most definitely Scriptural, it is not something that has to be administered for a person to be healed. Down through the centuries, millions, no doubt, have been healed while they were anointed with oil and others without being anointed with oil. In fact, the oil has no medicinal value, being only a Type of the Holy Spirit and, as well, a point of contact for our Faith.

IS HEALING IN THE ATONEMENT?

Yes!

I have preached the Gospel now for well over 50 years, and during that time I have read scores of sermons written by preachers who claimed that healing is not in the Atonement. Their conclusion is, if healing is in the Atonement, then there would be no sickness among Believers.

Such thinking is foolish!

These same preachers who claim that the Lord no longer heals, at the same time claim that forgiveness and cleansing from sin is definitely in the Atonement, and rightly so; however, that being the case, such does not guarantee that Believers do not again sin. In fact, there's never been a single Believer who has ever lived, no matter how gracious the Lord was to him or her, who in some way has not failed the Lord, not one time, but many times. So, forgiveness and cleansing from sin being in the Atonement, doesn't mean that Christians, although availing ourselves of the privileges of the Atonement, will not at times fail the Lord. This doesn't mean that the Atonement is deficient; it just means that we are deficient.

EVERYTHING LOST IN THE FALL WAS ANSWERED IN THE ATONEMENT

Not only did the Lord address everything in the Atonement that was lost in the Fall, and I mean everything, but, as well, the Atonement also addressed Satan and his revolution against God. Concerning that, Paul said:

"Having made known unto us the mystery of His Will *(refers to the secret purposes and counsels God intends to carry into effect in His Kingdom)*, according to His good pleasure *(extended to Believers)* which He has purposed in Himself *(originated in His Own Mind)*:

"That in the dispensation of the fulness of times *(concerns itself with a well-ordered plan)* He might gather together in one all things in Christ *(the Atonement addressed not only man's Fall, but the revolution of Lucifer as well)*, both which are in Heaven *(where the revolution of Lucifer began)*, and which are on earth *(the Fall of man)*; *even* in Him *(made possible by what Christ did at the Cross)*:

"In Whom *(Christ)* also we have obtained an inheritance *(the best Greek Texts have, 'we were designated as a heritage'; thus, the Saints are God's Heritage, His Possession through the Work of Christ on the Cross)*, being predestinated according to the purpose of Him *(pertains to the inheritance being predestinated, not the individual who would obtain the inheritance)* Who works all things after the Counsel of His Own Will *(therefore, it is perfect)*" (Eph. 1:9-11).

And then Paul wrote, and I continue to quote from THE

EXPOSITOR'S STUDY BIBLE:

SATAN'S DEFEAT AT THE CROSS

"**Beware lest any man spoil you through philosophy and vain deceit** *(anything that pulls the Believer away from the Cross is not of God)*, **after the tradition of men** *(anything that is not of the Cross is of men)*, **after the rudiments of the world, and not after Christ.** *(If it's truly after Christ, then it's after the Cross.)*

"**For in Him** *(Christ)* **dwells all the fulness of the Godhead bodily.** *(This is Godhead as to essence. Christ is the completion and the fullness of Deity, and in Him the Believer is complete.)*

"**And you are complete in Him** *(the satisfaction of every spiritual want is found in Christ, made possible by the Cross)*, **which is the Head of all principality and power** *(His Headship extends not only over the Church, which voluntarily serves Him, but over all forces that are opposed to Him as well [Phil. 2:10-11])*:

"**In Whom also you are circumcised with the Circumcision made without hands** *(that which is brought about by the Cross [Rom. 6:3-5])*, **in putting off the body of the sins of the flesh by the Circumcision of Christ** *(refers to the old carnal nature that is defeated by the Believer placing his Faith totally in the Cross, which gives the Holy Spirit latitude to work)*:

NOT WATER BAPTISM

"**Buried with Him in Baptism** *(does not refer to Water Baptism, but rather to the Believer baptized into the Death of Christ, which refers to the Crucifixion and Christ as our substitute [Rom. 6:3-4])*, **wherein also you are risen with *Him* through the Faith of the operation of God, Who has raised Him from the dead.** *(This does* *not refer to our future physical Resurrection, but to that Spiritual Resurrection from a sinful state into Divine Life. We died with Him, we are buried with Him, and we rose with Him [Rom. 6:3-5], and herein lies the secret to all Spiritual Victory.)*

"And you, being dead in your sins and the uncircumcision of your flesh *(speaks of spiritual death [i.e., 'separation from God'], which sin does!)*, **has He quickened together with Him** *(refers to being made spiritually alive, which is done through being 'Born-Again')*, **having forgiven you all trespasses** *(the Cross made it possible for all manner of sins to be forgiven and taken away)*;

THE LAW WAS ANSWERED

"Blotting out the handwriting of Ordinances that was against us *(pertains to the Law of Moses, which was God's Standard of Righteousness that man could not reach)*, **which was contrary to us** *(Law is against us, simply because we are unable to keep its precepts, no matter how hard we try)*, **and took it out of the way** *(refers to the penalty of the Law being removed)*, **nailing it to His Cross** *(the Law with its decrees was abolished in Christ's Death, as if Crucified with Him)*;

"*And* **having spoiled principalities and powers** *(Satan and all of his henchmen were defeated at the Cross by Christ Atoning for all sin; sin was the legal right Satan had to hold man in captivity; with all sin atoned, he has no more legal right to hold anyone in bondage)*, **He** *(Christ)* **made a show of them openly** *(what Jesus did at the Cross was in the face of the whole universe)*, **triumphing over them in it.** *(The triumph is complete and it was all done for us, meaning we can walk in power and perpetual victory due to the Cross)*" **(Col. 2:8-15).**

Let me say it again, yes, unequivocally so, Divine Healing

is in the Atonement, and so is everything else that man lost in the Fall.

THE FIRSTFRUITS

And yet, we do not now have all for which Jesus paid such a price at Calvary's Cross; actually, we presently only have *"the firstfruits,"* with the balance coming to us at the First Resurrection. Concerning this, Paul also said:

"For I reckon that the sufferings of this present time *(speaks of the world and its condition because of the Fall)* **are** not worthy *to be compared* with the glory *(the glory of the coming future time will bear no relation to the misery of this present time)* **which shall be revealed in us** *(our glory will be a reflective Glory, coming from Christ)*.

"For the earnest expectation of the creature *(should have been translated, 'for the earnest expectation of the Creation')* **waits for the manifestation of the sons of God** *(pertains to the coming Resurrection of Life)*.

"For the creature *(Creation)* **was made subject to vanity** *(Adam's Fall signaled the fall of Creation)***, not willingly** *(the Creation did not sin, even as such cannot sin, but became subject to the result of sin which is death)***, but by reason of Him Who has subjected** *the same* **in Hope** *(speaks of God as the One Who passed sentence because of Adam's Fall, but at the same time gave us a 'Hope'; that 'Hope' is Christ, Who will rectify all things)***,**

"Because the creature *(Creation)* **itself also shall be delivered** *(presents this 'Hope' as effecting that Deliverance, which He did by the Cross)* **from the bondage of corruption** *(speaks of mortality, i.e., 'death')* **into the glorious liberty of the Children of God** *(when man fell, Creation fell! when man shall be delivered, Creation will be delivered as well, and is expressed in the word 'also')*.

"For we know that the whole Creation *(everything*

has been *affected by Satan's rebellion and Adam's Fall)* **groans and travails in pain together until now** *(refers to the common longing of the elements of the Creation to be brought back to their original perfection).*

WE GROAN

"And not only *they (the Creation, and all it entails),* **but ourselves also** *(refers to Believers),* **which have the Firstfruits of the Spirit** *(even though Jesus addressed every single thing lost in the Fall at the Cross, we only have a part of that possession now, with the balance coming at the Resurrection),* **even we ourselves groan within ourselves** *(proclaims the obvious fact that all Jesus paid for in the Atonement has not yet been fully realized),* **waiting for the Adoption** *(should be translated, 'waiting for the fulfillment of the process, which Adoption into the Family of God guarantees'),* ***to wit,*** **the Redemption of our body** *(the glorifying of our physical body that will take place at the Resurrection)*" **(Rom. 8:18-23).**

THE REDEMPTION OF OUR BODY

As Paul mentioned *"the Redemption of our body"* in Romans 8:23, he gives us more details in I Corinthians. He said:

"Behold, I show you a mystery *(a new Revelation given by the Holy Spirit to Paul concerning the Resurrection, i.e., Rapture)*; We shall not all sleep *(at the time of the Resurrection [Rapture], many Christians will be alive),* but we shall all be changed *(both those who are dead and those who are alive),*

"In a moment, in the twinkling of an eye *(proclaims how long it will take for this change to take place),* at the last trump *(does not denote by the use of the word 'last' that there will be successive trumpet blasts, but rather denotes* *that this is the close of things, referring to the Church Age)***: for the trumpet shall sound** *(it is the 'Trump of God' [I Thess. 4:16])*, **and the dead shall be raised incorrupt- ible** *(the Sainted Dead, with no sin nature)*, **and we shall be changed** *(put on the Glorified Body).*

"**For this corruptible** *(sin nature)* **must put on incor- ruption** *(a Glorified Body with no sin nature)*, **and this mortal** *(subject to death)* ***must*** **put on immortality** *(will never die).*

"**So when this corruptible** *(sin nature)* **shall have put on incorruption** *(the Divine Nature in total control by the Holy Spirit)*, **and this mortal** *(subject to death)* **shall have put on immortality** *(will never die)*, **then shall be brought to pass the saying that is written, Death is swallowed up in victory** *([Isa. 25:8], the full benefits of the Cross will then be ours, of which we now have only the Firstfruits [Rom. 8:23]).*

"**O death, where** *is* **your sting?** *(This presents the Apostle looking ahead, and exulting in this great coming victory. Sin was forever Atoned at the Cross, which took away the sting of death.)* **O grave, where** *is* **your victory?** *(Due to death being conquered, the 'grave' is no more and, once again, all because of what Christ did at the Cross [Col. 2:14-15].)*

"**The sting of death** *is* **sin** *(actually says, 'The sting of the death is the sin'; the words 'the sin' refer to the sin nature, which came about at the Fall, and results in death [Rom. 6:23])*; **and the strength of sin** *is* **the Law.** *(This is the Law of Moses. It defined sin and stressed its penalty, which is death [Col. 2:14-15].)*

"**But thanks** *be* **to God, Who gives us the victory through our Lord Jesus Christ.** *(This victory was won exclusively at the Cross, with the Resurrection ratifying what had been done)*" **(I Cor. 15:51-57).**

When the Trump of God sounds, which will signal the Resur- rection of Life, then the *"corruptible"* **will put on incorruption,**

meaning that all Saints will have a Glorified Body, and will never again sin. As well, with the *"mortal putting on immortality,"* this means that we also will never be sick again and, in fact, will never die. It is called *"Eternal Life"* (Jn. 3:16).

DOES THE LORD HEAL TODAY?

Most definitely!

The Bible clearly says:

"Jesus Christ the same yesterday, and today, and forever" (Heb. 13:8).

Such a question would never have arisen were it not for unbelieving preachers who claim that the days of miracles are over, or that God doesn't answer prayer anymore, etc. Whatever the Lord did yesterday, He will do today, providing it is apropos for the time and the individual. For instance, the Lord renewed the youth, so to speak, of Abraham and Sarah, that he could father a child, and that she could conceive, even though their physical bodies had been *"as good as dead"* (Rom. 4:19; Heb. 11:11). The Lord did this thing for Abraham and Sarah for any number of reasons, but the main reason for the birth of Isaac, was the coming of the Messiah. In other words, that through Abraham's seed, our Lord would come. He has already come, so there is no need for such to be repeated as it regards Abraham and Sarah.

The Lord is limited only by the lack of faith on the part of those who claim to serve Him. The Holy Spirit said of Israel, *"Yes, they turned back and tempted God, and limited the Holy One of Israel"* (Ps. 78:41).

The Lord having subjected Himself, at least to a great degree, to the Faith or lack thereof, as it regards His Children, can be limited by unbelief. Unfortunately, that problem did not die with Israel of old, but continues to be rampant presently. James said:

"You lust, and have not *(such a person is not looking to God, but rather operating from self-will)*: you kill, and desire

to have, and cannot obtain *(the word 'kill' refers to destroying the reputation of another in order to gain advantage, and to do so by slander, etc.):* **you fight and war, yet you have not, because you ask not.** *(This refers to Believers who little seek the Lord for anything, but rather depend upon other sources that are irregular to say the least!)*" **(James 4:2).**

THE WORDS OF OUR LORD

Jesus said:

"**For verily I say unto you, That whosoever shall say unto this mountain, Be thou removed, and be thou cast into the sea; and shall not doubt in his heart, but shall believe that those things which he says shall come to pass; he shall have whatsoever he says** *(the 'mountain' is used as a symbol, i.e., 'mountain of difficulties,' etc.; God is a Miracle working God, and will do so for any of His Children, 'whosoever'; however, every petition must be predicated as well on the Will of God).*
"**Therefore I say unto you, What things soever you desire** *(one seeking to do the Will of God, will want only what God desires),* **when you pray** *(the value of prayer, without which these things cannot be done),* **believe** *(have Faith)* **that you receive them, and you shall have them** *(as is obvious here, the receiving of these things, whatever they might be, requires relationship, and that is the key)*" **(Mk. 11:23-24).**

The Believer must understand that these great Promises given by Christ, and many more, which we have not taken the time to point out, are just as real presently as they were when they were uttered.

IS IT ALWAYS THE WILL OF GOD TO HEAL THE SICK?

Yes! But it's not always His Wisdom.

I think once and for all as it regards His Will, such was settled, and recorded by Mark:

"And there came a leper to Him, beseeching Him *(begging Him)*, **and kneeling down to Him** *(this was not merely a rendering of honor to an earthly being; it was a rendering of reverence to a Divine Being)*, **and saying unto Him, If You will, You can make me clean** *(leprosy was so loathsome, that the leper didn't know if Jesus would heal him or not, even though he knew, that Jesus had the Power)*.

"And Jesus, moved with compassion *(is a portrayal of the Heart of God)*, put forth *His* Hand, and touched him, and said unto him, I will; be thou clean *(according to the Greek, His Word healed the man, and not His Touch; when He touched him, the healing had already been effected, and the man was 'clean'; the words 'I will' forever settled the question of the Will of God to heal the sick)*.

"And as soon as He had spoken, immediately the leprosy departed from him *(proclaiming the spoken Word to be enough)*, and he was cleansed" (Mk. 1:40-42).

As we have stated, while the Scripture teaches that it's always God's Will to heal the sick, the Word also proclaims the fact that His Wisdom enters into all of this as well.

For instance, Israel under the leadership of the Prophet Samuel, demanded a king. While it was the Will of God for Israel to have a king, it was not His Wisdom for them to have such at that time. Through Samuel, He warned them of the outcome, but they persisted. They ultimately got what they desired, but it was to their chagrin.

The Truth is it was the Will of God for David to be the first king of Israel. Had Israel waited and not demanded their own selfish desires, the Nation would have been a hundred times better off (I Sam., Chpt. 8).

As another example, every parent desires to do good things for their children; however, at times, despite the will of the parent and the desire of the child, the parent knows that to do such at that time, whatever it might be, would not be good for the child.

Every Believer must understand that we belong to the Lord. We have been purchased with a great price. He has nothing but our welfare at heart, and to be sure, He knows best, and greatly so!

Understanding that the Wisdom of God is of supreme significance, there certainly would be times, I think, where healing might be withheld, or delayed, because such is for our good.

That doesn't mean that the Believer is to pray, *"Lord heal me if it be Your Will,"* because He has already given His Will on the subject. Despite our petitions, if healing is withheld or delayed, we should seek to learn the lesson that the Lord is endeavoring to teach us by this delay, and at the same time, keep asking Him in Faith for that which we need.

IS FAILURE TO RECEIVE HEALING ALWAYS A LACK OF FAITH?

No!

While this certainly does enter the picture at times, it is definitely not the reason most of the time.

The Believer should understand, that the Lord will never allow us by our Faith to override His Will. So this completely debunks the idea that if a person has enough faith, they can do anything. While this has been taught in the last several decades, it is not Scriptural. If a person can take their Faith and override the Word of God with their Faith, this would make that person stronger than the Lord. And I think it should go without saying, that such is never the case, and never will God allow such to be the case.

As it regards Faith, Jesus taught His Disciples and all of us as well, that it's not the amount of Faith for which we should be seeking, but rather the correct object of Faith. The Scripture says:

"And the Apostles said unto the Lord, Increase our faith *(this is the request of many; however, the answer the Lord will give is extremely interesting)*.

"And the Lord said, If you had faith as a grain of mustard seed *(a very small seed, telling us, in effect, that it's not really the amount of faith, but rather the correct object of Faith; the correct Object is the Cross [I Cor. 1:18])*, you might say unto this sycamine tree, Be thou plucked up by the root, and be thou planted in the sea; and it should obey you *(the removal of trees and mountains were proverbial figures of speech among the Jews at that time, expressing the overcoming of great difficulties)*" (Lk. 17:5-6).

WHAT IS THE CORRECT OBJECT OF FAITH?

It always is and without exception, the Cross of Christ (Lk. 9:23; 14:27; Rom. 6:1-14; 8:1-2, 11; I Cor. 1:17, 18, 23; 2:2).

Why the Cross?

The meaning of the Cross, in essence, is the meaning of the New Covenant. It was there that all sin was atoned, making it possible for all to come directly to the Throne of God in the Name of Jesus. Due to what Christ did at the Cross, the Holy Spirit can now come into the hearts and lives of all Believers, which He does, there to abide forever (Jn. 14:16-17). All self-will, operation of the flesh, false doctrine, false direction, all and without exception, have their beginning because of a mis-understanding of the Cross of Christ, or ignoring the Cross of Christ, or outright denying the Cross of Christ!

While a lack of Faith can definitely cause problems, the reason there is a lack, is because it has an improper object.

ISN'T THE WORD OF GOD TO BE THE OBJECT OF OUR FAITH?

Most definitely!

But the Believer must understand, the Story of the Word of God, is the Story of Jesus Christ and Him Crucified. One can believe all the Word, but at the same time misunderstand much of the Word, and bring upon oneself difficulties. For Faith to be proper, it must always have as its Object the Cross of Christ. Then the correct understanding of the Word will be developed.

GIFTS OF HEALING

The Gift of which we speak, concerns one of the nine Gifts of the Spirit. Paul wrote,

"For to one is given by the Spirit . . . the Gifts of Healing" (I Cor. 12:8-9).

Now this doesn't mean that only those who have this Gift can pray for the sick. Jesus said,

"And these signs shall follow them who believe" (Mk. 16:17).

This means that any Believer can pray for the sick, and at times see great healings; however, for the individual to whom the Lord has entrusted the *"Gifts of Healing,"* such a person will see more healings, as should be obvious. Several things should be said here:

•   First of all, these are *"Gifts,"* meaning, that the Lord has bestowed one or more Gifts on an individual. They didn't earn it, they didn't merit such, for the Lord's Own reasons, He gives such.

•   These Gifts are totally in the domain of the Holy Spirit. Nine times in I Corinthians, Chapter 12 in Verses 1 through 11, the Holy Spirit is mentioned. He is mentioned nine times, and there are nine Gifts.

•   While there are diversities of Gifts, or rather, different types of Gifts, they are all of *"the same Spirit,"* i.e., the Holy Spirit.

•   It is the Holy Spirit Who distributes the Gifts, and not man. So, the idea that a man can impart a Gift of the Spirit to others is facetious indeed! Let me emphasize it again, these are

"Gifts of the Spirit," and not of men. The Scripture says, and concerning this:

> "But all these work that one and the selfsame Spirit *(refers to the fact that all the abilities and powers of the Gifts are produced and operated by the energy of the Spirit)*, dividing to every man severally as He *(the Holy Spirit)* will. *(All the distribution is within the discretion of the Holy Spirit, which means that men or women cannot impart Gifts to other individuals. That is the domain of the Spirit Alone!)*" (I Cor. 12:11).

Actually, the original Text says, *"Gifts of Healings."*
Why the plural?
Perhaps it refers to the fact, that some who are used of God in *"Gifts of Healings,"* have greater Faith for healing of certain diseases or problems, while another will have greater Faith for another type of disease or problem to be healed.
To be sure, all nine Gifts of the Spirit, which includes *"Gifts of Healings,"* are in operation in the modern Church, at least as it regards those who believe.

ARE DOCTORS, MEDICINE, OR HOSPITALS, A DETRIMENT TO DIVINE HEALING?

No!
Multiple thousands of people have been healed in hospitals, and while taking medicine, and if such were wrong, the Lord would not heal at all in such circumstances.
Believers should thank the Lord for doctors, for nurses, for medicine, for hospitals, etc.
In Old Testament times, most physicians were repudiated by the Lord; however, there was a reason for that. The Scripture says:

> "And Asa in the thirty and ninth year of his reign

was diseased in his feet, until his disease was exceeding great: yet in his disease he sought not to the LORD, but to the physicians. *(The Lord permitted this disease as a result of Asa's actions. I wonder how many presently fall into the same category?*

"*The idea of this Verse is that if Asa had sought the Lord, the Lord would have forgiven him and healed him.*

"*The 'physicians' who are spoken of here were probably Egyptian physicians, who were in high repute at foreign courts in ancient times, and who pretended to expel diseases by charms, incantations, and mystic arts. In other words, they were Satanic!)*" **(II Chron. 16:12).**

THE COMING KINGDOM AGE

In the coming Kingdom Age when Jesus will be ruling Personally from Jerusalem, and over the entirety of the world, concerning healing at that time, etc., the Scripture says:

"And by the River upon the bank thereof, on this side and on that side, shall grow all trees for meat, whose leaf shall not fade, neither shall the fruit thereof be consumed: it shall bring forth new fruit according to his months, because their waters they issued out of the Sanctuary: and the fruit thereof shall be for meat, and the leaf thereof for medicine. *(Ezekiel is now shown the purpose of these Miracle Trees which grow on either side of these Rivers. These 'Trees' shall perpetually bring forth new fruit because they are nourished by waters issuing from the Sanctuary. The fruit will heal as well as nourish. Such is the character of a Life and Ministry based upon Calvary and energized by the Holy Spirit.*

"*In fact, the population of the world [which will include all, with the exception of the Glorified Saints] will continue to live perpetually by the means of the 'fruit' and the 'leaf' of these Trees)*" **(Ezek. 47:12).**

In other words, the leaves from these trees will be a preventative medicine. To be sure, if it was against one's faith to take medicine, then most definitely it would not be appropriate in the coming Kingdom Age. In fact, most medicine presently comes from the bark or the leaves of trees or plants.

But in the midst of it all, and again we thank the Lord for the advancement of medical science, the Lord still continues to heal the sick. A long, long time ago, the Lord said to Moses, and to be sure, His Word has not changed. Although the following is somewhat lengthy, I think it would be profitable to quote it in full from THE EXPOSITOR'S STUDY BIBLE.

THE BITTER WATERS MADE SWEET

"So Moses brought Israel from the Red Sea, and they went out into the wilderness of Shur; and they went three days in the wilderness, and found no water. *(God tests Faith in order to strengthen and enrich it.)*

"And when they came to Marah, they could not drink of the waters of Marah, for they were bitter: therefore the name of it was called Marah. *(Marah means 'bitter.' Pink says: 'While the wilderness may and will make manifest the weakness of God's Saints and, as well, our failures, this is only to magnify the Power and Mercy of Him Who brought us into the place of testing. Further, and we must understand, God always has in view our ultimate good.' The bitter waters of Marah typify life and its disappointments.)*

"And the people murmured against Moses, saying, What shall we drink? *(Three days before, the Children of Israel were rejoicing on the shores of the Red Sea. Now, some 72 hours later, they are 'murmuring against Moses.' Such presents a lack of Faith. 'Tests' brought upon us by the Lord portray what is in us. Regrettably, it doesn't take much to bring out the unbelief.)*

MOSES IMPORTUNED THE LORD

"And he cried unto the LORD *(Moses set the example; there is no help outside of the Lord, but man, even the Church, seem to find difficulty in believing this)*; and the LORD showed him a Tree *(the 'tree' is a Type of the Cross [Acts 5:30; 10:39; 13:29; Gal. 3:13; I Pet. 2:24])*, which when he had cast into the waters, the waters were made sweet *(we must put the Cross into every difficulty and problem of life, which alone holds the answer; only by this means can the bitter waters be made 'sweet')*: there He *(God)* made for them a Statute and an Ordinance, and there He proved them *(tested them! We must understand that God doesn't give victory to men, only to Christ; His Victory becomes ours, as we are properly in Him [Jn. 14:20; Rom. 6:3-5])*,

NO MORE DISEASES

"And said, If you will diligently hearken to the Voice of the LORD your God, and will do that which is right in His Sight, and will give ear to His Commandments, and keep all His Statutes, I will put none of these diseases upon you, which I have brought upon the Egyptians: for I am the LORD Who heals you. *(It is demanded that all these 'Statutes' and 'Ordinances' be perfectly kept; however, no man can boast of such; Christ has perfectly kept all the Commandments and, as our Substitute, kept them perpetually. Looking to Him, we can claim this blessing. As well, the 'healing' Promised here has to do not only with physical diseases but, as well, of emotional and spiritual diseases. The Cross is to be put into the bitter waters of these problems, whatever they might be. They can then be made sweet. The name 'LORD,' in the Hebrew, as used here, is 'Jehovah-Ropheka,' which means 'Jehovah, the Healer.' Jehovah has proven Himself as the Deliverer of Israel, and now He proclaims Himself as their and our 'Healer')*" (Ex. 15:22-26).

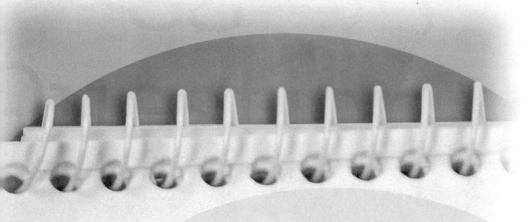

CHAPTER 5

The Doctrine Of Faith

THE DOCTRINE OF FAITH

There are three words in Christendom, which when used, stand as a synonym for the entire body of Bible Christianity. They are:
1. The Gospel;
2. The Cross; and,
3. The Faith.

The word *"Faith"* is mentioned over 240 times in the Bible, but only two times in the Old Testament, with the balance being in the New. The words, *"faithful," "faithfully,"* and *"faithfulness,"* along with *"faithless,"* are mentioned collectively over 100 times.

WHAT IS FAITH?

The Greek word for Faith is *"Pistis,"* and means, *"belief or a belief, which deals with relationships established by trust and maintained by trustworthiness."*

The words *"into faith,"* are unique to the New Testament, actually, an invention of the Early Church that expresses the inmost secret of our faith. This is never done, we are told, in secular Greek. In the New Testament it portrays a person committing himself or herself totally to the Person of Jesus Christ, for our Faith is *"into Jesus."*

Paul said:

"For the perfecting of the Saints *(to 'equip for service')*, for the work of the Ministry *(to proclaim the Message of Redemption to the entirety of the world)*, for the edifying of the Body of Christ *(for the Spiritual building up of the Church)*:

"Till we all come in the unity of the Faith *(to bring all Believers to a proper knowledge of Christ and the Cross)*, and of the knowledge of the Son of God *(which again refers to what He did for us at the Cross)*, unto a

perfect man *(the Believer who functions in maturity)*, **unto the measure of the stature of the fulness of Christ** *(the 'measure' is the 'fullness of Christ,' which can only be attained by a proper Faith in the Cross)*" **(Eph. 4:12-13).**

Paul also said:

"**Examine yourselves, whether you be in the Faith** *(the words, 'the Faith,' refer to 'Christ and Him Crucified,' with the Cross ever being the Object of our Faith)*; **prove your own selves.** *(Make certain your faith is actually in the Cross, and not other things.)* **Know you not your own selves, how that Jesus Christ is in you** *(which He can only be by our Faith expressed in His Sacrifice)*, **except you be reprobates** *(rejected)*?" **(II Cor. 13:5).**

THE OBJECT OF OUR FAITH

The Object of our Faith must always be the Cross of Christ (Rom. 6:1-14; 8:1-2, 11; I Cor. 1:17-18, 21, 23; 2:2).

Inasmuch as the Story of the Bible is *"Jesus Christ and Him Crucified,"* having Faith in the Cross of Christ, is actually having Faith in the entirety of the Word of God. We are given a compendium of this in the First Chapter of the Gospel according to John. He said:

"**In the beginning** *(does not infer that Christ as God had a beginning, because as God He had no beginning, but rather refers to the time of Creation [Gen. 1:1])* **was the Word** *(the Holy Spirit through John describes Jesus as 'the Eternal Logos')*, **and the Word was with God** *('was in relationship with God,' and expresses the idea of the Trinity)*, **and the Word was God** *(meaning that He did not cease to be God during the Incarnation; He 'was' and 'is' God from eternity past to eternity future)*.

IN HIM

"The same was in the beginning with God *(this very Person was in eternity with God; there's only one God, but manifested in Three Persons — God the Father, God the Son, God the Holy Spirit)*.

"All things were made by Him *(all things came into being through Him; it refers to every item of Creation one by one, rather than all things regarded in totality)*; and without Him was not any thing made that was made *(nothing, not even one single thing, was made independently of His cooperation and volition)*.

"In Him was Life *(presents Jesus, the Eternal Logos, as the first cause)*; and the Life was the Light of men *(He Alone is the Life Source of Light; if one doesn't know Christ, one is in darkness)*" (Jn. 1:1-4).

And then John said:

"And the Word was made flesh *(refers to the Incarnation, 'God becoming man')*, and dwelt among us *(refers to Jesus, although Perfect, not holding Himself aloft from all others, but rather lived as all men, even a peasant)*, (and we beheld His Glory, the Glory as of the Only Begotten of the Father,) *(speaks of His Deity, although hidden from the eyes of the merely curious; while Christ laid aside the expression of His Deity, He never lost the possession of His Deity)* full of Grace and Truth *(as 'flesh,' proclaimed His Humanity, 'Grace and Truth' His Deity)*" (Jn. 1:14).

THE LAMB OF GOD

And then John wrote as it regards John the Baptist introducing Christ. He said:

"The next day *(refers to the day after John had been*

questioned by the emissaries from the Sanhedrin) **John sees Jesus coming unto him** *(is, no doubt, after the Baptism of Jesus, and the temptation in the wilderness)*, **and said, Behold the Lamb of God** *(proclaims Jesus as the Sacrifice for sin, in fact, the Sin-Offering, Whom all the multiple millions of offered lambs had represented)*, **which takes away the sin of the world** *(animal blood could only cover sin, it could not take it away; but Jesus offering Himself as the Perfect Sacrifice took away the sin of the world; He not only cleansed acts of sin but, as well, addressed the root cause [Col. 2:14-15])"* **(Jn. 1:29).**

When one reads these Verses in this First Chapter of St. John, one is reading in a sense, the entirety of the Message of the Word of God.

As stated, the Object of Faith must be Jesus Christ and Him Crucified. Only twelve Verses in the New Testament have God as the Object of Faith (Jn. 12:44; 14:1; Acts 16:34; Rom. 4:3, 5, 17, 24; Gal. 3:6; I Thess. 1:8; Titus 3:8; Heb. 6:1; I Pet. 1:21).

Why?

The reason is clearly expressed by Jesus Himself. He said, *"I am the Way and the Truth and the Life. No one comes to the Father except by Me"* (Jn. 14:6). Actually, God the Father has revealed Himself in the Son. The Father has set Jesus and what He did for us at the Cross, before us as the One to Whom we must entrust ourselves for Salvation. It is Jesus and Him Crucified, Who is the focus of Christian Faith.

FAITH IS THE PRINCIPAL OF ALL THINGS
WHICH PERTAINS TO GOD

Paul said:

"Through Faith we understand that the worlds were framed by the Word of God *(refers to Creation, along with everything that goes with Creation)*, **so that things which**

are seen were not made of things which do appear. *(God began with nothing, thereby, speaking into existence the things needed to create the universe)*" **(Heb. 11:3).**

In fact, every person in the world has faith, whether they understand it or not. Everything is built on the premise of faith. That's the reason that Communism would never work. It excludes faith, which takes away the incentive of man. Every millionaire or billionaire in the world who became such, did so by faith, believing that what they did would bring forth rewards. Every scientist works on the premise of faith, whether he understands it or not, believing that his experiments will produce that for which he seeks.

However, none of this is faith that God recognizes, being only a carry-over from creation.

THE ONLY FAITH THAT GOD RECOGNIZES

The faith that God recognizes and, in fact, the only faith that He will recognize, is Faith that we place in Christ and His Finished Work of the Cross. Actually, when the words *"the Faith"* are used, it is always addressing itself to Christ and the Cross, i.e., what He did for us at the Cross, benefits that continue to come to us and, in fact, will ever continue to do so. That's the reason the Apostle told us to *"Examine yourselves, whether you be in the Faith"* **(II Cor. 13:5).**

The Scripture also says:

"**By Faith Enoch was translated that he should not see death** *(refers to God transferring Enoch to Heaven in his physical body while he was yet alive)*; **and was not found, because God had translated him** *(refers to his translation being well-known at that time)*: **for before his translation he had this testimony, that he pleased God.** *(He pleased God because he placed his Faith exclusively in Christ and the Cross.)*

    "But without Faith *(in Christ and the Cross; anytime Faith is mentioned, always and without exception, its root meaning is that its Object is Christ and the Cross; otherwise, it is faith God will not accept)* **it is impossible to please Him** *(faith in anything other than Christ and the Cross greatly displeases the Lord)***: for he who comes to God must believe that He is** *(places Faith as the foundation and principle of the manner in which God deals with the human race)***, and** *that* **He** *(God)* **is a rewarder of them who diligently seek Him** *(seek Him on the premise of Christ and Him Crucified)***"** **(Heb. 11:5-6).**

THE SACRIFICE

In fact, the Holy Spirit begins his great Hall of Fame regarding Faith in Hebrews, Chapter 11 by saying:

    "By Faith Abel offered unto God a more excellent Sacrifice than Cain *(immediately proclaims the fact that the Object of our Faith must be 'Jesus Christ and Him Crucified' [I Cor. 2:2])***, by which he obtained witness that he was Righteous** *(proclaims the fact that Righteousness comes exclusively from Christ, and is obtained by the Cross being the Object of our Faith)***, God testifying of his gifts** *(referring to the fact that the Sacrifice of the Lamb, which represented Christ was accepted by God; at the dawn of time it was 'the Cross,' and it is still 'the Cross')***: and by it he being dead yet speaks** *(speaks of that alone God will accept)***"** **(Heb. 11:4).**

FAITH CAN BE TURNED TO WORKS

Jesus said:

    "But if your eye be evil, your whole body shall be full of darkness *(if the spirit be evil, the entirety of the soul will* *be full of darkness).* **If therefore the light that is in you be darkness** *(the light is not acted upon, but rather perverted),* **how great** *is* **that darkness** *(the latter state is worse than if there had been no light at all)***!**

"**No man can serve two masters: for either he will hate the one, and love the other; or else he will hold to the one, and despise the other. You cannot serve God and mammon** *(this is flat out, stated as, an impossibility; it is total devotion to God, or ultimately it will be total devotion to the world; the word, 'mammon' is derived from the Babylonian 'Mimma,' which means 'anything at all')*" **(Mat. 6:23-24).**

HOW CAN FAITH BE TURNED TO WORKS?

If we truly evidence Faith in Christ and what He did for us at the Cross, understanding that this is God's Means of dealing with the human race, meaning, that everything we receive from the Lord is made possible by the Cross, understanding that, adhering to that, believing that with all of one's heart, placing one's Faith exclusively in the Cross of Christ, then thinking that God owes us something because of our Faith placed in the correct Object, we have just turned it into works. God doesn't owe us anything, in fact, He has nothing for sale. The Scripture plainly says:

"**For the wages of sin** *is* **death** *(speaks of spiritual death, which is separation from God)***; but the Gift of God** *is* **Eternal Life through Jesus Christ our Lord** *(as stated, all of this, without exception, comes to us by the means of what Christ did at the Cross, which demands that the Cross ever be the Object of our Faith, thus giving the Holy Spirit latitude to work within our lives and bring forth His Fruit)*" **(Rom. 6:23).**

Man must look at himself as being in the ocean without a life

raft, or any lifesaving device, thereby drowning, and holding up his hand asking for help. The Lord will always respond to that.

Pride has always been the major problem with man. It just might be the sin that God hates the most (Prov. 6:16-19).

I think one can say and without fear of exaggeration that pride has sent more people to Hell than anything else. As well, it has kept more Christians from receiving from God than anything else. This is why the Cross of Christ, which must be the Object of our Faith, is such an offense to many. It lays to waste all of our good works, leaving us with nothing but what we really are, which does not present a pretty picture. We don't like to see that or admit that. We like to think of ourselves as pretty good, even as did Job; however, when he saw the Lord, he then truly saw himself, and his reaction was, *"I am vile"* (Job 40:4). I think that one might say that pride is the greatest hindrance to Faith, and especially Faith in the correct Object, which is the Cross of Christ. It keeps many from going to the Cross, and then pride hinders many who actually do place their Faith and trust in the Cross, by making them think that God owes them something, due to the fact that the Cross of Christ is the Object of their Faith.

FAITH THAT GROWS

Paul said:

"So then Faith *comes* by hearing *(it is the publication of the Gospel which produces Faith in it)*, and hearing by the Word of God *(Faith does not come simply hearing just anything, but rather by hearing God's Word, and believing that Word)*" (Rom. 10:17).

This Passage simply means that we hear the Word of God and believe it; however, if our understanding is lacking as it regards the Cross of Christ, which, in effect, is the meaning of the New Covenant, then, as well, we will have a lack of under-standing concerning all of the Bible. That doesn't mean that in such a case one cannot understand some things about the Bible, and understand it correctly; however, if the truth be known, all error stems from an improper interpretation of the Cross of Christ. That being the case, our faith will be flawed as well. As should be obvious, flawed faith will hinder our understanding of the Word.

One might say that everything hinges on a proper under-standing of the New Covenant, to which the Old Covenant ever pointed, and which in reality is the Message of the Cross, which is the Story of the Bible.

God deals with everything on the premise of Faith; however, it must be Faith in the correct Object to be recognized by God. That correct Object is the Cross of Christ, which, in essence, is the Word of God.

CHAPTER 6

The Doctrine Of Grace

THE DOCTRINE OF GRACE

"**For by Grace** *(the Goodness of God)* **are you Saved through Faith** *(Faith in Christ, with the Cross ever as its Object)*; **and that not of yourselves** *(none of this is of us, but all is of Him)*: *it is* **the Gift of God** *(anytime the word 'Gift' is used, God is speaking of His Son and His Substitutionary Work on the Cross, which makes all of this possible)*:

"**Not of works** *(man cannot merit Salvation, irrespective what he does)*, **lest any man should boast** *(boast in his own ability and strength; we are allowed to boast only in the Cross [Gal. 6:14])*.

"**For we are His Workmanship** *(if we are God's Workmanship, our Salvation cannot be of ourselves)*, **created in Christ Jesus unto good works** *(speaks of the results of Salvation, and never the cause)*, **which God has before ordained that we should walk in them.** *(The 'good works' the Apostle speaks of has to do with Faith in Christ and the Cross, which enables the Believer to live a Holy life)*" **(Eph. 2:8-10).**

WHAT IS GRACE?

Some have defined Grace as *"unmerited favor."* That is a proper definition; however, to give it a broader perspective, one could also say that *"Grace is the Goodness of God extended to undeserving Believers."* While the Grace of God is most definitely available to all unredeemed, with some few exceptions, it stops at the word available.

God is Good! Everything about Him is Good, and the beautiful thing about this is He desires to give to us all of His good Things, whatever they might be.

It troubles me to hear Christians use terms such as *"greasy grace,"* or *"slippery grace,"* etc. The use of such terminology shows a complete misunderstanding of the Grace of God.

Grace is never a license to sin. It is, in fact, the means by which we can have Victory over sin and the only means.

THE CROSS OF CHRIST MAKES GRACE POSSIBLE!

God has always been a God of Grace. One could say He is Grace, because He is Goodness. This means that God had just as much Grace under the Old Covenant as He does under the New. It is the Cross of Christ which atoned for all sin that makes Grace much more available presently than it was under the old Law. It was not that God changed, for He cannot change, it was rather that conditions changed, which was brought about by the Cross of Christ.

Before the Cross God was greatly limited as to what He could do, and simply because animal blood was insufficient to take away the sin debt. When Jesus paid the price on Calvary's Cross, thereby shedding His Life's Blood, which was accepted by God as the Perfect Sacrifice for sin, this opened the door for the Lord to do many wonderful and great things. It is the Cross of Christ which makes Grace possible.

But, at the same time, everything that God has ever done for man, and in any capacity, even from the first page of human history, has been altogether because of His Grace, i.e., *"His Goodness."* That's the only way that He can function with man, simply because man does not merit anything that's good and, in fact, cannot merit anything that is good.

THE DISPENSATION OF GRACE

The Dispensation of Grace began when Jesus on the Cross said, *"It is finished"* (Jn. 19:30). At that moment the Law of God was completely satisfied. Paul said:

"Blotting out the handwriting of Ordinances that was against us *(pertains to the Law of Moses, which was God's Standard of Righteousness that man could not reach)*, which was contrary to us *(Law is against us, simply because we are unable to keep its precepts, no matter how hard we try)*, **and took it out of the way** *(refers to the penalty of the Law being removed)*, **nailing it to His Cross** *(the Law with its decrees was abolished in Christ's Death, as if Crucified with Him)"* **(Col. 2:14).**

Under the Old Covenant, God dealt with mankind, at least Israel, by the means of Law. The Law has now been satisfied by Christ, in the giving of Himself on the Cross, making it possible for God to now deal with mankind on the premise of Grace.

However, irrespective that this is the *"Dispensation of Grace,"* that doesn't mean that everyone is automatically under Grace. The potential is there, but sadly and regrettably most Believers, and we are speaking of Believers, are only enjoying a modicum of Grace because they are trying to live their Christian experience mostly by Law. So, irrespective that this is the Dispensation of Grace, it is not an automatic thing.

If one is to notice the writings of the Apostle Paul, even though he was living at the beginning of the Dispensation of Grace, still, he spoke of Law constantly.

Why?

It was because Believers were placing themselves under Law, whether they realized such or not, thereby forfeiting Grace. So, if it was a problem then, to be sure it is a problem now.

HOW DOES THE BELIEVER GUARANTEE A CONSTANT FLOW OF THE GRACE OF GOD IN HIS LIFE?

As we have stated, it is the Cross of Christ that ushered in this great Dispensation of Grace, making it possible for Believers to enjoy the Grace of God in an abundant way. Inasmuch as it is the Cross that has made the Grace of God possible even in an overflowing manner, because Jesus atoned for all sin there, thereby, lifting the sin debt, to guarantee this uninterrupted flow the Believer must ever make the Cross of Christ the Object of his Faith.

Paul said:

"Of how much sorer punishment, suppose you, shall he be thought worthy, who has trodden under foot the Son of God *(proclaims the reason for the 'sorer punishment')*, and has counted the Blood of the Covenant, wherewith he was Sanctified, an unholy thing *(refers to a person who has been Saved, but is now expressing unbelief toward that which originally Saved him)*, and has done despite unto the Spirit of Grace? *(When the Cross is rejected, the Holy Spirit is insulted)*" **(Heb. 10:29).**

John the Beloved wrote:

"For the Law was given by Moses, *but* Grace and Truth came by Jesus Christ *(proclaims Him as the Representative Law-Keeper for all humanity, i.e., to all who will believe; the Law manifested man [full of wickedness]; the Son manifested God [full of goodness])*" **(Jn. 1:17).**

THE THRONE OF GRACE

The Holy Spirit through Paul said:

"Seeing then that we have a Great High Priest *(Christ acts on our behalf to God)*, Who is passed into the Heavens *(has to do with a legal process)*, Jesus the Son of God *(presents the fact that Jesus is not only man, but is God as well)*, let us hold fast *our* profession. *(Let us hold fast to Christ and the Cross, which was necessary for our Lord to be our High Priest.)*

"For we have not an High Priest which cannot be touched with the feeling of our infirmities *(being Very Man as well as Very God, He can do such)*; but was in all points tempted like as *we are, yet* without sin *(His temptation, and ours as well, was to leave the Prescribed Will of*

God, which is the Word of God; but He never did, not even one time.)

"**Let us therefore come boldly unto the Throne of Grace** *(presents the Seat of Divine Power, and yet the Source of boundless Grace),* **that we may obtain Mercy** *(presents that which we want first),* **and find Grace to help in time of need** *(refers to the Goodness of God extended to all who come, and during any 'time of need'; all made possible by the Cross)*" **(Heb. 4:14-16).**

The *"Throne of Grace,"* could be called *"The Throne of the Goodness of God."* At any rate, we are speaking here of the Throne of God.

Under the old Law, God could be approached only in a particular way. As it regarded the Holy of Holies, where the Ark of the Covenant was, where God dwelt between the Mercy Seat and the Cherubim, it served as a Symbol of the Throne of God on Earth. No Israelite could enter the Holy of Holies. In fact, no Israelite could come into the Tabernacle at all. Only the Priests could come into the Tabernacle, but only the Great High Priest could come into the Holy of Holies, and that only once a year, the Great Day of Atonement, and not without blood. Due to the fact that the blood of bulls and goats could not take away sins, meaning that the sin debt remained despite the sacrifices, the Lord was inaccessible, except in a very limited way.

When Jesus died on the Cross, shedding His Life's Blood, which paid the price for all sin — past, present, and future — which God recognized and accepted, at the moment when He said, *"It is finished,"* the great Veil that hung between the Holy of Holies and the Holy Place in the Temple, ripped from top to bottom, in essence, saying, the way is now open.

Josephus, the Jewish historian, said that this Veil was some thirty feet high, some four inches thick, weighed over two thousand pounds, and four yoke of oxen could not pull it apart. But yet, it ripped from the top to the bottom, and was done so by God, because the price was forever paid. Now it can be said:

"And the Spirit and the Bride say, Come. *(This presents the cry of the Holy Spirit to a hurting, lost, and dying world. What the Holy Spirit says should also be said by all Believers.)* And let him who hears say, Come. *(It means if one can 'hear,' then one can 'come.')* And let him who is athirst come *(speaks of Spiritual Thirst, the cry for God in the soul of man)*. And whosoever will, let him take the Water of Life freely *(opens the door to every single individual in the world; Jesus died for all and, therefore, all can be Saved, if they will only come)*" **(Rev. 22:17).**

Once again, it is the Cross of Christ that has made the very Throne of God possible for any and all who will come. But all who come can only be admitted on the basis of the Grace of God, which is extended to all who place their Faith exclusively in Christ and what He did at the Cross. Otherwise, entrance will be barred. Paul said:

"But now in Christ Jesus *(proclaims the basis of all Salvation)* you who sometimes *(times past)* were far off *(far from Salvation)* are made nigh *(near)* by the Blood of Christ. *(The Sacrificial Atoning Death of Jesus Christ transformed the relations of God with mankind. In Christ, God reconciled not a nation, but 'a world' to Himself [II Cor. 5:19].)*

"For He *(Christ)* is our peace *(through Christ and what He did at the Cross, we have peace with God)*, Who has made both one *(Jews and Gentiles)*, and has broken down the middle wall of partition *between us* *(between Jews and Gentiles)*;

"Having abolished in His Flesh *(speaking of His Death on the Cross, by which He Redeemed humanity, which also means He didn't die spiritually, as some claim)* the enmity *(the hatred between God and man, caused by sin)*, *even* the Law of Commandments *contained* in Ordinances *(pertains to the Law of Moses, and more particularly the*

Ten Commandments); **for to make in Himself of twain** *(of Jews and Gentiles)* **one new man,** *so* **making peace** *(which again was accomplished by the Cross)*;

"**And that He** *(Christ)* **might reconcile both** *(Jews and Gentiles)* **unto God in one body** *(the Church)* **by the Cross** *(it is by the Atonement only that men ever become reconciled to God)*, **having slain the enmity thereby** *(removed the barrier between God and sinful man)*:

"**And came and preached peace to you which were afar off** *(proclaims the Gospel going to the Gentiles)*, **and to them who were nigh.** *(This refers to the Jews. It is the same Message for both.)*

"**For through Him** *(through Christ)* **we both** *(Jews and Gentiles)* **have access by One Spirit unto the Father.** *(If the sinner comes by the Cross, the Holy Spirit opens the door, otherwise it is barred [Jn. 10:1])*" **(Eph. 2:13-18).**

COME BOLDLY!

If we come in the Name of Jesus, understanding that He made all of this possible by the Cross, then we do not have to approach the Throne of Grace timidly, but can do so boldly.

The word *"boldly"* **in the Greek is** *"parrhesia,"* **and means several things; however, its basic meaning here is** *"confidence, freely, openly."* **The Blood of Jesus Christ has opened up the way; therefore, we can approach the Throne of God with confidence, knowing that it will be accessible to us, and no matter how many times we come.**

THRONE OF GRACE

We are speaking here of the very Throne of God. The idea that anyone can come to this Throne, and at any time, is overwhelming in its concept. But again we emphasize, it is all made possible by Christ and what He did for us at the Cross. We must never forget that.

As well, this is a *"Throne of Grace,"* i.e., *"the Goodness of God,"* which means, that it's not a Throne of Judgment. My sins were judged at Calvary and can never be judged again. In legal parlance, it is referred to as *"double jeopardy."* It means a person cannot be tried twice for the same crime. Jesus Christ was judged for my sins, and the price was paid by the giving of Himself in Sacrifice. As a result, the Law has no more claim on me, meaning, that I can approach with boldness, with confidence, the very Throne of God — but all because of Christ!

MERCY

As long as we come in the Name of Jesus, with the Cross of Christ as the Object of our Faith, Mercy will always be granted to us, and without exception. But we must ever understand, that none of this is because of any merit on our part, it is all because of Christ, and His Sacrificial, Atoning Death, on the Cross of Calvary. That's why the great Apostle said:

"But God forbid that I should glory *(boast)*, save in the Cross of our Lord Jesus Christ *(what the opponents of Paul sought to escape at the price of insincerity is the Apostle's only basis of exultation)*, by Whom the world is Crucified unto me, and I unto the world. *(The only way we can overcome the world, and I mean the only way, is by placing our Faith exclusively in the Cross of Christ and keeping it there)*" (Gal. 6:14).

TIME OF NEED

The *"need"* addressed here, could be forgiveness for sin, financial help, strength for the journey, Diving Healing, overcoming Grace, etc. In other words, this *"need"* has no limitations.

We are told here that the *"Goodness of God,"* is made available to us *"to help in time of need."* When we consider that God can do anything, then we are beginning to realize the most special privilege that we have as a Believer, once again, all because of the Cross of Christ.

FRUSTRATING THE GRACE OF GOD

The Greek word for *"frustrate"* is *"atheteo,"* and means, *"to set aside, to neutralize, to bring to nought."*

When the Believer places his faith in anything, and I mean anything, other than the Cross of Christ, considering that it is the Cross which makes possible the Grace of God, this frustrates the Grace of God, meaning that it stops its flow, or at least, greatly hinders it.

Paul said, and I continue to quote from THE EXPOSITOR'S STUDY BIBLE:

"I do not frustrate the Grace of God *(if we make anything other than the Cross of Christ the Object of our Faith, we frustrate the Grace of God, which means we stop its action, and the Holy Spirit will no longer help us)*: for if Righteousness *come* by the Law *(any type of Law)*, then Christ is dead in vain. *(If I can successfully live for the Lord by any means other than Faith in Christ and the Cross, then the Death of Christ was a waste)*" (Gal. 2:21).

Regrettably and sadly, the far greater majority of modern Christians, and I speak of those who are truly Born-Again, are constantly frustrating the Grace of God. How do I know that?

I know it simply because their Faith is not in Christ and the Cross, but it is rather in a religious law of some nature, whether a law devised by them personally, or preachers, or religious denominations, etc. That being the case, whether they realize it or not, and most don't realize it, they are functioning by Law and, thereby, frustrating the Grace of God. This means they are stopping all the good things that God wants to do for them, but cannot do because they have closed the door due to the incorrect object of faith.

I hear preachers over television telling their viewers to place their faith in the Lord's Supper, or the *"Purpose Driven Life"* book, or whatever! If it's not the Cross of Christ, then whatever it is, and no matter how useful it might be in its own right, the Believer will not see victory in this capacity.

Jesus said:

"And you shall know the Truth, and the Truth shall make you free *(this is the secret of all abundant Life in Christ; the 'Truth' is 'Jesus Christ and Him Crucified,' which alone is the answer to the problems of Man)*" **(Jn. 8:32).**

FALLING FROM GRACE

Paul said:

"Christ is become of no effect unto you *(this is a chilling statement, and refers to anyone who makes anything other than Christ and the Cross the Object of his Faith)*, whosoever of you are justified by the Law *(seek to be Justified by the Law)*; you are fallen from Grace *(fallen from the position of Grace, which means the Believer is trusting in something other than the Cross; it actually means, 'to apostatize')*" **(Gal. 5:4).**

There is a slight difference in *"frustrating the Grace of God,"* and *"falling from Grace."* The former has its flow greatly hindered, while in the latter Grace is stopped altogether.

Being *"fallen from Grace,"* means that the person has his Faith in something other than Christ and the Cross, meaning that he has willingly accepted a false way and, thereby, willingly rejecting or ignoring the Cross of Christ. Considering that the Cross of Christ is the means by which all Grace is given to us, such a person has just lost their way.

Concerning this, Paul also said:

"For *it is* impossible for those who were once en-lightened *(refers to those who have accepted the Light of the Gospel, which means accepting Christ and His great Sacrifice)*, and have tasted of the Heavenly Gift *(pertains to Christ and what He did at the Cross)*, and were made partakers of the Holy Spirit *(which takes place when a person comes to Christ)*,

"And have tasted the good Word of God *(is not language that is used of an impenitent sinner, as some claim; the unsaved have no relish whatsoever for the Truth of God, and see no beauty in it)*, and the powers of the world to come *(refers to the Work of the Holy Spirit within hearts and lives, which the unsaved cannot have or know)*,

"If they shall fall away *(should have been translated, 'and having fallen away')*, to renew them again unto Repentance *('again' states they had once repented, but have now turned their backs on Christ)*; seeing they crucify to themselves the Son of God afresh *(means they no longer believe what Christ did at the Cross, actually concluding Him to be an imposter; the only way any person can truly repent is to place his Faith in Christ and the Cross; if that is denied, there is no Repentance)*, and put *Him* to an open shame *(means to hold Christ up to public ridicule; Paul wrote this Epistle because some Christian Jews were going back into Judaism, or seriously contemplating doing so)*" (Heb. 6:4-6).

GRACE OR LAW

Paul said:

"For sin shall not have dominion over you *(the sin nature will not have dominion over us if we as Believers continue to exercise Faith in the Cross of Christ; otherwise, the sin nature most definitely will have dominion over the Believer)*: for you are not under the Law *(means that if we try to live this life by any type of law, no matter how good that law might be in its own right, we will conclude by the sin nature having dominion over us)*, **but under Grace** *(the Grace of God flows to the Believer on an unending basis only as long as the Believer exercises Faith in Christ and what He did at the Cross; Grace is merely the Goodness of God exercised by and through the Holy Spirit, and given to undeserving Saints)*" **(Rom. 6:14).**

Every person in the world, and without exception, is either under Law (and we speak of the moral part of the Law of Moses, namely, the Ten Commandments), or under Grace. Every unredeemed person in the world, even though they are not aware of such, is still under this Law. This means that unless they give their heart to Christ, Who suffered the penalty of the broken Law, and did it on our behalf, they will answer at the Great White Throne Judgment, and answer to this particular Law (Rev. 20:11-15).

But the tragedy is, most modern Christians, due to the fact of not understanding the Cross of Christ as it regards our Sanctification, i.e., *"how we live for God,"* are living, as well, under religious laws of some kind.

RELIGIOUS LAWS

While the laws of which I speak, are not the Law of Moses, but rather laws that we devise out of our own minds, which we think will help us live for God, still, they are laws, and the upshot is, the Holy Spirit will not function in such capacity.

Christians are bad about taking things which are legitimate in their own right, such as the Lord's Supper, or prayer, or the giving of money to the Work of the Lord, or witnessing to souls, etc., and turning them into laws. In other words, we think by doing these things, and thereby making it the object of our faith, which always happens, this will help us to live a cleaner life for the Lord. It won't! In fact, it will have the opposite affect.

Let me explain!

Anything and everything done in our lives for the Lord, which helps us to draw closer to the Lord, and I speak of Holiness and Righteousness, along with the Fruit of the Spirit, all, and without exception, must be done by the Power of the Holy Spirit. There is no way, even the best of us, whomever that might be, can bring about in our lives that which we need. It cannot be done that way. The Holy Spirit Alone can carry out this task.

Beside that, such a Believer, in such a case, is actually living in a state of spiritual adultery, which means that we are not being faithful to the Lord. Paul said in the first four Verses of the Seventh Chapter of Romans that we are married to Christ. As such, He is to meet our every need. He does that through the Cross, which demands our Faith. But when we ignore the Cross, thereby placing our faith in something else, even though the something else might be good in its own right, we are, in effect, committing spiritual adultery. That being the case, the Holy Spirit becomes greatly limited as to what He can do on our behalf. He loves us, and He will not depart, thank God, but, nevertheless, He is grieved, wounded, and actually hindered. In other words, He can only do a fraction for us as to what He could do if our faith was correct.

The way that I know that most of the modern Church is living under Law, and I'm speaking of those who are truly Born-Again, is because the Cross is not being preached. One would have to admit that the Apostle Paul preached the Cross (I Cor. 1:17-18, 21, 23; 2:2). In fact, Paul said to the Church at Corinth:

"For I determined not to know any thing among you *(with purpose and design, Paul did not resort to the knowledge or philosophy of the world regarding the preaching of the Gospel)*, **save Jesus Christ, and Him Crucified** *(that and that alone is the Message which will save the sinner, set the captive free, and give the Believer perpetual* *victory)*" **(I Cor. 2:2).**

For the Believer to get out from under Law, which brings all type of problems, the Believer must, and without fail, place his Faith exclusively in the Cross of Christ, and then Law will be replaced with Grace. Living for the Lord then becomes the greatest life there could ever be. Truly, even as Peter said, it becomes *"Joy unspeakable and full of glory."* This is the *"more abundant Life,"* of which Jesus spoke (Jn. 10:10). It then truly becomes what John Newton wrote about so long ago . . .

> *"Amazing Grace, how sweet the sound,*
> *"That Saved a wretch like me.*
> *"I once was lost, but now I'm found,*
> *"I was blind but now I see."*

CHAPTER 7

The Doctrine Of "Justification By Faith"

THE DOCTRINE OF *"JUSTIFICATION BY FAITH"*

First of all, allow us to establish the fact that *"Justification by Faith,"* is by far the greatest Gift that God has given to the fallen sons of Adam's lost race. In fact, there is nothing with which one can compare this great, glorious, and grand Gift from God, and it is a Gift.

Paul wrote:

"For the wages of sin is death; but the Gift of God is Eternal Life through Jesus Christ our Lord" (Rom. 6:23).

The great Apostle also said, *"Therefore being justified by Faith, we have peace with God through our Lord Jesus Christ: by Whom also we have access by Faith into this Grace wherein we stand, and rejoice in hope of the Glory of God"* (Rom. 5:1-2).

As well, this great Gift is available to all and, in fact, is that alone which can change the hearts of wicked men.

WHAT IS JUSTIFICATION?

The Hebrew root for Justification is *"sadag,"* and means, *"Righteous/Righteousness."*

The Greek word for Justification is *"dikaioo,"* which means *"to acquit,"* *"to vindicate,"* or *"to pronounce righteous."*

Justification is pure and simple, a legal work. Man owed a debt to God he could not hope to pay. In fact, it was, and is, impossible! The debt was and is a legal debt. So, the price that Jesus paid at Calvary's Cross, was accepted by God as legal payment for that which man owed, thereby meaning that the Work of Christ on the Cross was a legal work as well!

Someone has well said that Sanctification makes one clean, while Justification declares one clean.

THE END RESULT OF JUSTIFICATION

Justification declares one *"not guilty."* But it does more

than that. It declares one totally *"innocent."* But it does more than that. It declares one as such *"who has never sinned."* But it does more than that. It declares one to be like Christ, which speaks of perfection and, as well, that which has *"always been perfect."* Paul said:

"For such an High Priest became us *(presents the fact that no one less exalted could have met the necessities of the human race)*, *Who is Holy*, harmless, undefiled, separate from sinners *(describes the Spotless, Pure, Perfect Character of the Son of God as our Great High Priest; as well, this tells us Christ did not become a sinner on the Cross, as some claim, but was rather the Sin-Offering)*, and made higher than the Heavens *(refers to the fact that He is seated at the Right Hand of the Father, which is the most exalted position in Heaven or Earth)*;

"Who needs not daily *(refers to the daily Sacrifices offered by the Priests under the old Jewish economy)*, as those High Priests, to offer up sacrifice, first for his own sins, and then for the people's *(refers to the work of the Jewish High Priest on the Great Day of Atonement, which specified their unworthiness; Christ did not have to function accordingly)*: for this He did once, when He offered up Himself. *(This refers to His Death on the Cross, which Atoned for all sin — past, present, and future, making no further Sacrifices necessary)*" (Heb. 7:26-27).

Christ Personally said of Himself, and of Believers as well:

"At that day *(after the Resurrection, and the coming of the Holy Spirit on the Day of Pentecost)* you shall know that I *am* in My Father *(speaks of Deity; Jesus is God!)*, and you in Me *(has to do with our Salvation by Faith)*, and I in you *(enables us to live a victorious life [Gal. 2:20])*" (Jn. 14:20).

God could not and cannot accept anything less than the perfection of Christ. Such perfection is gained only by the believing sinner evidencing Faith in Christ and what He did for us at the Cross.

"For God so loved the world *(presents the God kind of love)*, that He gave His Only Begotten Son *(gave Him up to the Cross, for that's what it took to redeem humanity)*, that whosoever believes in Him should not perish, but have Everlasting Life" (Jn. 3:16).

JUSTIFICATION: THE SAME IN THE OLD TESTAMENT AS IN THE NEW TESTAMENT

Justification was first hinted at, at the very dawn of time, in fact, immediately after the Fall. The Lord said to Satan through the serpent:

"And I will put enmity *(animosity)* between you and the woman *(presents the Lord now actually speaking to Satan, who had used the serpent; in effect, the Lord is saying to Satan, 'You used the woman to bring down the human race, and I will use the woman as an instrument to bring the Redeemer into the world, Who will save the human race')*, and between your seed *(mankind which follows Satan)* and her Seed *(the Lord Jesus Christ)*; it *(Christ)* shall bruise your head *(the victory that Jesus won at the Cross [Col. 2:14-15])*, and you shall bruise His Heel *(the sufferings of the Cross)*" (Gen. 3:15).

However, this great Doctrine, all founded on the Cross, was first of all revealed to Abraham. The Scripture says:

"And he *(Abraham)* believed in the LORD *(exercised Faith, believing what the Lord told him)*; and He *(the Lord)* counted it to him *(Abraham)* for Righteousness. *(This is one of the single most important Scriptures in the entirety of the Word of God. In this simple term, 'Abraham believed the LORD,' we find the meaning of Justification by Faith. Abraham was Saved by Grace through Faith, not by his good works. There is no other way of Salvation anywhere in the Bible. God demands Righteousness; however, it is the Righteousness afforded strictly by Christ and Christ Alone. Anything else is self-righteousness, and totally unacceptable to God. Directly the sinner believes God's Testimony about His Beloved Son, he is not only declared righteous, but he is made a son and an heir)"* **(Gen. 15:6).**

But it awaited the Apostle Paul for this great Doctrine to be fully explained.

Paul proclaims the unrighteousness of man in Romans, Chapters 1 through 3. In Chapters 4 and 5 of Romans, he explains this great Doctrine of *"Justification by Faith."*

Paul tells us that *"Justification by Faith"* cannot in any measure be obtained by works. It is totally and fully obtained only by Faith in Christ. The great Apostle wrote:

"What shall we say then that Abraham our father, as pertaining to the flesh, has found? *(Having stated that the Old Testament teaches that God justifies the sinner on the Faith principle as opposed to the merit principle, the Holy Spirit now brings forward Abraham.)*

"For if Abraham were justified by works *(which he wasn't)***, he has *whereof* to glory; but not before God** *(the boasting of Salvation by works, which God will not accept).*

"For what says the Scripture? Abraham believed God, and it was counted unto him for Righteousness *([Gen. 15:6] if one properly understands this Verse, he properly understands the Bible; Abraham gained Righteousness by simple Faith in God, Who would send a Redeemer into the world [Jn. 8:56]).*

"Now to him who works *(tries to earn Salvation)* **is**

the reward *(Righteousness)* **not reckoned of Grace** *(the Grace of God),* **but of debt** *(claiming that God owes us something, which He doesn't!).*

"**But to him who works not** *(doesn't trust in works for Salvation),* **but believes on Him Who Justifies the ungodly** *(through Christ and the Cross),* **his Faith is counted for Righteousness** *(God awards Righteousness only on the basis of Faith in Christ and His Finished Work)*" **(Rom. 4:1-5).**

DAVID

David is used as the other example. Whereas Abraham symbolized the unredeemed coming to Christ, David epitomizes the Believer who has sinned. Both are justified on the same basis. Concerning David, the Scripture says:

"**Even as David** *(both Abraham and David were progenitors of the Promised Messiah, and as such they held a unique place in the Faith and veneration of the Work of God)* **also describes the blessedness of the man** *(a blessed man),* **unto whom God imputes Righteousness without works** *(works will never gain the Righteousness of God),*

"*Saying,* **Blessed** *are* **they whose iniquities are forgiven** *([Ps. 32:1-2] iniquities can only be forgiven by Faith in Christ),* **and whose sins are covered** *(the Cross made this possible).*

"**Blessed** *is* **the man to whom the Lord will not impute sin** *(the Lord will not impute sin to the person who places his Faith solely in Christ and what Christ did at the Cross)*" **(Rom. 4:6-8).**

THE CROSS ALONE HAS MADE
JUSTIFICATION POSSIBLE

Before the Cross, individuals were justified by their Faith in what the Sacrifices represented, namely the coming Redeemer.

In other words, they were justified by looking forward to the Cross. Since the Cross, man is justified solely by looking backward to that Finished Work. Before the Cross one might say that individuals were justified by God by looking forward to a Prophetic Jesus. Since the Cross individuals are justified by looking backward to a historical Cross. It is the Cross alone which has made and does make, Justification possible. Paul said:

"**Know you not, that so many of us as were baptized into Jesus Christ** *(plainly says that this Baptism is into Christ and not water [I Cor. 1:17; 12:13; Gal. 3:27; Eph. 4:5; Col. 2:11-13])* **were baptized into His Death?** *(When Christ died on the Cross, in the Mind of God, we died with Him; in other words, He became our Substitute, and our identification with Him in His Death gives us all the benefits for which He died; the idea is that He did it all for us!)*

"**Therefore we are buried with Him by baptism into death** *(not only did we die with Him, but we were buried with Him as well, which means that all the sin and transgression of the past were buried; when they put Him in the Tomb, they put all of our sins into that Tomb as well)*: **that like as Christ was raised up from the dead by the Glory of the Father, even so we also should walk in Newness of Life** *(we died with Him, we were buried with Him, and His Resurrection was our Resurrection to a 'Newness of Life').*

"**For if we have been planted together** *(with Christ)* **in the likeness of His Death** *(Paul proclaims the Cross as the instrument through which all Blessings come; consequently, the Cross must ever be the Object of our Faith, which gives the Holy Spirit latitude to work within our lives)*, **we shall be also** *in the likeness* **of** *His* **Resurrection** *(we can have the 'likeness of His Resurrection,' i.e., 'live this Resurrection Life,' only as long as we understand the 'likeness of His Death,' which refers to the Cross as the Means by which all* *of this is done)"* **(Rom. 6:3-5).**

The Apostle also said:

"For Christ sent me not to baptize *(presents to us a Cardinal Truth)***, but to preach the Gospel** *(the manner in which one may be Saved from sin)***: not with wisdom of words** *(intellectualism is not the Gospel)***, lest the Cross of Christ should be made of none effect.** *(This tells us in no uncertain terms that the Cross of Christ must always be the emphasis of the Message)"* **(I Cor. 1:17).**

He then said:

"For the preaching *(Word)* **of the Cross is to them who perish foolishness** *(Spiritual things cannot be discerned by unredeemed people, but that doesn't matter; the Cross must be preached just the same, even as we shall see)***; but unto us who are Saved it is the Power of God.** *(The Cross is the Power of God simply because it was there that the total sin debt was paid, giving the Holy Spirit, in Whom the Power resides, latitude to work mightily within our lives)"* **(I Cor. 1:18).**

And finally:

"But we preach Christ Crucified *(this is the Foundation of the Word of God and, thereby, of Salvation)***, unto the Jews a stumblingblock** *(the Cross was the stumblingblock)***, and unto the Greeks foolishness** *(both found it difficult to accept as God a dead Man hanging on a Cross, for such Christ was to them)"* **(I Cor. 1:23).**

And we might add:

"And I, Brethren, when I came to you, came not

with excellency of speech or of wisdom *(means that he depended not on oratorical abilities, nor did he delve into philosophy, which was all the rage of that particular day)*, **declaring unto you the Testimony of God** *(which is Christ and Him Crucified).*

"**For I determined not to know any thing among you** *(with purpose and design, Paul did not resort to the knowledge or philosophy of the world regarding the preaching of the Gospel)*, **save Jesus Christ, and Him Crucified** *(that and that alone is the Message which will save the sinner, set the captive free, and give the Believer perpetual victory)*" **(I Cor. 2:1-2).**

WHAT DOES IT MEAN *"BY FAITH,"* AS IN *"JUSTIFICATION BY FAITH"*?

Paul said, and as we have previously quoted:

"**Therefore being Justified by Faith** *(this is the only way one can be justified; refers to Faith in Christ and what He did at the Cross)*, **we have peace with God** *(justifying peace)* **through our Lord Jesus Christ** *(what He did at the Cross)*" **(Rom. 5:1).**

It is Faith as opposed to Works!
The Apostle also said:

"**Being justified freely by His Grace** *(made possible by the Cross)* **through the Redemption that is in Christ Jesus** *(carried out at the Cross):*
"**Whom God has set forth** *to be* **a propitiation** *(Atonement or Reconciliation)* **through Faith in His Blood** *(again, all of this is made possible by the Cross)*, **to declare His Righteousness for the remission of sins that are past** *(refers to all who trusted Christ before He actually came, which covers the entirety of the time from the Garden of*

Eden to the moment Jesus died on the Cross), **through the forbearance** *(tolerance)* **of God** *(meaning that God tolerated the situation before Calvary, knowing the debt would be fully paid at that time)*" **(Rom. 3:24-25).**

The idea is, for one to be Justified, the great Work can only be accomplished by Faith in Christ and what He did for us at the Cross. If one tries to earn Justification by works or by merit, he is automatically disqualified by the Lord.

The reason? It is not possible that one can be justified by works, simply because the debt was too great. So, Justification can come only by Christ Who suffered as our Substitute, thereby, placing our Faith exclusively in Him.

All of this means that the person who has Faith in Jesus stands acquitted *"now."* The Judge has spoken; no one can annul the Divine decision. Through Faith we are declared righteous and stand acquitted of every charge that might be brought against us.

Only by misunderstanding the Doctrine of Justification can Believers today imagine that they may become righteous by a modern struggle to live by law. Reliance on God both for Salvation and for power to live a righteous life is the only option the Believer has.

Thus, the Gospel offer of Salvation by Faith includes more than a pardon: it includes also a transformation. God will declare the sinner righteous, and then the Holy Spirit will act to make the sinner what God has declared him to be.

THERE IS NO SUCH THING AS A PARTIAL JUSTIFICATION

One is either justified fully, or one is not justified at all.

This means that when God forgives the believing sinner, He forgives in totality and in every capacity.

This means that the unredeemed individual coming to Christ is actually made into a new creation. The Scripture says concerning that:

> "**Therefore if any man** *be* **in Christ** *(Saved by the Blood),* *he is* **a new creature** *(a new creation):* **old things are passed away** *(what we were before Salvation);* **behold, all things are become new.** *(The old is no longer useable, with everything given to us now by Christ as 'new.')*
>
> "**And all things** *are* **of God** *(all these new things),* **Who has reconciled us to Himself by Jesus Christ** *(which He was able to do as a result of the Cross),* **and has given to us the Ministry of Reconciliation** *(pertains to announcing to men the nature and conditions of this Plan of being Reconciled, which is summed up in the 'preaching of the Cross' [I Cor. 1:21, 23])*" **(II Cor. 5:17-18).**

As it regards the Believer who has failed the Lord, once again, upon confession of sin to the Lord, forgiveness is complete. It is never partial! John the Beloved said:

> "**If we confess our sins** *(pertains to acts of sin, whatever they might be; the sinner is to believe [Jn. 3:16]; the Saint is to confess),* **He** *(the Lord)* **is faithful and just to forgive us** *our* **sins** *(God will always be true to His Own Nature and Promises, keeping Faith with Himself and with man),* **and to cleanse us from all unrighteousness.** *('All,' not some. All sin was remitted, paid for, and put away on the basis of the satisfaction offered for the demands of God's Holy Law, which sinners broke, when the Lord Jesus died on the Cross.)*
>
> "**If we say that we have not sinned** *(here, John is denouncing the claims of sinless perfection; he is going back to Verse 8, speaking of Christians who claimed they had no sin nature),* **we make Him a liar** *(the person who makes such a claim makes God a liar, because the Word says the opposite),* **and His Word is not in us.** *(If we properly know the Word, we will properly know that perfection is not*

in us at present, and will not be until the Trump sounds)"
(I Jn. 1:9-10).

INTERCESSION

"**As well, our Lord is ever interceding for us, and this speaks of failure, i.e., "***sin.*** " The Apostle wrote, "Wherefore He** *(the Lord Jesus Christ)* **is able also to save them to the uttermost** *(proclaims the fact that Christ Alone has made the only true Atonement for sin; He did this at the Cross)* **who come unto God by Him** *(proclaims the only manner in which man can come to God)*, **seeing He ever lives to make intercession for them.** *(His very Presence by the Right Hand of the Father guarantees such, with nothing else having to be done [Heb. 1:3])*" **(Heb. 7:25).**

HOW CAN GOD BE JUST AND AT THE SAME TIME JUSTIFY OBVIOUSLY GUILTY SINNERS?

Paul said regarding this very thing, and I continue to quote from THE EXPOSITOR'S STUDY BIBLE:

"**Being justified freely by His Grace** *(made possible by the Cross)* **through the Redemption that is in Christ Jesus** *(carried out at the Cross)*:
"**Whom God has set forth** *to be* **a propitiation** *(Atonement or Reconciliation)* **through Faith in His Blood** *(again, all of this is made possible by the Cross)*, **to declare His Righteousness for the remission of sins that are past** *(refers to all who trusted Christ before He actually came, which covers the entirety of the time from the Garden of Eden to the moment Jesus died on the Cross)*, **through the forbearance** *(tolerance)* **of God** *(meaning that God tolerated the situation before Calvary, knowing the debt would be fully paid at that time)*;
"**To declare,** *I say,* **at this time His Righteousness**

*(refers to God's Righteousness which must be satisfied at all time, and is in Christ and only Christ)***: that He** *(God)* **might be just** *(not overlooking sin in any manner)***, and the Justifier of him who believes in Jesus** *(God can justify a believing [although guilty] sinner, and His Holiness not be impacted, providing the sinner's Faith is exclusively in Christ; only in this manner can God be 'just' and at the same time 'Justify' the sinner)*" **(Rom. 3:24-26).**

IT'S ALL IN JESUS

The Lord can justify an obviously guilty sinner, declaring him to be not guilty, to be innocent, and even to be perfect, on the basis of the Sacrifice of Christ, and only on the basis of the Sacrifice of Christ, and Faith exhibited by the believing sinner in the Person of Christ.

That's the reason that Jesus must be accepted in order for a person to be Saved. Muhammad didn't die on that Cross and pay the price, and neither did Buddha, or a thousand and one other luminaries, so-called. It was God, made flesh, Who dwelt among us, and paid the price for our Redemption on Calvary's Cross, that makes all of this possible.

A DEATH

The idea is, when the person accepts Christ, in the Mind of God, what that person was before conversion, has died. And how did that happen?

Whenever you as a believing sinner expressed Faith in Christ, in the Mind of God, you were placed in Christ when He died on the Cross, when He was buried, and when He rose from the dead (Rom. 6:3-5). So, in the Mind of God, you died with Christ, and rose with Christ, actually rose as a new man, i.e., *"a new creation"* (II Cor. 5:17). Concerning this, Paul also said:

"**For he who is dead** *(He was our Substitute, and in the*

Mind of God, we died with Him upon Believing Faith) **is freed from sin** *(set free from the bondage of the sin nature).*

"Now if we be dead with Christ *(once again pertains to the Cross, and our being baptized into His Death),* **we believe that we shall also live with Him** *(have Resurrection Life, which is more Abundant Life [Jn. 10:10])*" **(Rom. 6:7-8).**

DOUBLE JEOPARDY

There is a phrase in legal parlance that is referred to as *"double jeopardy."* It means that a person cannot be tried for the same crime twice.

As an example, let's say that a man has murdered someone, and he stands before the Judge after the verdict of guilty has been given by the Jury, awaiting sentence. The Judge sentences him to die in the electric chair, and gives the date that this execution should be carried out.

On that particular date, the man is strapped into the electric chair and his life is forfeited.

A few days later, a member of the jury that convicted this man, is walking down the street, and all of a sudden he sees this man that died just a short time ago in the electric chair. He is nonplussed, flabbergasted, to say the least!

He runs to the house where the Judge lives, gets him out of bed, and says the following to him:

"Did you not sentence this certain man to death in the electric chair?" The Judge answers in the affirmative.

He then says, *"Well I know he died, because I read about it in the paper."* The Judge said, *"Yes, I did too, so what is it that you want?"*

"I just saw that same man walking down the street, so you had best go arrest him again."

The Judge would answer, and say, *"I don't know what happened, but I cannot arrest him. He's already been tried and sentenced, and the execution has been carried out. He is free, and there is nothing anyone can do."*

Now the only difference in that and what I'm about to say is the following:

It was Jesus Who died in my place. But, in essence, and according to the Word of God, by Faith, I died with Him. And when that happened, all of the past was taken away. I cannot be tried the second time for that which once was, but no longer is. Jesus died on the Cross, and Spiritually, I died with Him. So now, the Lord can continue to be just, *"and the Justifier of him which believes in Jesus."*

That is *"Justification by Faith."*

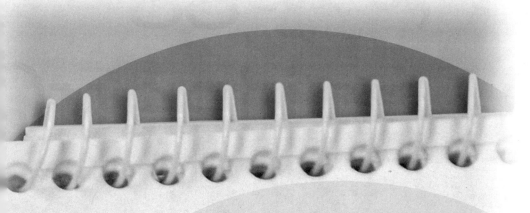

CHAPTER 8

The Doctrine Of Man

THE DOCTRINE OF MAN

In this Chapter we are going to look at man according to the following:

- His creation;
- His worth;
- His fall;
- His Salvation; and,
- His future.

I will begin this Chapter by placing the conclusion at the beginning. John the Beloved printed:

"And the Spirit and the Bride say, Come. And let him who hears say, Come. And let him who is athirst come. And whosoever will, let him take the Water of Life freely" (Rev. 22:17).

THE CREATION OF MAN

I quote from THE EXPOSITOR'S STUDY BIBLE:

"And God said, Let Us make man in Our Image, after Our Likeness *(the creation of man was preceded by a Divine consultation; as well, the pronouns 'Us' and 'Our' proclaim the consultation held by the Three Persons of the Divine Trinity, Who were One in the creative Work; 'image' and 'likeness' enable us to have fellowship with God; however, it does not mean we are gods, or can become gods; 'in Our Image after Our Likeness' actually refers to true Righteousness and Holiness [Eph. 4:24])*: and let them have dominion over the fish of the sea, and over the fowl of the air, and over the cattle, and over all the Earth, and over every creeping thing that creeps upon the Earth *(this dominion was given by God to man, and is always subject to God; the relationship of man to the balance of creation is now defined to be one of rule and supremacy; the sphere of His lordship is from the lowest to the highest of the subjects placed beneath his sway).*

THE IMAGE OF GOD

"So God created man in His Own Image *(the word 'man' should have the definite article, and should read 'the man,' that is, Adam — the same man Adam spoken of in 2:7; these are not, therefore, two accounts of the creation of man, but one Divine statement)***, in the Image of God created He him** *(the Image of God was lost at the Fall; however, the restoration of the Image was carried out at the Cross, but the completion of that restoration will not take place until the First Resurrection)***; male and female created He them** *(represents, at least as far as we know, the first time that God has created the female gender, at least as it regards intelligent beings; there is no record of any female Angels).*

"And God blessed them *(again, speaks of the ability to reproduce)***, and God said unto them, Be fruitful, and multiply, and replenish the Earth** *(the word 'replenish' carries the idea of a former creation on the Earth before Adam and Eve; according to Isaiah 14 and Ezekiel 28, Lucifer ruled this world for an undetermined period of time, and did so in Righteousness and Holiness as a beautiful Angel created by God; if, in fact, he did rule the world at that time, it would stand to reason that there had to be some type of creation on the Earth for him to rule; the word 'replenish' refers to that creation)***, and subdue it** *(and that man has done; however, he would have done it much sooner, but for the Fall)***: and have dominion over the fish of the sea, and over the fowl of the air, and over every living thing that moves upon the Earth.**

"And God said, Behold, I have given you every herb bearing seed, which is upon the face of all the Earth, and every tree, in the which is the fruit of a tree yielding seed; to you it shall be for meat *(refers to the fact that* *both animals and mankind were vegetarians before the Fall; incidentally, this was changed after the flood [Gen. 9:3]).*

"And to every beast of the Earth, and to every fowl of the air, and to every thing that creeps upon the Earth, wherein there is life, I have given every green herb for meat: and it was so *(this tells us that animals were not originally created as predators; in other words, all animals were then vegetarian as well, which means that all, and not just some, were docile).*

"And God saw every thing that He had made, and, behold, it was very good *(means that it was not simply good, but good exceedingly; it is not man alone whom God surveys, but the completed cosmos, with man as its crown and glory).* **And the evening and the morning were the sixth day** *(the word 'evening' signified the fact that the new day began at sunset, instead of 12 midnight as it presently does in our reckoning of time).*

THE CREATION OF WOMAN

"And the LORD God said, It is not good that the man should be alone *(doesn't mean that the idea of a companion for Adam suddenly presented itself to the Lord; God never intended that man should be alone)*; **I will make him an help meet for him** *(this is not meant to infer that the creation of woman was an afterthought; there is no Plan of God that is incomplete!).*

"And the LORD God caused a deep sleep to fall upon Adam, and he slept *(records the first anesthesia)*: **and He took one of his ribs** *(the word 'rib' here actually means 'side')*, **and closed up the flesh instead thereof** *(the woman is not merely of a rib, but actually of one side of man)*;

"And the rib *(side)*, **which the LORD God had taken from man, made He a woman** *(the Hebrew says, 'built He a woman'; Horton says, 'When God created the man, the word "form" was used, which is the same word used of a* *potter forming a clay jar; but the word "build" here seems to mean God paid even more attention to the creation of the woman')*, **and brought her unto the man** *(presents a formal presentation, with God, in essence, performing the first wedding; thus He instituted the bonds of the Marriage Covenant, which is actually called the Covenant of God [Prov. 2:17], indicating that God is the Author of this sacred institution; this is the marriage model, and was instituted by God; any other model, such as the homosexual marriages, so-called, can be constituted as none other than an abomination in the Eyes of God [Rom. 1:24-28]).*

THE FIRST MARRIAGE UNION

"And Adam said, This is now bone of my bones, and flesh of my flesh *(that is, she is man's counterpart, not merely in feeling and sense — his flesh — but in his solid qualities)*: **she shall be called Woman, because she was taken out of Man** *(God did not take the woman out of man's feet to be stepped on as an inferior; nor out of his head to be put on a pedestal as a superior; but from his side, close to his heart as an equal).*

"Therefore shall a man leave his father and his mother, and shall cleave unto his wife *(this Passage must be viewed as an inspired declaration of the law of marriage)*: **and they shall be one flesh** *(points to a unity of persons, not simply to a conjunction of bodies, or a community of interests, or even a reciprocity of affections).*

THE STATE OF INNOCENCE

"And they were both naked *(refers to an absence of clothing, at least as we understand such; they were actually enswathed in ethereal and transfiguring light)*, **the man and his wife, and were not ashamed** *(were not ashamed, because there was nothing of which to be ashamed)*"

(Gen. 1:26-31; 2:18, 21-25).

THE MANNER OF CREATION

The Lord created man, spirit, soul, and body. The Scripture says:

> "And the LORD God formed man of the dust of the ground *(proclaims the physical body made of clay)*, and breathed into his nostrils the breath of life *(the 'breath of life,' which comes from God, pertains to the soul and spirit of man; this was done with the first man, Adam, God breathing the soul and the spirit into man, and thereafter it comes automatically at conception)*; and man became a living soul" (Gen. 2:7).

The creation is as follows:

• Man is a living soul. The soul of man pertains to his passions and feelings. The soul addresses the physical body.

• Man has a spirit. With his spirit he addresses God. The spirit is the part of man which knows, which pertains to his intelligence, intellect, and mind (I Cor. 2:11).

• Man has a physical body. The physical body houses the soul and the spirit. With the physical body man addresses the world.

THE INTERPRETATION OF THE PHYSICAL BODY, THE SPIRIT, AND THE SOUL

While God originally created the human body, although of dust, to live forever, and to do so by virtue of the Tree of Life, the Fall of man plunged man from life to death. Concerning this, the Scripture says:

> "And the LORD God said, Behold, the man is become as one of Us, to know good and evil *(the Lord*

knew evil, not by personal experience, but rather through Omniscience; man now knows evil by becoming evil, which is the fountainhead of all sorrow in the world; the pronoun 'Us' signifies the Godhead, 'God the Father, God the Son, and God the Holy Spirit'): **and now, lest he put forth his hand, and take also of the Tree of Life, and eat, and live forever** *(this would have been the worst thing of all, to have an Adolf Hitler to live forever, etc.)*" **(Gen. 3:22).**

The physical body is merely a house, or a tent or tabernacle as Paul put it, which houses the spirit and the soul. He said concerning this:

"**For we know that if our earthly house of** *this* **tabernacle were dissolved** *(our physical body, which is not permanent)*, **we have a Building of God** *(refers to the Glorified Body, which all Saints will gain at the Resurrection)*, **an house not made with hands, eternal in the Heavens.** *(This Glorified Body is created by God, and will last and live forever.)*

"**For in this** *(this present physical body)* **we groan** *(not complaining, but rather seeing by Faith that which is to come and, thereby, longing for it to arrive)*, **earnestly desiring to be clothed upon with our house which is from Heaven** *(concerns the coming Resurrection, when the corruptible shall put on incorruption and the mortal will put on immortality)*:

"**If so be that being clothed we shall not be found naked** *(will not be destitute of covering, but will be clothed with light [I Cor. 15:41-42])*.

"**For we who are in** *this* **tabernacle do groan, being burdened** *(not for death, for death is an enemy, but rather for the coming Resurrection)*: **not for that we would be unclothed** *(we do not desire to die, nor are we unwilling to bear these burdens as long as God shall appoint)*, **but clothed upon, that mortality might be swallowed up of**

life. *(This refers to putting on immortality [I Cor. 15:35-54])"*
(II Cor. 5:1-4).

The spirit and the soul are the eternal parts of man, which will never die, and we speak of physical death, because the Spirit and the soul aren't physical.

When the Word of God speaks of the soul dying, it is speaking of separation from God, not a physical death as we think of such (Ezek. 18:4).

As it regards the physical body, Paul used the word *"dissolved,"* meaning, in effect, that with time, it is actually dissolving. In fact, the human body, as stated, was originally made to live forever, but because of the Fall in the Garden of Eden, sin entered, and the wages of sin is death; therefore, this present physical body is going to have to be replaced with an indestructible body, which will be done at the Resurrection, whether at the First Resurrection for the Saints, or the last Resurrection for the unredeemed. With the physical body, as also stated, we deal with the world. Regarding spiritual things, it is neutral. This means that, within itself, it is neither holy nor unholy, but is such according to the manner in which it is used.

THE MORTAL BODY

We are admonished, by the Holy Spirit through Paul, that we:

"Let not sin therefore reign (rule) in your mortal body, that you should obey it in the lusts thereof."

He went on to say:

"Neither yield you your members (the members of your physical body) as instruments of unrighteousness unto sin: but yield yourselves unto God, as those who are alive from the dead, and your members as instruments of Righteousness unto God" (Rom. 6:12-13).

Acts of sin or acts of Righteousness, begin in the heart (the soul and the spirit) and are carried out through the members of the physical body. In fact, in the Sixth Chapter of Romans, the Believer is told how to have victory over the sin nature, and thereby to *"yield our members as instruments of Righteousness unto God."*

THE CROSS OF CHRIST

Victory is obtained by the Child of God by the following means:
- All victory is found in the Cross of Christ (Rom. 6:1-14).
- Our Faith must ever have as its Object the Cross of Christ (I Cor. 1:17-18, 23; 2:2).
- The Holy Spirit, Who works entirely within the framework of the Finished Work of Christ, will then work mightily on our behalf (Rom. 8:1-2, 11).

So, man is a soul, he has a spirit, and the soul and the spirit live in the physical body, at least until the time of death, when they depart, whether to be with the Lord, or into eternal Hell.

SOUL SLEEP

The Scripture says, *"And many of them who sleep in the dust of the earth shall awake, some to everlasting life, and some to shame and everlasting contempt"* (Dan. 12:2).

From this Verse, and other verses, some teach a doctrine called *"soul sleep."* This means that when a person dies, their soul sleeps until the Resurrection, etc. However, the Word of God doesn't teach such a thing.

All Passages which allude to such are referring only to the body which sleeps at death, and not to the soul and the spirit.

The body is the only part of man that dies at physical death (James 2:26). As the body dies, the inner man, the life of the body, leaves. The body then goes back to dust and is spoken of as being asleep (Mat. 9:24; Jn. 11:11; I Cor. 11:30; 15:6; I Thess. 4:13-17).

Quite a number of Scriptures indicate that this sleep being referred to here is not of the soul and spirit, but, instead, of the body, such as: the body is asleep in the dust (Job 7:21; Ps. 22:15; 146:4); the body is made from dust and will return to the same as recorded in Genesis 2:7; 3:19. Conversely, the soul and the spirit are not made of a physical substance as the body, so they will not and, in fact, cannot, return to dust.

Due to what Christ did at the Cross, death, at least as far as the Child of God is concerned, has lost its sting, and is referred to as *"falling asleep"* (Acts 7:60; 13:36; I Cor. 15:6, 18-20, 51; I Thess. 4:13-17; 5:10; II Pet. 3:4).

INTERPRETATION

Some verses in the Bible regarding the subject of soul sleep have been misinterpreted. For instance, David wrote:

"For in death there is no remembrance of You: in the grave who shall give You thanks?" (Ps. 6:5).

This Passage doesn't refer to soul sleep, but, rather, when the physical body dies, which, as stated, is the only part of the human being that can die. The soul and the spirit then depart; consequently, there is nothing left in the physical body to retain memory and consciousness. Therefore, there can be no memory, etc.

Again, the Psalmist wrote:

"The dead praise not the LORD, neither any who go down into silence" (Ps. 115:17).

This is definitely true, as it regards the physical body, as should be obvious; however, the souls of all righteous people continue to praise the Lord after death (Heb. 12:22-23; Rev. 6:9-11).

EXAMPLES OF THE CONSCIOUSNESS OF THE SOUL AND THE SPIRIT AFTER DEATH

The Bible is replete with proof that the soul and the spirit do not die and, as well, that they do not sleep at the time of physical death, but, rather, go to their designated place.

Jesus gave a perfect example of this.

He told of two men, one a beggar and the other one, rich. He spoke of those men dying and, of the beggar, He said that he was *"carried by the Angels into Abraham's bosom: the rich man also died, and was buried."*

He then went on to talk about the rich man being in Hell and *"being in torments."* He also spoke of the rich man seeing Abraham, who was in Paradise, and *"Lazarus,"* which was the name of the beggar, *"in Abraham's bosom."*

He then gave an account of the conversation between the rich man and Abraham, etc. (Lk. 16:19-31).

Now, if the soul and the spirit sleep, as some teach, then Jesus didn't know what He was talking about. But, of course, we know that Jesus knew exactly what He was talking about.

The moment the Believer dies, the soul and the spirit of the Believer go to be with Christ. Paul said so (Phil. 1:23). The moment the unredeemed person dies, their soul and spirit instantly go into eternal Hell. Jesus said so (Lk. 16:19-31).

A CORRECT INTERPRETATION OF THE BIBLE

Many erroneous doctrines have come about simply because Scriptures have been pulled out of context. The way to interpret the Bible is to look at all Scriptures relative to a particular subject. To be sure, all Scriptures must harmonize on that particular subject, whatever it might be. There are no contradictions in the Bible.

If one or two Scriptures seem to point in another direction, other than the complete body of work on that particular subject, then we must understand what those isolated Texts say, and, once a proper study is made, we will find that they harmonize as well, with all other Passages on that particular subject.

If ten Scriptures say one particular thing on a given subject, and one or two other Scriptures seem to say differently, we must, first of all, lean toward the preponderance of weight which the ten Scriptures have proclaimed, etc. As stated, many erroneous doctrines have been brought about because the entirety of the subject matter was not considered. The Word of God harmonizes in every respect; and if a few Scriptures seem to be out of harmony, it is only because we do not properly understand what is being said.

SALVATION

There is a teaching that is quite strong that claims when a person comes to Christ, their spirit is then made perfect, while the soul is gradually saved over a period of time. The physical body, they teach, is brought into line along with the soul.

There is no teaching in the Word of God that substantiates that. When a person comes to Christ, they are Saved in totality, spirit, soul, and body. Likewise, when a person sins, whether a Believer or an unbeliever, their soul, their spirit, and their physical body are all affected the same. Paul said:

"**Having therefore these Promises** *(that we can draw all nourishment from the Lord)*, **dearly beloved, let us cleanse ourselves from all filthiness of the flesh and spirit** *(when one sins, he sins spirit, soul, and body; there is no such thing as the body sinning, and not the spirit, etc.)*, **perfecting holiness in the fear of God** *(to bring to a state of completion; we can do this only by 'walking after the Spirit' [Rom. 8:1-2], which refers to looking to the Cross, and looking to the Cross exclusively)*" **(II Cor. 7:1).**

Paul also said, and concerning this very subject:

"**And the very God of Peace Sanctify you wholly** *(this is 'progressive Sanctification,' which can only be brought about by the Holy Spirit, Who does such as our Faith is firmly anchored in the Cross, within which parameters the*

Spirit always works; the Sanctification process involves the whole man); and *I pray God* **your whole spirit and soul and body** *(proclaims the makeup of the whole man)* **be preserved blameless unto the coming of our Lord Jesus Christ.** *(This refers to the Rapture. As well, this one Verse proclaims the fact that any involvement, whether Righteous or unrighteous, effects the whole man, and not just the physical body or the soul as some claim)*" **(I Thess. 5:23).**

This teaching of the spirit being perfect and the soul being saved, etc., is just another effort to circumvent the Cross. If it is believed, whether the individual understands it or not, it is stating that what Jesus did at the Cross was not complete. In other words, it was not a Finished Work, and we have to add something to what He has done. Such borders on blasphemy!

MAN'S WORTH

Concerning the worth of man, David wrote:

"When I consider Your Heavens, the Work of Your Fingers, the moon and the stars, which You have ordained *(the argument of Verses 3-8 is the amazing love of Christ in coming forth from the Highest Glory to redeem a being so insignificant as man)*;

"What is man, that You are mindful of him? And the son of man, that You visit him? *(God became man and went to Calvary in order to redeem fallen humanity. The price that was paid for Redemption proclaims to us the worth of man, which, in fact, is God's highest creation.)*

"For You have made him a little lower than the Angels, and have crowned him with glory and honor *(the Hebrew word 'Elohim' here translated 'angels' should have been translated 'God,' for that's what the word actually means; there is no place in the Old Testament where 'Elohim' means 'Angels'; this means that man was originally created higher than the Angels, and through Christ will be restored to that lofty position [Rom. 8:14-17]).*

"You made him to have dominion over the works of Your hands; You have put all things under His Feet *(in their fullness, these words given here are only true of the God-Man, Jesus Christ [Mat. 28:18]; Christ has been exalted to a place higher than Angels or any other being except the Father; redeemed man is to be raised up to that exalted position with Him [Eph. 2:6-7]):*

"All sheep and oxen, yea, and the beasts of the field;

"The fowl of the air, and the fish of the sea, and whatsoever passes through the paths of the seas *(man was made to have dominion over all this).*

"O LORD, our Lord, how excellent is Your Name in all the Earth! *(Christ is the Head of the Church, which is His Body; ultimately, that which is given by Promise will, upon the Resurrection of Life, be carried to its ultimate victorious conclusion)*" **(Ps. 8:3-9).**

THE INTELLIGENCE OF ADAM

When Adam was originally created, his intelligence level was absolutely phenomenal. There is evidence that in the *"cool of the day,"* which was at twilight in the evening, God would come down and walk in the Garden with Adam and Eve (Gen. 3:8), in which He gave them instructions. Now think about that for a moment.

The Creator of all the Ages, Who is Omnipotent (all-powerful), Omniscient (all-knowing), and Omnipresent (everywhere), instructed Adam and Eve, which meant that their training was absolutely exceptional. They had God as their teacher, and on a daily basis.

Adam was delegated by God to give names to all of the animal creation. The intelligence that it took to do this was far beyond our comprehension. It was not merely a name that was given each animal, but a name that explained, in essence, what that animal was and what it could do. From then until now, the names haven't changed. Concerning this, the Scripture says:

"And out of the ground the LORD God formed every beast of the field, and every fowl of the air *(the animals and the fowls were created out of dust, exactly as man)*; and brought them unto Adam to see what he would call them: and whatsoever Adam called every living creature, that was the name thereof *(carried within the name that Adam gave to each one of these creatures are the characteristics of that particular animal or fowl; so we are speaking here of a man who had amazing intelligence; to do all of this, Adam had to have a distinct knowledge of speech, the meaning of all words, and the capacity of attaching words to ideas; why not? Adam had the greatest Teacher that man has ever had, 'the LORD God')*.

"And Adam gave names to all cattle, and to the fowl of the air, and to every beast of the field; but for Adam there was not found a help meet for him *(we learn from this that the animal creation was of far greater magnitude and intelligence than at the present; it was the Fall which changed that creation [Rom. 8:19-23])*" **(Gen. 2:19-20).**

HIGHER THAN THE ANGELS

As we've already stated, from Psalm 8, the Holy Spirit through David, proclaimed the fact that man was and is God's highest creation, originally created even higher than the Angels. Of course, when man is seen today, what is observed is a far cry from that which God originally created.

In fact, if one wants to know what man was originally like, one only has to study the four Gospels, Matthew, Mark, Luke, and John, which give the Life and Ministry of the Lord Jesus Christ. *"The Man Christ Jesus,"* although at the same time very God, as well as very Man, functioned, however, totally as a Man in his earthly sojourn. So, when one saw Jesus Christ, they were seeing both God and Man. In other words, if one wants to know what God the Father is like, one only has to look at Jesus. If one wants to know what man was when originally created, one only has to look at Jesus. He was the consummate man.

THE ABILITY TO REPRODUCE

As far as we know, when God created the Angels, He created all of them at the same time. In other words, there's never been such a thing as a baby Angel, because they were all created fully mature. But, when the Lord created man, He created only a pair, Adam and Eve, and gave them the power of procreation, i.e., to bring offspring into the world.

Originally it was the Plan of God that all sons and daughters which would be born into the world, were to be born as *"sons and daughters of God,"* but the Fall stopped all of that. Now, sons and daughters could be brought into the world only in the likeness of Adam. The Scripture says:

"This is the book of the generations of Adam *(corresponds with the phrase, 'The Book of the Generation of Jesus Christ,' Who was the Last Adam [Mat. 1:1])*. In the day that God created man, in the Likeness of God made He him *(the 'Likeness of God' is the 'Glory of God' [II Cor. 4:6]. Through the Fall, man lost that glory; however, at the First Resurrection of Life, every Believer will regain that glory [Rom. 8:17])*;

"Male and female created He them *(refers to the fact that homosexuality is a grievous sin before God)*; and blessed them *(the blessing was lost as a result of the Fall, but has been regained in Christ)*, and called their name Adam, in the day when they were created *(Adam, in the Hebrew, is the word for humankind in general beside the specific name for the first man)*.

"And Adam lived an hundred and thirty years, and begat *(fathered)* a son in his own likeness *(God originally intended for mankind to procreate 'sons and daughters of God' into the world; due to the Fall, sons and daughters could be brought into the world only in the likeness of their original parent, Adam, a product of his fallen nature; it is called 'original sin')*, **and after his image** *(means that Adam no longer had the Image of God; the 'likeness' and 'image' are now after Satan [Jn. 8:44])*; **and called his name Seth** *(even though Seth was not the Promised One, still, he represented a ray of hope; through him, rather his line, the Promised One would come)*" **(Gen. 5:1-3).**

THE ABILITY TO CREATE

There is no record that Angels have the ability to create anything; however, as is obvious, man can create certain things, which he has ably done, especially in the last century. There is a great difference, however, in the creation abilities of God and man. God can create things out of nothing, whereas man has to have the original material.

As well, when God creates things, He does not deplete something else, which would create a loss. When man creates something, he has to deplete the original product. For instance, if he builds a house, he has to deplete the forest of the trees needed for construction. He has to deplete sand and other materials in order to make concrete and brick, etc. Conversely, God needs nothing in order to begin something (Heb. 11:3).

MAN AND HIS FALL

God loved Adam and Eve very, very much; consequently, how it saddened His Heart at their disobedience and resultant Fall. Sadder still, there is no record that they ever made their way back to God, even though they were given every opportunity.

Concerning their Fall, the Holy Spirit through Moses said:

"And the LORD God planted a Garden eastward in

Eden *(it was actually planted before Adam was created; the area is believed by some Scholars to be the site where the city of Babylon would ultimately be built)*; **and there He put the man whom He had formed** *(the Garden of Eden was to be the home place of man).*

"And out of the ground made the LORD God to grow every tree that is pleasant to the sight *(beautiful trees),* **and good for food** *(every fruit tree imaginable, even those which bear nuts)*; **the Tree of Life also in the midst of the Garden** *(evidently contained a type of fruit; 3:22 says as much! the Tree of Life had the power of so renewing man's physical energies that his body, though formed of the dust of the ground and, therefore, naturally mortal, would, by its continual use, live on forever; Christ is now to us the 'Tree of Life' [Rev. 2:7; 22:2]; and the 'Bread of Life' [Jn. 6:48, 51])*, **and the Tree of Knowledge of Good and Evil** *(presents the tree of death).*

"And the LORD God took the man, and put him into the Garden of Eden to dress it and to keep it.

"And the LORD God commanded the man, saying, Of every tree of the Garden you may freely eat *(as stated, before the Fall, man was a vegetarian)*:

"But of the Tree of the Knowledge of Good and Evil, you shall not eat of it *(as for the 'evil,' that was obvious; however, it is the 'good' on this tree that deceives much of the world; the 'good' speaks of religion; the definition of religion pertains to a system devised by men in order to bring about Salvation, to reach God, or to better oneself in some way; because it is devised by man, it is unacceptable to God; God's answer to the dilemma of the human race is 'Jesus Christ and Him Crucified' [I Cor. 1:23])*: **for in the day that you eat thereof you shall surely die** *(speaks of spiritual death, which is separation from God; let it be understood that the Tree of the Knowledge of Good and Evil was not the cause of Adam's Fall; it was a failure to heed and obey the Word of God, which is the cause of every* *single failure; spiritual death ultimately brought on physical death, and has, in fact, filled the world with death, all because of the Fall)"* **(Gen. 2:8-9, 15-17).**

THE FOREKNOWLEDGE OF GOD

Now we have the account of the Fall of man, which has plunged the world into spiritual darkness, from which it has not recovered even yet. Because of the Fall, the world has consistently been filled with war, bloodshed, pain, sickness, suffering, starvation, loneliness, man's inhumanity to man, in fact, at times, a little bit of Hell on Earth, and all because of the Fall.

DID THE FALL TAKE GOD BY SURPRISE?

No!
Peter said concerning this very thing:

"Forasmuch as you know that you were not Redeemed with corruptible things, *as* **silver and gold** *(presents the fact that the most precious commodities [silver and gold] could not Redeem fallen man)*, **from your vain conversation** *(vain lifestyle)* **received** **by tradition from your fathers** *(speaks of original sin that is passed on from father to child at conception)***;**
"But with the Precious Blood of Christ *(presents the payment, which proclaims the poured out Life of Christ on behalf of sinners)*, **as of a Lamb without blemish and without spot** *(speaks of the lambs offered as substitutes in the Old Jewish economy; the Death of Christ was not an execution or assassination, but rather a Sacrifice; the Offering of Himself presented a Perfect Sacrifice, for He was Perfect in every respect [Ex. 12:5])***:**
"Who verily was foreordained before the foundation of the world *(refers to the fact that God, in His Omniscience, knew He would create man, man would Fall,*

and man would be redeemed by Christ going to the Cross; this was all done before the Universe was created; this means the Cross of Christ is the Foundation Doctrine of all Doctrine, referring to the fact that all Doctrine must be built upon that Foundation, or else it is specious), **but was manifest in these last times for you** *(refers to the invisible God Who, in the Person of the Son, was made visible to human eyesight by assuming a human body and human limitations)*" **(I Pet. 1:18-20).**

THE TERRIBLE FALL

Moses continues in giving us the account of this terrible act, the Fall of our First Parents, Adam and Eve, which plunged the world into spiritual darkness. The Scripture says:

"Now the serpent was more subtle than any beast of the field which the LORD God had made *(the word 'subtle,' as used here, is not negative, but rather positive; everything that God made before the Fall was positive; it describes qualities such as quickness of sight, swiftness of motion, activity of self-preservation, and seemingly intelligent adaptation to its surroundings)*. **And he said unto the woman** *(not a fable; the serpent before the Fall had the ability of limited speech; Eve did not seem surprised when he spoke to her!)*, **Yes, has God said, You shall not eat of every tree of the Garden?** *(The serpent evidently lent its faculties to Satan, even though the Evil One is not mentioned. That being the case, Satan spoke through the serpent, and questioned the Word of God.)*

EVE

"And the woman said unto the serpent *(proclaims Satan leveling his attack against Eve, instead of Adam; his use of Eve was only a means to get to Adam)*, **We may eat**

of the fruit of the trees of the Garden *(the trial of our First Parents was ordained by God, because probation was essential to their Spiritual Development and self-determination; but as He did not desire that they should be tempted to their Fall, He would not suffer Satan to tempt them in a way that would surpass their human capacity; the tempted might, therefore, have resisted the tempter)***:**

"But of the fruit of the tree which is in the midst of the Garden, God has said, You shall not eat of it, neither shall you touch it, lest you die *(Eve quoted what the Lord had said about the prohibition, but then added, 'neither shall you touch it')***.**

"And the serpent said unto the woman, You shall not surely die *(proclaims an outright denial of the Word of God; as God had preached to Adam, Satan now preaches to Eve; Jesus called Satan a liar, which probably refers to this very moment [Jn. 8:44])***:**

"For God does know that in the day you eat thereof, then your eyes shall be opened *(suggests the attainment of higher wisdom)***, and you shall be as gods, knowing good and evil.** *(In effect, says, 'You shall be Elohim.' It was a promise of Divinity. God is Omniscient, meaning that His Knowledge of evil is thorough, but not by personal experience. By His very Nature, He is totally separate from all that is evil. The knowledge of evil that Adam and Eve would learn would be by moral degradation, which would bring wreckage. While it was proper to desire to be like God, it is proper only if done in the right way, and that is through Faith in Christ and what He has done for us at the Cross.)*

THE TEMPTATION OF EVE

"And when the woman saw that the tree was good for food *(presents the lust of the eyes)***, and that it was pleasant to the eyes** *(the lust of the flesh)***, and a tree to be**

desired to make one wise *(the pride of life)*, she took of the
fruit thereof, and did eat *(constitutes the Fall)*, and gave
also unto her husband with her; and he did eat *(refers
to the fact that evidently Adam was an observer to all these
proceedings; some claim that he ate of the forbidden fruit,
which she offered him out of love for her; however, no one
ever sins out of love; Eve submitted to the temptation out of
deception, but 'Adam was not deceived' [I Tim. 2:14]; he
fell because of unbelief; he simply didn't believe what God
had said about the situation; contrast Verse 6 with Luke
4:1-13; both present the three temptations, 'the lust of the
flesh,' 'the lust of the eyes,' and 'the pride of life'; the first
man falls, the Second Man conquers)*.

"And the eyes of them both were opened *(refers to
the consciousness of guilt as a result of their sin)*, and they
knew that they were naked *(refers to the fact that they had
lost the enswathing light of purity, which previously had
clothed their bodies)*; and they sewed fig leaves together,
and made themselves aprons *(sinners clothe themselves
with morality, sacraments, and religious ceremonies; they
are as worthless as Adam's apron of fig leaves)*.

THE VOICE OF THE LORD

"And they heard the Voice of the LORD God walking in the Garden in the cool of the day *(the 'Voice' of the
Lord had once been a welcome sound; it is now a dreaded
sound, because of their sin; it is not that the Voice of the Lord
had changed, for it hadn't; it was the same Voice that they
had heard since creation; He hadn't changed, but they had)*:
and Adam and his wife hid themselves from the presence
of the LORD God amongst the trees of the Garden *(here
is the dawn of a new era in the history of humanity; the eye
of a guilt conscience is now opened for the first time, and
God and the universe appear in new and terrible forms)*.

"And the LORD God called unto Adam, and said

unto him, Where are you? *(This is the first question in the Old Testament. 'Where is he?' is the first question in the New Testament [Mat. 2:2]. The Old Testament, God seeking the sinner; the New Testament, the sinner seeking God.)*

ADAM'S RESPONSE

"And he *(Adam)* **said, I heard Your Voice in the Garden, and I was afraid** *(fear is the first reaction of fallen man; Adam's consciousness of the effects of sin was keener than his sense of the sin itself)*, **because I was naked; and I hid myself** *(he was naked to the Judgment of God, because of sin, which must be judged; he tried to hide himself from God, even as untold millions have, but never with any success; God wanted Adam to know that he who hides himself from Him is never hidden from Him, and that he who runs away from Him can never escape Him)*.

NO SIGN OF REPENTANCE

"And He said, Who told you that you were naked *(carries Adam's mind from the effect to the sin that had caused it; as long as a man feels sorrow only for the results of his action, there is no Repentance, and no wish to return to the Divine Presence)*? **Have you eaten of the tree, whereof I commanded you that you should not eat?** *(The way the question is framed removes the pretext of ignorance, and also points to the fact that the sin had been carried out in direct violation of the Divine prohibition.)*

"And the man said, The woman whom You gave to be with me, she gave me of the tree, and I did eat *(Adam first of all blamed God, and then blamed Eve; he recapitulates the history, as if, in his view, it was a matter of course that he should act as he had done; man has been doing this ever since)*.

"And the LORD God said unto the woman, What

is this that you have done? *(The two questions, 'Where are you?' and 'What is this that you have done?' comprise the human problem.)* **And the woman said, The serpent beguiled me, and I did eat** *(presents Eve blaming the serpent; in a sense, she was blaming God as well, simply because God had made the serpent).*

THE RESULTS OF THE FALL

"And the LORD God said unto the serpent *(as we shall see, presents no question or interrogation being posed toward the serpent at all; God judges him, and it is in listening to this judgment that the guilty pair hear the first great Promise respecting Christ),* **Because you have done this, you are cursed above all cattle, and above every beast of the field** *(refers to this animal being reduced from possibly the highest place and position in the animal kingdom to the lowest)*; **upon your belly shall you go, and dust shall you eat all the days of your life** *(if, in fact, the serpent was an unwitting tool in the hand of Satan, then I think that the Lord would not have placed a curse upon this animal)*:

THE FIRST MENTION OF CHRIST,
THE COMING REDEEMER

"And I will put enmity *(animosity)* **between you and the woman** *(presents the Lord now actually speaking to Satan, who had used the serpent; in effect, the Lord is saying to Satan, 'You used the woman to bring down the human race, and I will use the woman as an instrument to bring the Redeemer into the world, Who will save the human race'),* **and between your seed** *(mankind which follows Satan)* **and her Seed** *(the Lord Jesus Christ)*; **it** *(Christ)* **shall bruise your head** *(the victory that Jesus won at the Cross [Col. 2:14-15]),* **and you shall bruise His Heel** *(the* *sufferings of the Cross).*

THE CURSE ON THE WOMAN

"**Unto the woman He said, I will greatly multiply your sorrow and your conception** *(the original Plan of God was that husband and wife would bring sons and daughters of God into the world; due to the Fall, they can only bring sons and daughters into the world in the 'likeness of Adam' [Gen. 5:3])*; **in sorrow you shall bring forth children** *(as a result of the Fall, children would be born into a world of sorrow)*; **and your desire shall be to your husband, and he shall rule over you** *(her husband, instead of God, would now rule over her).*

THE CURSE UPON ADAM

"**And unto Adam He said, Because you have hearkened unto the voice of your wife** *(Adam hearkened unto his wife instead of God)*, **and have eaten of the tree, of which I commanded you, saying, You shall not eat of it** *(the tree itself contained no evil properties in the fruit; the Fall, as stated, was caused rather by disobedience to the Word of God)*: **cursed is the ground for your sake; in sorrow shall you eat of it all the days of your life** *(Earth was originally intended to be a paradise, but now it will give up its largesse reluctantly; as well, the phrase, 'all the days of your life,' proclaims the death sentence, which means that life is now terminal, all as a result of 'spiritual death,' which was, and is, separation from God)*;

"**Thorns also and thistles shall it bring forth to you** *(thorns and thistles were not originally in the creation of God, this being a result of the curse, which is a result of the sin of man)*; **and you shall eat the herb of the field** *(this would not now grow freely, as originally intended, but only now with great care and great labor)*;

"In the sweat of your face shall you eat bread *(food will be obtained by hard labor)*, till you return unto the ground *(the life-source, which was formerly in God, is now in food, and which is woefully insufficient)*; for out of it were you taken: for dust you are, and unto dust shall you return *(the Power of God alone could keep the dust alive; that being gone, to dust man returns)*.

"And Adam called his wife's name Eve; because she was the mother of all living. *(God named the man, and called him Adam, which means 'red earth.' Adam named the woman, and called her Eve, which means 'life.' Adam bears the name of the dying body, Eve of the living soul.)*

A TYPE OF CHRIST

"Unto Adam also and to his wife did the LORD God make coats of skins, and clothed them *(in the making of coats of skins, God, in effect, was telling Adam and Eve that their fig leaves were insufficient; as well, He was teaching them that without the shedding of blood, which pertained to the animals that gave their lives, which were Types of Christ, is no remission of sin; in this first sacrifice was laid the foundation of the entirety of the Plan of God as it regards Redemption; also, it must be noticed that it is the 'LORD God' Who furnished these coats, and not man himself; this tells us that Salvation is altogether of God and not at all of man; the Life of Christ given on the Cross, and given as our Substitute, provides the only covering for sin; everything else must be rejected)*" (Gen. 3:1-21).

And now begins man ruled by the sin nature instead of the Divine Nature. The results will not be pleasant.

When man fell, he fell from a position of total God-consciousness, to the far, far lower level, of total self-consciousness. And so now instead of being taken up with God, Who is the Fountain of all life, he is now taken up with self, and in every capacity.

THE RESULTS OF ADAM'S FALL

Due to the fact that the Lord made Adam to have dominion over the *"works of His Hands,"* this dominion seemingly covered everything that had to do with Adam, which definitely included the elements.

That means that the elements do not function as God originally made them. This is the reason for hurricanes, tornados, droughts, earthquakes, storms, etc. None of that was ever originally intended. Paul addressed this by saying:

THE GROANING OF CREATION

"For the creature *(Creation)* was made subject to vanity *(Adam's Fall signaled the fall of Creation)*, not willingly *(the Creation did not sin, even as such cannot sin, but became subject to the result of sin, which is death)*, but by reason of Him Who has subjected *the same* in Hope *(speaks of God as the One Who passed sentence because of Adam's Fall, but at the same time gave us a 'Hope'; that 'Hope' is Christ, Who will rectify all things)*,

"Because the creature *(Creation)* itself also shall be delivered *(presents this 'Hope' as effecting that Deliverance, which He did by the Cross)* from the bondage of corruption *(speaks of mortality, i.e., 'death')* into the glorious liberty of the Children of God *(when man fell, Creation fell! when man shall be delivered, Creation will be delivered as well, and is expressed in the word 'also')*.

"For we know that the whole Creation *(everything has been affected by Satan's rebellion and Adam's Fall)* groans and travails in pain together until now *(refers to the common longing of the elements of the Creation to be brought back to their original perfection)*.

"And not only *they* *(the Creation, and all it entails)*, but ourselves also *(refers to Believers)*, which have the Firstfruits of the Spirit *(even though Jesus addressed every single thing lost in the Fall at the Cross, we only have a part of that possession now, with the balance coming at the Resurrection)*, even we ourselves groan within ourselves *(proclaims the obvious fact that all Jesus paid for in the Atonement has not yet been fully realized)*, waiting for the Adoption *(should be translated, 'waiting for the fulfillment of the process, which Adoption into the Family of God guarantees')*, *to wit,* the Redemption of our body *(the glorifying of our physical body that will take place at the Resurrection)*" (Rom. 8:20-23).

THE SALVATION OF MAN

To understand the depths of the Fall of man, we only have to look at the price that had to be paid in order to redeem man, the Cross of Christ.

Due to His miraculous Power, some have asked, why would God not simply, because of the Fall, do away with Adam and Eve, and create another pair?

First of all, it was love that created man and, therefore, love would have to redeem man. It was Charles C. Wesley who wrote the song: *"Oh Love That Will Not Let Me Go"*.

Would you do away with your child simply because it was sick?

Of course not!

You would do everything within your power to save that child. God functions in the same capacity; consequently, the most oft quoted Scripture in the Bible, stands out starkly to us:

"For God so loved the world that He gave His Only Begotten Son *(gave Him up to the Cross, for that's what it took to redeem humanity)*, that whosoever believes in Him should not perish, but have Everlasting Life" (Jn. 3:16).

According to Simon Peter, the Fall of Adam and Eve came as no surprise to God. Through Omniscience, meaning that He is all-knowing, past, present, and future, He knew that He would create man, even before the world was created, and that man would Fall. It was then deemed necessary by the Godhead that man would be redeemed by God becoming man, and paying the price for man's Redemption, which meant that He would have to give His Life as a Sacrifice on the Cross, which He did! Even then, it took some 4,000 years before Christ could come to this world (I Pet. 1:18-20).

THE RIGHTEOUSNESS OF GOD

Why did it take so long for Redemption to be brought about? Couldn't God with His Omnipotence, simply speak the word and Redemption be effected?

Yes, He had the Power to do that; however, to have done such, would have been against His Nature, and against His Righteousness. While God is able to do all things, there are many things He will not do, simply because it is not in keeping with His Righteousness. His Nature of supreme Holiness must never be abrogated. So, if it was to be done right, and everything that God does is right, He would have to drink the bitter cup, in the Person of His Son and our Saviour, the Lord Jesus Christ.

THE SACRIFICIAL SYSTEM

The Salvation of mankind is all wrapped up in the Cross of Christ and, as well, the Sanctification of the Saint is also firmly in the Cross of Christ. The meaning of the New Covenant is the Cross of Christ, as the Cross of Christ is the meaning of the New Covenant. At Calvary Jesus atoned for all sin; past, present, and future, at least for those who will believe (Jn. 3:16). With all sin taken away, Satan's legal right to hold man captive was, as well, taken away. So, captivity presently, and ever since Calvary, is the result of the individual not taking advantage of what Christ has done for us. Through the Cross, Salvation awaits the sinner, and Sanctification awaits the Saint.

THE FOUNDATION OF ALL DOCTRINE

The foundation of every Doctrine in the Word of God, all that we teach, preach, and believe, everything and without exception, is built on the Foundation of the Cross. How do we know that?

As we've already stated, Simon Peter told us that through foreknowledge God knew that He would make man, and that man would fall. This was all before the foundation of the world (I Pet. 1:18-20). At that time, the Godhead determined that man would be redeemed, even as we've already stated, by God becoming man, going to the Cross, where there the price would be paid to satisfy the demands of a thrice-Holy God. So, we know from this, that the Cross of Christ is the literal foundation of everything, meaning that every Doctrine in the Bible must be built squarely on the Cross, and if it's not, it will fall out to false doctrine. There is no way that one could overstate this case as it regards the Cross.

THE CROSS, A MEANS OF FORGIVENESS AND FELLOWSHIP

To serve as a stopgap measure, so to speak, immediately after the Fall, and after Adam and Eve were driven from the Garden, God established the Sacrificial System, which would serve as a Symbol or a Type of the Redeemer, Who would ultimately come. Even though the First Family was fallen, still, the Cross, symbolized by the Sacrificial System, could provide a means of forgiveness of sins, and a restored fellowship after a fashion.

In the Fourth Chapter of Genesis, the standard was set. We find in this Chapter, as we will quote some of it verbatim momentarily, despite the fact that the Way of God was given, which was and is the Cross, that Cain wasn't satisfied with that way, and attempted to substitute that of his own making. So in this first example of Sacrifice, which was meant to epitomize Christ, we find the opposition already beginning. It has continued unto this hour, and if one wants to know the problem in the Church, one only has to study the Fourth Chapter of Genesis. I quote from THE EXPOSITOR'S STUDY BIBLE:

CAIN AND ABEL

"And Adam knew Eve his wife *(is the Biblical con-notation of the union of husband and wife in respect to the sex act)*; and she conceived, and bore Cain *(the first child born to this union, and would conclude exactly as the Lord said it would, with 'sorrow')*, and said, I have gotten a man from the LORD *(by Eve using the title 'LORD,' which means 'Covenant God,' and which refers to the 'Seed of the woman,' [Gen. 3:15], she thought Cain was the Promised One; she evidently didn't realize that it was impossible for fallen man to bring forth the Promised Redeemer)*.

"And she again bore his brother Abel *('Abel' means 'vanity'; Cain being the oldest, this shows that Eve by now had become disillusioned with her firstborn, undoubtedly seeing traits in him which she knew could not be of the Promised Seed; she was losing faith in God)*. And Abel was a keeper of sheep, but Cain was a tiller of the ground *(both were honorable professions)*.

THE SACRIFICIAL SYSTEM

"And in process of time it came to pass *(the phrase used here refers to a long indefinite period)*, that Cain brought of the fruit of the ground an offering unto the LORD. *(This was probably the first offering that he brought, even though the Lord had explained to the First Family the necessity of the Sacrificial System, that is, if they were to have any type of communion with God and forgiveness of sins. There is evidence that Adam, at least for a while, offered up sacrifices. Cain knew the type of sacrifice that the Lord would accept, but he rebelled against that admonition, demanding that God accept the labor of his hands, which, in fact, God could not accept. So we have, in the persons of Cain and Abel, the first examples of a religious man of the world and a genuine man of Faith.)*

"And Abel, he also brought of the firstlings of his flock and of the fat thereof *(this is what God demanded; it was a blood sacrifice of an innocent victim, a lamb, which proclaimed the fact that Abel recognized his need of a Redeemer, and that One was coming Who would redeem lost humanity; the Offering of Abel was a Type of Christ and the price that He would pay on the Cross of Calvary in order for man to be redeemed)*. And the LORD had respect unto Abel and to his offering: *(As stated, this was a Type of Christ and the Cross, the only Offering which God will respect. Abel's Altar is beautiful to God's Eye and repulsive to man's. Cain's altar is beautiful to man's eye and repulsive to God's. These 'altars' exist today; around the one, which is Christ and His atoning Work, few are gathered, around the other, many. God accepts the slain lamb and rejects the offered fruit; and the offering being rejected, so of necessity is the offerer.)*

THE RESPONSE OF THE LORD

"But unto Cain and to his offering He had not respect *(let us say it again, God has no respect for any proposed way of Salvation, other than 'Jesus Christ and Him Crucified' [I Cor. 1:23; 2:2])*. And Cain was very angry, and his countenance fell *(that which filled Abel with peace filled Cain with wrath; the carnal mind displays its enmity against all this Truth which so gladdens and satisfies the heart of the Believer)*.

"And the LORD said unto Cain *(God loves Cain, just*

as He did Abel, and wishes to bless him also), **Why are you angry** *(Abel's Altar speaks of Repentance, of Faith, and of the Precious Blood of Christ, the Lamb of God without blemish; Cain's altar tells of pride, unbelief, and self-righteousness, which always elicits anger)*? **and why is your countenance fallen** *(anger, in one form or the other, accompanies self-righteousness, for that is what plagued Cain; God's Righteousness can only come by the Cross, while self-righteousness is by dependence on works)*?

"**If you do well, shall you not be accepted** *(if you bring the correct sacrifice, and thereby place your faith)*? **and if you do not well, sin** *(a Sin-Offering)* **lies at the door** *(a lamb was at the door of the Tabernacle)*. **And unto you shall be his desire, and you shall rule over him** *(the Lord promised Cain dominion over the Earth of that day, if he would only offer up, and place his trust in, the right sacrifice; He promises the same presently to all who trust Christ [Mat. 5:5])*.

CAIN MURDERS ABEL

"**And Cain talked with Abel his brother: and it came to pass, when they were in the field, that Cain rose up against Abel his brother, and killed him** *(the first murder; Cain's religion was too refined to kill a lamb, but not too cultured to murder his brother; God's Way of Salvation fills the heart with love; man's way of salvation enflames it with hatred; 'Religion' has ever been the greatest cause of bloodshed)*" **(Gen. 4:1-8).**

THE STAGE IS SET

This Chapter, as we have already stated, sets the stage for all that will follow.

We have Abel offering up the correct sacrifice, a slain lamb, which typified the coming Redeemer, Who would give His Life on the Cross of Calvary, in order to save those who will believe.

And then we have Cain.

Cain did not deny that there was a God; actually, God conversed with him. He did not deny the altar or the need for a sacrifice. But what He did, was to substitute a sacrifice of his own making, instead of that which was demanded by God, which, in essence, said, *"I don't need a Redeemer."* That has been man's problem ever since.

Man offers up the labor of his own hands, whatever that might be, and demands that God accept it, which is impossible. As with Cain, rebellious man is not satisfied to go his own way, even though he will be lost in the end, he also attempts to stop the true Sacrifice of the Cross. All religious tension begins and ends at the Cross.

When the meaning of the New Covenant was given to the Apostle Paul, which was and is the meaning of the Cross (Gal. 1:1-12), immediately Satan sends forth false apostles, to pull people away from the Grace of God into Law. As it was the problem then, it is the problem now!

Nevertheless, despite the efforts of the Evil One, the Sacrificial System continued from the dawn of time, even until Noah, a time frame of approximately 1,600 years. Concerning Noah the Scripture says:

> "And Noah built an Altar unto the LORD; and took of every clean beast, and of every clean fowl, and offered **Burnt Offerings** on the Altar *(Civilization, as it sprang from the sons of Noah, has its foundation in the Cross of Christ, i.e., 'the Altar')*.
>
> "And the LORD smelled a sweet savor *(the burning of the Sacrifice was sweet unto the Lord, because it spoke of the Coming Redeemer, Who would lift man out of this morass of evil)*; and the LORD said in His Heart, I will not again curse the ground any more for man's sake *(the 'curse' of which God speaks here refers to the fact that He will not again visit the Earth with a flood)*; for the imagination of man's heart is evil from his youth;

neither will I again smite any more every thing living, as I have done *(it means that God will take into consideration the results of the Fall, over which man at the time has no control; however, there is a remedy, which is the Altar, i.e., 'the Cross')*" **(Gen. 8:20-21).**

ABRAHAM

We find by the time of Abraham, that the great Patriarch built so many Altars, that he is referred to by some as the *"Altar-builder."* The Scripture says:

"And the LORD appeared unto Abram *(though the hostile Canaanite was in the land, the Lord was there as well)*, and said, Unto your seed will I give this land *(the 'seed' through Isaac, and not Ishmael; Satan has contested this Promise from the very beginning, with the struggle continuing even unto this hour, as it regards Israel and the Palestinians)*: and there built he an Altar unto the LORD, Who appeared unto him. *(The 'Altar' and its Sacrifice represented the Lord Jesus Christ, and the price He would pay on the Cross in order to redeem humanity. The Promises of God to Abraham, as are all the Promises of God, are built upon the foundation of the 'Altar,' i.e., 'the Cross.')*

"And he removed from thence unto a mountain on the east of Beth-el, and pitched his tent, having Beth-el on the west, and Hai on the east *('Beth-el' means 'House of God,' while 'Hai' means 'the heap of ruins')*: and there he built an Altar unto the LORD, and called upon the Name of the LORD. *(The 'Altar' and the 'tent' give us the two great features of Abraham's character. He was a worshipper of God, hence the Cross, and a stranger in the world, hence the tent. Our prayers are based upon our Faith in Christ and what Christ has done for us at the Cross, of which the Altar was a Type)*" **(Gen. 12:7-8).**

THE GIVING OF THE LAW

The Sacrificial System continued unto the time of the Law, a time frame of some 2,500 years. Actually, the Law came in three parts:

- Ceremonial Law;
- Civil Law; and,
- Moral Law.

All of the Law in its entirety, and without exception, typified Christ in His Mediatorial, Intercessory, or Atoning Work. But the core of the Law was the moral part, which constitutes the Ten Commandments, found in Exodus, Chapter 20. But at the heart of the Law was the Sacrificial System.

In fact, the Lord plainly and consistently told Israel that they had to keep the Law, and the severe penalties involved if they didn't, but actually never told them how to do it.

Why?

The answer is obvious, no matter how hard they tried, they simply could not keep the Law. Concerning this, the Apostle Paul, who was possibly the greatest authority on the Law of Moses of his day, stated that the Lord *"blotted out the handwriting of Ordinances that was against us, which was contrary to us, and took it out of the way, nailing it to His Cross"* (Col. 2:14).

As it regards the Sacrificial System, which was Israel's only hope, because it symbolized the coming Redeemer, Who would be the Lord Jesus Christ, He explained this System to them in every way conceivable. This means that the Cross, of which the Sacrificial System was a Type, was Israel's only hope then, as the Cross is our only hope now. In fact, the Cross of Christ is the only thing standing between man and the Wrath of God, meaning it's the only thing standing between mankind and eternal Hell.

ABRAHAM AND MOSES

To Abraham, the Lord showed the Patriarch the manner in

which man would be redeemed, which would be by death. It was portrayed in the proposed offering up of Isaac as a Sacrifice, which was stopped at the last moment (Gen., Chpt. 22). But he didn't tell Abraham exactly as to how this death would be.

That information concerning what type of death this would be, would be given to Moses.

It was while the Children of Israel were in the wilderness, a time of terrible spiritual declension. The people were murmuring and complaining, and the Lord, Who normally swept reptiles all away, allowed them instead to bite the Children of Israel, which resulted in the death of many (Num., Chpt. 21; Deut. 8:15).

To save the people, the Lord told Moses, *"Make you a fiery serpent, and set it upon a pole: and it shall come to pass, that everyone who is bitten, when he looks upon it, shall live"* (Num. 21:8).

That fiery serpent on the pole was a Type of the manner in which Christ would die, i.e., *"the Cross."* Jesus said so when He spoke with Nicodemus saying, *"And as Moses lifted up the serpent in the wilderness, even so must the Son of Man be lifted up"* (Jn. 3:14).

And now the great Prophet Isaiah would be given the manner in which our Lord would pay the price.

ISAIAH, CHAPTER 53

"Who has believed our report? and to whom is the Arm of the LORD revealed? *('Our report,' refers to this very Prophecy, as well as the other Messianic Prophecies delivered by Isaiah. To Israel was 'the Arm of the LORD revealed.' And to Israel is ascribed the 'unbelief,' which destroyed them.*

"The Revelation of 'the Arm of the LORD' requires the eye of Faith to see it. Unbelief can always assign the most plainly providential arrangements to happy accident. It takes Faith to believe the report that is revealed.)

"For He shall grow up before Him as a tender plant,

and as a root out of a dry ground: He has no form nor comeliness; and when we shall see Him, there is no beauty that we should desire Him. *(To God's Eye, Israel, and the entirety of the Earth for that matter, was a 'dry ground,' but that Eye rested with delight upon one tender plant which had a living root. It was Jesus!*

"The Hebrew verbs in these Verses [through Verse 7] are to be regarded as 'perfects of prophetic certitude.' This means in the Mind of God all has been finished before the foundation of the world and done so in the Divine Counsels [I Pet. 1:18-20].

"The words, 'Before Him,' mean 'before Jehovah' — under the fostering care of Jehovah. God the Father had His Eye fixed upon the Son with a watchfulness and tenderness and love.

"This 'sapling' from the house of David shall become the 'root' out of which His Church will grow. The Messiah will be a fresh sprout from the stump of a tree that had been felled, i.e., from the destroyed Davidic Monarchy.

"The words, 'He has no form nor comeliness,' refer to the fact that He had none during His Sufferings, but now He has it more than anyone else except the Father and the Holy Spirit [Eph. 1:20-23; Phil. 2:9-11; Col. 1:15-18; I Pet. 3:22].

"The words, 'There is no beauty that we should desire Him,' refer to His Sufferings, which include His Peasant upbringing, and, as a consequence, His Poverty, as well as His lack of association with the aristocracy!)

DESPISED AND REJECTED

"He is despised and rejected of men; a man of sorrows, and acquainted with grief: and we hid as it were our faces from Him; He was despised, and we esteemed Him not. *(Him being 'rejected of men' means 'One from Whom men held themselves aloof.' Why? He was pure*

Holiness and they were pure corruption.

"'A man of sorrows,' refers to Jesus taking all the sorrows of humanity upon Himself.

"'Acquainted with grief' actually refers to diseases and sicknesses, for that's what the word 'grief' in the Hebrew means.

"'And we hid as it were our faces from Him,' describes the treatment of the Servant by His fellowmen. Again, Why? He was not the type of Messiah they wanted!

"'He was despised, and we esteemed Him not,' refers to the fact that the religious leadership of Israel esteemed Him not at all. He came to deliver men from sin, but that wasn't the type of deliverance they desired!)

SMITTEN OF GOD

"Surely He has borne our griefs, and carried our sorrows: yet we did esteem Him stricken, smitten of God, and afflicted. *(Twelve times within the space of nine Verses the Prophet asserts, with the most emphatic reiteration, that all the Servant's sufferings were vicarious; i.e., borne for man to save him from the consequences of his sins, to enable him to escape punishment. In other words, Jesus did this all for us.*

"'Yet we did esteem Him stricken, smitten of God, and afflicted,' proclaims the fact that because He died on a Cross, Israel assumed that He died under the curse of God, because Moses had said, 'For he who is hanged is accursed of God' [Deut. 21:23].

"What they did not understand was that He was not accursed, neither in Himself was cursed, but, in fact, was 'made a curse for us.'

"Israel assumed He was 'smitten of God,' and, in a sense, He was. He suffered in our stead, actually as our Substitute, which means that the blow that should have come to us instead went to Him. But yet, it was not

for His sins, because He had none, but instead was for our sins. He was 'afflicted' for us. As stated, He was our Substitute.)

WITH HIS STRIPES WE ARE HEALED

"But He was wounded for our transgressions, He was bruised for our iniquities: the chastisement of our peace was upon Him; and with His Stripes we are healed. *('He was wounded for our transgressions,' pertains to the manner in which He died, which was the price He paid for the Redemption of humanity.*

" 'He was bruised for our iniquities,' means that what He suffered was not at all for Himself, but all for us. It was for our iniquities. Look at the Cross, and then say, 'My sin did this.'

" 'The chastisement of our peace was upon Him,' means that if peace between God and man was to be restored, all which Adam lost, then Jesus would have to bring it about. Here is the simple Doctrine of the Gospel — the Death of Christ. All other founders of religions base their claims upon their life and their teaching — their death was a calamity, and without significance. But the Death of Christ was His Glory, and forms the imperishable foundation of the one and only Salvation. His purpose in coming was to die.

" 'And with His Stripes we are healed,' definitely pertains to physical healing, but is far greater in meaning than that. Its greater meaning refers to being healed of the terrible malady of sin.)

THE INIQUITY OF US ALL

"All we like sheep have gone astray; we have turned everyone to his own way; and the LORD has laid on Him the iniquity of us all. *(Sheep without a shepherd get lost* *easily. Man as sheep has wandered from the right path; he has become so hopelessly lost that it is impossible for him, within his own means, to come back to the right path. Therefore, the Lord had to come from Heaven down to this wilderness called Earth, and, thereby seek and save man, who is lost.*

" 'We have turned everyone to his own way,' refers to the fact that the whole world, collectively and individually, has sinned and come short of the Glory of God. This 'erroneous way' has led to death, suffering, sorrow, heartache, loneliness, despair, and pain. This is the reason that everything that man touches dies! Whereas everything that God touches lives! So man desperately needs God's Touch, i.e., 'the Atonement of Calvary.'

" 'And the LORD has laid on Him the iniquity of us all,' refers to the total price He paid for our total Salvation. The penalty for every sin for all of humanity and for all time was laid on Christ. God the Father, as primary disposer of all things, lays upon the Son the burden which the Son voluntarily accepts. He comes into the world to do the Father's Will and the Father's Will is to secure the Salvation of man, at least for those who will believe.)

AS A LAMB TO THE SLAUGHTER

"He was oppressed, and He was afflicted, yet He opened not His Mouth: He is brought as a lamb to the slaughter, and as a sheep before her shearers is dumb, so He opens not His Mouth. *(The first phrase refers to all that was done to Him in His Humiliation, Suffering, and Agony. He could so easily have vindicated Himself from every charge; therefore, He self-abased Himself.*

"It seems like an admission of guilt and, in fact, was, but not His guilt, but the guilt of those who were accusing Him, as well as the entirety of the world.

"Of all the Levitical Offerings [five total], the 'lamb'

was the animal most used; hence, John the Baptist would say, 'Behold the Lamb of God, which takes away the sin of the world' [Jn. 1:29].)

FOR THE TRANSGRESSION OF THE PEOPLE

"He was taken from prison and from judgment: and who shall declare His generation? For He was cut off out of the land of the living: for the transgression of My People was He stricken. *('He was taken from prison and from judgment,' refers to a violence which cloaked itself under the formalities of a legal process.*

"'And who shall declare His generation,' refers to the fact of Him being 'cut off' [Dan. 9:26], which means that He would have no posterity.

"'For the transgression of My People was He stricken,' can be summed up in what He suffered, and all on our behalf. This must never be forgotten: every single thing He suffered was not at all for Himself, or for Heaven in any capacity, but all for sinners.)

NO DECEIT IN HIS MOUTH

"And He made His grave with the wicked, and with the rich in His death; because He had done no violence, neither was any deceit in His Mouth. *('And He made His grave with the wicked,' means that He was appointed such by the religious hierarchy of Israel, but Joseph of Arimathea, a rich man, asked that Jesus be buried in his personal tomb instead, and so He was. 'Because He had done no violence, neither was any deceit in His Mouth,' proclaims the sinlessness of Christ, and forms the main argument in the Epistle to the Hebrews for the superiority of the New Covenant over the Old [Heb. 7:26-28; 9:14].*

"As no other man was ever without sin, it follows that

the Servant of this present Chapter is, and can be no other than, Christ.)

A SIN OFFERING

"Yet it pleased the LORD to bruise Him; He has put Him to grief: when You shall make His Soul an offering for sin, He shall see His Seed, He shall prolong His Days, and the pleasure of the LORD shall prosper in His Hand. *('Yet it pleased the LORD to bruise Him,' refers to the sufferings of Christ, which proceeded from the 'determinate counsel and foreknowledge of God' [Acts 2:23], and which, being permitted by Him, were in some way His doing. It 'pleased Him' moreover that they should be undergone, for the Father saw with satisfaction the Son's self-sacrifice, and He witnessed with joy man's Redemption and Deliverance effected thereby.*

" 'He has put Him to grief,' actually says, 'He has put Him to sicknesses' or 'He has made Him sick.' This spoke of the time He was on the Cross bearing our sins and 'sicknesses' [Mat. 8:16-17; I Pet. 2:24]. And yet, while all sin and sickness were atoned at the Cross, the total effects of such will not be completely dissipated until the coming Resurrection [Rom. 8:23].

" 'When You shall make His Soul an offering for sin,' is powerful indeed! The word 'offering' in the Hebrew is 'Asham,' and means 'a Trespass Offering,' an 'offering for sin.'

"Offerings for sin, or 'guilt offerings,' were distinct from 'sin offerings.' The object of the former was 'satisfaction'; of the latter, 'expiation.' The Servant of Jehovah was, however, to be both. He was both the 'Sin Offering' and the 'Guilt Offering.'

"This completely destroys the idea that Jesus died spiritually on the Cross, meaning that He became a sinner on the Cross, and died and went to Hell as all sinners,

and was born again in Hell after three days and nights of suffering, etc. None of that is in the Word of God. While Jesus definitely was a 'Sin Offering,' He was not a sinner, and did not become a sinner on the Cross. To have done so would have destroyed His Perfection of Sacrifice, which was demanded by God. In other words, the Sacrifice had to be perfect, and He was Perfect in every respect.

" 'He shall see His Seed,' refers to all His 'true followers,' which include all who have ever been Born-Again.

" 'He shall prolong His Days,' refers to His Resurrection.

" 'And the pleasure of the LORD shall prosper in His Hand,' refers to the great victory that He would win at Calvary, which will ultimately restore everything that Adam lost.)

THE TRAVAIL OF HIS SOUL

"He shall see of the travail of His Soul, and shall be satisfied: by His Knowledge shall My righteous Servant justify many; for He shall bear their iniquities. *(The 'travail of His Soul' pertains to His Sacrifice for sin, which has resulted in the Restoration of man, at least for those who will believe.*

" 'And shall be satisfied,' refers to the fact that even though the price was high, actually beyond comprehension, still, it was worth the Redemption it accomplished.

"What Jesus did at the Cross made it possible for man to be fully and totally 'justified' in the Eyes of God, which comes about by man exhibiting Faith in Christ and what Christ did at the Cross.)

HE MADE INTERCESSION FOR
THE TRANSGRESSORS

"Therefore will I divide Him a portion with the great, and He shall divide the spoil with the strong; because

He has poured out His Soul unto death: and He was numbered with the transgressors; and He bore the sin of many, and made intercession for the transgressors. *(To be appointed with the great and to divide the spoil with the strong is figurative language expressive of full victory. It means here that Christ, by His Death, delivers from Satan mankind who was held captive.*

" 'Because He has poured out His Soul unto death,' means that Christ not only died for man, but, as it were, 'poured out His Soul' with His Own Hand to the last drop. The expression emphasizes the duration and the voluntariness of the Messiah's sufferings. In other words, He laid down His Own life and no man took it from Him [Jn. 10:18].

" 'And He was numbered with the transgressors,' refers to the actions of the Jews toward Him. He was crucified between two thieves. He was condemned as a 'blasphemer' [Mat. 26:65], crucified with malefactors [Lk. 23:32], called 'that deceiver' [Mat. 27:63], and regarded generally by the Jews as accursed [Deut. 21:23].

" 'And He bore the sin of many, and made intercession for the transgressors,' is, in the Hebrew, an act, though begun in the past, not yet completed. The 'Intercession for transgressors' was begun on the Cross with the compassionate words, 'Father, forgive them; for they know not what they do' [Lk. 23:34]. This Intercession for Believers has continued ever since and will ever continue [Rom. 8:34; Heb. 7:25]; such Intercession is made possible by what Christ did at the Cross)" **(Isa. 53:1-12).**

THE STORY OF THE BIBLE

As we have previously stated, the Story of the Bible in its entirety is the Story of *"Jesus Christ and Him Crucified"* (I Cor. 1:23). The Cross of Christ stands at the apex of the great Plan of Redemption, the greatest Story ever told. All Salvation and Sanctification were affected at the Cross. And, as we also have previously stated, the only thing standing between mankind and eternal Hell is *"the Cross of Christ."* That rejected, there remains no escape otherwise.

"For God so loved the world that He gave His Only Begotten Son, that whosoever believes in Him should not perish, but have Everlasting Life" (Jn. 3:16).

THE FUTURE OF MAN

Man will yet realize that for which he was created, and that is to rule with Christ, and to do so forever.

Believers now await the Resurrection of Life. It could happen at any moment, and will include every Born-Again Believer who has ever lived, going all the way back to the very dawn of time, and we speak of righteous Abel. The Fall of man in the Garden of Eden, which has filled the world with blood, sorrow, and heartache, did not stop the Plan of God, it only delayed it. That which God originally planned will yet be realized, and in totality. In fact, there is every evidence that it will be even greater.

The Holy Spirit through Paul said:

"But where sin abounded, Grace did much more abound" (Rom. 5:20). The statement actually says, *"Where sin increased, Grace super-abounded, and then some on top of that."* So, how could it be greater than originally intended?

As far as we know, God intended our original parents to remain alive and young indefinitely, by virtue of the Tree of Life (Gen. 3:22-24).

Now, as a result of what Jesus did at the Cross, and all on our behalf, every Born-Again Believer will have part in the First Resurrection, and will, as well, have a Glorified Body. That is far better than the original intent.

THE GLORIFIED BODY

As to exactly what this will be like, we can only look at Christ

after His Resurrection. Suffice to say, in the words of John the Beloved:

> **"Beloved, now are we the sons of God** *(we are just as much a 'son of God' now as we will be after the Resurrection)*, **and it does not yet appear what we shall be** *(our present state as a 'son of God' is not at all like that we shall be in the coming Resurrection)*: **but we know that, when He shall appear** *(the Rapture)*, **we shall be like Him** *(speaks of being glorified)*; **for we shall see Him as He is.** *(Physical eyes in a mortal body could not look upon that Glory, only eyes in Glorified Bodies)*" **(I Jn. 3:2).**

THE RAPTURE OF THE CHURCH

Paul also told us of the fact of this coming Resurrection, i.e., *"Rapture."* He said:

> **"But I would not have you to be ignorant, Brethren, concerning them which are asleep** *(refers to Believers who have died)*, **that you sorrow not, even as others who have no hope.** *(This concerns those who do not know the Lord who will have no part in the First Resurrection of Life and, therefore, no hope for Heaven.)*
> **"For if we believe that Jesus died and rose again** *(the very Foundation of Christianity is the Death and Resurrection of Christ; it is the proof of life after death in a glorified state for all Saints in that life, which incidentally will never end)*, **even so them also which sleep in Jesus will God bring with Him.** *(This refers to the Rapture of the Church, or the Resurrection of all Believers, with both phrases meaning the same thing, even as Paul describes in I Cor., Chpt. 15. At death, the soul and the spirit of the Child of God instantly go to be with Jesus [Phil. 1:23], while the physical body goes back to dust. At the Rapture, God will replace what was the physical body with a Glorified*

Body, united with the soul and the spirit. In fact, the soul and the spirit of each individual will accompany the Lord down close to this Earth to be united with a Glorified Body, which will then make the Believer whole.)

THIS IS THE WORD OF THE LORD

"For this we say unto you by the Word of the Lord *(presents the Doctrine of the Rapture of the Church as the 'Word of the Lord')*, **that we which are alive *and* remain unto the coming of the Lord** *(all Believers who are alive at the Rapture)* **shall not prevent them which are asleep.** *(This refers to the fact that the living Saints will not precede or go before the dead Saints.)*

THE WAY IT WILL HAPPEN

"For the Lord Himself shall descend from Heaven with a shout *(refers to 'the same Jesus' which the Angels proclaimed in Acts 1:11)*, **with the voice of the Archangel** *(refers to Michael, the only one referred to as such [Jude, Vs. 9])*, **and with the Trump of God** *(doesn't exactly say God will personally blow this Trumpet, but that it definitely does belong to Him, whoever does signal the blast)***: and the dead in Christ shall rise first** *(the criteria for being ready for the Rapture is to be 'in Christ,' which means that all who are truly Born-Again will definitely go in the Rapture)***:**
"Then we which are alive *and* remain shall be caught up *(Raptured)* **together with them** *(the Resurrected dead)* **in the clouds** *(clouds of Saints, not clouds as we normally think of such)*, **to meet the Lord in the air** *(the Greek word for 'air' is 'aer,' and refers to the lower atmosphere, or from about 6,000 feet down; so, the Lord will come at least within 6,000 feet of the Earth, perhaps even lower, with all the Saints meeting Him there; but He, at that time, will not come all the way to the Earth, that awaiting the*

Second Coming, which will be seven or more years later): **and so shall we ever be with the Lord.** *(This presents the greatest meeting humanity will have ever known.)*

"Wherefore comfort one another with these words. *(This pertains to the future of the Child of God, which is Glorious indeed!)*" **(I Thess. 4:13-18).**

THE ULTIMATE VICTORY

Paul now tells us as to exactly what will take place with our physical bodies at the coming Resurrection. He said:

"Behold, I show you a mystery *(a new Revelation given by the Holy Spirit to Paul concerning the Resurrection, i.e., Rapture)*; **We shall not all sleep** *(at the time of the Resurrection [Rapture], many Christians will be alive)*, **but we shall all be changed** *(both those who are dead and those who are alive)*,

"In a moment, in the twinkling of an eye *(proclaims how long it will take for this change to take place)*, **at the last trump** *(does not denote by the use of the word 'last' that there will be successive trumpet blasts, but rather denotes that this is the close of things, referring to the Church Age)*: **for the trumpet shall sound** *(it is the 'Trump of God' [I Thess. 4:16])*, **and the dead shall be raised incorruptible** *(the Sainted Dead, with no sin nature)*, **and we shall be changed** *(put on the Glorified Body)*.

NO MORE SIN NATURE

"For this corruptible *(sin nature)* **must put on incorruption** *(a Glorified Body with no sin nature)*, **and this mortal** *(subject to death)* ***must*** **put on immortality** *(will never die)*.

"So when this corruptible *(sin nature)* **shall have put on incorruption** *(the Divine Nature in total control by the*

Holy Spirit), **and this mortal** *(subject to death)* **shall have put on immortality** *(will never die)*, **then shall be brought to pass the saying that is written, Death is swallowed up in victory** *([Isa. 25:8], the full benefits of the Cross will then be ours, of which we now have only the Firstfruits [Rom. 8:23])*" **(I Cor. 15:51-54).**

REIGNING WITH CHRIST

John the Beloved, as he closed out the Book of Revelation, gives us a little more information as it regards the coming Kingdom Age, and the Believer's part in that coming time. He said:

"And I saw Thrones, and they sat upon them, and judgment was given unto them *(refers to the 24 Elders who represent the entire Plan of God, which pertains to the Redeemed of all Ages; we aren't told who these men are)*: **and** *I saw* **the souls of them who were beheaded for the witness of Jesus, and for the Word of God, and which had not worshipped the Beast, neither his image, neither had received** *his* **mark upon their foreheads, or in their hands** *(categorizes the Tribulation Saints who gave their lives for the cause of Christ; the idea is that these will be included in the first Resurrection of Life, and will enjoy all its privileges)*; **and they lived and reigned with Christ a thousand years.** *(This is the Kingdom Age.)*

THE FIRST RESURRECTION

"But the rest of the dead lived not again until the thousand years were finished. *(This pertains to all the unsaved, in fact, all those who lived and died since the dawn of time. The souls and spirits of these people are now in Hell [Lk. 16:19-31].)* **This** *is* **the First Resurrection** *(proclaims the fact that these two Resurrections, the*

Resurrection of the Just and the Resurrection of the Unjust, will be separated by 1,000 years).

"**Blessed and Holy** *is* **he who has part in the First Resurrection** *(this is the Resurrection of Life, which will include every Saint of God who has ever lived from Abel to the last Tribulation Saint; all will be given Glorified Bodies)*: **on such the second death has no power** *(the 'second death' is to be cast into the Lake of Fire, and to be there forever and forever [Rev. 2:8]; all who are washed in the Blood of the Lamb need not fear the second death)*, **but they shall be Priests of God and of Christ, and shall reign with Him a thousand years.** *(All Believers who have part in the First Resurrection will at the same time serve as mediators, so to speak, between the population of the world and God and Christ. The 'thousand years' portrays the Kingdom Age, when Christ will reign supreme over the entire Earth)*" **(Rev. 20:4-6).**

THE ETERNAL AGE TO COME

As it regards the unredeemed, which speaks of all those who have not accepted Christ, their eternal destiny is eternal Hell, i.e., *"the Lake of Fire."* We are given the account in Revelation 20:11-15. And remember, it is eternal, which means ages without end.

As it regards the Redeemed, and we speak of those who have accepted Christ as their Saviour and Lord, which again, goes back all the way to the dawn of time, the last two Chapters of the Book of Revelation, as written by John the Beloved, give us this account. It as well is eternal, which means Ages without end.

It would be very simple to just make the reference to the last two Chapters of the Bible; however, considering the notes from THE EXPOSITOR'S STUDY BIBLE along with the Text, I think it would be profitable for us to print it in full and, as well, for you to carefully peruse its contents. It makes for most interesting reading, especially considering, this is the eternal abode of the Redeemed. John said:

THE NEW HEAVEN AND THE NEW EARTH

"And I saw a New Heaven and a New Earth *('New' in the Greek is 'kainos,' and means 'freshness with respect to age'; when it is finished, it will be new, as is obvious, but the idea is it will remain new and fresh forever and forever because there is no more sin)*: **for the first Heaven and the first Earth were passed away** *(refers to the original Creation, which was marred by sin; 'passed away' in the Greek is 'parer-chomai,' and means 'to pass from one condition to another'; it never means annihilation)*; **and there was no more sea** *(refers to the giant oceans, such as the Pacific and the Atlantic; however, there will continue to be lakes, bodies of water, rivers, streams, etc.)*.

THE NEW JERUSALEM

"And I John saw the Holy City, New Jerusalem *(presents a New City for this New Earth)*, **coming down from God out of Heaven** *(in effect, God will change His Headquarters from Heaven to Earth)*, **prepared as a Bride adorned for her husband** *(proclaims the Eternal Home of the Redeemed as a dwelling place)*.

"And I heard a great Voice out of Heaven saying *(according to the best manuscripts, the Voice now heard was heard 'out of the Throne')*, **Behold, the Tabernacle of God *is* with men, and He will dwell with them, and they shall be His People, and God Himself shall be with them, *and be* their God.** *(Finally proclaims that which God intended from the beginning.)*

ALL SORROW IS FOREVER OVER

"And God shall wipe away all tears from their eyes

*(actually says in the Greek, 'every teardrop,' and refers to tears of sorrow)***; and there shall be no more death, neither sorrow, nor crying, neither shall there be any more pain** *(addresses sin and all its results)***: for the former things are passed away** *(refers to the entire effect of the Fall).*

"And He Who sat upon the Throne said *(presents, for the second time in this Book, God Himself as the Speaker)***, Behold, I make all things new** *(refers to the fact of changing from one condition to another).* **And He said unto me, Write: for these words are true and faithful.** *(All said is 'true,' and God will be 'faithful' to bring it all to pass as well.)*

"And He said unto me, It is done. I am Alpha and Omega, the beginning and the end. *(The mighty declaration 'Finished' heard at the morning of Creation, at Calvary, and now repeated here for the last time, closes all Prophecy. What He began, He now finishes.)* **I will give unto him who is athirst of the Fountain of the Water of Life freely.** *(This statement doesn't pertain to the coming Perfect Age, for all then will have the Water of Life, but rather to the present. This 'Fountain of the Water of Life' is tied directly to the Cross of Calvary in that it is free to all who will believe [Jn. 3:16].)*

THE OVERCOMER

"He who overcomes shall inherit all things *(the only way one can overcome is to place one's Faith exclusively in the Cross of Christ, which gives the Holy Spirit latitude to work in one's life, bringing about the Fruit of the Spirit)***; and I will be his God, and he shall be My son.** *(The overcomer is adopted into the Family of God and God treats him as a son, exactly as He does His Son, the Lord Jesus Christ.)*

"But the fearful, and unbelieving, and the abominable, and murderers, and whoremongers, and sorcerers,

and idolaters, and all liars *(all of this corresponds with the 'works of the flesh,' as outlined in Gal. 5:19-21)*, **shall have their part in the lake which burns with fire and brimstone: which is the second death** *(proclaims the eternal destiny of Christ-rejecters)*.

THE LAMB'S WIFE

"And there came unto me one of the seven Angels which had the seven Vials full of the seven last plagues, and talked with me, saying, Come hither, I will show you the Bride, the Lamb's Wife. *(By use of the word 'Lamb,' we are taken back to the Cross, which has made all of this possible.)*

"And he carried me away in the Spirit to a great and high mountain *(the 'Spirit' referred to here is the Holy Spirit)*, **and showed me that great city, the Holy Jerusalem, descending out of Heaven from God** *(John saw it 'descending,' meaning that it is coming down to Earth; this will be after the Lord has made the 'New Heavens and New Earth,' in fact, when God changes His Headquarters from Heaven to Earth)*,

"Having the Glory of God *(this is what makes the city what it is)*: **and her light *was* like unto a stone most precious, even like a jasper stone, clear as crystal** *(presents the radiance of God's Glory)*;

THE HOLY CITY

"And had a wall great and high *(this wall is 216 feet high, counting 18 inches to the cubit; it is decorative only)*, ***and* had twelve gates** *(signifies three gates on the North, three on the South, three on the East, and three on the West; the gates on each side will be about 375 miles apart from each other)*, **and at the gates twelve Angels** *(proclaims the Glory of the City and, as well, the Glory of*

God's Government), **and names written thereon, which are *the names* of the Twelve Tribes of the Children of Israel** *(proclaims the fact that 'the Lamb's Wife' is made up of every single Believer, whether on this side or the other side of the Cross; every gate will have the name of one of the Twelve Tribes; as well, this tells us how precious Israel is to the Heart of God)*:

"On the east three gates *(will probably have the names Joseph, Benjamin, and Dan)*; **on the north three gates** *(will probably have the names Reuben, Judah, and Levi)*; **on the south three gates** *(will probably have the names Simeon, Issachar, and Zebulun)*; **and on the west three gates** *(will probably have the names Gad, Asher, and Naphtali).*

"And the wall of the city had twelve foundations *(the way of Salvation was shown to the Jews, hence, the gates and the names of the Twelve Tribes inscribed on those gates; however, the foundation of Salvation was not really given until after the Cross, because it could not be given until after the Cross)*, **and in them the names of the Twelve Apostles of the Lamb.** *(On each foundation is the name of one of the Twelve Apostles. The foundation of the Salvation Message is based 100% on Christ and the Cross, hence, the word 'Lamb' being used.)*

"And he who talked with me *(this is not the Angel who talked with John in Verse 9; the one now speaking identifies himself as a Prophet [Rev. 22:9])* **had a golden reed to measure the city, and the gates thereof, and the wall thereof.** *(The measuring is done for a reason. It reveals the perfection, fulfillment, and completion of all God's Purposes for His Redeemed People.)*

MEASUREMENTS

"And the city lies foursquare, and the length is as large as the breadth: and he measured the city with the reed, twelve thousand furlongs *(translates into about*

1,500 miles per side). **The length and the breadth and the height of it are equal.** *(This presents astounding dimensions. It is about half the size of the United States, regarding length and breadth. If that is not enough to take one's breath away, it will also be about 1,500 miles tall. The mind cannot comprehend this, but Faith believes.)*

"**And he measured the wall thereof, an hundred** *and* **forty** *and* **four cubits** *(translates into about 216 feet, that is if we are using 18 inches to the cubit; as stated, the wall is strictly for ornamentation)***, according to the measure of a man, that is, of the Angel.** *(The designation of 'Angel' is sometimes given to men, God, and the Creatures we refer to as Angels. This man, as Rev. 22:9 proclaims, is a Prophet.)*

"**And the building of the wall of it was** *of* **jasper** *(presents a precious stone of several colors)***: and the city** *was* **pure gold, like unto clear glass** *(takes us beyond the imagination, beyond comprehension! but yet, this is literal).*

"**And the foundations of the wall of the city** *were* **garnished with all manner of precious stones** *(describes beauty upon beauty)***. The first foundation was jasper; the second, sapphire; the third, a chalcedony; the fourth, an emerald;**

"**The fifth, sardonyx; the sixth, sardius; the seventh, chrysolyte; the eighth, beryl; the ninth, a topaz; the tenth, a chrysoprasus; the eleventh, a jacinth; the twelfth, an amethyst.** *(The flooding of color in that incomparable City is beyond imagination. All of these stones named here are exquisite in color.)*

"**And the twelve gates** *were* **twelve pearls** *(probably means each gate, which is about 216 feet tall, is made of untold thousands of pearls)***; every several gate was of one pearl** *(seems to indicate that this particular gate, which is probably every third or fourth one, is made out of one gigantic pearl)***: and the street of the city** *was* **pure gold,**

as it were transparent glass *(refers to the fact that not only are all the buildings of 'pure gold,' [Rev. 21:18], but even the streets are made of pure gold)*.

THE LIGHT

"**And I saw no Temple therein** *(refers to a Temple such as in Old Testament times; actually there is a literal Temple in the New Jerusalem, but it will not serve the same purpose as the Temple on Earth [Rev. 3:12; 7:15; 11:19; 14:15, 17; 15:1-8; 16:1, 17])*: **for the Lord God Almighty and the Lamb are the Temple of it.** *(Before the Cross, a Temple on Earth was necessary because God could not dwell with man at that time, at least directly. Since the Cross, the Holy Spirit can dwell within man, because the terrible sin debt has been paid [Jn. 14:17; I Cor. 3:16].)*

"**And the city had no need of the sun, neither of the moon, to shine in it** *(proclaims the fact that the Creator is not in need of His Creation; God has need of nothing, but all have need of God)*: **for the Glory of God did lighten it, and the Lamb** *is* **the Light thereof.** *(The word 'Lamb' signifies that all of this is made possible for Believers as a result of what Christ did at the Cross.)*

"**And the nations of them which are saved shall walk in the light of it** *(should have been translated, 'and the nations shall walk by means of its light'; the words 'of them which are saved' are not actually in the best manuscripts; in fact, there will be no one in the world in that day who isn't Saved)*: **and the kings of the Earth do bring their glory and honour into it.** *(This refers to leaders of nations, whatever they might be called at that particular time. All will give Glory to God, and all will Honor the Lord, and do so forever.)*

"**And the gates of it shall not be shut at all by day** *(in fact, they will never be shut)*: **for there shall be no night there.** *(This speaks of the City only, for outside the City* *there will be day and night eternally [Gen. 1:14-18; 8:22; Ps. 89:2-3; Jer. 31:35-36].)*

"**And they shall bring the glory and honour of the nations into it** *(proclaims a Righteous commerce, and in every capacity)*.

"**And there shall in no wise enter into it any thing that defiles, neither *whatsoever* works abomination, or *makes* a lie** *(this means that all sin is forever banished, and will never return)*: **but they who are written in the Lamb's Book of Life** *(refers to the Book of the Redeemed; the word 'Lamb' refers to the fact that all are Saved by placing their Faith and Trust in Christ and what He did for us at the Cross)*.

THE WATER OF LIFE

"**And he showed me a pure river of Water of Life, clear as crystal** *(symbolic of the Holy Spirit [Jn. 7:37-39])*, **proceeding out of the Throne of God and of the Lamb.** *(This 'Water of Life' is made possible by what Jesus did at the Cross, hence, the word 'Lamb.')*

"**In the midst of the street of it** *(proclaims the fact that this 'pure River of Water of Life, clear as crystal' flows in the middle of this street of pure gold)*, **and on either side of the river, *was there* the Tree of Life** *(the fruit of this Tree of Life must be eaten every month, and we're speaking of the part of the population who don't have Glorified Bodies)*, **which bear twelve *manner of* fruits, *and* yielded her fruit every month** *(we have the number '12' again, which signifies the Government of God as it relates to the manner of Eternal Life; there are twelve different types of fruit, but we aren't told what they are)*: **and the leaves of the tree *were* for the healing of the nations.** *(This pertains to the stopping of any type of sickness before it even begins. As stated, the population on Earth, which will never die and will not have Glorified Bodies, will need these things.*

These are they who were Saved during the Kingdom Age, and thereafter.)

NO MORE CURSE

"**And there shall be no more curse** *(a curse was placed on the Earth at the Fall; it is being said here that there will be no more curse because there will be no more sin)*: **but the Throne of God and of the Lamb shall be in it** *(the authority of rulership will be as great with God the Son as it is with God the Father; in fact, by the use of the word 'Lamb,' we are made to realize that all of this is made possible because of what Jesus did at the Cross)*; **and His Servants shall serve Him** *(the idea is that every Believer in the Perfect Age will so love the Lord and the Lamb that they will gladly 'serve Him')*:

"**And they shall see His Face** *(shows intimate relationship)*; **and His Name *shall be* in their foreheads** *(refers to ownership; we were bought 'with a price,' and that price was the Blood of the Lamb).*

"**And there shall be no night there** *(this speaks of the New Jerusalem only, for night and day will be in the balance of the Earth forever)*; **and they need no candle, neither light of the sun; for the Lord God gives them light** *(presents the Source of this Light)*: **and they shall reign forever and ever.** *(It has never been known for servants to 'reign' like kings; however, these servants shall!)*

THESE SAYINGS ARE FAITHFUL AND TRUE

"**And he said unto me, These sayings *are* faithful and true** *(proclaimed in this fashion simply because many of the statements made are so absolutely astounding they defy description)*: **and the Lord God of the Holy Prophets sent his Angel to show unto His Servants** *(the Greek word 'Aggelos' is translated 'Angel' here, but should have been* *translated 'Messenger'; we know this man is not an Angel, nor is he Christ)* **the things which must shortly be done** *(is not speaking of John's day, but rather the setting of the Vision is a time frame which has not come about even yet; it will take place immediately after the Rapture of the Church; from that point forward, which is what is meant here, we have 'the things which must shortly be done,' referring to the Great Tribulation).*

"Behold, I come quickly *(has more to do with the manner of His Coming than anything else; when He does come, which will be at the height of the Battle of Armageddon, it will be sudden, even immediate)*: **blessed** *is* **he who keeps the sayings of the Prophecy of this Book.** *(This is the only Book in the world that gives a preview of the future. Consequently, every Believer ought to study the Book of Revelation as much as they do any other Book in the entire Bible.)*

THE TIME IS AT HAND

"And I John saw these things, and heard *them (presents an impeccable witness).* **And when I had heard and seen, I fell down to worship before the feet of the Angel which showed me these things.** *(John, it seems, will make the same mistake twice.)*

"Then says he unto me, See *you do it* **not** *(presents the same words used by the previous man when John did the same thing [Rev. 19:10])*: **for I am your fellowservant, and of your Brethren the Prophets, and of them which keep the sayings of this Book.** *(He evidently is one of the Great Prophets of the Old Testament, who eagerly awaits the fulfillment of these Prophecies as well)*: **worship God** *(includes both God the Father and God the Son.)*

"And he said unto me, Seal not the sayings of the Prophecy of this Book *(refers to the fact that the things given in this Book are meant to be known and understood;*

they are not hidden truths): **for the time is at hand** *(speaks of the immediate fulfillment of the events, which were to happen in consecutive order from John's day to eternity; it began with the Church Age, which is now almost over; the Great Tribulation will follow, concluding with the Second Coming, which will usher in the Kingdom Age, followed by the Perfect Age).*

THE REWARD

"He who is unjust, let him be unjust still: and he which is filthy, let him be filthy still *(proclaims the fact that men are building up their destiny by the actions and habits of their lives)*: **and he who is Righteous, let him be Righteous still: and he who is Holy, let him be Holy still.** *(Records that which the Spirit of God can bring about in a person's life, irrespective that they have once been 'unjust and morally filthy.' This is all done through the Cross, and only through the Cross.)*
"And, behold, I come quickly *(is not meant to portray the 'time' of His Coming, but rather the suddenness of His Coming; the idea is that whatever we are at His Coming, whenever that Coming takes place, is what we will be forever)*; **and My reward *is* with Me** *(the word 'reward' can either be positive or negative)*, **to give every man according as his work shall be.** *(Our Faith, however placed, will produce a certain type of works. Only Faith in the Cross is accepted.)*
"I am Alpha and Omega *(presents the first letter in the Greek Alphabet [Alpha], and the last letter in the Greek Alphabet [Omega]; it is another way of saying, 'the first and the last,' which includes all in-between)*, **the beginning and the end, the first and the last.** *(This doesn't mean Christ as God had a beginning, for He didn't. It is speaking of whatever is in question. Christ is the beginning of all things and the end of all things.)*

BLESSED

"**Blessed** *are* **they** *(presents the seventh and last Beatitude in the Book of Revelation)* **who do His Commandments** *(should have been translated, 'who washed their robes in the Blood of the Lamb'; the Greek Text used for the King James Version of the Bible was the Textus Receptus; it is the Text that Erasmus, the famous Renaissance scholar, published in A.D. 1516; it was the first New Testament Greek Text ever published; since 1516, the world of scholarship and Archaeology has discovered thousands of earlier Greek Texts; by comparing these thousands of Manuscripts, the scholars can easily ascertain the original Text the Apostle wrote)*, **that they may have the right to the Tree of Life** *(proclaims the fact that this 'right' can be attained in only one way, 'by washing our robes in the Blood of the Lamb')*, **and may enter in through the gates into the city** *(proclaims the Eternal abode of the Redeemed; we shall enter that city by means of His Grace, which is the Cross of Christ).*

THE BRIGHT AND MORNING STAR

"**For without** *are* **dogs** *(homosexuals)*, **and sorcerers** *(witchcraft)*, **and whoremongers** *(pertains to all type of immorality)*, **and murderers** *(pertains not only to killing in cold blood, but, as well, murdering one's reputation through gossip)*, **and idolaters** *(pertains to placing anything above God, or on a par with God; religion is the greatest idolatry of all)*, **and whosoever loves and makes a lie** *(refers to anything that's untrue).*

"**I Jesus** *(this short phrase is found only here in Scripture, emphasizing its importance; Christ is closing out the Book of Revelation here, but most of all, He is testifying to the Truth of what has been given)* **have sent My Angel to testify unto you these things in the Churches.** *(The* *word 'Angel' here means 'Messenger,' and actually refers to the Pastors of the respective Churches in question, and actually for all time.)* **I am the Root and the Offspring of David** *(is meant to project the Incarnation of Christ)*, **and the Bright and Morning Star.** *(The 'Morning Star' speaks of a new beginning that any person can have, irrespective of their present situation, if they will only look to Christ.)*

THE GREAT INVITATION

"And the Spirit and the Bride say, Come. *(This presents the cry of the Holy Spirit to a hurting, lost, and dying world. What the Holy Spirit says should also be said by all Believers.)* **And let him who hears say, Come.** *(It means if one can 'hear,' then one can 'come.')* **And let him who is athirst come** *(speaks of spiritual thirst, the cry for God in the soul of man).* **And whosoever will, let him take the Water of Life freely** *(opens the door to every single individual in the world; Jesus died for all and, therefore, all can be Saved, if they will only come).*

"For I testify unto every man who hears the words of the Prophecy of this Book *(proclaims the inerrancy of the Book of Revelation; in other words, John testifies that it is the Word of God)*, **If any man shall add unto these things, God shall add unto him the plagues that are written in this Book** *(proclaims the fact that changing the meaning of the Prophecies in this Book can bring upon one the Judgment of God)*:

THE WORDS OF THE BOOK OF THIS PROPHECY

"And if any man shall take away from the words of the Book of this Prophecy *(the idea is that the 'words of the Prophecy' should not be changed in any manner, whether by addition or deletion)*, **God shall take away his part out of the Book of Life, and out of the Holy**

City, and *from* the things which are written in this Book. *(This is a warning given to Believers, and should be understood accordingly!)*

"He which testifies these things *(proclaims the fact that the Office of the Messiah as Saviour is repeated again and again throughout the Prophecy; He is the Lamb Who was slain, and His Blood washes from sin, and Alone makes fit for entrance into the Eternal City)* says, Surely I come quickly *(leaves the Promise to come as the last Message from the Lord Jesus to the Believers' hearts; and on this sweet note, the Prophecy ends).* Amen. Even so, come, Lord Jesus *(proclaims the answer of the True Church to the Promise of Christ regarding the Second Coming).*

GRACE

"The Grace of our Lord Jesus Christ *(presents John using the very words of Paul in his closing benediction; Christ is the Source, but the Cross is the means)* be with you all. Amen. *(This proclaims the fact that it is the same Message for all, and is available to all. The word 'Amen' closes out the Book of Revelation and, in fact, the entire Canon of Scripture, which took about 1,600 years to bring forth in its entirety. It gives acclaim to the Finished Work of Christ. It is done. And, thereby, all of Heaven, along with all the Redeemed, must say: 'Amen')"* **(Rev. 21:1-27; Rev. 22:1-21).**

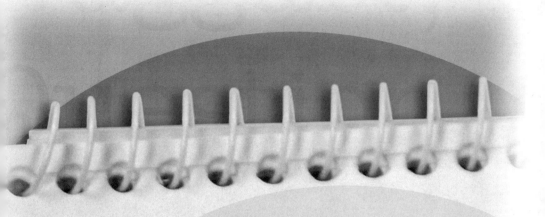

CHAPTER 9

The Doctrine Of Our Lord Jesus Christ

THE DOCTRINE OF OUR LORD JESUS CHRIST

If Jesus Christ was no more than a man, despite being ever so charismatic, ever so talented, ever so gifted, ever so educated, ever so noble, that would be one thing; however, if Jesus Christ, although a Man, but at the same time God manifest in the flesh, the Son of the Living God, the Creator of the Ages, then that is something else altogether. That puts Him in a place and position totally unlike any other human being who has ever existed.

The truth is, Jesus Christ is very God and very Man which means that He is not half God and half Man, but rather totally God and totally Man.

As one Greek Scholar put it, *"When God became Man, He laid aside His expression of Deity, while never losing possession of His Deity."* Pure and simple, Jesus Christ is God!

EVERY HUMAN BEING WILL ONE DAY FACE JESUS CHRIST

Every human being will face Him either at the Cross of Calvary, or at the Great White Throne Judgment, but face Him you will.

As it regards Salvation, the making of Heaven as one's eternal Home, Jesus Christ Alone is the way. Emphatically and dogmatically, He stated the following of Himself:

"Jesus said unto Him, I am the Way, the Truth, and the Life *(proclaims in no uncertain terms exactly Who and What Jesus is)*: no man comes unto the Father, but by Me *(He declares positively that this idea of God as Father, this approach to God for every man is through Him — through what He is and what He has done).*

"If you had known Me, you should have known My Father also *(means, 'If you had learned to know me spiritually and experientially, you should have known that I and the Father are One,' i.e., One in essence and unity, and not in number)*: **and from Henceforth you know Him, and have seen Him** *(when one truly sees Jesus, one truly sees the Father; as stated, they are 'One' in essence).*

"Philip said unto Him, Lord, show us the Father, and it suffices us *(like Philip, all, at least for the most part, want to see God, but the far greater majority reject the only manner and way to see Him, which is through Jesus).*

WHEN YOU SEE ME YOU HAVE SEEN THE FATHER

"Jesus said unto Him, Have I been so long with you, and yet have you not known Me, Philip? *(Reynolds says, 'There is no right understanding of Jesus Christ until the Father is actually seen in Him.')* **He who has seen Me has seen the Father** *(presents the very embodiment of Who and What the Messiah would be; if we want to know what God is like, we need only look at the Son)*; **and how do you say then, Show us the Father?**

"Do you believe not that I am in the Father, and the Father in Me? *(The key is 'believing.')* **the words that I speak unto you I speak not of Myself** *(the words which came out of the mouth of the Master are, in fact, those of the Heavenly Father)*: **but the Father who dwells in Me, He does the works** *(the Father does such through the Holy Spirit).*

"Believe Me that I *am* in the Father, and the Father in Me *(once again places Faith as the vehicle and Jesus as the Object)*: **or else believe Me for the very works' sake** *(presents a level which should be obvious to all, and includes present observation as well)*" **(Jn. 14:6-11).**

BEFORE THE FOUNDATION OF THE WORLD

The Incarnation of the Lord Jesus Christ, which means that God became man and dwelt among us, was decided in the Mind of the Godhead, even before the foundation of the world. The

Incarnation of Christ and Him going to the Cross to redeem mankind are the foundation of the Faith. This means that every Doctrine of the Bible must be built on the foundation of the Incarnation of Christ and the price He paid at the Cross, or else in some way it will be spurious. In fact, not understanding that the Cross of Christ is the foundation of Redemption is the cause of all false doctrine.

Both Peter and John the Beloved gave us some information concerning this.

SIMON PETER

"Forasmuch as you know that you were not redeemed with corruptible things, *as* silver and gold *(presents the fact that the most precious commodities [silver and gold] could not redeem fallen man)*, from your vain conversation *(vain lifestyle)* **received** by tradition from your fathers *(speaks of original sin that is passed on from father to child at conception)*;

THE CROSS OF CHRIST

"But with the Precious Blood of Christ *(presents the payment, which proclaims the poured out Life of Christ on behalf of sinners)*, as of a Lamb without blemish and without spot *(speaks of the lambs offered as substitutes in the Old Jewish economy; the Death of Christ was not an execution or assassination, but rather a Sacrifice; the Offering of Himself presented a Perfect Sacrifice, for He was Perfect in every respect [Ex. 12:5])*:

"Who verily was foreordained before the foundation of the world *(refers to the fact that God, in His Omniscience, knew He would create man, man would Fall, and man would be redeemed by Christ going to the Cross; this was all done before the Universe was created; this means the Cross of Christ is the Foundation Doctrine of all Doctrine, referring* to the fact that all Doctrine must be built upon that Foundation, or else it is specious), **but was manifest in these last times for you** *(refers to the invisible God Who, in the Person of the Son, was made visible to human eyesight by assuming a human body and human limitations)*,

"Who by Him do believe in God *(it is only by Christ and what He did for us at the Cross that we are able to 'Believe in God')*, **Who raised Him** *(Christ)* **up from the dead** *(His Resurrection was guaranteed insomuch as He Atoned for all sin [Rom. 6:23])*, **and gave Him Glory** *(refers to the exaltation of Christ)*; **that your Faith and Hope might be in God.** *(This speaks of a heart Faith in God, Who saves sinners in answer to our Faith in the Resurrected Lord Jesus Who died for us)*" **(I Pet. 1:18-21).**

JOHN THE BELOVED

John addressed himself to Who Christ was before the Incarnation, what He did, and the reason why He became man, i.e., *"the Incarnation."* He gives it to us in the First Chapter of his great Gospel. He said:

"In the beginning *(does not infer that Christ as God had a beginning, because as God He had no beginning, but rather refers to the time of Creation [Gen. 1:1])* **was the Word** *(the Holy Spirit through John describes Jesus as 'the Eternal Logos')*, **and the Word was with God** *('was in relationship with God,' and expresses the idea of the Trinity)*, **and the Word was God** *(meaning that He did not cease to be God during the Incarnation; He 'was' and 'is' God from eternity past to eternity future)*.

"The same was in the beginning with God *(this very Person was in eternity with God; there's only one God, but manifested in Three Persons — God the Father, God the Son, God the Holy Spirit)*.

"All things were made by Him *(all things came into*

being through Him; it refers to every item of Creation one by one, rather than all things regarded in totality)*; **and without Him was not any thing made that was made** *(nothing, not even one single thing, was made independently of His cooperation and volition).*

"**In Him was Life** *(presents Jesus, the Eternal Logos, as the first cause)*; **and the Life was the Light of men** *(He Alone is the Life Source of Light; if one doesn't know Christ, one is in darkness)*" **(Jn. 1:1-4).**

THE FACT OF THE INCARNATION

Concerning the Incarnation, God becoming Man, John the Beloved wrote:

"**And the Word was made flesh** *(refers to the Incarnation, 'God becoming man')*, **and dwelt among us** *(refers to Jesus, although Perfect, not holding Himself aloft from all others, but rather lived as all men, even a peasant)*, **(and we beheld His Glory, the Glory as of the Only Begotten of the Father,)** *(speaks of His Deity, although hidden from the eyes of the merely curious; while Christ laid aside the expression of His Deity, He never lost the possession of His Deity)* **full of Grace and Truth** *(as 'flesh,' proclaimed His Humanity, 'Grace and Truth' His Deity)*" **(Jn. 1:14).**

John the Beloved, now quotes John the Baptist. He said:

THE TESTIMONY

"**John bear witness of Him** *(John the Baptist was raised up for this very purpose)*, **and cried, saying, This was He of Whom I spoke** *(concerns the Ministry of John regarding the Person of Jesus)*, **He who comes after me is preferred before me** *(should have been translated, 'existed before me')*: **for He was before me** *(once again, a testimony to* the Deity of Christ; as God, He has always been).

"And of His fulness have all we received *(John has told us Who Jesus is, now he tells us what He does)***, and Grace for Grace** *(should have been translated, 'Grace upon Grace'; this is the provision of His Love heaped one upon another in this supply of His People's needs).*

"For the Law was given by Moses, *but* **Grace and Truth came by Jesus Christ** *(proclaims Him as the Representative Law-Keeper for all humanity, i.e., to all who will believe; the Law manifested man [full of wickedness]; the Son manifested God [full of goodness]).*

"No man has seen God at any time *(better translated, 'No man has ever comprehended or experienced God at any time in all His fullness')***; the Only Begotten Son** *(Jesus Christ and the Incarnation, Who Alone could perfectly declare the Father)***, which is in the bosom of the Father** *(proclaims the most intimate and loving fellowship with the Father)***, He has declared** *Him (in essence, God the Father and God the Son are One)"* **(Jn. 1:15-18).**

THE REASON FOR THE INCARNATION

John the Beloved continues to quote John the Baptist. He said:

"The next day *(refers to the day after John had been questioned by the emissaries from the Sanhedrin)* **John sees Jesus coming unto him** *(is, no doubt, after the Baptism of Jesus, and the Temptation in the wilderness)***, and said, Behold the Lamb of God** *(proclaims Jesus as the Sacrifice for sin, in fact, the Sin-Offering, Whom all the multiple millions of offered lambs had represented)***, which takes away the sin of the world** *(animal blood could only cover sin, it could not take it away; but Jesus offering Himself as the Perfect Sacrifice took away the sin of the world; He not only cleansed acts of sin but, as well, addressed the root cause [Col. 2:14-15])"* **(Jn. 1:29).**

The reason for the Incarnation, God becoming man, was in order to pay the price for man's Redemption, which man could not pay. That price would be and was the Cross of Christ; hence, John referring to Jesus as *"the Lamb of God."*

Two things are said in this Verse about Jesus that was never said, and, in fact, could not be said about any other human being. They are:

1.   Jesus was referred to, as stated, as *"the Lamb of God."* Why wasn't He called *"the Lion of the Tribe of Judah,"* which He later would definitely be called? (Rev. 5:5).

Before Jesus can be known and had as *"the Lion of the Tribe of Judah,"* which speaks of supremacy and power, first of all, one must accept Him as *"the Lamb of God."* In other words, Christ was referred to as the Lamb of God, simply because He would be the Sacrifice, which speaks of the Cross, which speaks of the foundation of all that we know and are in God.

2.   This Man Christ Jesus, this Son of the Living God, would do what no other human being had ever done or could do; he would *"take away the sin of the world."* That term had never been used, because the blood of bulls and goats could not take away sins. But Jesus would take those sins away, and do so by the giving of Himself in Sacrifice on the Cross, which would pay the price demanded by a thrice-Holy God. It's called, *"Justification by Faith."*

It means that God, upon the sinner expressing Faith in Christ and what Christ has done for us at the Cross, can declare an obviously guilty sinner as not guilty, even declaring him innocent and, in effect, declaring him perfect. That's what Justification means. It is obtained by Faith in Christ and what He did for us at the Cross, and obtained only by Faith in Christ and what Christ did for us at the Cross.

THE FIRST PROPHECY

The Fall of Adam in the Garden of Eden did not catch God by surprise, as should be obvious. As we've already stated, the

Lord through foreknowledge knew all of this would happen, even before man was created, even before the world was created. So, concerning the Fall, the Lord addresses Satan through the serpent, and says to him:

> "And I will put enmity *(animosity)* **between you and the woman** *(presents the Lord now actually speaking to Satan, who had used the serpent; in effect, the Lord is saying to Satan, 'You used the woman to bring down the human race, and I will use the woman as an instrument to bring the Redeemer into the world, Who will save the human race'),* **and between your seed** *(mankind which follows Satan)* **and her Seed** *(the Lord Jesus Christ)*; **it** *(Christ)* **shall bruise your head** *(the victory that Jesus won at the Cross [Col. 2:14-15]),* **and you shall bruise His Heel** *(the sufferings of the Cross)*" **(Gen. 3:15).**

In this one Verse, we now see the reason for the animosity against God, and especially the Lord Jesus Christ.

In this nation of America, which is supposed to be a Christian nation, but regrettably is far from that, among those who aren't redeemed, which, of course, makes up the far, far greater majority of the population, one could probably say, and without much fear of contradiction, that there is greater animosity among these against Jesus Christ than against Mohammed, who gave us September 11, 2001 (9/11).

Why?

THE ANGER AGAINST THE LORD

The anger against our Lord is present, even as predicted by the Lord at the dawn of time, simply because the Lord Jesus Christ, the *"Seed of the woman,"* is truly God. Every other leader of world religions, Mohammed included, are no more than fake luminaries. In fact, the unbelievers in this nation, or any nation, come from the same source as the religion of Islam

— demon powers.

Jesus said to the religious leaders of His Day:

"You are of *your* father the Devil, and the lusts of your father you will do *(presents the Lord repudiating in terrible language the spiritual claims made by these Jews respecting their association with Jehovah; this is the cause of all the problems in the world)*. He was a murderer from the beginning *(refers to the fact that Satan originated sin, and sin brings forth death)*, and abode not in the truth *(it means he was actually in truth, for a time, until he rebelled against God)*, because there is no truth in him *(no truth in him since his rebellion)*. When he speaks a lie, he speaks of his own: for he is a liar, and the father of it *(Satan is the originator of the 'lie'; consequently, his entire kingdom of darkness, in totality, is built on the 'lie')*.

"And because I tell *you* the truth, you believe Me not *(truth can only be believed and accepted by one's Faith being exclusively in Christ, and the price He paid on the Cross)*" (Jn. 8:44-45).

So, we find in this statement given by God to Satan through the serpent, the reason for the animosity against the Lord that has existed from then until now. Jesus Christ is God, and naturally, the followers of Satan, which includes almost all the world, are opposed to Him. In fact, most of them don't even really know why they are opposed to Him, but they are.

ADAM, THE FEDERAL HEAD

One might say that Adam was given by God the prerogative of being the father of the entirety of the human race. So, whatever happened to him would be passed down to all who would be born thereafter. Concerning all of this, Paul said:

"For since by man *came* death *(refers to Adam and the*

Fall in the Garden of Eden, and speaks of spiritual death, separation from God), **by Man** *came* **also the Resurrection of the dead.** *(This refers to the Lord Jesus Christ Who Atoned for all sin, thereby, making it possible for man to be united once again with God, which guarantees the Resurrection.)*

"For as in Adam all die *(spiritual death, separation from God)*, **even so in Christ shall all be made alive.** *(In the first man, all died. In the Second Man, all shall be made alive, at least all who will believe [Jn. 3:16])*" **(I Cor. 15:21-22).**

And then the great Apostle said: **"And so it is written** *(Gen. 2:7)*, **The first man Adam was made a living soul** *(the natural body)*; **the last Adam** *(Christ)* **was made a quickening Spirit.** *(The word 'last' is used. No other will ever be needed. 'Quickening' refers to making all alive who trust Him.)*

"Howbeit that *was* **not first which is spiritual, but that which is natural** *(Adam came first)*; **and afterward that which is spiritual.** *(Christ, as the Last Adam, came second in order to undo that which occurred at the Fall.)*

"The first man *(Adam)* **is of the earth, earthy** *(materialistic)*: **the Second Man** *(Christ)* **is the Lord from Heaven** *(a vast difference between the 'first man' and the 'Second Man')*" **(I Cor. 15:45-47).**

In all of this is the reason for the Incarnation.

THE NECESSITY OF THE INCARNATION

God, it seems, in the creation of Adam and Eve, invested more in this man than in all of His Creation. For instance, when God created the Angels, it seems that He created all of them at one time, and fully mature. In other words, there's never been such a thing as a baby Angel.

But when He created man, He created only a pair, thereby

giving them the ability of procreation, which was to bring off-spring into the world. So, whatever Adam did as our first parent so to speak, would pass down to the whole of the human race. When Adam fell, then original sin came into being, which was passed down to all the offspring thereafter, and is the cause of all the pain, sickness, death, dying, war, suffering, hunger, etc., in the world today and, in fact, ever has been.

To undo this thing, God would have to become man, function as a man, but without giving up His Deity and, thereby, pay the price for man to be redeemed, which was the Cross.

That's the reason that Jesus is referred to as the *"Second Man,"* and the *"Last Adam."* He did what the first Adam did not do, which was to render a perfect obedience to God, and He did not do what the first Adam did, which was to fail the Lord. In fact, our Lord never failed in thought, word, or deed, even one time.

Upon Faith in Him, and what He did for us at the Cross, we literally become one with Christ. Paul addressed this by saying:

THE MANNER IN WHICH BELIEVERS ARE IN CHRIST

I continue to quote from THE EXPOSITOR'S STUDY BIBLE:

"Know you not, that so many of us as were baptized into Jesus Christ *(plainly says that this Baptism is into Christ and not water [I Cor. 1:17; 12:13; Gal. 3:27; Eph. 4:5; Col. 2:11-13])* were baptized into His Death? *(When Christ died on the Cross, in the Mind of God, we died with Him; in other words, He became our Substitute, and our identification with Him in His Death gives us all the benefits for which He died; the idea is that He did it all for us!)*

"Therefore we are buried with Him by baptism

into death *(not only did we die with Him, but we were buried with Him as well, which means that all the sin and transgression of the past were buried; when they put Him in the Tomb, they put all of our sins into that Tomb as well)*: **that like as Christ was raised up from the dead by the Glory of the Father, even so we also should walk in newness of life** *(we died with Him, we were buried with Him, and His Resurrection was our Resurrection to a 'Newness of Life').*

LIVING THIS RESURRECTION LIFE

"For if we have been planted together *(with Christ)* **in the likeness of His Death** *(Paul proclaims the Cross as the instrument through which all Blessings come; consequently, the Cross must ever be the Object of our Faith, which gives the Holy Spirit latitude to work within our lives)*, **we shall be also** *in the likeness* **of** *His* **Resurrection** *(we can have the 'likeness of His Resurrection,' i.e., 'live this Resurrection Life,' only as long as we understand the 'likeness of His Death,' which refers to the Cross as the means by which all of this is done)*:
"Knowing this, that our old man is crucified with *Him* *(all that we were before conversion)*, **that the body of sin might be destroyed** *(the power of sin broken)*, **that henceforth we should not serve sin** *(the guilt of sin is removed at conversion, because the sin nature no longer rules within our hearts and lives)*" **(Rom. 6:3-6).**

IN CHRIST

John the Beloved quoted the Words of Christ, as to what would happen as a result of the Cross. He said:

"At that day *(after the Resurrection, and the coming of the Holy Spirit on the Day of Pentecost)* **you shall know**

that I *am* in My Father *(speaks of Deity; Jesus is God!)*, and you in Me *(has to do with our Salvation by Faith)*, and I in you *(enables us to live a victorious life [Gal. 2:20])*" (**Jn. 14:20**).

All Believers are *"in Christ,"* by virtue of what Jesus did at the Cross, and that alone, and our Faith expressed in His atoning Sacrifice of Himself. This is the reason that the Cross of Christ is so very, very important. What Jesus did on the Cross was not for Himself, for He did not need such, neither was it for Angels, or God the Father, except to pay the ransom to Him that was owed by man, which man could not pay, but was rather for you and me.

WHAT JESUS DID

We must ever understand that everything that Jesus did, and I mean everything, was not at all for Himself, but altogether for sinners. He did everything for you and me.

He kept the Law perfectly in His Life and Living, never failing even one time, whether in thought, word, or deed, and He did it all for us. Our accepting Him, consequently, considering that He kept the Law in every respect, makes us law-keepers as well, instead of lawbreakers.

As it regarded the terrible sin debt against us, which was committed against God, in other words, we had broken the Law, and the severe penalty of eternal death was upon us, He went to the Cross, gave of Himself as a Sacrifice, with the shedding of His Precious Blood, which atoned for all sin, and satisfied the demands of a thrice-Holy God. Upon my Faith in Christ, not a single sin is held against me. It's all gone, taken away, washed away, cleansed, and by the Precious Blood of Christ (**Jn. 1:29; I Jn. 1:7**).

So, our Lord as the Last Adam did what the first Adam failed to do, which was to render a perfect obedience to God. Again I state, He did it all on our behalf.

224 Brother Swaggart, How Can I Understand The Bible?

ABRAHAM AND THE PROMISE

While the knowledge that a Redeemer was to come into the world was understood by some, possibly only a few, still, the knowledge was vague. The First Family was told that the sacrifices represented the coming Redeemer and, as well, they had, no doubt, heard the Prophecy given by the Lord and recorded in Genesis 3:16. In essence, we have the account given to us in the Fourth Chapter of Genesis as it regarded Cain and Abel.

And then, Jude, the brother of our Lord, said, *"And Enoch also, the seventh from Adam, prophesied of these, saying, Behold, the Lord comes with ten thousands of His Saints"* (Jude 14). Incidentally, Enoch lived about six hundred years after Adam. In this Prophecy given by Enoch, when it is fleshed out, there would have to be some understanding of a coming Redeemer. But it was to Abraham that the knowledge was given by the Lord, that the Redeemer would come and, as well, how He would come.

THE ABRAHAMIC COVENANT

"Now the LORD had said unto Abram *(referring to the Revelation which had been given to the Patriarch a short time before; this Chapter is very important, for it records the first steps of this great Believer in the path of Faith)*, Get thee out of your country *(separation)*, and from your kindred *(separation)*, and from your father's house *(separation)*, unto a land that I will show you *(refers to the fact that Abraham had no choice in the matter; he was to receive his orders from the Lord, and go where those orders led him)*:

"And I will make of you a great Nation *(the Nation which God made of Abraham has changed the world, and exists even unto this hour; in fact, this Nation 'Israel' still has a great part to play, which will take place in the coming Kingdom Age)*, and I will bless you, and make your

name great *(according to Scripture, 'to bless' means 'to increase'; the builders of the Tower of Babel sought to 'make us a name,' whereas God took this man, who forsook all, and 'made his name great')*; **and you shall be a blessing:** *(Concerns itself with the greatest blessing of all. It is the glory of Abraham's Faith. God would give this man the meaning of Salvation, which is 'Justification by Faith,' which would come about through the Lord Jesus Christ, and what Christ would do on the Cross. Concerning this, Jesus said of Abraham, 'Your father Abraham rejoiced to see My Day: and he saw it, and was glad' [Jn. 8:56].)*

THE BLESSING AND THE CURSE

"And I will bless them who bless you *(to bless Israel, or any Believer, for that matter, guarantees the Blessings of God)*, **and curse him who curses you** *(to curse Israel, or any Believer, guarantees that one will be cursed by God)*: **and in you shall all families of the Earth be blessed.** *(It speaks of Israel, which sprang from the loins of Abraham and the womb of Sarah, giving the world the Word of God and, more particularly, bringing the Messiah into the world. Through Christ, every family in the world who desires blessing from God can have that Blessing, i.e., 'Justification by Faith')*" **(Gen. 12:1-3).**

ISAAC

Now more knowledge is given as to how the Redeemer is to come into the world, and more particularly, through whom He would come. The Scripture says:

"And Abraham said unto God, O that Ishmael might live before You! *(Abraham asked the Lord that Ishmael might have some place, and not be completely left out.)*
"And God said, Sarah your wife shall bear you a

son indeed; and you shall call his name Isaac *(the name Isaac means 'laughter')*: **and I will establish My Covenant with him for an Everlasting Covenant, and with his seed after him.** *(The Covenant is to be established with Isaac and not Ishmael. This completely shoots down the contention of the Muslims that Ishmael was the chosen one, unless you don't believe the Bible. Through Isaac the Lord Jesus Christ, the Saviour of mankind, would ultimately come)"* **(Gen. 17:18-19).**

Abraham now knows that through the lineage of his family the Redeemer would ultimately come. He did not know how long it would be, but he did now know how it would be.

THE MANNER OF REDEMPTION
WOULD BE BY DEATH

The Twenty-second Chapter of Genesis records one of the greatest tests that God ever laid upon a human being. Abraham was told by the Lord to go to a certain place and offer up Isaac as a sacrifice. Considering that human sacrifices were abhorrent to God, and Abraham knew this, the manner and way in which God revealed Himself to the Patriarch, must have been convincing indeed!

At any rate, Abraham fully obeyed, in which he was stopped at the last minute.

After the Lord stopped Abraham from carrying out the deed, the Scripture says:

"**And Abraham lifted up his eyes, and looked, and behold behind him a ram caught in a thicket by his horns** *(this is the Doctrine of Substitution plainly laid out; the ram was offered up in sacrifice instead of his son; likewise, Jesus was offered up as our Substitute)*: **and Abraham went and took the ram, and offered him up for a Burnt Offering in the stead of his son** *(even though the Doctrine* *of Substitution is clearly set forth here, its corresponding Doctrine of Identification is not so clearly stated, that awaiting Moses [Num. 21:9]; but still, we are seeing here the very heart of the Salvation Plan).*

"**And Abraham called the name of that place Jehovah-jireh** *(meaning 'the Lord will provide')*: **as it is said to this day, In the mount of the LORD it shall be seen** *(should read 'in this mount Jehovah shall be seen'; this was fulfilled in II Sam. 24:25; I Chron. 21:26; II Chron. 7:1-3)*" **(Gen. 22:13-14).**

While the Lord told Abraham the manner in which Redemption would be carried out, which would be by God giving His Only Son, he was told it would be by death, but the Patriarch wasn't told how that death would be, that awaiting the time of Moses.

THE MOSAIC LAW

The entirety of the Law, and in every capacity, excluding nothing, presented itself as a Type of Christ, whether in His Atoning Work, His Intercessory Ministry, or His Mediatorial capacity. We know this because Paul said:

"**For Christ** *is* **the end of the Law for Righteousness** *(Christ fulfilled the totality of the Law)* **to everyone who believes** *(Faith in Christ guarantees the Righteousness which the Law had, but could not give)*" **(Rom. 10:4).**

But, if it is to be noticed, while the Lord told Moses and the Children of Israel that they must obey the Law and, as well, told of the tremendous penalty involved if they didn't, still, the Lord never really told Israel how to keep the Law.

Why?

Due to the Fall, it was and is impossible for man to keep the Law. So, the Sacrificial System was given in the very heart of the Law, and in fact, was the driving force of the Law. The Sacrificial System provided a way for sins to be forgiven, of which all were a Type of the coming Redeemer. While the Lord did not tell Israel how to keep the Law, He did provide for them a way of escape. That way out was the Sacrificial System which was a Type of the Crucifixion of Christ (Lev., Chpts. 1-7).

REDEEMED FROM THE CURSE OF THE LAW

The curse of the Law was death, and actually eternal separation from God. Concerning this terrible penalty which hung over mankind, Paul said:

"**For as many as are of the Works of the Law are under the curse** *(the Believer can only be under Law or Grace; it is one or the other; one can only come to Grace through the Cross; if one is trusting in Law, whatever kind of Law, one is cursed)*: **for it is written, Cursed *is* every one who continues not in all things which are written in the Book of the Law to do them** *(Deut. 27:26). (To attain the Righteousness of the Law, one must keep the Law perfectly, thereby never failing. Such is impossible, so that leaves only the Cross as the means of Salvation and Victory.)*
"**But that no man is justified by the Law in the Sight of God, *it is* evident** *(because it is impossible for man to perfectly keep the Law)*: **for, The just shall live by Faith** *([Hab. 2:4], Faith in Christ and what He did at the Cross)*.
"**And the Law is not of Faith** *(the two principles of Law and of Faith as a means of Justification are mutually exclusive of one another)*: **but, The man who does them shall live in them.** *(The Believer has a choice. He can attempt to live this life by either Law or Faith. He cannot live by both.)*
"**Christ has redeemed us from the curse of the Law** *(He did so on the Cross)*, **being made a curse for us** *(He*

took the penalty of the Law, which was death): **for it is written, Cursed** *is* **every one who hangs on a tree** *(Deut. 21:22-23)*:

"**That the blessing of Abraham** *(Justification by Faith)* **might come on the Gentiles through Jesus Christ** *(what He did at the Cross)*; **that we might receive the Promise of the Spirit through Faith.** *(All sin was atoned at the Cross which lifted the sin debt from believing man, making it possible for the Holy Spirit to come into the life of the Believer and abide there forever [Jn. 14:16-17])*" **(Gal. 3:10-14).**

THE TRIBE OF JUDAH

Jacob on his dying bed, so to speak, prophesied concerning all of the Tribes of Israel, which would go by the names of his sons. As it regards the Tribe of Judah, the Holy Spirit through him gave us something most remarkable. He said:

"**Judah, you are he whom your brethren shall praise** *(the name Judah means 'praise,' and it is from this Tribe that the Messiah would come)*: **Your hand shall be in the neck of Your enemies** *(speaks of the great victory that Christ would win over Satan and all the powers of darkness at the Cross [Col. 2:14-15])*; **your father's children shall bow down before You** *(Israel will do this at the Second Coming).*

"**Judah is a lion's whelp** *(refers to a young lion, in the power of its youth, absolutely invincible; this represented Christ in the flower of His manhood, full of the Holy Spirit, healing the sick, casting out demons, raising the dead, and doing great and mighty things, with every demon spirit trembling at His Feet)*: **from the prey** *(the lion is always seeking the prey, never the prey seeking the lion)*, **My Son** *(Jesus is the Son of God)*, **You are gone up** *(meaning that Christ is always on the offensive)*: **He stooped down, He couched as a lion** *(a rampant lion, standing on his hind* *feet, ready to pounce, which, in fact, was the emblem of the Tribe of Judah)*, **and as an old lion** *(referring to one ripening into its full strength and ferocity)*; **who shall rouse Him up?** *(Who would be so foolish as to contest the absolute invincibility of Christ?)*

SHILOH

"The sceptre shall not depart from Judah *(the 'Sceptre' is defined as 'a staff of office and authority,' which pertains to Christ)*, **nor a Law-Giver from between His Feet** *(refers to the fact that Judah was meant to be a guardian of the Law, which they were; the Temple was in Jerusalem, which was a part of the Tribe of Judah, and which had to do with the Law)*, **until Shiloh come** *(when Jesus came, typified by the name 'Shiloh,' Who, in fact, was, and is, the True Law-Giver, He fulfilled the Law in totality by His Life and His Death, thereby satisfying all of its just demands)*; **and unto Him shall the gathering of the people be** *(the only way to God the Father is through Christ the Son; the only way to Christ the Son is through the Cross; the only way to the Cross is through an abnegation of self [Lk. 9:23-24])*.

"Binding his foal unto the vine *(the 'Vine' speaks of fruit, and, in fact, 'the blood of grapes,' which speaks of what He did on the Cross in the shedding of His Life's Blood, in order to bring forth this fruit [Jn. 15:1])*, **and his animal's colt unto the choice vine; He washed His Garments in wine, and His Clothes in the blood of grapes** *(all of this speaks of the Cross, and Him washing His Garments in wine, i.e., 'in blood')*:

"His Eyes shall be red with wine *(His eyes ever toward the Cross)*, **and His Teeth white with milk** *(speaks of the Righteousness of Christ; it is Righteousness which He has always had, but now is made possible to us, due to what He did in His Sufferings, i.e., 'the blood of grapes')*" **(Gen. 49:8-12).**

THE FAMILY IN THE TRIBE OF JUDAH
THROUGH WHICH JESUS WOULD COME

The Lord meant for David to be the first king of Israel; however, Israel wouldn't wait on the Lord, demanded a king then, and the Lord let them have Saul, which was one of the worst things that could have ever happened. At any rate, the Plan of God will be fulfilled, although Satan did everything within his power to hinder it and even stop it, and without success. Despite the efforts of the Evil One, little by little the coming of the Redeemer is getting closer.

• The Lord had promised a Redeemer for the lost sons of Adam's fallen race.

• From the womb of Sara and the loins of Abraham, He had raised up a people through whom this Redeemer would come.

• Through the Patriarch Jacob, He had proclaimed the fact that the Redeemer would be born through the Tribe of Judah.

• Now the Holy Spirit proclaims that through the family of David of the Tribe of Judah, the Redeemer will come. In fact, the Redeemer would be referred to as *"The Son of David."*

DAVID

And it came to pass that night, that the Word of the Lord came unto Nathan, saying:

"And it came to pass that night, that the Word of the LORD came unto Nathan, saying,

"Go and tell My servant David, Thus says the LORD, Shall you build Me an house for Me to dwell in? *(There is no disapproval of David's purpose as such; but only the deferring of its full execution unto the days of his son, Solomon. But there is more than this. The idea which runs through the Divine Message is that the dwelling of Jehovah in a tent was a fitting symbol of Israel's unsure possession of the land. In fact, they had conquered the land a long time before, but had never been able to maintain their liberty unimpaired. David would rectify that.)*

"Whereas I have not dwelt in any house since the time that I brought up the Children of Israel out of Egypt, even to this day, but have walked in a tent and in a Tabernacle.

"In all the places wherein I have walked with all the Children of Israel spoke I a word with any of the Tribes *(Judges)* of Israel, whom I commanded to feed My People Israel, saying, Why build you not Me an house of cedar? *(For a proper House for the Lord to be built, proper leadership must first be established — leadership that would properly feed the people. To properly feed is to properly govern. David was the first one to fit this bill, so to speak; therefore, the plans would be given to him, but not the right to actually build. That would go to Solomon.)*

THE CONQUESTS OF DAVID

"Now therefore so shall you say unto My servant David, Thus says the LORD of Hosts, I took you from the sheepcote, from following the sheep, to be ruler over My People, over Israel *(now the Lord tells David that admittance into this House will be by the way of humility and the shed blood, hence, 'the sheep')*:

"And I was with you wheresoever you went, and have cut off all your enemies out of your sight, and have made you a great name, like unto the name of the great men who are in the Earth. *(The widespread conquests of David, and his great empire, were not for the sake of mere Earthly dominion. It was, first of all, a Type of Messiah's reign, to Whom God has promised the heathen for His Inheritance, and that His Gospel shall be carried to the ends of the Earth [Mk. 16:15].)*

"Moreover I will appoint a place for My People Israel, and will plant them, that they may dwell in a place of their own, and move no more; neither shall the children of wickedness afflict them any more, as before-time *(in Genesis, Chapter 15, God promised the land to Abraham's Seed. In this Chapter, He promises the Throne to David's Seed. The Seed is Christ; and, therefore, in each instance the Covenant is unconditional, for there can be no failure on Christ's part),*

"And as since the time that I commanded Judges to be over My People Israel, and have caused you to rest from all your enemies. Also the LORD tells you that He will make you an house. *(In Genesis 49:10, through Jacob, the Lord promised that the Messiah would come from the Tribe of Judah. And now, He selects the family in Judah which will bring forth the Messiah, and David is clearly chosen. David had thought to build the Lord a house, but, instead, the Lord tells him that He [the Lord] will build David a house.)*

"And when your days be fulfilled, and you shall sleep with your fathers, I will set up your seed after you, which shall proceed out of your bowels, and I will establish His Kingdom *(this speaks of the Lord Jesus Christ).*

"He shall build an house for My Name, and I will stablish the Throne of His Kingdom for ever *(as stated, this is an unconditional Promise; it will most definitely come to pass).*

THE THRONE ESTABLISHED FOREVER

"I will be his father, and he shall be my son. If he commit iniquity, I will chasten him with the rod of men, and with the stripes of the children of men *(this pertains to Solomon and those who would follow after him in the lineage of David, through whom the Messiah would come, which pertains to the first phrase of the Verse)*:

"But My Mercy shall not depart away from him, as I took it from Saul, whom I put away before you *(this means that whatever happened, the Messiah would come through the lineage of David).*

"And your house and your kingdom shall be established for ever before you: your throne shall be established for ever *(and so shall it be in Christ, and will be established at the Second Coming).*

"According to all these Words, and according to all this Vision, so did Nathan speak unto David *(no doubt, we only have a small portion here of what Nathan actually said, but yet the full ingredients).*

DAVID'S THANKSGIVING TO GOD

"Then went king David in, and sat before the LORD, and he said, Who am I, O LORD God? and what is my house, that You have brought me hitherto? *(The magnitude of all this overwhelms David, as well it should! God's Thoughts are always so much bigger than our thoughts.)*

"And this was yet a small thing in Your Sight, O LORD God; but You have spoken also of Your servant's house for a great while to come. And is this the manner of man, O LORD God? *(While there is no direct reference here to the Messiah in David's words, yet the Psalms indicate that he did connect the duration of his house with the Messiah's advent [Ps. 2:8; 89:27]. In effect, he was saying, 'So this is the manner in which You will redeem man. You will do so by God becoming Man, fulfilling Genesis 3:15.')*

"And what can David say more unto You? for You, LORD God, know Your servant *('LORD God,' in the Hebrew, is 'LORD Jehovah,' signifying Covenant relationship).*

"For Your Word's sake, and according to Your Own Heart, have You done all these great things, to make Your servant know them *(from this statement we know that David knew that the Lord had chosen him for this great honor, not because He saw something good in David, but because of the good within Himself)*" **(II Sam. 7:4-21).**

THE VIRGIN BIRTH

Some 750 years before Christ was born, the Holy Spirit through the great Prophet Isaiah, proclaimed the manner of His Birth. It would be totally unlike anything that had ever been and, as well, nothing would ever be that way again. The Scripture says:

"... Behold, a virgin shall conceive, and bear a son, and shall call His Name Immanuel. *(Without a doubt, this Prophecy is one of the greatest, if not the greatest, in the Bible.*

"In Hebrew, the 'virgin' is 'haalmah,' which means 'the virgin — the only one that ever was or ever will be a mother in this way.'

"The 'Son' Who would be born would be the 'Son of God.' The word 'Immanuel' means 'God with us.' Such was fulfilled in Christ.

"This Prophecy was given by God as a rebuttal to the efforts of Satan working through the kings of Syria and Israel to unseat Ahaz. In other words, their efforts to make void the Promise of God given to David would come to naught)" (Isa. 7:14).

To redeem mankind, God would have to become man. There had to be a sacrifice on the Cross, and God cannot die. So, God would become man, The Man Christ Jesus.

However, this man could not be born by the natural method of procreation, in other words, as all other human beings were born. Had that been so, He would have been born with original sin, which was unacceptable. So, the manner of His Conception, would have to be supernatural. In fact, the Holy Spirit would decree His Conception, and it would be done.

THE ACCOUNT AS GIVEN BY LUKE

When the time came for this conception, the Scripture says:

"**And in the sixth month** *(refers to six months after Elisabeth had conceived; consequently, John was six months older than Jesus)* **the Angel Gabriel was sent from God unto a city of Galilee, named Nazareth** *(strangely enough, Nazareth was held in scorn by Israel at that time)*,

"**To a virgin** *(in the Greek Text is 'parthenos,' which refers to a pure virgin who has never known a man, and never experienced a marriage relationship; in the Hebrew, the word is 'Ha-alma,' which means, 'the Virgin — the only one who ever was, or ever will be a mother in this way')* **espoused** *(engaged)* **to a man whose name was Joseph, of the house of David** *(he was in the direct lineage of David through Solomon)*; **and the Virgin's name** *was* **Mary** *(Mary went back to David through another of David's sons, Nathan; so their lineage was perfect as it regards the Prophecies that the Messiah would come from the House of David [II Sam., Chpt. 7])*.

"**And the Angel came in unto her, and said** *(presents the greatest moment in human history, the announcement of the coming Birth of the Lord of Glory in the Incarnation, i.e., 'God becoming man')*, **Hail,** *you that are* **highly favoured** *(means 'much engraced,' not 'full of grace,' as the Catholic Church teaches, but one who, herself meritless, had received signal Grace from God)*, **the Lord** *is* **with you** *(signals her position of humility)*: **blessed** *are* **you among women** *(does not say 'above women,' as the Catholics teach; however, she definitely was much blessed)*.

"**And when she saw** *him,* **she was troubled at his saying** *(a total disturbance; not a partial, or light agitation)*, **and cast in her mind what manner of salutation this should be** *(she in no way understood the reason that he addressed her as he did)*.

"**And the Angel said unto her, Fear not, Mary: for you have found favour with God** *(should have been translated, 'you have received Grace from God')*.

"**And, behold, you shall conceive in your womb**

(should have been translated, 'You shall forthwith conceive in your womb,' meaning immediately), **and bring forth a Son** *(proclaims the Incarnation, 'God manifest in the flesh, God with us, Immanuel' [Isa. 7:14; 9:6])*, **and shall call His Name JESUS** *(the Greek version of the Hebrew, 'Joshua'; it means 'Saviour,' or 'The Salvation of Jehovah').*

"He shall be great, and shall be called the Son of the Highest *(actually means 'The Most High,' and refers to 'Jehovah')*: **and the Lord God shall give unto Him the throne of His father David** *(II Sam., Chpt. 7)*:

"And He shall reign over the house of Jacob forever; and of His Kingdom there shall be no end *(this will begin at the Second Coming, and will last forever; it could have begun at the beginning of His Ministry, but He was rejected by Israel; but at the Second Coming, they will accept Him as their Saviour, Messiah, and King [Zech., Chpts. 12-14]).*

THE HOLY SPIRIT

"Then said Mary unto the Angel, How shall this be, seeing I know not a man? *(She was probably in her late teens.)*

"And the Angel answered and said unto her, The Holy Spirit shall come upon you *(has the same connotation as, 'the Spirit of God moved upon the face of the waters' [Gen. 1:2])*, **and the power of the Highest shall overshadow you** *(has the same reference as, 'And God said, let there be light: and there was light' [Gen. 1:3])*: **therefore also that Holy thing which shall be born of you shall be called the Son of God** *(constitutes the Incarnation, 'God becoming Man'; He would be Very God and Very Man).*

"And, behold, your cousin Elisabeth *(the word, 'cousin,' in the Greek Text is 'suggenes,' which means 'countryman,' and not necessarily a cousin in the sense of a blood relative; however, Mary definitely could have been* *personally kin to Elisabeth)*, **she has also conceived a son in her old age: and this is the sixth month with her, who was called barren.**

"For with God nothing shall be impossible *(what is impossible with man is very much possible with God)*.

"And Mary said, Behold the handmaid of the Lord *(beautifully portrays the humility of this young lady; I think she would be greatly grieved at the unscriptural manner in which Catholicism has elevated her — even to the place of Deity)*; **be it unto me according to your word** *(she gives this consent in a word that was simple and sublime, which involved the most extraordinary act of Faith that a woman ever consented to accomplish)*. **And the Angel departed from her"** **(Lk. 1:26-38).**

BETHLEHEM, THE PLACE OF HIS BIRTH

Some 700 years before Christ, the Prophet Micah foretold the place of His Birth. He said:

"But you, Beth-lehem Ephratah, though you be little among the thousands of Judah, yet out of you shall He come forth unto Me Who is to be Ruler in Israel; Whose goings forth have been from old, from everlasting. *(The question could be asked as to why the Holy Spirit would give these Prophecies in this fashion, having little or no chronological order? The answer probably falls into the same category as to why the Lord, in His earthly Ministry, mostly spoke in Parables [Lk. 8:10].*

"'But you, Beth-lehem Ephratah,' speaks of the birth-place of Christ. 'Though you be little among the thousands of Judah,' signifies a small place, though the birthplace of David, as well! 'Yet out of you shall He come forth unto Me, Who is to be Ruler in Israel,' speaks of Christ coming from the Tribe of Judah. This was prophesied by Jacob long before [Gen. 49:10].

" '*Whose goings forth have been from old, from ever-lasting,*' *is meant to portray to any and all that this is not just any person, but rather, as Isaiah prophesied, 'Immanuel, God with us' [Isa. 7:14])*" **(Mic. 5:2).**

THE BIRTH OF JESUS CHRIST

As we shall see, the Prophecy of Micah came to pass exactly as predicted. The Scripture says:

"And it came to pass in those days, that there went out a decree from Caesar Augustus *(Caius Octavius, the adopted son and successor of Julius Caesar; he reigned 29 B.C. to A.D. 14)* **that all the world should be taxed** *(a figure of speech; a whole is put for a part; it was only the part of the world of which it spoke.)*
"(And this taxing was first made when Cyrenius was governor of Syria. *(This Verse should have been translated, 'this census was before Cyrenius was Governor of Syria.')*
"And all went to be taxed, every one into his own city.
"And Joseph also went up from Galilee, out of the city of Nazareth, into Judaea, unto the city of David, which is called Bethlehem; because he was of the house and lineage of David:) *(It was a distance of about 80 miles.)*
"To be taxed with Mary his espoused wife, being great with child *(the trip must have been very difficult for her).*
"And so it was, that, while they were there, the days were accomplished that she should be delivered *(this concerned the most important deliver of a baby in human history; God would become flesh, and offer up Himself on the Cross as a Perfect Sacrifice in order to deliver humanity).*
"And she brought forth her Firstborn Son *(this is meant to emphasize the fact that there were no other children up to this time; as well, it refutes the error of the Catholic Church, which claims that Mary, thereafter, had no other children, and remained a Virgin throughout her life; actually, Jesus*

had four brothers, 'James, Joseph, Simon, and Jude,' as well as two or three sisters [Mat. 13:55-56]), **and wrapped Him in swaddling clothes, and laid Him in a manger** *(spoke of a feeding place for animals)*; **because there was no room for them in the inn** *(the Inn of Bethlehem was of ancient duration, being mentioned in Jer. 41:17; this type of 'Inn' was for the poorest of the poor, and offered little more than the shelter of its walls and roof)*" **(Lk. 2:1-7).**

It should be obvious, that there is no way that this could be faked. This is another irrefutable proof of the Divinity of Christ.

THE LIFE OF THE LORD JESUS CHRIST

If it is to be noticed, the detractors of the Lord, of which there seemed to have been many, namely the religious leaders of Israel, never accused Christ of any type of specific sin. While they claimed that He did cast out demons by the power of Satan, this was only a wicked observation on their part. To be sure, had He done anything wrong, spying on Him constantly, it would have been heralded far and wide. The Truth is His Life was impeccable. He never sinned, never failed in even one aspect of life and living, whether in thought, word, or deed.

In fact, Jesus said to His detractors, and publicly, *"Which of you convinces Me of sin?"* (Jn. 8:46).

His Life had to be perfect in every respect, that is, if He was to be a Sacrifice for sin. God could not accept anything less than perfection.

Some may think this is relatively insignificant due to the fact that Jesus was God. Yes, He was! However, even though He was Very God, still, He never performed one single Miracle, or functioned in any capacity as God, but only as a Man filled with the Holy Spirit. The Scripture says of Jesus:

"**How God anointed Jesus of Nazareth with the Holy Spirit and with Power** *(as a Man, Christ needed the Holy*

*Spirit, as we certainly do as well! in fact, everything He did was by the Power of the Spirit)***: who went about doing good** *(everything He did was good)***, and healing all who were oppressed of the Devil** *(only Christ could do this, and Believers can do such only as Christ empowers them by the Spirit)***; for God was with Him** *(God is with us only as we are 'with Him')***" (Acts 10:38).**

God doesn't need the Anointing of the Holy Spirit to do anything; however, Jesus as a Man, did need the Holy Spirit. In other words, He functioned in His earthly sojourn, exactly as we do, with one exception:

Whereas every human being that's ever been born, due to Adam's Fall, has been born with a sin nature, Jesus, not being conceived by man, was not born with a sin nature; however, we must remember, that Adam was not created with a sin nature either.

The sin nature, in fact, does not cause the Believer to fail the Lord. Failure comes from the fact of disobedience and originates in the heart. If the Believer then places his faith in something other than the Cross of Christ, the sin nature, however, will then begin to dominate such a person, making life miserable, to say the least (Rom. 6:12).

THE MINISTRY OF OUR LORD

Jesus did not begin His Ministry until He was thirty years of age. This was the age at the beginning, when members of the Tribe of Levi could become a Priest. In fact, He did not engage in any type of Ministry before this time, and concerning this time, the Scripture says:

"Then came Jesus from Galilee to Jordan unto John, to be baptized of him *(signifying the greatest moment in human history thus far; the earthly Ministry of Christ would now begin).*

"But John forbad Him, saying, I have need to be baptized of You, and come You to me?

"And Jesus answering said unto him, Suffer *it to be so* now *(permit Me to be baptized)*: for thus it becomes us to fulfill all Righteousness *(Water Baptism is a Type of the death, burial, and Resurrection of Christ [Rom. 6:3-5])*. Then he suffered Him.

"And Jesus, when He was baptized *(this was the beginning of His earthly Ministry)*, went up straightway *(immediately)* out of the water *(refers to Baptism by immersion and not by sprinkling)*: and, lo, the Heavens were opened unto Him *(the only One, the Lord Jesus Christ, to Whom the Heavens would be opened)*, and he saw the Spirit of God *(Holy Spirit)* descending like a dove, and lighting upon Him *(John saw a visible form that reminded him of a dove)*:

"And lo a Voice from Heaven, saying *(the Voice of God the Father)*, This is My Beloved Son, in Whom I am well pleased *(the Trinity appears here: the Father speaks, the Spirit descends, and the Son prays [Lk. 3:21])*" (Mat. 3:13-17).

So, before Jesus began His earthly Ministry, He was first baptized with the Holy Spirit. Now the question should loom large, if He our Perfect Lord, had to have the Holy Spirit, how in the world do we think we could get by with less?

This is the reason that Jesus said to His followers, in His last Message before His Ascension:

"And, being assembled together with *them* *(speaks of the time He ascended back to the Father; this was probably the time of the 'above five hundred' [I Cor. 15:6])*, Commanded them *(not a suggestion)* that they should not depart from Jerusalem *(the site of the Temple where the Holy Spirit would descend)*, but wait for the Promise of the Father *(spoke of the Holy Spirit which had been promised by the Father [Lk. 24:49; Joel, Chpt. 2])*, **which, said *He*, you have heard of Me** *(you have also heard Me say these things [Jn. 7:37-39; 14:12-17, 26; 15:26; 16:7-15]).*

"**For John truly baptized with water** *(merely symbolized the very best Baptism Believers could receive before the Day of Pentecost)*; **but you shall be baptized with the Holy Spirit not many days hence** *(spoke of the coming Day of Pentecost, although Jesus did not use that term at that time)*" **(Acts 1:4-5).**

GREAT LIGHT

The Scripture further says as it regards the beginning of the Ministry of the Master:

"**Now when Jesus had heard that John was cast into prison** *(John's Ministry was now finished; he had properly introduced Christ)*, **He** *(Jesus)* **departed into Galilee** *(where the central core of His Ministry would be)*;

"**And leaving Nazareth** *(refers to His rejection there [Lk. 4:16-30])*, **He came and dwelt in Capernaum** *(made this city His Headquarters)*, **which is upon the sea coast** *(refers to the Sea of Galilee)*, **in the borders of Zabulon and Nephthalim** *(refers to these two Tribes bordering the Sea of Galilee)*:

"**That it might be fulfilled which was spoken by Isaiah the Prophet, saying** *(Isaiah prophesied of Christ more than any other Prophet)*,

"**The land of Zabulon, and the land of Nephthalim,** *by* **the way of the sea** *(Sea of Galilee)*, **beyond Jordan, Galilee of the Gentiles** *(the great Roman Road ran near the Sea of Galilee from Damascus; almost all Gentiles traveling in this direction did so on this road; the Headquarters of Christ was within the confines of the Tribe of Naphtali)*;

"**The people which sat in darkness** *(implies a settled acceptance of this darkness; the moral darkness was even* *greater than the national misery)* **saw great Light** *(Christ is the Light of the world, and the only True Light)*; **and to them which sat in the region and shadow of death** *(spiritual death is the result of this spiritual darkness)* **light** *(spiritual illumination in Christ)* **is sprung up.**

"**From that time** *(the move to Capernaum)* **Jesus began to preach** *(the major method of the proclamation of the Gospel)*, **and to say, Repent** *(beginning His Ministry, the first word used by Christ, as recorded by Matthew, was 'Repent')*: **for the Kingdom of Heaven is at hand** *(the Kingdom from Heaven, headed up by Christ, for the purpose of reestablishing the Kingdom of God over the Earth; the Kingdom was rejected by Israel)*" **(Mat. 4:12-17).**

THE MISSION OF CHRIST

Concerning the purpose of His Ministry, He said of Himself:

"**The Spirit of the Lord** *is* **upon Me** *(we learn here of the absolute necessity of the Person and Work of the Holy Spirit within our lives)*, **because He has anointed Me** *(Jesus is the ultimate Anointed One; consequently, the Anointing of the Holy Spirit actually belongs to Christ, and the Anointing we have actually comes by His Authority [Jn. 16:14])* **to preach the Gospel to the poor** *(the poor in spirit)*; **He has sent Me to heal the brokenhearted** *(sin breaks the heart, or else is responsible for it being broken; only Jesus can heal this malady)*, **to preach Deliverance to the captives** *(if it is to be noticed, He didn't say to 'deliver the captives,' but rather 'preach Deliverance,' which refers to the Cross [Jn. 8:32])*, **and recovering of sight to the blind** *(the Gospel opens the eyes of those who are spiritually blind)*, **to set at liberty them who are bruised** *(the vicissitudes of life at times place a person in a mental or spiritual prison; the Lord Alone, and through what He did at the Cross, can open this prison door)*,

"To preach the acceptable Year of the Lord *(it is be-lieved that the day, on which Jesus delivered this Message was the first day of the year of Jubilee)*" **(Lk. 4:18-19).**

JESUS, THE FULFILLMENT OF THE PROPHECY

Luke went ahead to say:

"And He closed the book, and He gave *it* again to the Minister, and sat down *(portrays the custom of that time).* And the eyes of all them who were in the Synagogue were fastened on Him *(even though most there would fail to see it, this represented a moment far exceeding anything these people had ever known).*

"And He began to say unto them, This day is this Scripture fulfilled in your ears *(in effect, He is saying, 'I am the Messiah,' the fulfillment of these Scriptures).*

"And all bear Him witness *(all understood exactly what He said, but all did not believe Him),* and wondered at the gracious words which proceeded out of His Mouth *(means that we are given only a small portion of the things He actually said).* . ." **(Lk. 4:20-22).**

THE HEALINGS AND MIRACLES OF OUR LORD

There is no way that vocabulary can properly describe the healings and Miracles carried out by our Lord. In fact, concerning this, John the Beloved said:

"And there are also many other things which Jesus did *(speaks, no doubt, of the many Miracles He performed, some which are not recorded in any of the four Gospels),* the which, if they should be written every one *(lends credence to the idea that there were far more Miracles performed by Jesus and not recorded, than those which were recorded),* I

suppose that even the world itself could not contain the
books that should be written. **Amen** *(Christ is infinite,
the Earth finite; hence, the supposition of the Verse is most
reasonable)*" **(Jn. 21:25).**

No one, not even his most strident enemies, refuted His
Miracles. In fact, the veracity of these Miracles was irrefutable. They were obvious for all to see. While His enemies did
claim that He performed the Miracles by the power of Satan,
they never questioned the validity of the Miracles themselves.
But yet, the following should be noted:

While His miraculous Conception was absolutely necessary, still, had it all stopped there, no one would have ever
been Saved. While His Perfect Life was absolutely necessary
as well, still, had it stopped there, no one would have ever
been Saved. While His Healings and Miracles were necessary
as well, still, had it all stopped there, still, no one would have
been Saved.

For man to be redeemed, Jesus would have to go to the
Cross, give Himself as a Sacrifice, which alone would satisfy
the demands of a thrice-Holy God.

THE DEATH OF THE LORD JESUS CHRIST

The Truth is He came to die! That was His Purpose. That
was the reason for the Incarnation. While everything else was
important, in fact, everything He did was of the utmost significance, still, His primary objective was *"death,"* and not just any
type of death, it had to be death on a Cross.

WHY THE CROSS?

The price that would be paid for our sins had to be a price
that would cover every sin, no matter how vile.

The Law stated that if certain types of sins were committed, the person was to be stoned to death, and then their body

placed on a tree, as a sign that they were cursed by God, and because of the vileness of their sin and crime. Concerning this, Moses wrote:

"And if a man have committed a sin worthy of death, and he be to be put to death, and you hang him on a tree:
"His body shall not remain all night upon the tree, but you shall in any wise bury him that day; (for he who is hanged is accursed of God;) that your land be not defiled, which the LORD your God gives you for an inheritance. *(This is the reason that the religious leaders of Israel demanded that Jesus be put on the Cross [Mat. 27:23]. They knew that one put on the tree was accursed of God, and so they reasoned that the people would then think, were He really the Messiah, God would never allow Him to be put on a Cross. They did not realize that the Lord had foretold the event of the Cross some 1,500 years earlier, as it concerned the brazen serpent on the pole [Num. 21:8-9]. It was necessary that Jesus go to the Cross, in order that He might atone for all the sins of mankind, at least for all who will believe [Jn. 3:16]. So, Jesus was made a curse on the Cross, not because of His sins, for He had none, but for the sin of the whole world, and for all time [Jn. 1:29; Gal. 3:13])"* **(Deut. 21:22-23).**

THIRTY PIECES OF SILVER

The great Prophet Zechariah prophesied the worth that the religious leaders of Israel placed on Christ. It was the price of a slave. The Prophet said, and nearly 500 years before Christ:

"And I said unto them, If you think good, give Me My price; and if not, forebear. So they weighed for My price thirty pieces of silver.
"(The first phrase of this Verse refers to the Lord speaking, even though He uses the Prophet as His Instrument. The

Lord is speaking in the Person of the Great Shepherd. He asks His hire of the flock, because the flock represents men.

" 'And if not, forebear,' means 'I leave it to you to decide.'

"The phrase, 'So they weighed for My price thirty pieces of silver,' proclaims what Israel thought of their Messiah and His care through all the many centuries. They valued Him at thirty shekels, the price of an injured slave [Ex. 21:32].

"It is amazing that the Pharisees, who claimed to be such sticklers for the Law, would read these words, especially after the act had been performed, and still not relate it to themselves. Such is the marvel of unbelief!)" (**Zech. 11:12**).

THE POTTER'S FIELD

And then Zechariah prophesied as to what would be done with the money that Judas received for betraying the Lord. He said:

"And the LORD said unto me, Cast it unto the potter: a goodly price that I was prised at of them. And I took the thirty pieces of silver, and cast them to the potter in the House of the LORD. *('And the LORD said unto me,' now refers to His Response to their actions. This was all prophesied about 500 years before it would actually take place. The phrase, 'Cast it unto the potter,' implies the contemptuous rejection of the paltry sum; at the same time, it intimates the ultimate destination i.e., a field in which to bury the penniless [Mat. 27:3-10]. This was fulfilled to the letter by the action of Judas Iscariot.*

" 'A goodly price that I was prised at of them,' is used as sarcasm. Such was the 'price' that they valued Him. The pronoun 'them' is used strongly by the Holy Spirit, and of contempt; it speaks of the leadership of Israel at that time!

" 'And I took the thirty pieces of silver . . . ,' is quoted

in Matthew 27:9. The phrase, 'And cast them to the potter in the House of the LORD,' represents that all of this took place in the Temple)" **(Zech. 11:13).**

THE CROSS OF CHRIST

The Cross of Christ was not an afterthought, it was not an incident, and neither was it an execution. As we have previously stated, it was a Sacrifice. In fact, while everything that Christ did was of the utmost significance, and played its part in the great Plan of God regarding the redemption of man, still, the Cross of Christ was the apex. That's where all sin was atoned. That's where Satan and all of his cohorts were totally and completely defeated.

At the Cross, Jesus addressed every single thing that Adam lost in the Fall and, as well, Satan's rebellion, which is the cause of all problems to begin with. Nothing was left out, nothing was unattended. The Cross answered it all. And yet, as it regards what Christ did there, presently, we only have the *"firstfruits"* (Rom. 8:23). At the First Resurrection, the Resurrection of Life, we will then gain all for which Jesus paid such a price (I Cor. 15:51-57).

Concerning this great victory, Paul wrote:

"And you, being dead in your sins and the uncircumcision of your flesh *(speaks of spiritual death [i.e., 'separation from God'], which sin does!)*, has He quickened together with Him *(refers to being made spiritually alive, which is done through being 'Born-Again')*, having forgiven you all trespasses *(the Cross made it possible for all manner of sins to be forgiven and taken away)*;

THE DEMANDS OF THE LAW WERE ANSWERED

"Blotting out the handwriting of Ordinances that was against us *(pertains to the Law of Moses, which was*

God's Standard of Righteousness that man could not reach), **which was contrary to us** *(Law is against us, simply because we are unable to keep its precepts, no matter how hard we try)*, **and took it out of the way** *(refers to the penalty of the Law being removed)*, **nailing it to His Cross** *(the Law with its decrees was abolished in Christ's Death, as if Crucified with Him)*;

THE DEFEAT OF SATAN

"**And** **having spoiled principalities and powers** *(Satan and all of his henchmen were defeated at the Cross by Christ Atoning for all sin; sin was the legal right Satan had to hold man in captivity; with all sin atoned, he has no more legal right to hold anyone in bondage)*, **He** *(Christ)* **made a show of them openly** *(what Jesus did at the Cross was in the face of the whole universe)*, **triumphing over them in it.** *(The triumph is complete and it was all done for us, meaning we can walk in power and perpetual victory due to the Cross)*" **(Col. 2:13-15).**

THE FINISHED WORK OF THE CROSS

Just before He died, Jesus said: *"It is finished"* (Jn. 19:30). This means the world's debt was paid, the debt owed to God, but which mankind could not pay. Every iota of the Law was fulfilled.

It should be understood that no one took the Life of Jesus from Him. He laid it down freely. Concerning this, Jesus said:

"**Therefore does My Father love Me** *(proclaims that what Christ was to do held a special value in God's Heart)*, **because I lay down My Life** *(the entirety of the idea of the Incarnation was to purposely 'lay down His Life')*, **that I might take it again** *(the Resurrection)*.

"**No man takes it from Me, but I lay it down of**

Myself *(His Death was not an execution or an assassination, it was a Sacrifice; the idea is that He allowed His Death to take place).* **I have power to lay it down, and I have power to take it again** *(proclaims that what He did, He did voluntarily; He did not step out of the path of obedience, for He died as commanded).* **This Commandment have I received of My Father** *(this means that God the Father gave Him the latitude to do what He desired, and His desire was to do the Will of God; so He purposely laid down His Life)*" **(Jn. 10:17-18).**

THE RENT VEIL

When Jesus died, the Scripture says:

"**And, behold, the Veil of the Temple** *(that which hid the Holy of Holies; Josephus said it was sixty feet high from the ceiling to the floor, four inches thick, and was so strong, that four yoke of oxen could not pull it apart)* **was rent in twain from the top to the bottom** *(meaning that God Alone could have done such a thing; it also signified, that the price was paid completely on the Cross; signified by the rent Veil; regrettably, some say, the Cross — didn't finish the task with other things required; this Verse says differently)*; **and the earth did quake, and the rocks rent** *(represented an earthquake, but had nothing to do with the renting of the Veil, which took place immediately before this phenomenon)*" **(Mat. 27:51).**

The *"rent Veil"* was extremely important! This meant that the way was now open to the very Throne of God, with the only requirement being that man comes by Faith, and we speak of Faith in Christ and what Christ did at the Cross. The Cross opened the door to the very heart of God; consequently, the Scripture beautifully says: *"Whosoever will, let him take the Water of Life freely"* **(Rev. 22:17).**

WHAT HAPPENED FROM THE TIME OF THE DEATH OF CHRIST TO THE RESURRECTION OF CHRIST?

The Scripture only records two things that took place from the time of the Death of Jesus, unto His Resurrection. They are:

1. The Scripture says:

"**By which also He went** *(between the time of His Death and Resurrection)* **and preached** *(announced something)* **unto the spirits in prison** *(does not refer to humans, but rather to fallen Angels; humans in the Bible are never referred to in this particular manner; these were probably the fallen Angels who tried to corrupt the human race by co-habiting with women [II Pet. 2:4; Jude, Vss. 6-7]; these fallen Angels are still locked up in this underworld prison)*;

"**Which sometime** *(in times past)* **were disobedient** *(this was shortly before the Flood)*, **when once the long-suffering of God waited in the days of Noah** *(refers to this eruption of fallen Angels with women taking place at the time of Noah; this was probably a hundred or so years before the Flood)*, **while the Ark was a preparing** *(these fallen Angels were committing this particular sin while the Ark was being made ready, however long it took; the Scripture doesn't say!)*, **wherein few, that is, eight souls were saved by water.** *(This doesn't refer to being saved from sin. They were saved from drowning in the Flood by being in the Ark)*" **(I Pet. 3:19-20).**

What our Lord said to these fallen Angels we aren't told.

2. The second thing that Jesus did, possibly immediately before His Resurrection, was to deliver all of the souls in Paradise, which included every Believer from the time of Adam unto the time of His entrance into this place. The Scripture says concerning this:

"**Wherefore He said** *(Ps. 68:18)*, **When He ascended up on high** *(the Ascension)*, **He led captivity captive** *(liberated the souls in Paradise; before the Cross, despite being Believers, they were still held captive by Satan because the blood of bulls and goats could not take away the sin debt; but when Jesus died on the Cross, the sin debt was paid, and now He makes all of these His Captives)*, **and gave Gifts unto men.** *(These 'Gifts' include all the Attributes of Christ, all made possible by the Cross.)*

"**(Now that He ascended** *(mission completed)*, **what is it but that He also descended first into the lower parts of the earth?** *(Immediately before His Ascension to Glory, which would be done in total triumph, He first went down into Paradise to deliver all the believing souls in that region, which He did!)*" **(Eph. 4:8-9).**

THE RESURRECTION

The Resurrection of Christ was never in doubt. Some have claimed that He had to fight demons, etc., in order to be resurrected. There is nothing in the Scripture about that. The Truth is, if He had failed to atone for even one sin, He could not have been raised from the dead, because the Bible says, *"The wages of sin is death"* **(Rom. 6:23). But due to the fact that He most definitely did atone for all sin, past, present, and future, death had no claim on Him. There were no demons to fight they were all defeated at the Cross!**

Concerning the Resurrection, the Scripture says:

"**In the end of the Sabbath** *(the regular weekly Sabbath, which was every Saturday)*, **as it began to dawn toward the first** *day* **of the week** *(this was just before daylight on Sunday morning; Jesus rose from the dead some time after sunset on Saturday evening; the Jews began the new day at sunset, instead of midnight, as we do presently)*, **came Mary Magdalene and the other Mary to see the sepulcher** *(they* *wanted to put spices on the Body of Christ).*

"**And, behold, there was a great earthquake** *(presents the second earthquake, with the first taking place, when Christ died [27:51]):* **for the Angel of the Lord descended from Heaven** *(was probably observed by the Roman soldiers, who alone witnessed it and gave the account),* **and came and rolled back the stone from the door** *(Christ had already risen from the dead and had left the Tomb when the stone was rolled away; His Glorified Body was not restricted by obstacles),* **and sat upon it** *(this was done as a show of triumph; in other words, death was vanquished!).*

THE ANGEL

"**His countenance was like lightning, and his raiment white as snow** *(there is no evidence that any of the women or Disciples saw this glorious coming of the Angel; however, the next Verse tells us that the Roman guards did see it, and were terrified!):*

"**And for fear of Him** *(the Angel)* **the keepers** *(guards)* **did shake, and became as dead** *men (inasmuch as this happened at night, the situation was even more frightful).*

"**And the Angel answered and said unto the women** *(this was just before dawn, and after the soldiers had run away),* **Do not fear: for I know that you seek Jesus, Who was crucified** *(the Angel now uses this word, 'Crucified,' in a most glorious manner; it is now 'the Power of God and the Wisdom of God' [I Cor. 1:23-24]).*

"**He is not here** *(is the beginning of the most glorious statement that could ever fall upon the ears of mere mortals):* **for he is risen** *(a dead and risen Saviour is the life and substance of the Gospel [I Cor. 15:1-4]),* **as He said** *(the Angel brought to the attention of the women, the fact that Christ had stated several times that He would be crucified and would rise from the dead).* **Come, see the place where the Lord lay** *(they were looking for a corpse, but instead,*

*would find a risen Lord; they were looking for a Tomb con-
taining a corpse, but instead, would find it empty).*

"**And go quickly, and tell His Disciples that He is
risen from the dead** *(the Disciples should have been the
ones telling others, but because of unbelief, the women
will tell them; this is the greatest Message that humanity
has ever received)***; and, behold, He goes before you into
Galilee; there shall you see Him** *(He would reveal Himself
to whom and to where He so desired)***: lo, I have told you**
(guarantees the certitude of this action)" **(Mat. 28:1-7).**

THE ASCENSION OF CHRIST

**From the Resurrection of Christ to His Ascension, was a pe-
riod of forty days (Acts 1:3). During that time our Lord appeared
to His Disciples, and to others, even to** *"above 500 at one time,"*
which was probably the time of His Ascension (I Cor. 15:6).
Concerning His Ascension, the Scripture says:

"**And when He had spoken these things** *(refers to His
last instructions to His followers)*, **while they beheld, He
was taken up** *(refers to Him ascending before their very
eyes)***; and a cloud received Him out of their sight** *(represents the Shekinah Glory of God, which enveloped Christ
as He ascended).*

"**And while they looked stedfastly toward Heaven as
He went up** *(these statements are important because they
affirm His actual Ascension testified to by eyewitnesses)*,
behold, two men stood by them in white apparel *(these
two 'men' were actually Angels)*;

"**Which also said, You men of Galilee, why do you
stand gazing up into Heaven?** *(This does not mean that
it was only men who were present, but rather that this was
a common term used for both men and women.)* **this same
Jesus, Who is taken up from you into Heaven** *(refers to
the same Human Body with the nail prints in His Hands*

*and Feet, etc.)***, shall so come in like manner as you have seen Him go into Heaven** *(refers to the same place, which is the Mount of Olivet)*" **(Acts 1:9-11).**

THE INTERCESSION OF CHRIST

After the Ascension, the Scripture says concerning Christ:

"Who being the brightness of *His* Glory *(the radiance of God's Glory)***, and the express Image of His Person** *(the exact reproduction)***, and upholding all things by the Word of His Power** *(carries the meaning of Jesus not only sustaining the weight of the universe, but also maintaining its coherence and carrying on its development)***, when He had by Himself purged our sins** *(which He did at the Cross, dealing with sin regarding its cause, its power, and its guilt)***, sat down on the Right Hand of the Majesty on high** *(speaks of the Finished Work of Christ, and that the Sacrifice was accepted by the Father)*" **(Heb. 1:3).**

It seems from the Scriptures, that the main function of Christ at this present time is intercession for the Saints. The Scripture says concerning this:

"Wherefore He *(the Lord Jesus Christ)* **is able also to save them to the uttermost** *(proclaims the fact that Christ Alone has made the only true Atonement for sin; He did this at the Cross)* **who come unto God by Him** *(proclaims the only manner in which man can come to God)***, seeing He ever lives to make intercession for them.** *(His very Presence by the Right Hand of the Father guarantees such, with nothing else having to be done [Heb. 1:3])*" **(Heb. 7:25).**

To be sure, every single Believer, excepting none, needs this intercession as afforded by our Lord. Actually, this is intercession for failure, for disobedience, for sin! Again I emphasize

the fact, that we are foolish, if we think that we don't need such. The truth is, if there was no need for such, it would not be provided. By the very fact that it is provided, that tells us that it is needed, and by all Believers.

THE LORD JESUS CHRIST AND HIS CHURCH

During the earthly Ministry of Christ, He said to His Disciples regarding the building of His Church:

". . . Whom do men say that I the Son of Man am?" *(The third form of unbelief manifested itself in popular indifference, indolence, or mere curiosity respecting the Messiah Himself. Upon the answer to this all-important question, hinges the Salvation of man.)*
"And they said, Some *say that you are* John the Baptist: some, Elijah; and others, Jeremiah, or one of the Prophets" *(this form of unbelief manifests itself in the frivolity of the natural heart)*.
"He said unto them, But whom say you that I am?" *(Addressed personally to the Twelve.)*
"And Simon Peter answered and said, You are the Christ, the Son of the Living God" *(the Great Confession)*.
"And Jesus answered and said unto him, Blessed are you, Simon Bar–jona" *(Peter is the son of Jonah, as Jesus is the Son of God)*: **for flesh and blood have not revealed** *it* **unto you** *(mere human ingenuity)*, **but My Father which is in Heaven** *(all Spiritual Knowledge must be by Revelation)*.
"And I say also unto you, That you are Peter" *(the Lord changed his name from Simon to Peter, which means 'a fragment of a rock')*, **and upon this rock** *(immovable mass; Jesus is the Living Rock on which the Redeemed as living stones are built; for other foundation can no man lay [I Cor. 3:11])* **I will build My Church** *(the Church belongs to Christ, and He is the Head [Col. 1:18])*; **and the gates of Hell shall not prevail against it** *(the power of death caused*

by sin, shall not prevail against it, which victory was won at the Cross [Vss. 21, 24]).

"**And I will give unto you** *('you' refers to all Believers)* **the keys of the Kingdom of Heaven** *(refers to symbols of authority, the privilege of preaching or proclaiming the Gospel, which is the privilege of every Believer)*: **and whatsoever you shall bind on earth shall be bound in Heaven** *(Christ has given the authority and power to every Believer to bind Satan and his minions of darkness, and to do so by using the Name of Jesus [Mk. 16:17-18; Lk. 10:19])*: **and whatsoever you shall loose on earth shall be loosed in Heaven** *(looses the Power of God according to the usage of the Name of Jesus; this is the authority of the Believer)*" **(Mat. 16:13-19).**

CHRIST THE HEAD OF THE CHURCH

It must be understood, that Christ is not a passive head, but rather an active Head, and through the Person and Office of the Holy Spirit. Paul said:

"**And He is before all things** *(preexistence)*, **and by Him all things consist.** *(All things come to pass within this sphere of His Personality, and are dependent upon it.)*

"**And He is the Head of the Body, the Church** *(the Creator of the world is also Head of the Church)*: **Who is the Beginning** *(refers to Christ as the Origin or Beginning of the Church)*, **the firstborn from the dead** *(does not refer to Jesus being Born-Again as some teach, but rather that He was the first to be raised from the dead as it regards the Resurrection, never to die again)*; **that in all *things* He might have the preeminence.** *(He is the First and Foremost as it relates to the Church.)*

"**For it pleased *the Father* that in Him should all fulness dwell** *(this 'fullness' denotes the sum total of the Divine Powers and Attributes)*" **(Col. 1:17-19).**

THE RAPTURE OF THE CHURCH

The words *"Rapture"* and *"Resurrection,"* are merely two different words describing the same event — when Believers, both those who are dead and those who are now alive, will be changed from the mortal to the immortal (I Cor. 15:51-57).

Concerning this event, the Scripture says:

"For the Lord Himself shall descend from Heaven with a shout *(refers to 'the same Jesus' which the Angels proclaimed in Acts 1:11)*, with the voice of the Archangel *(refers to Michael, the only one referred to as such [Jude, Vs. 9])*, and with the Trump of God *(doesn't exactly say God will personally blow this Trumpet, but that it definitely does belong to Him, whoever does signal the blast)*: and the dead in Christ shall rise first *(the criteria for being ready for the Rapture is to be 'in Christ,' which means that all who are truly Born-Again will definitely go in the Rapture)*:

"Then we who are alive *and* remain shall be caught up *(Raptured)* together with them *(the Resurrected dead)* in the clouds *(clouds of Saints, not clouds as we normally think of such)*, to meet the Lord in the air *(the Greek word for 'air' is 'aer,' and refers to the lower atmosphere, or from about 6,000 feet down; so, the Lord will come at least within 6,000 feet of the Earth, perhaps even lower, with all the Saints meeting Him there; but He, at that time, will not come all the way to the Earth, that awaiting the Second Coming, which will be seven or more years later)*: and so shall we ever be with the Lord. *(This presents the greatest meeting humanity will have ever known)*" (I Thess. 4:16-17).

First of all, we are here told that the Lord Himself is going to head up this event.

He will not come to the Earth at this time, only coming approximately within a mile of the Planet.

The Greek word for *"air"* as used in Verse 17, is *"aer,"* and refers to the lower atmosphere, or from about 6,000 feet down; so, the Lord will come at least within 6,000 feet of the Earth at that time, perhaps even lower, with all the Saints meeting Him there; but He, at that time, will not come all the way to the Earth, that awaiting the Second Coming, which will be seven or more years later.

He will come to receive the Saints, as stated, both dead and alive.

THE JUDGMENT SEAT OF CHRIST

This event, *"The Judgment Seat of Christ,"* will take place in Heaven, no doubt, immediately before the Second Coming. Concerning this event, Paul said:

"Wherefore we labour *(are ambitious)*, that, whether present *(with Christ)* or absent *(still in this world)*, we may be accepted of Him *(approved by Him, which we will be if our Faith is in Christ and the Cross)*.

"For we must all appear before the Judgment Seat of Christ *(this will take place in Heaven, and will probably transpire immediately before the Second Coming)*; that every one may receive the things *done* in *his* body, according to that he has done, whether *it be* good or bad. *(This concerns our life lived for the Lord. Sins will not be judged here, but rather our motivation and faithfulness, for sin was judged at Calvary)*" (II Cor. 5:9-10).

As should be obvious, Christ will officiate at this Judgment. No doubt, at this time, as well, rewards will be handed out to all Believers. While no one will lose their soul at this time, and no one will be judged of sins, and as also stated, that already having been handled at Calvary, still, every Believer will then be judged for our life and living on this Earth. What did we do with this great Gift of Eternal Life given to us by the Lord?

How did we acquit ourselves? What was our motivation?

All of this will come up before Christ at that time, and to be certain, His Judgment will be perfect.

We should consider all of this in our life and living now, realizing, that one day, we will answer for every action regarding our stewardship.

THE SECOND COMING

The Nineteenth Chapter of Revelation portrays the Second Coming of our Lord. It will be the most cataclysmic, the most startling, the most powerful, and the most striking event the world will have ever known. Actually, the Second Coming of the Lord will take place in the midst of the Battle of Armageddon. Concerning this, the great Prophet Zechariah said:

"**Behold, the Day of the LORD comes, and your spoil shall be divided in the midst of you.** *('Behold, the Day of the LORD comes,' presents this day as beginning with the Second Coming and lasting until the end of the Millennium. At that time, the end of the Millennium, the 'Day of God' begins and will continue through eternity [I Cor. 15:24-28; Eph. 1:10; II Pet. 3:10-13].)*

" 'And your spoil shall be divided in the midst of you,' concerns the Antichrist coming against Israel [Ezek. 38:11-12].)

"**For I will gather all nations against Jerusalem to battle; and the city shall be taken, and the houses rifled, and the women ravished; and half of the city shall go forth into captivity, and the residue of the people shall not be cut off from the city.** *(The first phrase refers to the mobilization of the nations to Armageddon [Ezek., Chpts. 38-39; Joel, Chpt. 3; Rev. 16:13-16; 19:11-21]. 'And the city shall be taken,' actually means that the Antichrist will prepare to take Jerusalem, with actually half of it being taken. The phrase, 'And the houses rifled, and the women ravished,' expresses extreme cruelty practiced by the army* *of the Antichrist.*

" 'And half of the city shall go forth into captivity,' means that half of Jerusalem will fall to the advances of the Antichrist, with the other half fighting furiously to save themselves, but with futility, other than the Coming of the Lord. Actually, the phrasing of the sentence structure portrays Israel fighting with a ferocity that knows no bounds, but yet not able to stand against the powerful onslaught of the combined armies of the man of sin.

" 'And the residue of the people shall not be cut off from the city,' refers to the army of Israel already cut to pieces, but determined to defend the city, even house to house, and, if necessary, to die to the last man.)

JESUS CHRIST THE WARRIOR

"Then shall the LORD go forth, and fight against those nations, as when He fought in the day of battle. *('Then' is the key word!*

"1. 'Then': when Israel will begin to cry to God for Deliverance, knowing that He is their only hope.

"2. 'Then': when half of Jerusalem has fallen and it looks like the other half is about to fall.

"3. 'Then': when it looks like every Jew will be annihilated, with two-thirds already killed.

"4. 'Then': when it looks like the Promises of God made to the Patriarchs and Prophets of old will fall down.

"5. 'Then': when it looks like the Antichrist will win this conflict, which will make Satan the lord of the Earth.

" 'Then shall the LORD go forth,' refers to the Second Coming, which will be the most cataclysmic event that the world has ever known. 'And fight against those nations,' pertains to the nations under the banner of the Antichrist, which have set out to destroy Israel, and actually with annihilation in mind.

" 'As when He fought in the day of battle,' probably

refers to the time when the Lord led the Children of Israel out of Egypt by way of the Red Sea [Ex. 14:14; 15:3]. This was Israel's first battle when Jehovah Messiah 'went forth' and fought for them. Israel then passed through a valley between mountains of water; in this, their last battle, they will escape through a valley between mountains of rock, which the next Verse proclaims.)

THE ACTUAL EVENT OF THE SECOND COMING

"And His Feet shall stand in that day upon the Mount of Olives, which is before Jerusalem on the east, and the Mount of Olives shall cleave in the midst thereof toward the east and toward the west, and there shall be a very great valley; and half of the mountain shall move toward the north, and half of it toward the south. *(The first phrase refers to Christ literally standing on the Mount of Olives, which will be His landing point at the Second Coming, fulfilling the prediction of the two Angels at His Ascension [Acts 1:10-11]. 'And the Mount of Olives shall cleave in the midst thereof toward the east and toward the west,' actually speaks of a great topographical change, which Israel will use at that hour as a way of escape from the Antichrist. With every road blocked, the Lord will open a way through the very center of the mountain, as He opened a path through the Red Sea.*

" 'And there shall be a very great valley,' refers to the escape route of Israel. 'And half of the mountain shall remove toward the north, and half of it toward the south,' refers to the wall of rock on either side of escaping Israel, which makes it similar to the wall of water on either side when Israel escaped Egypt)" **(Zech. 14:1-4).**

THE LORD JESUS CHRIST AND THE KINGDOM AGE

The coming Kingdom Age which will last for 1,000 years

will begin immediately at the Second Coming. Our Lord will Personally set up His Headquarters in a beautifully rebuilt Jerusalem, described by the great Prophet Ezekiel in the last nine Chapters of the Book that bears his name.

The Prophet Isaiah had more to say about this coming time than any other Prophet. It will be a time of prosperity and freedom such as the world has never known before. There will be no more war, and as well, no more want. Jesus Christ will reign supreme, and Israel at that time, will finally do that for which they were raised up to do.

Concerning the administration of our Lord, the Scripture says:

"But with Righteousness shall He judge the poor, and reprove with equity for the meek of the Earth: and He shall smite the Earth with the rod of His Mouth, and with the breath of His Lips shall He slay the wicked. *(The 'smiting of the Earth' might be better stated 'the oppressor of the land,' referring to the Antichrist. The word 'reprove' means 'to set right with equity,' or 'to administer justice on behalf of the meek.')*

"And Righteousness shall be the girdle of His Loins, and Faithfulness the girdle of His Reins. *(This Verse presents Immanuel as Priest. The 'loins' speak of the physical, with the 'reins' speaking of the heart and, therefore, the spiritual. For the first time, the human family in Christ will witness perfection. In fact, the Man Christ Jesus will be girdled with Perfection)*" (Isa. 11:4-5).

THE LORD JESUS CHRIST AND
THE PERFECT AGE TO COME

John the Beloved gives us the description of this coming Age, referred to as the *"Perfect Age,"* which, in fact, will last forever. At that time, God will transfer His Headquarters, so to speak, from Planet Heaven to Planet Earth, where it will there abide forever. In fact, He will bring down the entirety of the New Jerusalem, a city 1,500 miles wide, 1,500 miles long, and 1,500 miles high (Rev. 21:16). A city 1,500 miles wide, and 1,500 miles long, is almost incomprehensible; however, a city 1,500 miles high is beyond the pale of one's imagination.

Concerning that city, the Scripture says:

"**And the city had no need of the sun, neither of the moon, to shine in it** *(proclaims the fact that the Creator is not in need of His Creation; God has need of nothing, but all have need of God)*: **for the Glory of God did lighten it, and the Lamb** *is* **the Light thereof.** *(The word 'Lamb' signifies that all of this is made possible for Believers as a result of what Christ did at the Cross)*" (**Rev. 21:23**).

THE KINGDOM DELIVERED UP TO THE FATHER

When all evil has been expunged from the Universe, which will take place after the Millennial Reign. Concerning this time, the Scripture says:

"**Then** *comes* **the end** *(does not refer to the time immediately following the Rapture or even the Second Coming, but rather to when all Satanic rule and authority have been put down, which will take place at the conclusion of the Millennial Reign [Rev., Chpt. 20])*, **when He** *(Jesus)* **shall have delivered up the Kingdom to God, even the Father; when He shall have put down all rule and all authority and power.** *(He will have put down all of Satan's rule, etc.; the means of which were made possible by the Cross and the Resurrection.)*

"**For He** *(Jesus)* **must reign** *(refers to the 1,000 year reign of Christ on Earth after He returns)*, **till He has put all enemies under His Feet** *(the subjugation of all evil powers, which will take place at the conclusion of the Millennial Reign [Rev., Chpt. 20])*.

"The last enemy *that* shall be destroyed *(abolished)* is
death *(Death is the result of sin [Rom. 6:23], and the Cross
addressed all sin. After the Resurrection, when all Saints
are given glorified bodies, it will be impossible to sin. Even
during the Millennial Reign, sin will still be in the world,
but not in the Glorified Saints. It will be eradicated when
Satan and all his fallen Angels and demon spirits, plus all
people who followed him, are cast into the Lake of Fire,
where they will remain forever [Rev., Chpt. 20]. Death will
then be no more.)*

"For He has put all things under His Feet. *(God the
Father has put all things under the Feet of Jesus.)* But when
He said all things are put under *Him, it is* manifest that
He is excepted, which did put all things under Him. *(This
has reference to the fact that 'all things' do not include God
the Father being made subject to Jesus. God is excepted,
as should be obvious.)*

"And when all things shall be subdued unto Him
*(implies that in Paul's day, this total dominion had not yet
been exercised and, in fact, has not done so unto this present hour; but the time will come when it definitely shall be,
which will be at the close of the Millennial Reign)*, then
shall the Son also Himself be subject unto Him Who put
all things under Him, that God may be all in all. *(There
will be no trace of evil left anywhere in the Universe)*"
(I Cor. 15:24-28).

AMEN

John the Beloved closed out the Canon of Scripture with
the following words. He said:

"The Grace of our Lord Jesus Christ *(presents John
using the very words of Paul in his closing benediction;
Christ is the Source, but the Cross is the Means)* be with
you all. Amen. *(This proclaims the fact that it is the same*

Message for all, and is available to all. The word 'Amen' closes out the Book of Revelation, and, in fact, the entire Canon of Scripture, which took about 1,600 years to bring forth in its entirety. It gives acclaim to the Finished Work of Christ. It is done. And, thereby, all of Heaven, along with all the Redeemed, must say: 'Amen')" **(Rev. 22:21).**

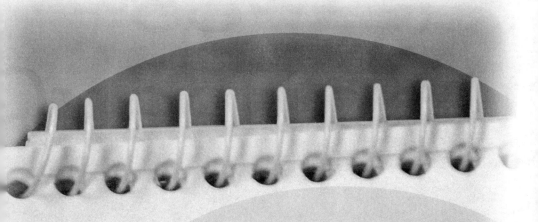

CHAPTER 10

The Doctrine Of Prayer

THE DOCTRINE OF PRAYER

If there is anything the Bible clearly and plainly teaches, it is prayer and the fact that God answers prayer.

Our Lord taught His Disciples, and you and me as well, how to pray. He said:

THE MANNER IN WHICH WE SHOULD PRAY

"**And in that day** *(after the Day of Pentecost)* **you shall ask Me nothing** *(will not ask Me Personally, as you now do)*. **Verily, verily, I say unto you, Whatsoever you shall ask the Father in My Name** *(according to what He did at the Cross, and our Faith in that Finished Work)*, **He will give** *it* **you** *(He places us in direct relationship with the Father, enjoying the same access as He Himself enjoys)*.

"**Hitherto have you asked nothing in My Name** *(while He was with them, the Work on the Cross had not been accomplished; so His Name could not be used then as it can be used now)*: **ask, and you shall receive** *(ask in His Name, which refers to the fact that we understand that all things are given unto us through and by what Christ did at the Cross)*, **that your joy may be full** *(it can only be full when we properly understand the Cross)*.

"**These things have I spoken unto you in Proverbs** *(concerns the Parables and, as well, His portraying Truths to them in a veiled way, and for purpose)*: **but the time comes, when I shall no more speak unto you in Proverbs, but I shall show you plainly of the Father** *(this could not be done until the Cross was a Finished Work; then the Holy Spirit could reveal things plainly, but only if one properly understands the Cross)*.

"**At that day** *(after the Day of Pentecost)* **you shall ask in My Name** *(in a sense, we are given the power of attorney)*: **and I say not unto you, that I will pray the Father for you** *(His very Presence before the Father guarantees* *that the Sacrifice of the Cross was accepted; therefore, all who truly follow Christ are instantly accepted as well; if Jesus had to pray to the Father for us, that would mean the Cross was not a Finished Work)*:

"For the Father Himself Loves you, because you have loved Me *(acceptance of Christ is acceptance by the Father)*, **and have believed that I came out from God** *(concerns the Faith of the Believer as it is registered in Christ)*.

"I came forth from the Father *(speaks of His Deity, and the Mission for which He was sent)*, **and am come into the world** *(but for one purpose, that was to go to the Cross that man might be Redeemed [I Pet. 1:18-20])*: **again, I leave the world, and go to the Father** *(the Mission is complete)*" (Jn. 16:23-28).

In these Passages, our Lord tells us several things.

THINGS WE NEED TO KNOW

• The words, *"in that day,"* refer to the time after the Cross is a fact, and more particularly, after the Day of Pentecost, for that's the Day that the Holy Spirit came in a new dimension, that is, to fill the hearts and lives of all Believers, and to do so permanently (Jn. 14:16-18).

• The phrase, *"You shall ask Me nothing,"* means that the mode of prayer, petitions, and requests, was to be changed. During His earthly Ministry, the Disciples were accustomed to asking Jesus Personally whatever it was they wanted or desired. He now tells them that that is about to change.

• They are now told when they pray that whatever it is that is needed, they should petition the Father directly in the Name of Jesus. Due to the Cross, Faith in Christ gives us instant access to the Father, which was not the case before the Cross.

• We are to ask in the *"Name of Jesus,"* simply because He is the One Who paid the price at Calvary's Cross. This means that we should not pray directly to the Holy Spirit, and neither should we pray directly to Jesus, but rather to the Father in the Name of Jesus.

• Praying in that manner, to the Father in the Name of Jesus, guarantees that the requests will be granted, that is, if it is the Will of God, because Jesus has paid for all of this at the Cross.

• These Passages completely lay to rest the idea that we pray to Mary, or some Saint, or even to Jesus, with Him taking our petition to the Father. He said, *"And I say not unto you, that I will pray the Father for you,"* meaning, inasmuch as we now have, due to what Christ did at the Cross, immediate access to the Father, the very Presence of Christ at the Throne, guarantees that we are heard, and that our petition is granted. As we stated in the notes, if Christ had to pass on our petition to the Father, this would mean that the Cross of Christ was not a Finished Work.

• The Cross opened up the way to the Throne of God, that all may come and drink of the water of life freely (Jn. 7:37-39; Heb. 4:15-16; Rev. 22:17).

The magnitude of what our Lord did for us in the giving of Himself as a Sacrifice on the Cross, has never yet been fully realized, and I doubt ever shall be. To truly plumb its depths, or to scale its heights, presents itself as beyond the scale of human proportion.

JESUS' TEACHING ON PRAYER

"And when you pray *(the necessity of prayer)*, you shall not be as the hypocrites *are*: for they love to pray standing in the Synagogues and in the corners of the streets, that they may be seen of men *(they do it for show)*. Verily I say unto you, They have their reward *(meaning that there will be no reward from God in any capacity)*.

"But you *(sincere Believer)*, when you pray, enter into your closet, and when you have shut your door, pray to your Father which is in secret; and your Father Who sees in secret shall reward you openly *(the word 'closet' is not to be taken literally, but means that our praying must not be done for show; if we make God's interests our own, we are assured that He will make our interest His Own).*

"But when you pray, use not vain repetitions, as the heathen *do (repeating certain phrases over and over, even hundreds of times)*: for they think that they shall be heard for their much speaking *(they will not be heard by God).*

"Be not you therefore like unto them: for your Father *(Heavenly Father)* knows what things you have need of, before you ask Him *(He is omniscient, meaning that He knows all things, past, present, and future)*" (Mat. 6:5-8).

Several things are said here in these Passages. They are:
• Don't pray for show, which Jesus said is hypocrisy. The Lord is not going to answer such.
• We are to seek the Face of the Lord with our petitions being in secret. In other words, it's between the Believer and the Heavenly Father.
• *"Vain repetition"* will not be heard either. Prayer must be from the heart, not merely repeating some phrase over and over. This means, as well, that prayer beads are out.

Jesus now gives us the model prayer that we should pray, in other words, that which gives us direction.

THE MODEL PRAYER

I will copy directly from **THE EXPOSITOR'S STUDY BIBLE**. Jesus said:

"After this manner therefore pray you *(is meant to be in total contrast to the heathen practice; as well, it is to be prayed in full confidence, that the Heavenly Father will hear and answer according to His Will)*: **Our Father** *(our prayer should be directed toward our Heavenly Father, and* *not Christ or the Holy Spirit)* **Who is in Heaven, Hallowed be Your Name** *(we reverence His Name)*.

"**Your Kingdom come** *(this will definitely happen at the Second Coming)*, **Your Will be done in Earth, as** *it is* **in Heaven** *(the Will of God is all-important; it will be carried out on Earth, beginning with the Kingdom Age)*.

"**Give us this day our daily bread** *(we are to look to the Lord for sustenance, both natural and spiritual)*.

"**And forgive us our debts, as we forgive our debtors** *(the word 'debts' here refers to 'trespasses' and 'sins'; His forgiveness on our part is predicated on our forgiving others)*.

"**And lead** *(because of self-confidence)* **us not into temptation** *(help us not to be led into testing — the idea is, in my self-confidence, which stems from the flesh and not the Spirit, please do not allow me to be led into temptation, for I will surely fail!)*, **but deliver us** *(the trap is more powerful than man can handle; only God can deliver; He does so through the Power of the Holy Spirit, according to our Faith in Christ and the Cross [Rom. 8:1-2, 11])* **from evil** *(the Evil One, Satan himself)*: **For Yours is the Kingdom** *(this Earth belongs to the Lord and not Satan; he is an usurper)*, **and the Power** *(God has the Power to deliver, which He does, as stated, through the Cross)*, **and the Glory** *(the Glory belongs to God, and not Satan)*, **forever** *(none of this will ever change)*. **Amen** *(this Word expresses a solemn ratification; in the Mind of God, the defeat and destruction of Satan and, therefore, all evil in the world, is a foregone conclusion)*" **(Mat. 6:9-13).**

THE CONDITIONS OF ANSWERED PRAYER

The idea of being able to call on the Lord, knowing that He is all-powerful, and all-knowing, and that He will answer our prayers, presents a help that is beyond comprehension. My grandmother taught me when I was a child that God heard

and answered prayer. Countless times she told me, *"Jimmy, God is a big God, so ask big!"* I have never forgotten that. To be frank, it has helped me to touch this world for Christ.

And yet, there are conditions for prayer to be heard and answered.

UNCONFESSED SIN

1. If there is unconfessed sin in our life, the Lord will not hear and answer prayer. He said through John the Beloved:

> "And hereby we know that we are of the Truth *(the evidence of love is the guarantee of Truth)*, and shall assure our hearts before Him. *(Am I loving as I ought to be? Our hearts will tell us!)*
>
> "For if our heart condemn us *(our failures in duty and service rise up before us, and our heart condemns us)*, God is greater than our heart *(the worst in us is known to God, and still He cares for us and desires us; our discovery has been an open secret to Him all along)*, and knows all things *(presents God Alone knowing our hearts; this is the true test of a man)*.
>
> "Beloved, if our heart condemn us not *(does not claim sinless perfection, but represents the heart attitude of a Saint that, so far as he knows, has no unconfessed sin in his life)*, ***then*** have we confidence toward God *(implies no condemnation)*.
>
> "And whatsoever we ask, we receive of Him *(speaks of prayer, and that we must keep asking for that which is desired)*, because we keep His Commandments *(Christ has already kept all of the Commandments; our Faith in Him and the Cross gives us His Victory, and is guaranteed by the Holy Spirit [Rom. 8:1-2, 11])*, and do those things that are pleasing in His Sight *(pertains to the fact that the Cross is ever the Object of our Faith [Heb. 11:6])*" (I Jn. 3:19-22).

BITTERNESS

2. If there is bitterness in our heart toward others, the Lord will not hear and answer prayer: John the Beloved also said:

"For this is the Message that you heard from the beginning, that we should love one another. *(The first attribute made evident in the new Christian is 'Love.')*

"Not as Cain, *who* was of that wicked one, and slew his brother *(presents the prototype of evil).* And wherefore slew he him? *(Cain was not a murderer because he killed his brother, but killed his Brother because he was a murderer.)* Because his own works were evil, and his brother's Righteous *(points directly to the Cross; the rejection of God's Way [the Cross], which Cain did, is labeled by the Holy Spirit as 'evil'; Abel accepted the Cross [Gen., Chpt. 4]).*

"Marvel not, my Brethren, if the world hate you *(expect no better treatment from the world than Abel received from Cain).*

"We know that we have passed from death unto life, because we love the Brethren *(love for the Brethren is the first sign of 'Spiritual Life').* He who loves not *his* Brother abides in death. *(Love for the Brethren must characterize the Salvation profession. Otherwise, our claims are false)*" (I Jn. 3:11-14).

FAITH

3. For prayer to be answer, as should be obvious, we must have Faith. Paul said:

"But without Faith *(in Christ and the Cross; anytime Faith is mentioned, always and without exception, its root meaning is that its Object is Christ and the Cross; otherwise,*

278 Brother Swaggart, How Can I Understand The Bible?

*it is faith God will not accept) **it is** impossible to please* ***Him*** *(faith in anything other than Christ and the Cross greatly displeases the Lord)*: **for he who comes to God must believe that He is** *(places Faith as the foundation and principle of the manner in which God deals with the human race)*, **and** *that* **He** *(God)* **is a rewarder of them who diligently seek Him** *(seek Him on the premise of Christ and Him Crucified)*" **(Heb. 11:6).**

UNFORGIVENESS

4. **Unforgiveness on our part will stop the Lord from answering prayer: Jesus said:**

"For if you forgive men *(it must be the God kind of forgiveness)* **their trespasses** *(large sins)*, **your Heavenly Father will also forgive you** *(forgiveness rests totally on the Atoning Work of Christ; it is an act of sheer Grace)*:
"But if you forgive not men their trespasses, neither will your Father forgive your trespasses *(if we want God to forgive us, we must at the same time forgive others; if not, His Forgiveness for us is withheld; consequently, such a person is in jeopardy of losing their soul)*" **(Mat. 6:14-15).**

THE WILL OF GOD

Should the Believer always preface his petitions to the Lord by the words *"If it be Your Will?"*
Sometimes yes, most of the time no!
Every Believer should be close enough to the Lord that they know and understand somewhat about His Ways. As a result, they should know His Will in most things. But to preface every petition with the words *"If it be Your Will,"* **is wrong, and actually hinders our faith, which means that it hinders us from receiving a positive answer.**
The Child of God, as stated, should know enough about

the Lord and His Ways to know what He wants and desires. That being the case, if the Believer asks for something amiss, as sometimes all of us have done, the Lord will step in and stop the situation. And that's exactly what we want Him to do.

A PERSONAL ILLUSTRATION

Sometime back, the Lord began to move upon my heart about obtaining a Radio Station in a particular city. We actually had looked at the Station a year earlier, but simply did not have the money to close the deal. And so now a year had passed, and I thought surely they had already sold the Station.

But feeling very strongly that I should give the owners a call, that I did. His answer was revealing.

He said, *"Brother Swaggart, we signed the papers yesterday to sell the Station to someone else; however, if he cannot live up to the contract, and you want the Station at the same price, it is yours."*

In prayer, I felt it even more strongly, so strong in fact, that I told my associate, *"The other man is going to fall down on the contract, and we'll get the Station."*

That's exactly what happened. Two days later the owner called, and said, *"If you want the Station, it's yours."*

But during the meantime I was seeking the Lord ardently. I found myself over and over again, saying, or words to this effect, *"Lord, we want this Station, that is if it's Your Will."*

Now that sounds right; however, it wasn't right.

The day before the Brother called and offered us the Station, in prayer, I greatly sensed that afternoon the Spirit of God. In praying about the Station, I once again said, *"Lord we want this Station if it be Your Will."* And the Lord spoke to my heart very forcibly and said, *"Don't use that terminology anymore."* When you say, *"If it be Your Will,"* you are hindering your Faith and, thereby, hindering Me from doing what I want to do.

"Have I not been dealing with you about this Station?" Of

course He had. He then said, *"Would I have been dealing with your heart about it if I didn't want you to have it?"* Of course, He wouldn't!

He said *"Now change your praying and say, 'Lord I claim this Station for the Glory of God, and I count it as mine.'"*

The Lord then told me, *"I know that you want My Will in all things. And if at times you make a mistake, and claim something that is not My Will, I will step in and stop the situation."*

THE DOUBLE-MINDED MAN

Forever prefacing our petition with the words, *"If it be Your Will,"* puts us into the position of a *"double-minded man."* And James said as it regards such:

"If any of you lack wisdom *(pertains to proper knowledge of the Word of God)*, **let him ask of God, Who gives to all** *men* **liberally** *(the Lord gives to those who ask, providing they ask the right thing; a greater knowledge of the Word of God is always the right thing)*, **and upbraideth not; and it shall be given him.** *(This means when we ask wisdom of Him, He will not reproach or chide us for our past conduct. He permits us to come in the freest manner, and meets us with a spirit of entire kindness, and with promptness in granting our requests.)*

"But let him ask in Faith *(some accuse James of denigrating Faith; however, he actually does the very opposite, making Faith a criteria for all things)*, **nothing wavering** *(nothing doubting).* **For he who wavers is like a wave of the sea driven with the wind and tossed.** *(He who continuously veers from one course to another only reveals his own instability and lack of a sense of being under Divine control.)*

"For let not that man think that he shall receive any thing of the Lord. *(This points to a particular type of individual, one who has a 'doubting heart.')*

"A double minded man *is* unstable in all his ways. *(One cannot place one's Faith in the Cross and something else at the same time. Such produces instability, a type of Faith that will never be honored by the Lord)*" **(James 1:5-8).**

ONE MORE HURDLE . . .

Now that the man had told us we could have the Station and, in fact, after we had signed the papers, I had to come up with the money. The truth was we didn't have any more money now than we had had a year before. But I took it to the Lord in prayer, as we take everything to the Lord in prayer.

In a few minutes time, He told me exactly what to do as it regarded raising the funds, which we did!

We as Believers have a mighty resource at our beck and call. With Faith, we need to take advantage of this mighty resource.

What a mighty God we serve!

THE WAY WE SHOULD PRAY

When we come before the Lord, we must always keep it in mind, that we are coming before the Throne of God, that which is so high and mighty as to defy all description. As a result, we should treat it accordingly.

First of all, and as stated, we should come to the Heavenly Father in the Name of Jesus. And then we should begin to thank Him for the many Blessings He has given us, and is giving at the present. In fact, the entire 100th Psalm proclaims this. It says, and we continue to quote from THE EXPOSITOR'S STUDY BIBLE:

"Make a joyful noise unto the LORD all ye lands. *(Seven times in these Psalms, men are commanded to make a 'joyful noise unto the LORD' [66:1; 81:1; 95:1-2; 98:4-6; 100:1]. 'Seven' is God's Number, speaking of totality, completion, perfection, fulfillment, and universality. This speaks of Christ reigning supreme in the Kingdom Age. Every country in the world will then serve Him.)*

"**Serve the LORD with gladness: come before His Presence with singing.** *(Then the theme of the world will be 'gladness and singing.')*

"**Know you that the LORD He is God: it is He Who has made us, and not we ourselves; we are His People, and the sheep of His Pasture.** *(Several things are said in this Verse:*

"*1. Jesus Christ is God, not Buddha, Muhammad, etc.;*

"*2. We are the product of His Hand, not a product of senseless, mindless evolution;*

"*3. He Saved us; we could not save ourselves;*

"*4. We are His People; and,*

"*5. We will forage in His Pasture, and a wonderful pasture it is!)*

"**Enter into His Gates with thanksgiving, and into His Courts with praise: be thankful unto Him, and bless His Name.** *(Even though this Verse refers to the old economy of God, in essence, it means that every Believer, when coming into our Lord's Presence in prayer, should begin with 'thanksgiving' and 'praise.')*

"**For the LORD is good; His Mercy is everlasting; and His Truth endures to all generations.** *(Everything else falls by the wayside, while 'His Truth' marches on, and does so forever)*" **(Ps. 100).**

Picking up on the Fourth Verse, before we start asking the Lord for everything, we should thank Him, as stated, for what He has already done for us, and for what He is presently doing. This is exactly what the Holy Spirit tells us to do. Many times in thanking Him and praising Him for that which He has done, He will bring to our mind a great moment in our Christian experience, where He waxed Himself great on our behalf, and renew it again in our spirit. This gives us Faith; it helps us to believe for the present and for the future.

LEADING AND GUIDANCE

We should then ask the Lord for leading and guidance in all things. The Holy Spirit wants total control in our lives; however, it must be control that we purposely give to Him. Even though He is God, and can do anything, as would be obvious, still, He will not take by force anything of ours, awaiting our humbling before Him, and acquiescing to His Desires and His Will. As the song says, *"The Lord knows the way through the wilderness."*

PETITION

After thanking the Lord for what He has done for us, and seeking for His Leading and Guidance in all things, we should then make known our needs to the Lord. We should be specific, because the Lord is able to do all things. We should pray in Faith believing that He is able. And then we should thank Him for hearing us, and allowing us to come into His Presence.

PRAISE

All throughout the time of prayer, following the guidelines we have laid down, everything should be interspersed with praise. For He is worthy to be praised. In fact, over half of our praying, the seeking of His Face, and the bringing of our petitions to Him, should be given over to Praise and Worship. We will find at times, as well, as the Spirit of the Lord comes upon us that we will begin to praise the Lord in Tongues, which means that now we are praying solely from our spirit (I Cor. 14:14). The truth is, when we *"pray solely in the Spirit,"* there is no danger of a mistake; nevertheless, most of our praying will be in our native language, as should be obvious.

INTERCESSORY PRAYER

Prayer intercessors are quite possibly the most valuable

people in the Kingdom of God. I know of no higher place or Calling.

Almost always when the Lord is going to do something, and irrespective as to where it may be done in the world, He will begin to lay a burden on the hearts and lives of Intercessors, as they begin to pray about things, many times of which they have little knowledge of. But the Spirit of God will pray through them.

The burden He lays upon such hearts may be for a mission's effort somewhere in the world. It may be for Revival in general. It might be something respecting a particular need regarding an individual. In fact, I personally believe that anything and everything that's done for the Lord on this Earth, is when the Holy Spirit moves upon Intercessors as it regards the situation, with them praying this thing through, whatever it might be. It might be something that would last only for a short period of time, and it may be a burden that would last for months. But until intercessory prayer goes forth, I personally feel that this Work for God, whatever it might be, and whatever direction it might take, cannot be carried out.

AN EXAMPLE

Back when we were conducting Crusades all over the nation and, in fact, around the world, we had just finished a Meeting in Norfolk, Virginia. The Lord had given us a great meeting with many people Saved, and many baptized with the Holy Spirit.

In those days, the Ministry owned an old DC3. It was a twin engine airplane, actually built during WWII, and used as a transport in the service of this great conflict. It was a comfortable plane, but not very fast. At any rate, as we left that night out of Norfolk on our way to Baton Rouge, Louisiana, we ran into a line of thunderstorms. Actually, some 37 people were killed in plane crashes that night as a result of those storms.

Physically exhausted from the meeting, I had laid down on the floor between the seats to try to drift off to sleep. I actually don't remember whether I had drifted off or not, but I do remember all of a sudden, the plane began to be bounced all over the sky. And then I heard it, the left engine was missing. It was raining so hard that I couldn't even see the wing tips on the plane. But I could certainly hear that engine missing.

I looked ahead and the door was open to the cockpit, and I could see the radar with the lights swinging back and forth. I found out just a little later that the storm had knocked out our radar. In effect, we were flying blind.

My pilots were calling frantically, *"Mayday, Mayday!"*

They finally got through to a 737 passenger jet. The pilot hearing the distress call answered my pilots and said, *"My radar is working fine, and I know exactly where you are."* He then went on to say, *"I will slow down my plane just above stall speed, and hopefully I can keep you on my radar and show you a way through this storm."* And that's exactly what he did.

INTERCESSION ON OUR BEHALF

Some days later, Frances and I were in Lakeland, Florida, in a Crusade. An Evangelist friend of mine was on the platform along with other preachers as well.

At a particular time, he turned to me and quietly whispered, *"Brother Swaggart, on the Sunday night* (and he gave the date), *were you in an airplane, and were you in trouble?"*

I quickly turned and looked at him with astonishment, knowing that he knew nothing about this situation, because we had not related it to anyone.

I said to him, *"Yes, we were in a storm, but how did you know?"*

He said, *"I didn't know. Sunday night after getting home from Church, my wife and I had retired to bed, and then I felt it so very strongly. I said to my wife. The Lord has just laid Brother Swaggart on my heart. He's in an airplane, and he's in trouble. Let's pray."*

He then told me that he and his wife fell on their knees and began to intercede before the Lord on my behalf. He said they prayed until they felt victory in their soul.

Now that's what I'm talking about! I've had such to happen to me any number of times, as people, as much as a thousand miles away from where we were, would feel led of the Lord to hold Frances and I up to the Lord in prayer. Sometimes the Lord would tell them the problem, and sometimes He wouldn't. But at any rate that is the Holy Spirit empowering a person to intercede on behalf of another. As we have stated, it might be for an individual, it might be for a Revival, it might be for an entire nation, but it's that which is so very, very important.

Actually, this is the crying need of the hour, and I speak of God-called Intercessors, who can hear from Heaven, and can pray a situation through. Many of you reading this may not know exactly what I'm talking about, but many of you will. This is the strength of the Church! This is the Power of the Holy Spirit in action! This is Intercessory Prayer! If Abraham had not interceded for Lot, quite possibly his nephew would have been forever lost (Gen. Chpt. 18).

PRAYING IN THE SPIRIT

While we have briefly alluded to praying in other Tongues this, as well, is quite possibly one of the most important aspects of the Lord helping and strengthening one of His Children. Worshipping the Lord in Tongues, as we have stated, presents our spirit praying, which means that we do not know exactly what we are saying, but we do know that it is *"the wonderful Works of God"* (Acts 2:11).

Stress, nervous disorders, emotional lows, etc., are just a few of the problems facing the modern Believer. But the Lord has an answer for that. Beautifully enough, He gave us the solution to these problems some 750 years before Christ, and did so through the great Prophet Isaiah.

He said:

REST AND REFRESHING

"For with stammering lips and another tongue will He speak to this people. *(The phrase, 'stammering lips,' refers to a proper language being spoken, but yet the people hearing it would not understand it. Paul quoted this same Passage as it regards the Gift of Tongues as a sign to unbelievers [I Cor. 14:21-22]. Oftentimes, the Holy Spirit used strange circumstances to present Prophecy proclaiming tremendously important coming events, even as this Prophecy does.*

"Such also was the Prophecy given through Isaiah of the Birth of Christ through a 'virgin' [Isa. 7:14]. The occasion would be the unbelief, ridicule, and scorn of wicked Ahaz.

"Therefore, it seems that the Holy Spirit designed both these Prophecies [the Virgin Birth of Christ and the Baptism with the Holy Spirit], to occasion Faith in Believers and unbelief in mockers!)

"To whom He said, this is the rest wherewith you may cause the weary to rest; and this is the refreshing: yet they would not hear. *(Coupled with Verse 11, this tells us that speaking with other Tongues brings about a 'rest' from the tiredness of the journey of life. As well, speaking with other Tongues brings about a 'refreshing,' which rejuvenates the person. Many people ask, 'What good is there in speaking with other Tongues?' This mentioned by Isaiah presents two Blessings, of which there are many. Regrettably, despite this tremendous Gift given to the people of God, at least to those who will believe, like Judah of old, most 'will not hear' even as Paul quoted Isaiah [I Cor. 14:21])"* (Isa. 28:11-12).

PERSONAL

Coming from my house to the office, I generally leave the house at approximately 6 a.m. each morning. At that time, over the SonLife Radio Network of some 80 Stations scattered all across the nation, my grandson Gabe and Jill, his wife, are always reading from **THE EXPOSITOR'S STUDY BIBLE.** Gabe reads the Text, while Jill reads the notes. They read for one hour.

At any rate, my radio is always on at this time, as I listen to them read the Word. There is nothing in the day that refreshes me more than this. Almost every morning, the Spirit of God, as I hear them read the Scriptures plus the comments, will come upon me, and I will begin to worship the Lord in Tongues. Almost all the time it's done subconsciously, meaning that it's not done out loud at all, but to be sure, it brings about the *"rest"* and the *"refreshing."*

While the problems do not leave, somehow I sensed a peace, which comes to me from the Spirit of God as it flows through my soul as I worship the Lord in Tongues and that lets me know that these problems will be handled, irrespective as to what they are.

This is God's Answer, as stated, for emotional disturbances, for nervous disorders, for stress, and for the pressures of life. And yet, all too few Believers take advantage of this most glorious privilege.

I think it would be most appropriate for us to close this Chapter on prayer, with the Shepherd's Psalm.

THE SHEPHERD'S PSALM

"**The LORD is My Shepherd; I shall not want.** *(Even though this beautiful Psalm applied to David and to all Believers as well, more than all it applied to Christ.*

"Williams says, 'Only one voice sang this Psalm in perfect tune. It was the Voice of Jesus. When walking through the dark valley of His earthly Life, Jehovah was His Shepherd. There is no suggestion of sin in the Psalm. Its great theme is not so much what Jehovah gives or does, as What and Who He is.'

"And yet, at the same time, as Christ presents Himself as the Sheep, He is also presented as the Great Shepherd of His People, for He was raised from the dead in order to be such [Heb. 13:20]).

"He makes me to lie down in green pastures *(any other voice that is followed will lead only to barren pastures)*: **He leads me beside the still waters.** *(The 23rd Psalm makes it abundantly clear that the Church is not the Saviour, neither is religious hierarchy the Saviour, neither are rules and regulations the Saviour. Only the Lord is. We can follow Him, or we can follow other things; we cannot follow both.)*

"He restores my soul *(when the sheep skin their forehead foraging for grass, the shepherd would pour oil over the wounds)*: **He leads me in the paths of Righteousness for His Name's sake.** *(At times the lamb will leave the appointed path, even doing so several times, being retrieved each time by the shepherd. But if it leaves too many times, the Shepherd upon retrieving it from the rocky crevices will take his staff and break one of the legs. He then carefully 'sets' the leg, and then lays the lamb on his shoulder, close to his heart. He carries it until the wound is healed. That is a symbol of chastisement [Heb. 12:5-11.])*

"Yea, though I walk through the valley of the shadow of death, I will fear no evil *(the powers of darkness, constituting powerful attacks by Satan)*: **for You are with me; Your Rod and Your Staff they comfort me.** *(The ideal position for the 'lamb' is to allow the shepherd to fight for him. In fact, the only fight we are told to fight is the 'good fight of Faith' [I Tim. 6:12].*

"What a comfort it is to know that the 'rod' and 'staff' are constantly beating back the powers of darkness on our behalf.)

"You prepare a table before me in the presence of my enemies *(and these 'enemies' cannot touch this 'prepared table')*: **You anoint my head with oil** *(a Type of the Holy*

Spirit); **my cup runs over** *(a figure of speech that refers to abundance)*.

"**Surely goodness and mercy shall follow me all the days of my life** *('goodness' gives us green pastures and still waters; 'mercy' retrieves us when we foolishly leave the 'paths of Righteousness')*: **and I will dwell in the House of the LORD forever** *(as long as the Lord is our Shepherd, we can expect all of this, 'all the days of our lives')*" **(Ps. 23).**

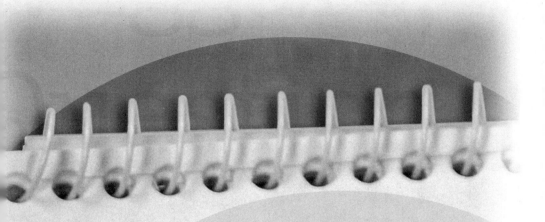

CHAPTER 11

The Doctrine Of Sanctification

THE DOCTRINE OF SANCTIFICATION

The Greek word for Sanctification is *"hagiazo,"* and means *"to make holy."* In fact, the word *"Holiness,"* basically means the same thing. To help us understand it a little better, it can be said to mean *"the setting apart from something to something."* In other words, we as Believers upon Faith in Christ and what He has done for us at the Cross are *"set apart from the world and unto Christ exclusively."*

Sanctification refers to *"making one clean, while Justification refers to declaring one clean."* In fact, one cannot be declared clean (Justified) until one has been made clean (Sanctified).

SANCTIFICATION, A POSITION IN CHRIST

The Truth is, we have been Sanctified as Believers, and we are being Sanctified as Believers.

Let me explain!

When the believing sinner comes to Christ, several things happen, and instantly. I'll quote from THE EXPOSITOR'S STUDY BIBLE:

> "Do you not know that the unrighteous shall not inherit the Kingdom of God? *(This shoots down the unscriptural Doctrine of Unconditional Eternal Security.)* Be not deceived *(presents the same Words of our Lord, 'let no man deceive you' [Mk. 13:5])*: neither fornicators, nor idolaters, nor adulterers, nor effeminate, nor abusers of themselves with mankind *(the proof of true Christianity is the changed life)*,
>
> "Nor thieves, nor covetous, nor drunkards, nor revilers, nor extortioners, shall inherit the Kingdom of God *(refers to those who call themselves 'Believers,' but yet continue to practice the sins mentioned, whom the Holy Spirit says are not Saved, irrespective of their claims).*
>
> "And such were some of you *(before conversion)*:

but you are washed *(refers to the Blood of Jesus cleansing from all sin)*, **but you are Sanctified** *(one's position in Christ)*, **but you are Justified** *(declared not guilty)* **in the Name of the Lord Jesus** *(refers to Christ and what He did at the Cross, in order that we might be Saved)*, **and by the Spirit of our God** *(proclaims the Third Person of the Triune Godhead as the Mechanic in this great Work of Grace)*" **(I Cor. 6:9-11).**

As is obvious from the Scripture, when the believing sinner comes to Christ, three things take place. They are:

1. We are Washed: This refers to the Blood of Christ, pertaining to His Death, Burial, and Resurrection, and our being placed in Him in all of this procedure, upon our conversion. John the Beloved said, *"Unto Him Who loved us, and washed us from our sins in His Own Blood"* (Rev. 1:5).

2. We are Sanctified: Inasmuch as we have been made clean by the Blood of Christ, we are now given a position of Sanctification, which is a position of perfection, and because it is all in Christ (Jn. 14:20). In fact, God cannot accept anything less. This position never changed, irrespective of our conduct. Paul said, *"For by one Offering, He has perfected forever them who are Sanctified"* (Heb. 10:14).

3. We are then Justified: As Sanctification made us clean, thereby giving us a position in Christ, Justification then declares us clean, declaring the work as a legal entity.

All of this, the Washing, the Sanctification, and the Justification, come instantly at conversion. Thank the Lord that soon, we will be *"Glorified,"* which will be the last step in this great process of Redemption (I Cor. 15:51-53).

SANCTIFICATION IS A PROCESS

As we have stated, we have been Sanctified and we are being Sanctified. The *"position"* of Sanctification given to us at conversion, is a position of perfection. As also stated, God can

accept nothing less. This is given to us only because of our Lord
Jesus Christ, and what He did for us at the Cross, and our Faith
in His Finished Work (Rom. 5:1-2). But we very soon find out
as a new Believer, that our *"condition"* is not exactly up to our
"position." And this is where the process of Sanctification
takes place, the process of *"being sanctified,"* as it regards our
daily life and living. In fact, this is a process that never ends.
Paul said:

> **"And the very God of Peace Sanctify you wholly** *(this
> is 'progressive Sanctification,' which can only be brought
> about by the Holy Spirit, Who does such as our Faith is
> firmly anchored in the Cross, within which parameters the
> Spirit always works; the Sanctification process involves the
> whole man)*; **and *I pray God* your whole spirit and soul
> and body** *(proclaims the makeup of the whole man)* **be
> preserved blameless unto the coming of our Lord Jesus
> Christ.** *(This refers to the Rapture. As well, this one Verse
> proclaims the fact that any involvement, whether Righteous
> or unrighteous, affects the whole man, and not just the
> physical body or the soul as some claim.)*
> **"Faithful *is* He Who calls you** *(God will do exactly what
> He has said He will do, if we will only believe Him)*, **Who also
> will do *it*** *(will Sanctify us wholly)*" **(I Thess. 5:23-24).**

HOW IS THE ONGOING PROCESS OF
SANCTIFICATION CARRIED OUT?

First of all, the Believer must understand that it's not possible for us to Sanctify ourselves. In fact, Churches have been
making up rules almost from the beginning, as it pertains to
the Sanctification process. It is the Holy Spirit Alone, Who can
bring about this process. In fact, at the moment of conversion,
the Holy Spirit comes into our hearts and lives in order to do
any number of things. But His greatest work is to *"Sanctify us
wholly."* Paul said:

"**For if ye live after the flesh** *(after your own strength and ability, which is outside of God's Prescribed Order)*, **you shall die** *(you will not be able to live a victorious, Christian life)*: **but if you through the Spirit** *(by the Power of the Holy Spirit)* **do mortify the deeds of the body** *(which the Holy Spirit Alone can do)*, **you shall live** *(shall walk in victory; but once again, even at the risk of being overly repetitive, we must never forget that the Spirit works totally and completely within the confines of the Cross of Christ; this means that we must ever make the Cross the Object of our Faith, giving Him latitude to work)*" **(Rom. 8:13).**

THE MANNER IN WHICH
THE HOLY SPIRIT WORKS

As we said in the notes above, and quoting from THE EXPOSITOR'S STUDY BIBLE, the Holy Spirit works exclusively by and through the Cross of Christ. In fact, this is so much a position of the Holy Spirit that He refers to it as a *"Law."* He said through Paul, and again I quote from THE EXPOSITOR'S STUDY BIBLE:

"**For the Law** *(that which we are about to give is a Law of God, devised by the Godhead in eternity past [I Pet. 1:18-20]; this Law, in fact, is 'God's Prescribed Order of Victory')* **of the Spirit** *(Holy Spirit, i.e., 'the way the Spirit works')* **of Life** *(all life comes from Christ, but through the Holy Spirit [Jn. 16:13-14])* **in Christ Jesus** *(any time Paul uses this term or one of its derivatives, he is, without fail, referring to what Christ did at the Cross, which makes this 'life' possible)* **has made me free** *(given me total Victory)* **from the Law of Sin and Death** *(these are the two most powerful Laws in the Universe; the 'Law of the Spirit of Life in Christ Jesus' alone is stronger than the 'Law of Sin and Death'; this means that if the Believer attempts to live for God by any manner other than Faith in Christ and the*

Cross, he is doomed to failure)" **(Rom. 8:2).**

THE CROSS OF CHRIST

This means that our Faith as a Believer must always and without exception rest in the Cross of Christ, for that's where all victory was purchased, and by the precious, shed Blood of Jesus Christ (Rom. 6:1-14; 8:1-2, 11; I Cor. 1:17-18, 23; 2:2; Gal., Chpt. 5; 6:14; Eph. 2:13-18; Col. 2:14-15).

When the Believer places his Faith exclusively in Christ and the Cross (Lk. 9:23), then the Holy Spirit, Who works exclusively within the parameters of the Cross of Christ, i.e., *"The Finished Work of Christ,"* will then begin to work mightily on behalf of the Believer. He doesn't require much of us, but He does require that our Faith be exclusively in Christ and the Cross. Then and only then can He bring about the Sanctification process in our lives, in that we will *"grow in Grace and in the Knowledge of the Lord"* (II Pet. 3:18).

This is the only manner in which the Sanctification process, in other words to bring our *"condition"* up to our *"position"* can be brought about.

IS SANCTIFICATION A WORK OF GRACE?

Everything we receive from the Lord, including Sanctification, is a work of Grace. Grace is simply the Goodness of God extended to undeserving people. The whole process is by Faith, as the whole process can only be by Faith. More than all, it refers to the correct Object of Faith, which must be the Cross of Christ. Unfortunately, Believers make everything and anything the object of their faith, except the Cross of Christ. When this is done, even though the Holy Spirit remains with us, and will do all He can to help us, still, we greatly limit Him when we make something other than the Cross the object of our Faith. Again we emphasize:

Everything that's done in our hearts and lives can only be

done by the Holy Spirit. Rules and regulations, no matter how sincere, will never bring about Righteousness (Gal. 2:21). We must never forget, while Jesus Christ is always the *"Source"* of all things that we receive from God, the Cross of Christ is the *"Means"* by which these things are received, all superintended by the Holy Spirit (Rom. 8:1-2, 11).

IS THERE SUCH A THING AS ENTIRE SANCTIFICATION?

The term *"entire Sanctification"* is meant to imply, that the Believer can have a particular experience with the Lord, where he is entirely sanctified, meaning as some understand it, that such a person has attained to sinless perfection. The Bible does not teach such! It does teach Sanctification as a *"position,"* even as we have already explained, and it teaches *"progressive Sanctification,"* but it does not teach *"entire Sanctification."*
Concerning all of this, Paul said:

"Not as though I had already attained, either were already perfect *(the Apostle is saying he doesn't claim sinless perfection)*: but I follow after *(to pursue)*, if that I may apprehend *(Paul is pursuing absolute Christlikeness)* that for which also I am apprehended of Christ Jesus. *(He was Saved by Christ for the purpose of becoming Christlike, and so are we!)*

"Brethren, I count not myself to have apprehended *(in effect, repeats what he said in the previous Verse)*: but *this* one thing *I do,* forgetting those things which are behind *(refers to things the Apostle had depended upon to find favor with God, and the failure that type of effort brought about [3:5-6])*, reaching forth unto those things which are before *(all our attention must be on that which is ahead, and not on what is past; 'those things' consists of all the victories of the Cross),*

"I press toward the mark *(this represents a moral and*

Spiritual Target) **for the prize of the high Calling of God** *(Christlikeness)* **in Christ Jesus** *(proclaims the manner and means in which all of this is done, which is the Cross [I Cor. 1:17-18; 2:2])*" **(Phil. 3:12-14).**

If the Apostle Paul did not consider himself to be entirely Sanctified, I certainly don't think we should either. In Truth, the process of being Sanctified, is a work carried on by the Holy Spirit, which will continue until the Lord calls us home, or the Trump sounds. The Holy Spirit carries this forth according to our Faith ever being in Christ and what He did for us at the Cross.

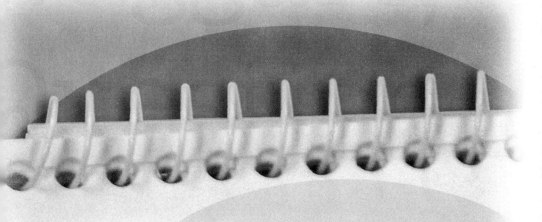

CHAPTER 12

The Doctrine Of Satan

THE DOCTRINE OF SATAN

"Be sober, be vigilant; because your adversary the Devil, as a roaring lion, walks about, seeking whom he may devour" (I Pet. 5:8).

WHO IS SATAN?

The Bible presents Satan as a personal being. He is an Angel, created by God, perhaps as the most wise and the most beautiful of all the Angels. The evidence is, he served the Lord in Righteousness and Holiness for an undetermined period of time.

He was named *"Lucifer,"* which means *"light bearer,"* or *"son of the morning."* He carries a number of names in the Old Testament and the New Testament. These include the Devil, the Serpent, the Accuser of the brethren, and the Prince of the power of the air.

The Hebrew word is *"Satan,"* which means *"adversary."* The Greek carries the same meaning. The common name of Satan in the New Testament is *"diabolos,"* which means *"Devil,"* meaning *"one who slanders or accuses."*

All of this means that Satan is not merely a principal, or a figure of speech, but actually a personal being who heads up his kingdom of darkness. His pride and warped desire to take God's place in the universe introduced sin. His initial rebellion, whenever that occurred, included the defection of many Angels, possibly as many as one-third (Rev. 12:4).

Although the Bible clearly pronounces his doom, he is so deceived, that he believes that he will ultimately be the god of Heaven, and the god of this world, and actually the entirety of the universe. In fact, his greatest effort of usurping God is yet ahead. It will be the time when he will invest in a man, the Antichrist, greater power than previously invested in anyone.

Some may ask the question as to how he thinks that as a created being, he can win out over the Creator. While that aim is preposterous to Believers, it is not at all preposterous to him. As stated, he is so deceived, even as are his billions of followers, that he actually thinks he will succeed.

He is the cause of all evil, all war, all pain and suffering, all heartache, all destruction in the world today and, in fact, ever has been. Sin is the means by which all of this is brought about. In fact, as far as we know, Satan is the originator of sin.

WHY DID SATAN FALL?

The only information we have on that subject is found in the Bible, and the Holy Spirit was very sparse in His enlightenment on this subject. Actually, the Bible is not the story of the creation, and fall of Lucifer and the Angels who threw in their lot with him, but rather the story of man's Fall and Redemption, which, of course, is by the Lord Jesus Christ and what He did at Calvary. But what information is given does let us in on certain things. I'm going to copy directly from THE EXPOSITOR'S STUDY BIBLE. It says:

THE PERFECTION OF BEAUTY AND WISDOM

"Son of man, take up a lamentation upon the king of Tyrus, and say unto him, Thus says the Lord GOD; You seal up the sum, full of wisdom, and perfect in beauty. *(As is obvious, even though the king of Tyrus is used as a symbol, the statements made could not refer to any mere mortal. In fact, they refer to Satan.*

"The phrase, 'You seal up the sum,' means that Lucifer, when originally created by God, was the perfection of wisdom and beauty. In fact, the phrase intimates that Lucifer was the wisest and most beautiful Angel created by God, and served the Lord in Holiness and Righteousness for a given period of time.

"'Perfect in beauty,' means that he was the most beautiful of God's Angelic creation. The Holy Spirit even labeled his beauty as 'perfect.')

"You have been in Eden the Garden of God; every precious stone was your covering, the sardius, topaz, and the diamond, the beryl, the onyx, and the jasper, the sapphire, the emerald, and the carbuncle, and gold: the workmanship of your tabrets and of your pipes was prepared in you in the day that you were created. *('You have been in Eden the Garden of God,' does not actually refer to the 'Eden' of Gen., Chpt. 3, but rather to the 'Eden' which existed on this Planet before Adam and Eve, which evidently was ruled by Lucifer before his rebellion.*

MUSIC?

" 'Every precious stone was your covering,' presents itself as very similar to the dress of the High Priest of Israel [Ex. 28:19].

" 'The workmanship of your tabrets and of your pipes,' has to do with music. There is every indication that Lucifer's leadership had something to do with the worship of God. As well, he is called, 'O Lucifer, son of the morning' [Isa. 14:12]. When the Earth was originally created, the Scripture says, 'The morning stars sang together, and all the sons of God shouted for joy' [Job 38:4-7]. So, if the idiom, 'son of the morning,' can be linked to the 'morning stars,' these Passages tell us that Lucifer, at least before his fall, was greatly used in leading the Worship of God.

"In fact, this is the reason that Satan has done everything within his power to corrupt the music of the world, and to corrupt the music of the Church above all. Inasmuch as the Book of Psalms is the longest Book in the Bible, we learn from this that music and singing are among the highest forms of worship of the Lord.)

THE ANOINTED CHERUB

"You are the anointed Cherub who covers; and I

have set you so: you were upon the Holy Mountain of God; you have walked up and down in the midst of the stones of fire.

"('You are the anointed Cherub who covers,' means that Lucifer was chosen and 'anointed' by God for a particular task and service. This probably was the 'worship' to which we have just alluded.

"'You were upon the Holy Mountain of God,' speaks of his place and position relative to the Throne [Rev. 4:2-11]. 'You have walked up and down in the midst of the stones of fire,' has reference to his nearness to the Throne [Ezek. 1:26-27]. As well, the phrase, 'Walked up and down,' seems to imply that not just any Angel would have been given such latitude.)

INIQUITY

"You were perfect in your ways from the day that you were created, till iniquity was found in you *(pride was the form of this iniquity [Lk. 10:17-18]. The rebellion of Lucifer against God probably caused the catastrophe which occurred between the First and Second Verses of Gen. Chpt. 1),*

"By the multitude of your merchandise they have filled the midst of you with violence, and you have sinned; therefore I will cast you as profane out of the Mountain of God: and I will destroy you, O covering Cherub, from the midst of the stones of fire. *('Violence' has been the earmark of Satan's rule and reign in the world of darkness [Jn. 10:10]. Lucifer being 'cast out' of the 'Mountain of God' refers to him losing his place and position, which he held with God since his creation. It was because 'he had sinned,' which spoke of pride that caused him to lift himself up against God.)*

"Your heart was lifted up because of your beauty, you have corrupted your wisdom by reason of your

brightness: I will cast you to the ground, I will lay you before kings, that they may behold you. *('Your heart was lifted up because of your beauty,' tells us the reason for his fall. As stated, it was pride. He took his eyes off of Christ, noticing his own beauty as it grew more and more glorious in his eyes. At some point in time, his 'heart' was changed from Christ to himself. As far as we know, this was the origin of evil in all of God's Creation.*

CORRUPTED WISDOM

" 'You have corrupted your wisdom by reason of your brightness,' does not refer to the loss of wisdom, but instead refers to wisdom corrupted, hence, the insidious design practiced upon the human family [Jn. 10:10].

" 'I will cast you to the ground,' refers to his ultimate defeat [Rev. 12:7-12]. 'I will lay you before kings, that they may behold you,' refers to him ultimately being cast into the Lake of Fire, where all the kings of the Earth who have died lost will behold him in his humiliation [Mat. 25:41; Rev. 20:10].)

"You have defiled your sanctuaries by the multitude of your iniquities, by the iniquity of your traffic; therefore will I bring forth a fire from the midst of you, it shall devour you, and I will bring you to ashes upon the Earth in the sight of all them who behold you. *(When Satan at long last will be thrown into the Lake of Fire [Rev. 20:10], all the billions he has duped, who also are in Hell because of him, will hate him with a passion that words cannot begin to express, and a hatred which will last forever and forever.)*

"All they who know you among the people shall be astonished at you: you shall be a terror, and never shall you be any more. *(Then the prayer of Christ, 'Your Will be done in Earth, as it is in Heaven,' will finally be answered and brought to pass [Mat. 6:9-10])"* **(Ezek. 28:12-19).**

PRIDE

As we have stated in the notes, Verse 17 proclaims to us the fact that it was pride which caused Lucifer's Fall. As a result, pride could very well be the sin that has caused more people to be lost than anything else.

As it regards the billions of unredeemed, it is pride that keeps them from Christ. They immerse themselves in other religions, of which all present their multitude of works, which appeal to the pride of man. So, most of the world thinks they're going to Heaven, and as they put it, if there is a Heaven, because of all the good things they have done, or the bad things they haven't done.

Unfortunately, pride continues to be the problem for the Believer. It is the greatest hindrance to the acceptance of the Cross. As *"works"* plague the unredeemed, likewise, they plague the redeemed also.

We like to think that our good works, whatever they might be, earn us something with God. To be told they don't, not at all, goes against our pride, in fact, greatly impacts our pride. It doesn't sit well!

THE CROSS OF CHRIST

The Cross of Christ lays man bare as nothing else! It shows him how worthless are his works, how worthless is his religion, how worthless is his personal righteousness, i.e., *"self-righteousness."* That is an offense. Paul said, and concerning this very thing:

"And I, Brethren, if I yet preach Circumcision, why do I yet suffer persecution? *(Any message other than the Cross draws little opposition.)* then is the offence of the Cross ceased. *(The Cross offends the world and most of the Church. So, if the preacher ceases to preach the Cross as the only way of Salvation and Victory, then opposition and persecution will cease. But so will Salvation!)"* **(Gal. 5:11).**

If the preacher is not preaching the Cross, then whatever it is he is preaching is not the Gospel, which means that no souls will be Saved, and no lives will be changed. That's why Paul said, *"We preach Christ Crucified"* **(I Cor. 1:23).**

Other than the Cross of Christ, there is no defense against sin, against Satan, against his cohorts of darkness, meaning that all Salvation, all victory, all answer to prayer, all blessing, come by and through the Cross of Christ. Let us say it again:

• Jesus Christ is the Source of all things that we receive from God (Jn. 14:6).

• The Cross of Christ is the Means by which these things are given (Rom. 6:3-5).

• Faith in Christ and the Cross is, as well, the Means by which all things are received (Rom. 6:1-3; I Cor. 1:17-18; 2:2; Col. 2:14-15).

• The Holy Spirit superintends all of this great Plan (Jn. 7:37-39; Eph. 2:18).

WHAT DOES SATAN HOPE TO ACCOMPLISH?

Once again, the answer to that question is given to us in the Word of God. And again, we quote directly from THE EXPOSITOR'S STUDY BIBLE. As the Prophet Isaiah said:

"How are you fallen from Heaven, O Lucifer, son of the morning! how are you cut down to the ground, which did weaken the nations! *(Isaiah's Prophecy now switches from the Antichrist to his unholy sponsor, Satan Himself.*

" *'Lucifer' is the name of Satan. Actually, he is an Angel, originally created by God, who served the Lord in Righteousness for an undetermined period of time.*

"*When he fell, he led a revolution against God, with about one-third of the Angels, it seems, throwing in their lot with him [Rev. 12:4]. Therefore, all the pain, suffering, misery, heartache, death, and deception, which have ruled the nations from the very beginning, can be laid at the doorstep of this revolution headed up by Satan.)*

"For you have said in your heart, I will ascend into Heaven, I will exalt my throne above the stars of God: I will sit also upon the mount of the congregation, in the sides of the north:

"I will ascend above the heights of the clouds, I will be like the Most High. *(In these two Verses, we see the foment of Satan's rebellion and revolution against God. It seems that Lucifer, while true to the Lord, was given dominion of the Earth, which was before Adam. After his fall, he worked deceitfully to get other angelic rulers to follow him in his war against God.)*

"Yet you shall be brought down to Hell, to the sides of the pit. *(This would be the lot of Satan and all who seek to be like God, but in a wrong way, in effect, by making themselves god)*" **(Isa. 14:12-15).**

WHY HAS GOD ALLOWED SATAN TO CONTINUE THESE THOUSANDS OF YEARS?

That's a good question! While we can speculate, that's the best that can be done. The Bible tells us that the reason that God has allowed Satan to continue these many millennia is a mystery.

Satan is a creature while God is the Creator. God can do away with the Evil One at any time with just one spoken Word. He has the Power to do so, as should be obvious. In fact, God's Power is totally unlimited, hence, Him being referred to as *"Almighty."*

So, considering all the heartache, the war, the pain, sickness, and suffering that this world has endured, I suppose that every Believer has asked himself, knowing that Satan is the cause of all this, as to why the Lord hasn't stopped him before now?

The Scripture says, and concerning this very thing:

"**But in the days of the voice of the seventh Angel, when he shall begin to sound** *(proclaims the beginning of the last half of the Great Tribulation, which will be worse than ever)*, **the Mystery of God should be finished** *(this 'Mystery' pertains to the reason God has allowed Satan to continue his reign over this Earth for these thousands of years [II Cor. 4:4])*, **as He has declared to His servants the Prophets** *(Isa. 14:12-20; Ezek. 28:11-19)*" **(Rev. 10:7).**

THE REASON!

Looking at the situation from a practical point of view, at least one of the reasons that the Lord has allowed the Evil One to continue, is that God uses the Devil, as He, in a sense, uses everything. Of course, this doesn't mean that the Lord is party to any of Satan's doings, as should be overly obvious, but that He allows Satan certain latitude in order that all the Saints of God be tested, which every one of us has been, and every one of us continues to be. Satan tempts in order to get us to fail, while the Lord tests in order for us to succeed. The opposition brought on by our adversary, is the greatest strengthening force for the Child of God, as we learn how to use our Faith, and to believe and trust the Lord.

VICTORY OVER SATAN

Paul tells us how this victory is brought about. He said:

"**Finally, my Brethren, be strong in the Lord** *(be continually strengthened, which one does by constant Faith in the Cross)*, **and in the power of His Might.** *(This power is at our disposal. The Source is the Holy Spirit, but the means is the Cross [I Cor. 1:18].)*

"**Put on the whole Armour of God** *(not just some, but*

all), **that you may be able to stand against the wiles of the Devil.** *(This refers to the 'stratagems' of Satan.)*

"For we wrestle not against flesh and blood *(our foes are not human; however, Satan constantly uses human beings to carry out his dirty work)*, **but against principalities** *(rulers or beings of the highest rank and order in Satan's kingdom)*, **against powers** *(the rank immediately below the 'Principalities')*, **against the rulers of the darkness of this world** *(those who carry out the instructions of the 'Powers')*, **against spiritual wickedness in high** *places.* *(This refers to demon spirits.)*

THE WHOLE ARMOUR OF GOD

"Wherefore take unto you the whole Armour of God *(because of what we face)*, **that you may be able to withstand in the evil day** *(refers to resisting and opposing the powers of darkness)*, **and having done all, to stand.** *(This refers to the Believer not giving ground, not a single inch.)*

"Stand therefore, having your loins gird about with Truth *(the Truth of the Cross)*, **and having on the Breastplate of Righteousness** *(the Righteousness of Christ, which comes strictly by and through the Cross)*;

"And your feet shod with the preparation of the Gospel of Peace *(peace comes through the Cross as well)*;

"Above all, taking the Shield of Faith *(ever making the Cross the Object of your Faith, which is the only Faith God will recognize, and the only Faith Satan will recognize)*, **wherewith you shall be able to quench all the fiery darts of the wicked.** *(This represents temptations with which Satan assails the Saints.)*

"And take the Helmet of Salvation *(has to do with the renewing of the mind, which is done by understanding that everything we receive from the Lord, comes to us through the Cross)*, **and the Sword of the Spirit, which is the Word of God** *(the Word of God is the Story of Christ and* *the Cross)*" **(Eph. 6:10-17).**

THE BELIEVER AND THE HOLY SPIRIT

When our Faith is placed exclusively in the Cross of Christ, understanding that it was there that all victory was won, and the Cross ever remains the Object of our Faith, the Holy Spirit, Who works exclusively within the parameters of the Finished Work of Christ, meaning that this gives Him the legal right and means to do all that He does, one will find Him working mightily within our hearts and lives, giving us victory over the world, the flesh, and the Devil. In brief, that is God's Prescribed Order of Victory.

SATAN'S ULTIMATE END

The Bible emphatically tells us, and in no uncertain terms, what the ultimate end of the Evil One is going to be. While he was totally defeated at Calvary's Cross, and in every capacity, yet the Lord has allowed him to continue. In fact, Satan's greatest effort at domination of the world is just ahead. And how does he think that he can succeed?

He knows what our Lord has said about the Word of God. I quote:

"**Think not that I am come to destroy the Law** *(this was the Law of Moses)*, **or the Prophets** *(the predictions of the Prophets of the Old Testament)*: **I am not come to destroy, but to fulfill** *(Jesus fulfilled the Law by meeting its just demands with a Perfect Life, and satisfying its curse by dying on the Cross [Gal. 3:13])*.

"**For verily I say unto you** *(proclaims the ultimate authority!)*, **Till Heaven and Earth pass** *(means to be changed, or pass from one condition to another, which will take place in the coming Perfect Age [Rev., Chpts. 21-22])*, **one jot** *(smallest letter in the Hebrew alphabet)* **or one**

tittle *(a minute ornamental finish to ancient Hebrew letters)* **shall in no wise pass from the Law, till all be fulfilled** *(the Law was meant to be fulfilled in Christ and was, in fact, totally fulfilled by Christ, in His Life, Death, and Resurrection, with a New Testament or New Covenant being brought about [Acts 15:5-29; Rom. 10:4; II Cor. 3:6-15; Gal. 3:19-25; 4:21-31; 5:1-5, 18; Eph. 2:15; Col. 2:14-17])"* **(Mat. 5:17-18).**

Satan knowing and realizing what Jesus said, and knowing that the Word of God is sacrosanct on all counts, knows that if he can cause one of the predictions to fail, then he has won the day. He will select the greatest prediction of all, and that is the restoration of Israel.

In other words, if he can destroy Israel, then he will have won this conflict, and for time and eternity. In other words, if he can destroy Israel, Satan will then be God, because God's Word has failed. So, while he has tried repeatedly to destroy these people even from the very beginning, his greatest effort is just ahead. It will be in the last half of the Great Tribulation and above all in the Battle of Armageddon.

Concerning this Battle, which will, no doubt, be the greatest ever fought, the Lord says:

ARMAGEDDON

"For I will gather all nations against Jerusalem to battle; and the city shall be taken, and the houses rifled, and the women ravished; and half of the city shall go forth into captivity, and the residue of the people shall not be cut off from the city. *(The first phrase refers to the mobilization of the nations to Armageddon [Ezek., Chpts. 38-39; Joel, Chpt. 3; Rev. 16:13-16; 19:11-21]. 'And the city shall be taken,' actually means that the Antichrist will prepare to take Jerusalem, with actually half of it being taken. The phrase, 'And the houses rifled, and the women ravished,' expresses extreme cruelty practiced by the army of the Antichrist.*

"*'And half of the city shall go forth into captivity,' means that half of Jerusalem will fall to the advances of the Antichrist, with the other half fighting fiercely to save themselves, but with futility, other than the Coming of the Lord. Actually, the phrasing of the sentence structure portrays Israel fighting with a ferocity that knows no bounds, but yet not able to stand against the powerful onslaught of the combined armies of the man of sin.*

"*'And the residue of the people shall not be cut off from the city,' refers to the army of Israel already cut to pieces, but determined to defend the city, even house to house, and, if necessary, to die to the last man.)*

THEN!

"Then shall the LORD go forth, and fight against those nations, as when he fought in the day of battle. *('Then' is the key word!*

"*1. 'Then': when Israel will begin to cry to God for Deliverance, knowing that He is their only hope.*

"*2. 'Then': when half of Jerusalem has fallen and it looks like the other half is about to fall.*

"*3. 'Then': when it looks like every Jew will be annihilated, with two-thirds already killed.*

"*4. 'Then': when it looks like the Promises of God made to the Patriarchs and Prophets of old will fall down.*

"*5. 'Then': when it looks like the Antichrist will win this conflict, which will make Satan the Lord of the Earth.*

"*6. 'Then shall the LORD go forth,' refers to the Second Coming, which will be the most cataclysmic event that the world has ever known. 'And fight against those nations' pertains to the nations under the banner of the Antichrist, which have set out to destroy Israel, and actually with annihilation in mind.*

" *'As when He fought in the day of battle,' probably refers to the time when the Lord led the Children of Israel out of Egypt by the way of the Red Sea [Ex. 14:14; 15:3]. This was Israel's first battle when Jehovah Messiah 'went forth' and fought for them. Israel then passed through a valley between mountains of water; in this, their last battle, they will escape through a valley between mountains of rock, which the next Verse proclaims)*" **(Zech. 14:2-3).**

THE SECOND COMING OF THE LORD

The Second Coming of the Lord will be the most cataclysmic event the world has ever known, and by far. In fact, there is no way that mere vocabulary could even begin to explain or to portray that which will take place at that particular time.

He will come in the very middle of the Battle of Armageddon when Satan will think that he has won the day. But that's when Israel will begin to cry to the Lord for help, and to be sure, the Lord will hear their cry. The Scripture says:

"And His Feet shall stand in that day upon the Mount of Olives, which is before Jerusalem on the east, and the Mount of Olives shall cleave in the midst thereof toward the east and toward the west, and there shall be a very great valley; and half of the mountain shall remove toward the north, and half of it toward the south. *(The first phrase refers to Christ literally standing on the Mount of Olives, which will be His landing point at the Second Coming, fulfilling the prediction of the two Angels at His Ascension [Acts 1:10-11]. 'And the Mount of Olives shall cleave in the midst thereof toward the east and toward the west,' actually speaks of a great topographical change, which Israel will use at that hour as a way of escape from the Antichrist. With every road blocked, the Lord will open a way through the very center of the mountain, as He opened a path through the Red Sea.*

" '*And there shall be a very great valley,' refers to the escape route of Israel. 'And half of the mountain shall remove toward the north, and half of it toward the south,' refers to the wall of rock on either side of escaping Israel, which makes it similar to the wall of water on either side when Israel escaped Egypt.)*

ALL THE SAINTS

"And you shall flee to the valley of the mountains; for the valley of the mountains shall reach unto Azal: yes, you shall flee, like as you fled from before the earthquake in the days of Uzziah king of Judah: and the LORD my God shall come, and all the Saints with you. *('And you shall flee to the valley of mountains,' should read 'through the valley.' As stated, this will be Israel's escape route from the Antichrist. 'For the valley of the mountains shall reach unto Azal,' probably refers to Bethezel, mentioned in Micah 1:11 as a village on the east of Olivet.*

" '*Yes, you shall flee,' is that the people might not be involved in the judgments which shall fall upon the enemy. The phrase, 'Like as you fled from before the earthquake in the days of Uzziah king of Judah,' also pertains to an earthquake, which the Lord will use to produce this phenomenon.*

" '*And the LORD my God shall come, and all the Saints with you,' pertains to the Lord coming at this particular time, which will have caused the cataclysmic events in the first place. The Passage, 'All the Saints with you,' refers to every Saint of God who has ever lived being with the Lord at the Second Coming [Rev. 19:14])*" **(Zech. 14:4-5).**

SATAN'S DEFEAT!

At that time, the time of the Battle of Armageddon, the Scripture says as it concerns Satan:

"And I saw an Angel come down from Heaven *(continues with the idea that Angels are very prominent in the Plan and Work of God)*, having the key of the bottomless pit *(speaks of the same place recorded in Rev. 9:1; however, there the key is given to Satan, but this Angel of Rev. 20:1 'has the key,' implying he has had it all along; more than likely, God allows this Angel to give the key to Satan in Rev. 9:1)* and a great chain in his hand *(should be taken literally)*.

"And he laid hold on the dragon, that old serpent, which is the Devil, and Satan *(as a 'dragon,' he shows his power; as a 'serpent,' he shows his cunning; as the 'Devil,' he is the accuser; and as 'Satan,' he is the adversary)*, and bound him a thousand years *(refers to being bound by the great chain carried by the Angel)*,

THE BOTTOMLESS PIT

"And cast him into the bottomless pit, and shut him up, and set a seal upon him *(speaks of the abyss being sealed to keep him there)*, that he should deceive the nations no more, till the thousand years should be fulfilled: and after that he must be loosed a little season. *(At the end of the thousand-year period, Satan will be loosed out of his prison. He will make another attempt to deceive the nations, in which he will not succeed. We aren't told how long this 'little season' will be)*" (Rev. 20:1-3).

The world will then enjoy a thousand year respite from Satan and all demon spirits, because the Evil One will be locked away in the bottomless pit for the entirety of this thousand year period. And then the Scripture says:

THE LAKE OF FIRE FOREVER AND FOREVER

Now we are told as to exactly what is going to happen to Satan and all who follow him, which will last forever and forever.

"And when the thousand years are expired *(should have been translated, 'finished')*, **Satan shall be loosed out of his prison** *(is not meant to infer a mere arbitrary act on the part of God; He has a very valid reason for doing this)*,

"And shall go out to deceive the nations which are in the four quarters of the Earth, Gog and Magog *(the main reason the Lord allows Satan this latitude is, it seems, to rid the Earth of all who oppose Christ; George Williams says: 'The Creation Sabbath witnessed the first seduction, and the Millennial Sabbath will witness the last'; the 'Gog and Magog' spoken of by John is a Hebrew term expressive of multitude and magnitude; here it embraces all nations, 'the four quarters of the Earth')*, **to gather them together to battle: the number of whom** *is* **as the sand of the sea** *(proclaims the fact that virtually all of the population at that particular time, which did not accept Christ during the Kingdom Age, will throw in their lot with Satan)*.

"And they went up on the breadth of the earth, and compassed the camp of the Saints about, and the beloved city *(pictures Satan coming against Jerusalem with his army, which will be the last attack against that city)*: **and fire came down from God out of Heaven, and devoured them.** *(Stipulates that the Lord will make short work of this insurrection. In fact, very little information is given regarding this event, as is obvious.)*

"And the Devil who deceived them was cast into the Lake of Fire and brimstone *(marks the end of Satan regarding his influence in the world and, in fact, in any part of the Creation of God)*, **where the Beast and the False Prophet** *are (proclaims the fact that these two were placed in 'the Lake of Fire and Brimstone' some one thousand years earlier [Rev. 19:20])*, **and shall be tormented day and night forever and ever.** *(This signifies the Eternity of this place. It is a matter of interest to note that Satan's* *first act is recorded in Gen., Chpt. 3 [the third Chapter from the beginning], whereas his last act on a worldwide scale is mentioned in Rev., Chpt. 20 [the third Chapter from the end])"* **(Rev. 20:7-10).**

Thus, the Word of God proclaims the final destination of the Evil One!

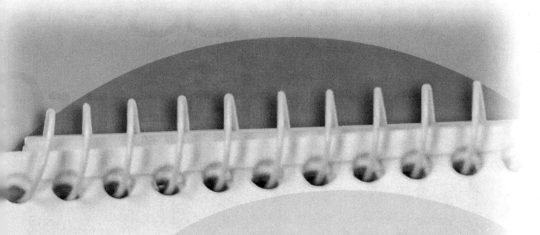

CHAPTER 13

The Doctrine Of Sin

THE DOCTRINE OF SIN

This subject, as distasteful as it is, is without a doubt, one of the single most important subjects in the entirety of the Word of God, i.e., *"Life and living."* The cause of all the heartache in the world, all the pain, sickness, suffering, death, hunger, war, man's inhumanity to man, is sin. The world doesn't understand that, and, therefore, continuously produces one panacea after the other which is supposed to solve the problem, but has no lasting affect at all. In fact, the answer to sin is not found in this world per se, it's not found in the mind of man and, in fact, cannot be found accordingly, but there is a remedy for sin. That remedy is, *"Jesus Christ and Him Crucified"* (I Cor. 1:23; 2:2). Regrettably, the world will not believe that, and sadder still, much of the Church doesn't believe it either. Nevertheless, there are literally multiplied millions of people down through the centuries, and even alive today, who have experienced the fact of the Heavenly Remedy, namely the Lord Jesus Christ, and have had their lives gloriously and wondrously changed. One might say it this way:
- The problem as it regards mankind is sin.
- The solution to that problem, and the only solution, is Jesus Christ and Him Crucified.

THE ORIGIN OF SIN

As far as we know, sin had its beginning with Lucifer, known as *"Satan."* From that origin of sin, the entirety of the heavens and the Earth, even the Creation, have been tainted. While the Bible does not give us much information regarding the origin of sin, instead specializing in its remedy, still, what it does give is revealing.

The great Prophet Ezekiel said the following, and I quote from THE EXPOSITOR'S STUDY BIBLE:

THE CREATION OF LUCIFER

"Moreover, the Word of the LORD came unto me,

saying *(the tenor of this Chapter will now change from the earthly Monarch, the 'Prince of Tyre,' to his sponsor, Satan, of which the earthly king was a symbol),*

"Son of man, take up a lamentation upon the king of Tyrus, and say unto him, Thus says the Lord GOD; You seal up the sum, full of wisdom, and perfect in beauty. *(As is obvious, even though the king of Tyrus is used as a symbol, the statements made could not refer to any mere mortal. In fact, they refer to Satan.*

"The phrase, 'You seal up the sum,' means that Lucifer, when originally created by God, was the perfection of wisdom and beauty. In fact, the phrase intimates that Lucifer was the wisest and most beautiful Angel created by God, and served the Lord in Holiness and Righteousness for a given period of time.

" 'Perfect in beauty,' means that he was the most beautiful of God's Angelic creation. The Holy Spirit even labeled his beauty as 'perfect.')

THE MANNER OF HIS CREATION

"You have been in Eden the Garden of God; every precious stone was your covering, the sardius, topaz, and the diamond, the beryl, the onyx, and the jasper, the sapphire, the emerald, and the carbuncle, and gold: the workmanship of your tabrets and of your pipes was prepared in you in the day that you were created. *('You have been in Eden the Garden of God,' does not actually refer to the 'Eden' of Gen., Chpt. 3, but rather to the 'Eden' which existed on this Planet before Adam and Eve, which evidently was ruled by Lucifer before his rebellion.*

" 'Every precious stone was your covering,' presents itself as very similar to the dress of the High Priest of Israel [Ex. 28:19].

" 'The workmanship of your tabrets and of your pipes,' has to do with music. There is every indication that Lucifer's

leadership had something to do with the worship of God. As well, he is called, 'O Lucifer, son of the morning' [Isa. 14:12]. When the Earth was originally created, the Scripture says, 'The morning stars sang together, and all the sons of God shouted for joy' [Job 38:4-7]. So, if the idiom, 'son of the morning,' can be linked to the 'morning stars,' these Passages tell us that Lucifer, at least before his fall, was greatly used in leading the Worship of God.

"In fact, this is the reason that Satan has done everything within his power to corrupt the music of the world, and to corrupt the music of the Church above all. Inasmuch as the Book of Psalms is the longest Book in the Bible, we learn from this that music and singing are among the highest forms of worship of the Lord.)

THE ANOINTED CHERUB

"You are the anointed Cherub who covers; and I have set you so: you were upon the Holy Mountain of God; you have walked up and down in the midst of the stones of fire.

"('You are the anointed Cherub who covers,' means that Lucifer was chosen and 'anointed' by God for a particular task and service. This probably was the 'worship' to which we have just alluded.

" 'You were upon the Holy Mountain of God,' speaks of his place and position relative to the Throne [Rev. 4:2-11]. 'You have walked up and down in the midst of the stones of fire,' has reference to his nearness to the Throne [Ezek. 1:26-27]. As well, the phrase, 'Walked up and down,' seems to imply that not just any Angel would have been given such latitude.)

INIQUITY

"You were perfect in your ways from the day that

you were created, till iniquity was found in you *(pride was the form of this iniquity [Lk. 10:17-18]. The rebellion of Lucifer against God probably caused the catastrophe which occurred between the First and Second Verses of Gen., Chpt. 1),*

"By the multitude of your merchandise they have filled the midst of you with violence, and you have sinned; therefore I will cast you as profane out of the Mountain of God: and I will destroy you, O covering Cherub, from the midst of the stones of fire. *('Violence' has been the earmark of Satan's rule and reign in the world of darkness [Jn. 10:10]. Lucifer being 'cast out' of the 'Mountain of God' refers to him losing his place and position, which he held with God since his creation. It was because 'he had sinned,' which spoke of pride that caused him to lift himself up against God.)*

PRIDE

"Your heart was lifted up because of your beauty, you have corrupted your wisdom by reason of your brightness: I will cast you to the ground, I will lay you before kings, that they may behold you. *('Your heart was lifted up because of your beauty,' tells us the reason for his fall. As stated, it was pride. He took his eyes off of Christ, noticing his own beauty as it grew more and more glorious in his eyes. At some point in time, his 'heart' was changed from Christ to himself. As far as we know, this was the origin of evil in all of God's Creation.*

" 'You have corrupted your wisdom by reason of your brightness,' does not refer to the loss of wisdom, but instead refers to wisdom corrupted, hence, the insidious design practiced upon the human family [Jn. 10:10].

" 'I will cast you to the ground,' refers to his ultimate defeat [Rev. 12:7-12]. 'I will lay you before kings, that they may behold you,' refers to him ultimately being cast into

the Lake of Fire, where all the kings of the Earth who have died lost will behold him in his humiliation [Mat. 25:41; Rev. 20:10])" **(Ezek. 28:11-17).**

THE DEFINITION OF SIN

While there are several words in the Old Testament used for sin, the principal word is *"Hata,"* and simply means *"to miss the mark."* It speaks of missing the standard that God sets for man.

The structure of human nature and the revelation of Divine expectations both provide valid standards to humanity. Violation of these standards, by falling short of performing what is expected, is sin.

In the Hebrew language, what addresses sin, is after a fashion, what addressed Redemption as well. An example of this is the word *"Hatta't."* This word means both *"sin"* and *"Sin Offering."* It speaks of both the fact of failure and the wonderful reality of a forgiveness provided by God through the Sin Offering in Old Testament times that removed guilt. Thank God, Jesus became an Offering for Sin on the Cross. The great Prophet Isaiah said:

"Yet it pleased the LORD to bruise Him; He has put Him to grief: when You shall make His Soul an offering for sin, He shall see His Seed, He shall prolong His Days, and the pleasure of the LORD shall prosper in His Hand" (Isa. 53:10).

JESUS AS THE SIN OFFERING

The notes on Verse 10 in THE EXPOSITOR'S STUDY BIBLE proclaim the following:

" *'Yet it pleased the LORD to bruise Him,' refers to the sufferings of Christ, which proceeded from the 'determinate counsel and foreknowledge of God' [Acts 2:23], and which, being permitted by Him, were in some way His doing. It 'pleased Him' moreover that they should be undergone, for the Father saw with satisfaction the Son's self-sacrifice, and He witnessed with joy man's Redemption and Deliverance effected thereby.*

" 'He has put Him to grief,' actually says 'He has put Him to sicknesses' or 'He has made Him sick.' This spoke of the time He was on the Cross bearing our sins and 'sicknesses' [Mat. 8:16-17; I Pet. 2:24]. And yet, while all sin and sickness were atoned at the Cross, the total effects of such will not be completely dissipated until the coming Resurrection [Rom. 8:23].

" 'When You shall make His Soul an offering for sin,' is powerful indeed! The word 'offering' in the Hebrew is 'Asham,' and means 'a Trespass Offering,' an 'offering for sin.'

TRESPASS OFFERINGS AND SIN OFFERINGS

"Offerings for sin, or 'guilt offerings,' were distinct from 'Sin Offerings.' The object of the former was 'satisfaction'; of the latter, 'expiation.' The Servant of Jehovah was, however, to be both. He was both the 'Sin Offering' and the 'Guilt or Trespass Offering.'

"This completely destroys the idea that Jesus died spiritually on the Cross, meaning that He became a sinner on the Cross, and died and went to Hell as all sinners, and was born again in Hell after three days and nights of suffering, etc. None of that is in the Word of God. While Jesus definitely was a 'Sin Offering,' He was not a sinner, and did not become a sinner on the Cross. To have done so would have destroyed His Perfection of Sacrifice, which was demanded by God. In other words, the Sacrifice had to be perfect, and He was Perfect in every respect.

" 'He shall see His Seed,' refers to all His 'true followers,' which include all who have ever been Born-Again.

" 'He shall prolong His Days,' refers to His Resurrection.

" 'And the pleasure of the LORD shall prosper in His Hand,'

refers to the great victory that He would win at Calvary, which will ultimately restore everything that Adam lost."

THE GREEK WORD FOR SIN

That word is *"Hamartia,"* and basically means the same thing as the Hebrew word, *"missing the mark."* *"Hamartia"* assumes a Divine standard or norm and portrays humanity as missing the mark. Yet sin is also seen in the New Testament as rebellion and as conscious deviation from known right.

"Sin" is used in a descriptive sense in the Gospels, and there it is almost always associated with forgiveness. The Epistles, especially those of Paul, penetrate beyond observation of human behavior to explore its cause. Paul takes the concept of sin hinted at in Psalms 51:5 and implied in the Old Testament Doctrine of the New Covenant and develops the portrait of a humanity distorted and twisted by the brutal power of sin. Therefore, sin is not only missing God's Mark; it is an inner reality, a warped inhuman nature, and a malignant power that holds each individual in an unbreakable grip (some of these thoughts on sin were taken from the book, *"Expository Dictionary of Bible Words,"* by Dr. Larry Richards.)

ADAM AND ORIGINAL SIN

We should say original as far as this Planet Earth is concerned. As stated, sin began, at least as far as we know, with the rebellion of Lucifer against God, which originally took place in Heaven.

As it regards the account of the Fall of Adam and Eve, we could just give the Scriptural reference; however, I feel that the quotation of the Text, along with the expository notes, provide more information. So, even though we have given this in other doctrines, still, in the context of that which we are addressing, the Doctrine of Sin, it is imperative that we give this account in its totality. It came through Moses. The great Law-Giver said:

THE TEMPTATION

"**Now the serpent was more subtle than any beast of the field which the LORD God had made** *(the word 'subtle,' as used here, is not negative, but rather positive; everything that God made before the Fall was positive; it describes qualities such as quickness of sight, swiftness of motion, activity of self-preservation, and seemingly intelligent adaptation to its surroundings)*. **And he said unto the woman** *(not a fable; the serpent before the Fall had the ability of limited speech; Eve did not seem surprised when he spoke to her!)*, **Yes, has God said, You shall not eat of every tree of the Garden?** *(The serpent evidently lent its faculties to Satan, even though the Evil One is not mentioned. That being the case, Satan spoke through the serpent, and questioned the Word of God.)*

"**And the woman said unto the serpent** *(proclaims Satan leveling his attack against Eve, instead of Adam; his use of Eve was only a means to get to Adam)*, **We may eat of the fruit of the trees of the Garden** *(the trial of our first parents was ordained by God, because probation was essential to their spiritual development and self-determination; but as He did not desire that they should be tempted to their Fall, He would not suffer Satan to tempt them in a way that would surpass their human capacity; the tempted might, therefore, have resisted the tempter)*:

"**But of the fruit of the tree which is in the midst of the Garden, God has said, You shall not eat of it, neither shall you touch it, lest you die** *(Eve quoted what the Lord had said about the prohibition, but then added, 'neither shall you touch it')*.

THE LIE OF SATAN

"**And the serpent said unto the woman, You shall not surely die** *(proclaims an outright denial of the Word of*

God; as God had preached to Adam, Satan now preaches to Eve; Jesus called Satan a liar, which probably refers to this very moment [Jn. 8:44]):

"For God does know that in the day you eat thereof, then your eyes shall be opened *(suggests the attainment of higher wisdom),* **and you shall be as gods, knowing good and evil.** *(In effect says, 'You shall be Elohim.' It was a promise of Divinity. God is Omniscient, meaning that His Knowledge of evil is thorough, but not by personal experience. By His very Nature, He is totally separate from all that is evil. The knowledge of evil that Adam and Eve would learn would be by moral degradation, which would bring wreckage. While it was proper to desire to be like God, it is proper only if done in the right way, and that is through Faith in Christ and what He has done for us at the Cross.)*

THE LUST OF THE FLESH, THE LUST OF THE EYES, AND THE PRIDE OF LIFE

"And when the woman saw that the tree was good for food *(presents the lust of the eyes),* **and that it was pleasant to the eyes** *(the lust of the flesh),* **and a tree to be desired to make one wise** *(the pride of life),* **she took of the fruit thereof, and did eat** *(constitutes the Fall),* **and gave also unto her husband with her; and he did eat** *(refers to the fact that evidently Adam was an observer to all these proceedings; some claim that he ate of the forbidden fruit which she offered him out of love for her; however, no one ever sins out of love; Eve submitted to the temptation out of deception, but 'Adam was not deceived' [I Tim. 2:14]; he fell because of unbelief; he simply didn't believe what God had said about the situation; contrast Verse 6 with Luke 4:1-13; both present the three temptations, 'the lust of the flesh,' 'the lust of the eyes,' and 'the pride of life'; the first man falls, the Second Man conquers).*

"And the eyes of them both were opened *(refers to*

the consciousness of guilt as a result of their sin), **and they knew that they were naked** *(refers to the fact that they had lost the enswathing light of purity, which previously had clothed their bodies)*; **and they sewed fig leaves together, and made themselves aprons** *(sinners clothe themselves with morality, sacraments, and religious ceremonies; they are as worthless as Adam's apron of fig leaves)*" **(Gen. 3:1-7).**

THE DESTRUCTIVE POWER OF SIN

Sin is more, much more, than a mere act that is committed. Sin in its most simple form, is disobedience to the Word of God. But in that disobedience, is a rebellion against the Word of God, a rebellion against God Personally, and a rebellion against His Creation.

Sin contains a malignant power that never remains static, but always grows in intensity. It is like a fungus, if it's not rooted out, it will ultimately take over and spoil everything. It is the cause of all the destruction in the world. In fact, when Adam and Eve fell, the very Creation of God suffered a Fall as well. That's why Paul wrote:

"**For the earnest expectation of the creature** *(should have been translated, 'for the earnest expectation of the Creation')* **waits for the manifestation of the sons of God** *(pertains to the coming Resurrection of Life)*.

"**For the creature** *(Creation)* **was made subject to vanity** *(Adam's Fall signaled the Fall of Creation)*, **not willingly** *(the Creation did not sin, even as such cannot sin, but became subject to the result of sin which is death)*, **but by reason of Him Who has subjected** *the same* **in** **Hope** *(speaks of God as the One Who passed sentence because of Adam's Fall, but at the same time gave us a 'Hope'; that 'Hope' is Christ, Who will rectify all things)*,

"**Because the creature** *(Creation)* **itself also shall be delivered** *(presents this 'Hope' as effecting that Deliverance,* *which He did by the Cross)* **from the bondage of corruption** *(speaks of mortality, i.e., 'death')* **into the glorious liberty of the Children of God** *(when man fell, Creation fell! when man shall be delivered, Creation will be delivered as well, and is expressed in the word 'also').*

"For we know that the whole Creation *(everything has been affected by Satan's rebellion and Adam's Fall)* **groans and travails in pain together until now** *(refers to the common longing of the elements of the Creation to be brought back to their original perfection)"* **(Rom. 8:19-22).**

THE CAUSE

Due to the fact that the Creation has suffered as a result of the Fall, this means that it doesn't function properly. This is the reason for all storms, hurricanes, tornados, earthquakes, etc. It is all because of the Fall of man in the Garden of Eden.

Part of the reason, and perhaps a very major part, is because of the following.

David said:

"When I consider Your Heavens, the Work of Your Fingers, the moon and the stars, which You have ordained *(the argument of Verses 3-8 is the amazing Love of Christ in coming forth from the Highest Glory to redeem a being so insignificant as man)***;**

"What is man, that You are mindful of him? And the son of man, that You visit him? *(God became man and went to Calvary in order to redeem fallen humanity. The price that was paid for that Redemption proclaims to us the worth of man, which, in fact, is God's highest Creation.)*

"For You have made him a little lower than the Angels, and have crowned him with glory and honor *(the Hebrew word 'Elohim' here translated 'angels' should have been translated 'God,' or 'Godhead,' for that's what the word actually means; there is no place in the Old Testament where*

*'Elohim' means 'Angels'; this means that man was origi-
nally created higher than the Angels, and through Christ
will be restored to that lofty position [Rom. 8:14-17]).*
**"You made him to have dominion over the works
of Your Hands; You have put all things under his feet**
*(in their fullness, these words given here are only true of
the God-Man, Jesus Christ [Mat. 28:18]; Christ has been
exalted to a place higher than Angels or any other being
except the Father; redeemed man is to be raised up to that
exalted position with Him [Eph. 2:6-7])"* **(Ps. 8:3-6).**

Inasmuch as the Lord gave Adam *"dominion over the work
of His Hands,"* this included the Creation. So, when Adam fell,
the Creation suffered as well.

All of this means that nothing presently functions as the Lord
originally intended and, in fact, originally created it to function.
That will be remedied at the Second Coming of the Lord.

ORIGINAL SIN

Due to the Fall, man is now born in sin, which is called
"original sin," which the Apostle Paul personifies as a ruling
principal in human life (Rom. 5:12; 6:12, 14; 7:17, 20; 8:2). It
expresses moral and spiritual depravity (Lk. 11:39; Acts 8:22;
Rom. 1:29; Eph. 6:12). It is associated with Satan, the Evil
One (Mat. 13:19; I Jn. 3:12). It is translated variously as *"in-
justice"* (Rom. 9:14), *"unrighteousness"* (Lk. 18:6), *"falsehood"*
(Jn. 7:18), *"wickedness"* (Rom. 2:8), *"iniquity"* (II Tim. 2:19).

ALL SIN IS AGAINST GOD

The most characteristic feature of sin and all its aspects is
that it is directed against God (Ps. 51:4; Rom. 8:7). Any conception of sin that does not have in the forefront the contradiction,
which it offers to God, is a deviation from the Biblical repre-
sentation.

The common notion that sin is mere selfishness betrays a false assessment of its nature and gravity. Essentially, sin is directed against God, and this perspective alone accounts for the diversity of its form and activities. It is a violation of that which God's Glory demands and is, therefore, in its essence the contradiction of God.

As we have stated, sin was present in the universe before the Fall of Adam and Eve (Gen. 3:1; Jn. 8:44; II Pet. 2:4; I Jn. 3:8; Jude 6).

The Bible, however, does not deal directly with the origin of evil in the Universe, being concerned rather with sin and its origin in human life (I Tim. 2:14; James 1:13).

THE MANNER OF SATAN'S ATTACK

The real thrust of the demonic temptation in the account of the Fall in Genesis, Chapter 3, lies in its subtle suggestion of man's aspiring to equality with his Maker (*"You will be like God"* — Gen. 3:5). Satan's attack was directed against the integrity, veracity, and loving provision of God, and consisted in an enticement to wicked and blasphemous rebellion against man's proper Lord. In this act man snatched at equality with God (Phil. 2:6), attempted to assert his independence of God and, hence, to call into question the very nature and ordering of existence whereby he lived as a creature in utter dependence upon the Grace and provision of his Creator. Man's sin lies in his pretension to be God.

In this act, further, man blasphemously withheld the worship and adoring love which is ever his proper response to God's Majesty and Grace, and instead paid homage to the enemy of God and to his own foul ambitions.

Thus, the origin of sin according to Genesis, Chapter 3 ought not to be sought so much in an overt action (Gen. 2:17; 3:6), but in an inward, God-denying aspiration of which the act of disobedience was the immediate expression.

As to the problem of how Adam and Eve could have been

subject to temptation had they not previously known sin, Scripture does not enter into extended discussion; however, in the Person of Jesus Christ, it witnesses to a Man, Who, though without sin, was subject to temptation *"in every respect as we are"* (Mat. 4:3; Heb. 2:17; 4:15; 5:7; I Pet. 1:19; 2:22).

PERSONAL GUILT

The ultimate origin of evil is part of the mystery of lawlessness (II Thess. 2:7), but an arguable reason for Scripture's relative silence is that a *"rational explanation"* of the origin of sin would have the inevitable result of directing attention away from the Scripture's primary concern, the confession of *"my personal guilt."*

The consequences of sin, regarding Adam and Eve were immediate.

THE CONSEQUENCES OF SIN

The changed attitude toward God on the part of Adam indicates the revolution that took place in their minds. They *"hid themselves from the Presence of the LORD God"* (Gen. 3:8). Made for the Presence and Fellowship of God, they now dreaded encounter with Him. Shame and fear were now the dominate emotions (Gen. 2:25; 3:7, 10), indicating the disruption that had taken place.

GOD'S ATTITUDE TO MAN

Not only was there a change in man's attitude toward God, but also in God's Attitude toward man. Reproof, condemnation, curse, expulsion from the Garden, are all indicative of this. Sin is one-sided, but its consequences are not. Sin elicits God's Wrath and Displeasure, and necessarily so, because it is in contradiction of what He is. For God to be complacent toward sin is an impossibility, since it would be for God to cease to take

Himself seriously. He cannot deny Himself. The consequences for the entirety of the human race, regarding the Fall of Adam and Eve, which was in their loins, furnishes a catalog of vices (Gen. 4:8, 19, 23; 6:2-3, 5). The sequel of abounding iniquity results in the virtual destruction of mankind (Gen. 6:7, 13; 7:21-24). The Fall had abiding effect not only upon Adam and Eve, but upon all who descended from them, because all were in the loins of Adam. As well, there is a racial solidarity in sin and evil.

The effects of the Fall also extended to the physical cosmos. *"Cursed is the ground because of you"* (Gen. 3:17; Rom. 8:20). Man, as stated, is the crown of Creation, made in God's Image and, therefore, God's Vice-regent (Gen. 1:26). The catastrophe of man's Fall brought the catastrophe of the curse upon that over which he was given dominion. Sin was an event in the realm of the human spirit, but it has its repercussions on the whole of Creation.

THE APPEARANCE OF DEATH

Death is the epitome of sin's penalty. This was the warning attached to the prohibition of Eden (Gen. 2:17), and it is the direct expression of God's Curse upon man the sinner (Gen. 3:19). Death in the phenomenal realm consists in the separation of the integral elements of man's being. This dissolution exemplifies the principle of death, namely, separation and it comes to its most extreme expression in separation from God (Gen. 3:23). Because of sin death is infested with a fear and terror for man (Lk. 12:5; Heb. 2:15).

THE IMPUTATION OF SIN

The first sin of Adam had unique significance for the whole human race (Rom. 5:12, 14:19; I Cor. 15:22). Here there is sustained emphasis upon the one trespass of the one man, and that by which sin, condemnation, and death came upon all

338 Brother Swaggart, How Can I Understand The Bible?

mankind. The sin is identified as *"the transgression of Adam,"* *"the trespass of the one,"* *"one trespass,"* *"the disobedience of the one,"* and there can be no doubt that the first trespass of Adam is intended.

Hence, the clause, *"Because all men sinned,"* in Romans 5:12 refers to the sin of all and the sin of Adam. It cannot refer to the actual sins of all men, far less to the hereditary depravity with which all are afflicted, for in Romans 5:12 the clause in question clearly says why *"death spread to all men,"* and in the succeeding Verses *"one man's trespass"* (Rom. 5:17) is stated to be the reason for the universal reign of death. If the same sin were not intended, Paul would not be affirming two things with reference to the same subject in the same context.

The only explanation of the two forms of statement is that all sinned in the sin of Adam. The same inference is to be drawn from I Cor. 15:22, *"in Adam all die."* If all die in Adam, it is because all sinned in Adam.

According to Scripture, the kind of solidarity with Adam, which explains the participation of all in Adam's sin is the kind of solidarity which Christ sustains to those united to Him.

In Christ is a representative Headship, and this is all that is necessary to ground the solidarity of all in the sin of Adam. To say that the sin of Adam is imputed to all is but to say that all were involved in his sin by reason of his representative headship.

As well, to say that the Victory of Christ over sin is imputed to all is but to say that all are involved (all who believe in His Victory at Calvary and the Resurrection by reason of His representative Headship).

The history of all mankind is, therefore, finally subsumed under two complexes:

1. Sin-condemnation and
2. Justification-life.

The former arises from our union with Adam, the latter from union with Christ. These are the two orbits within which we live and move. God's Government of men is directed in terms of these relationships. If we do not reckon with Adam we are thereby excluded from a proper understanding of Christ. All who die, die in Adam; all who are made alive, are made alive in Christ.

THE DEPRAVITY OF MAN

Sin never consists merely in a voluntary act of transgression. Every volition proceeds from something that is more deep-seated than the volition itself. A sinful act is the expression of a sinful heart (Prov. 4:23; 23:7; Mk. 7:20-23). Sin must always include, therefore, the perversity of heart, mind, disposition, and will. This was true, as we saw in Adam in the case of the first sin, and it applies to all sin.

From whatever angle man is viewed, there is the absence of that which is well-pleasing to God. Considered more positively, all are turned aside from God's Way and become corrupted. In Romans 8:5-7, Paul refers to the mind of the flesh, and nature directed and governed by sin. Further, according to Romans 8:7, *"the mind that is set on the flesh is hostile to God."* No stronger condemnatory judgment could be arrived at, for it means that the thinking of the natural man is conditioned and governed by enmity directed against God. Nothing less than a judgment of total depravity is the clear implication of these Passages; consequently, there is no area or aspect of human life which is resolved from the somber effects of man's fallen state and, hence, no area which might serve as a possible ground for man's justification of himself in the Face of God and His Law.

RESTRAINING FACTORS

Depravity, however, is not registered in actual transgression to an equal extent in all. There are multiple restraining factors. God does not give over all men to uncleanness, to a base mind, and to improper conduct (Rom. 1:24, 28). Total depravity (total that is, in the sense that it touches everything) is not incompatible with the exercise of the natural virtues and the promotion of civil righteousness. Unregenerate men are still endowed with conscience, and the work of the Law is written upon their heart so that in measure and at points they fulfill its requirement (Rom. 2:14).

The doctrine of depravity, however, means that these works, though formerly in accord with what God commands, are not good and well-pleasing to God in terms of the full and ultimate criteria by which His Judgment is determined. The criteria of love to God is the animating motive, the Law of God as the directing principal, and the Glory of God as the controlling purpose (Mat. 6:2, 5, 16; Mk. 7:6-7; Rom. 8:7; 13:4; I Cor. 2:14; 10:31; 13:3; Titus 1:15; Heb. 11:4, 6). In other words, unregenerate man may do certain things in accord with God's Will and Principal, but nevertheless, always according to the wrong motive.

INABILITY

Inability is concern with the incapacity arising from the nature of depravity. If depravity is total, i.e., affecting every aspect and area of man's being, then inability for what is good and well-pleasing to God is likewise comprehensive in its reference.

We are not able within ourselves, to change our character or act differently from it, which within itself debunks humanistic psychology. In the matter of understanding, *"the natural man cannot know the things of the Spirit of God"* because *"they are spiritually discerned"* (I Cor. 2:14). In respect of obedience to the Law of God, the unregenerate man is not subject to the Law of God and, in fact, cannot be (Rom. 8:7). They who are in the flesh cannot please God (Rom. 8:8). A corrupt tree cannot bring forth good fruit (Mat. 7:18). The impossibility in each case is undeniable. It is our Lord Who affirms that even Faith in Him is impossible apart from the gift and drawing of the Father (Jn. 6:44, 65).

This witness on His Part is to the same effect as His insistence that apart from the supernatural birth of the Born-Again experience, no one can have intelligent appreciation of, or entrance into, the Kingdom of God (Jn. 1:13; 3:3, 5, 8; I Jn. 2:29; 3:9; 4:7; 5:1, 4, 18).

The necessity of so radical and momentous a transformation and re-creation as regeneration is proof of the whole witness of Scripture to the bondage of sin and the hopelessness of our sinful condition. This bondage implies that it is a moral and spiritual impossibility for the natural man to receive the things of the Spirit, to love God, and to do what is well-pleasing to Him, or to believe in Christ to the Salvation of the soul, apart from the Work of the Spirit. It is this enslavement to which is the Promise of the Gospel, and the Glory of the Gospel which lies precisely in the fact that it provides release from the bondage and slavery of sin. It is the Gospel of Grace and Power, all which is made possible by the Cross, and for the helpless.

THE LIABILITY OF SIN

Since sin is against God, He cannot be complacent towards it or indifferent with respect to it. He reacts inevitably against it. This reaction is specifically His Wrath. The frequency with which Scripture mentions the Wrath of God compels us to take account of its reality and meaning, exactly as is portrayed in Jeremiah 33:5, as well as scores of other Scriptures.

Various terms are expressed regarding the sense of God's *"anger,"* and *"fury"* against sin. The Old Testament is permeated with these types of references to the Wrath of God. Often more than one of these terms appears together, as in Jeremiah 33:5, in order to strengthen and confirm the thought expressed. There is intensity in the terms themselves and in the constructions in which they occur to convey the notions of displeasure, fiery indignations and holy vengeance, i.e., *"anger and fury."*

The Wrath of God is, therefore, a reality, and the language and teaching of Scripture are calculated to impress upon us the severity by which it is characterized.

THREE OBSERVATIONS

There are three observations which particularly require mention:

1. The Wrath of God must not be interpreted in terms of the fitful passions so commonly associated with anger in us. It is the deliberate, resolute displeasure, which the contradiction of His Holiness demands.

2. It is not to be construed as vindictiveness but as Holy indignation; nothing of the nature of malice attaches to it. It is not malignant hatred but righteous detestation.

3. We must not reduce the Wrath of God to merely His Will to punish. Wrath is a positive outgoing of dissatisfaction as sure as that which is pleasing to God involves complacency. We must not eliminate from God what we term emotion. The Wrath of God finds its parallel in the human heart, exemplified in a perfect manner in our Lord Jesus Christ (Mk. 3:5; 10:14).

The epitome of sin's liability is, therefore, the Holy Wrath of God. Since sin is never impersonal, but exists in, and is committed by persons, the Wrath of God consists in the displeasure to which we are subjected; we are the objects. The penal infliction, which we suffer are the expressions of God's Wrath. The sense of guilt and torment of conscience are the reflections in our consciousness of the displeasure of God. The essence of final perdition will consist in the infliction of God's indignation (Isa. 30:33; 66:24; Dan. 12:2; Mk. 9:43, 45, 48).

THE LAW OF GOD IS THE DIVINE STANDARD

The Law of God, at times referred to as the *"Law of Moses,"* was given for many reasons, one of the most important, that it defined sin.

The Hebrew word for Law is *"Torah."* Its basic meaning is *"teaching"* or *"instruction."* It denotes instruction focused on how one should live, rather than on abstract or academic subjects. In other words, it was very pointed, plain, and clear in its demands.

The Law, as given to Moses by Jesus Christ in a preincarnate appearance was a Code, with its Ten Commandments and with instructions covering every aspect of Israel's personal and national life. It was broken up, one might say, in three parts. They were:

1. Moral, which basically consisted of the Ten Commandments.

2. Ceremonial, which pertained to the sacrifices, and all of the activities of the Priests.

3. Civil, which addressed itself to government.

In fact, the Law was ordained by God for His Covenant People.

In this sense, the Law consisted of all the Statutes, Ordinances, Precepts, Commandments, and Testimonies given by God to guide His People. But this Law, the Mosaic Law, these Teachings included in the first five Books of the Old Testament include even more.

GOD'S REVELATION

It included Moses' review of an interpretation of history, his record of God's mighty Acts, and his report of Creation.

When the word *"Law"* in the Old Testament is read, it is helpful to remember that it may have many references.

It may refer to God's Revelation in a general way. It may point to a specific set of instructions — e.g., the Law of Passover, or the Ten Commandments, etc. It may indicate the moral or ceremonial codes, or the writings of Moses.

What is clear, however, is that whatever a particular use of *"Law"* points to, the Old Testament views it as Divine Instruction. It is God's Gift, intended to show Israel how to live a holy and happy life in this world.

To be sure, the Law of Moses was not the only law in the world, as other codes of law had been given previously; however, it was the only Law given by God and, as such, it so far exceeded the viability of all other law, that there was no comparison. It was the only Law in the world of that day that truly taught man how to live, and gave a complete code directing attention to every facet of life, and, thereby, put Israel light-years ahead of everyone else.

THE EXTENT OF THE LAW

To be sure, the Law was a moral code as delivered by Moses; however, it encompassed far more than that. It functioned as follows:
- The Constitution of the Nation of Israel.
- The basis for determining civil and criminal cases.
- A guide to worship.
- A personal guide to good family and social relationships.
- A personal guide to relationship with the Lord.

It comprised not only those regulations that defined sin and established guilt, but also the Sacrificial System through which the Believer might find Atonement for sins. In essence, everything in the experience of the people of Israel was to be guided by the Law.

Despite the all-encompassing nature of Law, and despite the fact that Law is seen in the Old Testament as one of God's Great Gifts, Israel fell far short of becoming a just and holy community.

In effect, and even though the Law was a pattern for living, and, given by God, still, it contained no Salvation, nor did it offer any power to give man the ability to keep it.

Even though the keeping of it was the objective, and demanded by God, still, all fell short, which brought upon Israelites its penalty, which is the custom of all law.

WHY DIDN'T THE LORD GIVE POWER
TO KEEP THE LAW?

As someone has well said, the Law was like a mirror which

showed man what he was, but gave him no power to change what he was.

The Law was God's Standard for Righteousness. As stated, it was the Moral Code of God. It was:

- To define sin.
- To show man his inability to keep the Law.
- Thereby, he should look to the coming Redeemer, typified by the Sacrificial System, which was at the very heart of the Law.

Man's problem always has been, and is, pride. So, if God had given man the power to keep the Law, obedience, due to man's pride, would not have been the outcome, but rather the very opposite. Man would have been further lifted up in his pride, which would have made the situation even worse.

All of this means that man's problem as the result of the Fall, could not be addressed so easily. Man's condition is terminal, meaning that it is beyond the pale of any type of Law. For man to be Saved, something far greater would have to be offered, and that something greater was God's only Son, Who would keep the Law perfectly, and all on our behalf, and then would address the broken law, which was incumbent upon every human being, and do so by going to the Cross and paying the price that God demanded. This was and is, the Death of Christ on the Cross, God's Answer to fallen man, and His Answer to the Law.

Even though the keeping of the Law was the objective, and demanded by God, still, all fell short, which brought upon Israel its penalty, which is the custom of all law.

In effect, the Law was not meant to save man from sin, but was meant to show man, as stated, his inability to keep the Law, and that despite all his efforts, he still needed a Redeemer. That Redeemer was Christ!

Consequently, the Law in the Old Testament was good. But it was not meant to be permanent, for Law has never been effective in making the People of God righteous.

JESUS AND THE LAW

At the time of Christ the Rabbis (the teachers of the Law), focused their Faith on the Law.

They taught that the first five Books of the Old Testament were the Law, and all the other Writings and Prophets were but Commentary on this core.

The Religious Leaders in Jesus' Day were sure not only that these Mosaic Books were the key to life and death, but also that the individual could keep the Law and please God. The young ruler's question, *"What shall I do to inherit Eternal Life?"* (Lk. 18:18), sums up the understanding of religion held by most of the religious people in his generation.

When Jesus appeared, He did not deny the Law (the Books of Moses). But He did directly challenge the understanding of the Old Testament on which contemporary Jewish Faith was based. To understand the challenge and to sense Jesus' own view of *"Law"* as the term is used in the Gospels, we need to examine several significant Gospel Passages.

FULFILLING THE LAW

Jesus began by stating His Own Allegiance to the Old Testament. But then He made this dramatic declaration concerning His Purpose for coming to Earth. He told them that He had not come to abolish the Law or the Prophets, but to fulfill them.

Jesus continued with the warning: the Commandments are to be practiced, but then He said, *"I tell you that unless your righteousness surpasses that of the Pharisees and the teachers of the Law, you will certainly not enter the Kingdom of Heaven"* (Mat. 5:20).

This, of course, exploded like a bombshell and, if possible, only exacerbated the anger of these groups against Him.

Jesus further taught that the Law and the Prophets could be summed up simply: *"In everything, do to others what you would have them do to you"* (Mat. 7:12).

An expansion on this statement came when Jesus was questioned by one *"expert in the Law."* When asked, which is the greatest Commandment, Jesus answered, *"Love the Lord your God with all your heart, and with all your soul, and with all your mind. This is the first and greatest Commandment. And the second is like it: Love your neighbor as yourself. All the Law and the Prophets hang on these two Commandments"* (Mat. 22:37-40). Again, Jesus shifted the issue from strict compliance with the detailed instructions of the Old Testament, of which the Pharisees demanded, to one's heart attitude. Love for God and love for others is the key to Godliness, He says!

When He said that He had come to *"fulfill the Law,"* in effect, He was saying that the day the Mosaic Law would be superseded has arrived.

In a sense, one could say that Jesus was the Law, but when He came to this Earth as God manifested in the flesh, He did not come to bring the Law, but, instead, Grace and Truth. As such, the *"Grace"* and *"Truth"* would fulfill the Law.

THE NEW COVENANT

The Old Testament economy was not rejected. Not at all. Instead, all that the Old Testament foretold had come with Jesus. He was the Prophet Who was destined to bring the Message that superseded that of Moses (Deut. 18:15); consequently, the way of life He introduced did not abolish the Mosaic Code, but superseded it with a new and better Code called the *"New Covenant,"* in which the Prophets had promised (Jer., Chpt. 31).

When the Pharisees came to Jesus to raise a point of Law concerning divorce, Jesus answered them by stating God's intentions for marriage, which preceded the Law. From the time of Creation God had intended marriage to be a permanent union.

The Pharisees then questioned Him by asking, *"Why then did Moses command that a man give his wife a certificate of divorce and send her away?"* (Mat. 19:7).

Jesus' response is stunning, cutting the ground from underneath those who saw the Mosaic Law as a perfect expression of God's Righteousness. He said, *"Moses permitted you to divorce your wives because your hearts were hard"* (Mat. 19:8).

THE POINT OF WHAT JESUS SAID

The point of Jesus' response is this: God, in the Law, established a requirement for His People that was less than ideal. Rather than being the highest possible standard, the Mosaic Law was what one might call a Divine compromise.

What God truly desired was utterly beyond the possibility for people whose hearts were hardened by sin. To make it possible for Israel to even approximate God's real Standards, He gave them a Law that made allowances for less than — perfect Righteousness!

No wonder, then, Jesus taught that our righteousness must surpass that of the Scribes and Pharisees. God called on the Believer to find a Righteousness that is greater than that expressed in Law: a Righteousness that flows from and finds expression in love for God and love for others.

Consequently, Jesus fulfilled the Old Testament Law, both in the sense of explaining it correctly and in the sense of being Himself the Goal toward which the Old Testament points. As far as the specific Commands contained in the Mosaic Law are concerned, Jesus introduced a Righteousness surpassing them.

This is possible because the moral regulations of the Law are simply practical guidelines on how to love God and neighbor. When love fills the Believer's heart, the reality to which the Law points will come.

THE TEACHING OF OUR LORD

Jesus' teaching shifted the focus of Righteousness from behavior to character and motivation. God was concerned with a Righteousness that surpassed that of the Rabbi and the Pharisee, who concluded their righteousness as being in what they called obedience to the Law, but, in effect, was no obedience at all.

That it is not necessary to express such Righteousness by detailed Commandments did show in Jesus' response when He was asked about the greatest Commandment. *"Love God and love others,"* Jesus replied. And He added, *"All the Law and the Prophets hang on these two Commandments"* (Mat. 22:40).

The Gospels show us that the Old Testament way was to be superseded and transformed by Jesus. Actually, He is the focus of the Old Testament, the One of Whom it testifies. Now that He has come, that era is brought to a close. It is fulfilled, because it pointed to Him, Who would bring a better way and, therefore, a new era with new patterns of life would replace it.

THE EPISTLES OF PAUL

To be sure, that new era was explained and developed in the Epistles of Paul. The Apostle showed that the Law's statements of Righteousness in Commandments and as an aid to being good, could not function in the Believer's life. Faith, not Law, was always the way to Salvation. Reliance on the Spirit, not a struggle to keep the Law, is the way to live a righteous life. We must learn that Jesus is the Source of all things that we receive from God, and that the Cross, and not Law, is the Means by which we receive these things, all superintended by the Holy Spirit (Rom. 6:1-14; 8:1-2, 11; I Cor. 1:17-18, 23; 2:2).

It seems clear from Paul's analysis of the weakness of the Law, that the Old Testament Saint, like the Christian today, lived a Godly life by trusting God and having a personal relationship with Him, rather than by looking to Law in order that it might save by trying to keep it.

Of course, the Old Testament Saint was to try to keep the Law, but the idea was that the Law could not save, but only the One to whom it pointed, namely Christ, and what He would do at the Cross, which was symbolized in the Sacrifices.

As a result of what Christ did, and that which He gave in the

Epistles through the Apostle Paul, and others, Christians today are to understand that the *"do's"* and *"do not's"* of Scripture, can only be fulfilled in our lives by us giving ourselves over to Christ, and what He did at the Cross, all on our behalf, which makes possible the Power of the Holy Spirit on our behalf.

THE TRUTH

We then find that in our loving God and others, we suddenly realize the Truth. The requirements of the Law begin to find expression in our lives — not because we're trying to be good, but because the Love of Jesus is working to transform us from within, and the Holy Spirit is prompting us to acts of love that fulfill every demand of the Law, but which the Law, within itself, could never do!

To sum up, Jesus *"fulfilled the Law,"* by meeting its requirements, which meant to walk perfect in its demands, which we could never do.

As a startling example, when the woman was caught in the act of adultery, the Law demanded that she be stoned (Jn. 8:1-11). Jesus satisfied the Law by dying in her place, as He did in the place of all of us; therefore, He fulfilled it down to its most minute detail, and then, in turn, freely gives His Victory to all who will believe Him, and allow His Life to become our life.

JESUS CHRIST AND THE CROSS, THE ONLY ANSWER FOR SIN

As we have stated, while the Law of God was His Standard of Righteousness, still, even though the Law contained Righteousness, and because it was solely from God, still, for that Righteousness to be obtained, one had to perfectly keep the Law, which was beyond the pale of any mere mortal. So, in effect, the Law could not save. Paul bluntly stated:

"For *it is* not possible that the blood of bulls and of

goats should take away sins. *(The word 'impossible' is a strong one. It means there is no way forward through the blood of animals. As well, it applies to all other efforts made by man to address the problem of sin, other than the Cross)*" **(Heb. 10:4).**

The Apostle Paul gave us the means and the way that sin is addressed, and the only way it can be addressed. He said:

"**What shall we say then?** *(This is meant to direct attention to Rom. 5:20.)* **Shall we continue in sin, that Grace may abound?** *(Just because Grace is greater than sin doesn't mean that the Believer has a license to sin.)*
"**God forbid** *(presents Paul's answer to the question, 'Away with the thought, let not such a thing occur')*. **How shall we, who are dead to sin** *(dead to the sin nature)*, **live any longer therein?** *(This portrays what the Believer is now in Christ.)*

WE DIED WITH CHRIST

"**Know you not, that so many of us as were baptized into Jesus Christ** *(plainly says that this Baptism is into Christ and not water [I Cor. 1:17; 12:13; Gal. 3:27; Eph. 4:5; Col. 2:11-13])* **were baptized into His Death?** *(When Christ died on the Cross, in the Mind of God, we died with Him; in other words, He became our Substitute, and our identification with Him in His Death gives us all the benefits for which He died; the idea is that He did it all for us!)*

WE ARE BURIED WITH HIM

"**Therefore we are buried with Him by baptism into death** *(not only did we die with Him, but we were buried with Him as well, which means that all the sin and transgression* *of the past were buried; when they put Him in the Tomb, they put all of our sins into that Tomb as well)***:**

RAISED WITH HIM

"That like as Christ was raised up from the dead by the Glory of the Father, even so we also should walk in Newness of Life *(we died with Him, we were buried with Him, and His Resurrection was our Resurrection to a 'Newness of Life')*.

LIVING THE RESURRECTION LIFE

"For if we have been planted together *(with Christ)* **in the likeness of His Death** *(Paul proclaims the Cross as the instrument through which all Blessings come; consequently, the Cross must ever be the Object of our Faith, which gives the Holy Spirit latitude to work within our lives)***, we shall be also** *in the likeness* **of** *His* **Resurrection** *(we can know the 'likeness of His Resurrection,' i.e., 'live this Resurrection Life,' only as long as we understand the 'likeness of His Death,' which refers to the Cross as the Means by which all of this is done)***:**

THE OLD MAN IS CRUCIFIED

"Knowing this, that our old man is crucified with *Him* *(all that we were before conversion)***, that the body of sin might be destroyed** *(the power of the sin nature broken, made ineffective)***, that henceforth we should not serve sin** *(the guilt of sin is removed at conversion, because the sin nature no longer rules within our hearts and lives)*.

DEAD WITH CHRIST

"For he who is dead *(He was our Substitute, and in the*

Mind of God, we died with Him upon Believing Faith) **is freed from sin** *(set free from the bondage of the sin nature).*

"Now if we be dead with Christ *(once again pertains to the Cross, and our being baptized into His Death)***, we believe that we shall also live with Him** *(have Resurrected Life, which is more Abundant Life [Jn. 10:10]):*

DEATH AND SIN HAVE NO MORE DOMINION

"Knowing that Christ being raised from the dead dies no more *(means that His Work was a Finished Work, and will require nothing else)***; death has no more dominion over Him** *(because all sin has been Atoned; inasmuch as Christ is our Substitute, if death has no more dominion over Him, it has no more dominion over us; this means that the power of the sin nature is broken).*

"For in that He died, He died unto sin *(the sin nature)* **once** *(actually means, 'He died unto the sin nature, once, for all')***: but in that He lives** *(the Resurrection)***, He lives unto God** *(refers to the fact that all life comes from God, and that we receive that life by virtue of the Cross and our Faith in that Finished Work).*

"Likewise reckon *(account)* **you also yourselves to be dead indeed unto** *(the)* **sin** *(while the sin nature is not dead, we are dead unto the sin nature by virtue of the Cross and our Faith in that Sacrifice, but only as long as our Faith continues in the Cross)***, but alive unto God** *(living the Resurrection Life)* **through Jesus Christ our Lord** *(refers to what He did at the Cross, which is the means of this Resurrection Life).*

SANCTIFICATION

"Let not sin *(the sin nature)* **therefore reign** *(rule)* **in your mortal body** *(showing that the sin nature can once again rule in the heart and life of the Believer, if the*

Believer doesn't constantly look to Christ and the Cross; the 'mortal body' is neutral, which means it can be used for Righteousness or unrighteousness), **that you should obey it in the lusts thereof** (ungodly lusts are carried out through the mortal body, if Faith is not maintained in the Cross [I Cor. 1:17-18]).

"Neither yield you your members (of your mortal body) **as instruments of unrighteousness unto sin** (the sin nature): **but yield yourselves unto God** (we are to yield ourselves to Christ and the Cross; that alone guarantees victory over the sin nature), **as those who are alive from the dead** (we have been raised with Christ in 'Newness of Life'), **and your members as instruments of Righteousness unto God** (this can be done only by virtue of the Cross and our Faith in that Finished Work, and Faith which continues in that Finished Work from day-to-day [Lk. 9:23-24]).

THE DOMINION OF THE SIN NATURE BROKEN

"For sin shall not have dominion over you (the sin nature will not have dominion over us if we as Believers continue to exercise Faith in the Cross of Christ; otherwise, the sin nature most definitely will have dominion over the Believer): **for you are not under the Law** (means that if we try to live this life by any type of law, no matter how good that law might be in its own right, we will conclude by the sin nature having dominion over us), **but under Grace** (the Grace of God flows to the Believer on an unending basis only as long as the Believer exercises Faith in Christ and what He did at the Cross; Grace is merely the Goodness of God exercised by and through the Holy Spirit, and given to undeserving Saints)" **(Rom. 6:1-14).**

FORGIVENESS OF SIN

First of all we must understand that forgiveness of sin is not

deliverance from sin. They are two different things altogether. Unfortunately, many Believers mistake forgiveness of sin for deliverance from sin, because fellowship is restored upon proper Repentance and forgiveness. While the Bible does not teach sinless perfection, it most definitely does teach, even as we have just stated, that sin is not to have dominion over the Believer. Such Victory, again as we have already explained, comes only by and through the Cross of Christ. The Believer must ever make the Cross of Christ the Object of his Faith, and maintain the Cross of Christ as the Object of his Faith. That being done, the Holy Spirit Who works exclusively within the parameters of the Finished Work of Christ, will set about to remove sin from our lives, in that the dominion of sin will no longer exist. While the Christian will then at times, sin inadvertently, that is altogether different than being dominated by the sin nature. And to be sure, if the Christian doesn't have the Cross of Christ solely as the Object of his faith, the sin nature will most definitely have dominion over him, and on a continuing basis.

THE APOSTLE JOHN

John had much to say about the sin nature, sin, and forgiveness. It is as follows:

"If we say that we have fellowship with Him, and walk in darkness, we lie *(to claim Salvation while at the same time 'walking in darkness' automatically dismisses our claims)*, and do not the Truth *(such a life is a 'lie,' and is not 'true')*:

"But if we walk in the Light, as He is in the Light, we have fellowship one with another *(if we claim fellowship with Him, we will at the same time walk in the Light, which is the sphere of His Walk)*, and the Blood of Jesus Christ His Son cleanses us from all sin. *(Our Faith being in the Cross, the shed Blood of Jesus Christ, constantly cleanses us from all sin.)*

SIN

"If we say that we have no sin *(refers to 'the sin nature')*, we deceive ourselves *(refers to self-deception)*, and the Truth is not in us. *(This does not refer to all Truth as it regards Believers, but rather that the Truth of the indwelling sinful nature is not in us.)*

"If we confess our sins *(pertains to acts of sin, whatever they might be; the sinner is to believe [Jn. 3:16]; the Saint is to confess)*, He *(the Lord)* is faithful and just to forgive us *our* sins *(God will always be true to His Own Nature and Promises, keeping Faith with Himself and with man)*, and to cleanse us from all unrighteousness. *('All,' not some. All sin was remitted, paid for, and put away on the basis of the satisfaction offered for the demands of God's Holy Law, which sinners broke, when the Lord Jesus died on the Cross.)*

"If we say that we have not sinned *(here, John is denouncing the claims of sinless perfection; he is going back to Verse 8, speaking of Christians who claimed they had no sin nature)*, we make Him a liar *(the person who makes such a claim makes God a liar, because the Word says the opposite)*, and His Word is not in us. *(If we properly know the Word, we will properly know that perfection is not in us at present, and will not be until the Trump sounds.)*

THE ADVOCATE

"My little children, these things write I unto you, that you sin not. *(This presents the fact that the Lord saves us from sin, not in sin. This Passage tells us that, as Believers, we don't have to sin. Victory over sin is found exclusively in the Cross.)* And if any man sin, we have an Advocate with the Father, Jesus Christ the Righteous *(Jesus is now seated at the Right Hand of the Father, signifying that*

His Mission is complete, and His very Presence guarantees intercession [Heb. 7:25-26; 9:24; 10:12]):

"And He is the propitiation *(satisfaction)* **for our sins: and not for ours only, but also for** *the sins of* **the whole world.** *(This pertains to the fact that the satisfaction is as wide as the sin. If men do not experience its benefit, the fault is not in its efficacy, but in man himself)"* **(I Jn. 1:6-10; 2:1-2).**

TRANSGRESSION OF THE LAW

John continues and says:

"And every man who has this hope in Him *(the Resurrection)* **purifies himself** *(takes advantage of what Christ did for us at the Cross, which is the only way one can be pure)***, even as He** *(Christ)* **is pure** *(places Christ as our example).*

"Whosoever commits sin transgresses also the Law *(the Greek Text says, 'the sin,' and refers to Believers placing their Faith in that other than the Cross; such constitutes rebellion against God's Prescribed Order and is labeled as 'sin')***: for sin is the transgression of the Law.** *(This refers to the moral Law — the Ten Commandments. Rebelling against God's Order, which is the Cross, opens the door for works of the flesh [Gal. 5:19-21].)*

JESUS TOOK AWAY OUR SINS

"And you know that He was manifested to take away our sins *(He did so at the Cross; the Christian cannot practice what Christ came to take away and destroy)***; and in Him is no sin.** *(This presents the fact that He was able to be the Perfect Sacrifice to take away the sin of the world, which completely destroys the erroneous doctrine that Jesus died spiritually, as some claim.)*

THE PRACTICING OF SIN

"**Whosoever abides in Him sins not** *(does not practice sin)*: **whosoever sins** *(practices sin)* **has not seen Him, neither known Him.** *(As stated, Jesus saves from sin, not in sin. If we look to the Cross, 'sin will not have dominion over us' [Rom. 6:14].)*

"**Little children, let no man deceive you** *(the entirety of this Epistle is a warning against antinomianism, which teaches that sin doesn't matter because Grace covers it)*: **he who does Righteousness is Righteous** *(truly being Righteous will truly do Righteousness, i.e., 'live Righteously')*, **even as He is Righteous.** *(We have been granted the Righteousness of Christ, so we should live Righteous, which we can if our Faith Eternally abides in the Cross [Rom. 6:1-14].)*

"**He who commits sin** *(practices sin)* **is of the Devil** *(whoever is truly born of God does not live a life of habitual sinning)*; **for the Devil sinneth from the beginning** *(from the beginning of his rebellion against God)*. **For this purpose the Son of God was manifested, that He might destroy the works of the Devil.** *(This proclaims what was done at the Cross [Col. 2:14-15].)*

"**Whosoever is born of God does not commit sin** *(does not practice sin)*; **for his seed remains in him** *(refers to the Word of God)*: **and he cannot sin** *(cannot continue to practice sin)*, **because he is born of God.** *(This refers to the repugnancy of sin in the heart of the true Christian)*" (**I Jn. 3:3-9**).

BIBLICAL REPENTANCE

Without a doubt, the Fifty-first Psalm proclaims Repentance as nothing else found in the Bible. It has four characteristics. They are:

1. It refers to David asking forgiveness.

2. This Psalm presents the Son of David, the Lord Jesus Christ, standing in our place, repenting for us, as if He actually sinned, which, of course, He did not. This is the Intercessory role of Christ.

3. It presents Israel in a coming day, actually at the Second Coming, pleading with the Lord for mercy and forgiveness, because of the terrible sins that she has committed, and especially her Crucifixion of Christ.

4. It serves in a sense, as a prayer for forgiveness for you and me.

Even though including the notes from THE EXPOSITOR'S STUDY BIBLE, which are quite lengthy, still, I think it would be profitable to quote the entirety of the Psalm.

THE FIFTY-FIRST PSALM

"Have mercy upon me, O God, according to Your lovingkindness: according unto the multitude of Your tender mercies blot out my transgressions. *(This is a Psalm of David, written when Nathan the Prophet came unto him after the sin with Bath-sheba and the murder of Uriah [II Sam., Chpt. 12]. This Psalm was given by the Holy Spirit to David when, his heart broken and contrite because of his sin against God, he pleaded for pardon through the Atoning Blood of the Lamb of God, foreshadowed in Exodus, Chapter 12. Thus, he was not only fittingly provided with a vehicle of expression in Repentance and faith, but he was also used as a channel of prophetic communication.*

"David, in his sin, Repentance, and Restoration, is a forepicture of Israel. For as he forsook the Law and was guilt of adultery and murder, so Israel despised the Covenant, turned aside to idolatry [spiritual adultery], and murdered the Messiah.

"Thus the scope and structure of this Psalm goes far beyond David. It predicts the future confession and forgiveness of Israel in the day of the Messiah's Second Coming,

when, looking upon Him Whom they pierced, they shall mourn and weep [Zech., Chpts. 12-13].

"As well, this is even more perfectly a vivid portrayal of the Intercessory Work of Christ on behalf of His People. Even though David prayed this prayer, the Son of David would make David's sin [as well as ours] His Own, and pray through him that which must be said.

"This means that this is the truest prayer of Repentance ever prayed, because it symbolizes the Intercessory Work of the Son of David.)

CLEANSING

"Wash me thoroughly from my iniquity, and cleanse me from my sin *(man's problem is sin, and man must admit that; the only remedy for sin is 'Jesus Christ and Him Crucified,' to which David, in essence, appealed [Heb. 10:12]; the Blood of Jesus Christ alone cleanses from all sin [I Jn. 1:7]).*

THE CONDITION OF DIVINE FORGIVENESS

"For I acknowledge my transgressions: and my sin is ever before me *(the acknowledgement of Verses 3 through 4 is the condition of Divine forgiveness; all sin, in essence, is committed against God; therefore, God demands that the transgressions be acknowledged, placing the blame where it rightfully belongs — on the perpetrator; He cannot and, in fact, will not, forgive sin that is not acknowledged and for which no responsibility is taken).*

"Against You, You only, have I sinned, and done this evil in Your Sight: that You might be justified when You speak, and be clear when You judge. *(While David's sins were against Bath-sheba, her husband Uriah, and all of Israel, still, the ultimate direction of sin, perfected by Satan, is always against God.*

"All sin is a departure from God's Ways to man's ways.

"David is saying that God is always 'justified' in any action that He takes, and His 'judgment' is always perfect.)

ORIGINAL SIN

"Behold, I was shaped in iniquity; and in sin did my mother conceive me. *(Unequivocally, this Verse proclaims the fact of original sin. This Passage states that all are born in sin, and as a result of Adam's Fall in the Garden of Eden.*

"When Adam, as the federal head of the human race, failed, this means that all of humanity failed. It means that all who would be born would, in effect, be born lost.

"As a result of this, the Second Man, the Last Adam, the Lord Jesus Christ, had to come into this world, in effect, God becoming Man, to undo what the original Adam did. He would have to keep the Law of God perfectly, which He did, all as our Substitute, and then pay the penalty for the terrible sin debt owed by all of mankind, for all had broken the Law, which He did by giving Himself on the Cross of Calvary [Jn. 3:16].

"To escape the judgment of original sin, man must be 'born again,' which is carried out by the believing sinner expressing Faith in Christ and what Christ did at the Cross [Jn. 3:3; Eph. 2:8-9].)

THE TRUTH

"Behold, You desire truth in the inward parts: and in the hidden part You shall make me to know wisdom *(man can only deal with the externals, and even that not very well; God Alone can deal with the 'inward parts' of man, which is the source of sin, which speaks of the heart; in other words, the heart has to be changed, which the Lord Alone can do [Mat. 5:8]).*

"Purge me with hyssop, and I shall be clean: wash me, and I shall be whiter than snow. *(The petition, 'purge* *me with hyssop,' expresses a figure of speech. 'Purge me with the blood which on that night in Egypt was sprinkled on the doorposts with a bunch of hyssop' [Ex. 12:13, 22] portrays David's dependence on 'the Blood of the Lamb.'*

"*David had no recourse in the Law, even as no one has recourse in the Law. The Law can only condemn. All recourse is found exclusively in Christ and what He did for us at the Cross, of which the slain lamb and the blood on the doorposts in Egypt were symbols [Ex. 12:13].)*

A CLEAN HEART

"**Make me to hear joy and gladness; that the bones which You have broken may rejoice.** *(Forgiveness for the past never exhausts the fullness of pardon. There is provision for the future.*

"*The expression 'bones which You have broken,' presents a figure of speech meaning that one cannot proceed until things have been made right with God. It is as though a man's leg is broken, and he cannot walk. Unforgiven sin immobilizes the soul the same as a broken bone immobilizes the body.)*

"**Hide Your face from my sins, and blot out all my iniquities.** *(Unforgiven sin stares in the Face of God. This can only be stopped when the sins are put away, which can only be done by proper Confession and Repentance, with the Blood of Jesus being applied by faith. When this is done, the 'iniquities' are 'blotted out' as though they had never existed. This is 'Justification by Faith' [Rom. 5:1].)*

"**Create in me a clean heart, O God: and renew a right spirit within me.** *(David's heart was unclean. Sin makes the heart unclean. The word 'create' is interesting. It means the old heart is infected by sin, is diseased, and cannot be salvaged. God must, spiritually speaking, 'create a clean heart' [Ezek. 18:31].*

"*Also, it is impossible for any individual to have a 'right spirit' if there is unconfessed sin.)*

THE HOLY SPIRIT

"Cast me not away from Your Presence; and take not Your Holy Spirit from me. *(If sin is unconfessed and rebellion persists, God will ultimately 'cast away' the individual 'from His Presence.' He will also 'take the Holy Spirit' from the person. This refutes the doctrine of unconditional eternal security.)*

"Restore unto me the joy of Your Salvation; and uphold me with Your free Spirit. *(Part of the business of the Holy Spirit is 'restoration,' but only if the individual meets God's conditions, as David did, and as we must do. With unconfessed sin, all 'joy' is lost. With sin confessed, cleansed, and put away, the 'joy of Salvation' returns. A clean heart, a willing spirit, and a steadfast will are then given by the Holy Spirit.)*

"Then will I teach transgressors Your Ways; and sinners shall be converted unto You. *(Before Repentance, David was in no condition to proclaim God's Truth to 'transgressors,' because he was a transgressor himself.*

"Upon true Repentance, David was now ready to teach and to preach, and the Holy Spirit attested to that.)

FORGIVENESS

"Deliver me from blood guiltiness, O God, Thou God of my Salvation: and my tongue shall sing aloud of Your Righteousness. *(This refers to the terrible sin of having Uriah, the husband of Bath-sheba, killed [II Sam. 11:14-21].*

"Only the consciously pardoned sinner can 'sing aloud' of God's Righteousness. Unpardoned men can speak of His Mercy, but their thoughts about it are unholy thoughts.)

"O LORD, open Thou my lips; and my mouth shall show forth Your Praise. *(Proper praise to the Lord cannot* *go forth as long as there is unconfessed sin. This is the reason for such little praise in most Churches, and far too often the praise which actually is offered is hollow. True praise can only come from a true heart!)*

THE SACRIFICES OF GOD

"For You desire not Sacrifice; else would I give it: You delight not in Burnt Offering. *(No penance, sacraments, or costly gifts of Churches or men, regarding expiation of past sins, are desired or accepted by God. Only Faith and trust in Christ and what He has done for us at the Cross can be accepted by the Lord.*

"Unfortunately, the world tries to create a new god, while the Church tries to create another sacrifice. There is only one Sacrifice for sin [Heb. 10:12].)

"The sacrifices of God are a broken spirit: a broken and a contrite heart, O God, You will not despise. *(True Repentance will always include a 'broken spirit' and a 'broken and contrite heart.' Such alone will accept Christ and what Christ has done at the Cross. God will accept nothing less.)*

A FUTURE DAY FOR ISRAEL

"Do good in Your Good Pleasure unto Zion: build Thou the walls of Jerusalem. *(Verses 18-19 are not, as some think, a meaningless addition to the Psalm by some later writer. They both belong to the structure and prophetic scope of the Psalm.*

"David's sin, confession, and Restoration illustrate this future chapter in Israel's history. With their idolatry [spiritual adultery] and murder forgiven, they will go forth as messengers of the Gospel to win other nations to whole-hearted faith and service in and for Christ.

"Upon Israel's Repentance, the Lord will once again

'build Thou the walls of Jerusalem.')

"Then shall You be pleased with the sacrifices of righteousness, with Burnt Offering and Whole Burnt Offering: then shall they offer bullocks upon Your Altar. *(The sacrificial program under the old system was lawful, because it pointed to the coming Redeemer. Since Christ and the Cross, they are no longer necessary, and for all the obvious reasons. Why the symbol when the substance is available?*

"During the Millennial Reign, the Sacrificial System will be restored, but only as a memorial of what Christ has done at the Cross [Ezek., Chpts. 40-48])" **(Ps. 51:1-19).**

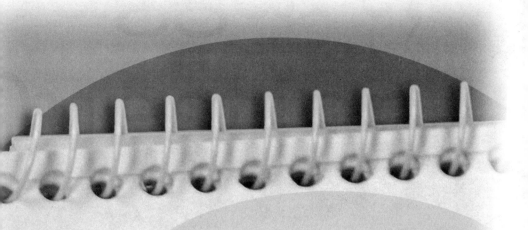

CHAPTER 14

The Doctrine Of The Baptism With The Holy Spirit

THE DOCTRINE OF THE BAPTISM WITH THE HOLY SPIRIT

"And they were all filled with the Holy Spirit *(all were filled, not just the Apostles; due to the Cross, the Holy Spirit could now come into the hearts and lives of all Believers to abide permanently [Jn. 14:16])*, and began to speak with other Tongues *(the initial physical evidence that one has been baptized with the Spirit, and was predicted by the Prophet Isaiah [Isa. 28:9-12], and by Christ [Mk. 16:17; Jn. 15:26; 16:13])*, as the Spirit gave them utterance *(meaning they did not initiate this themselves, but that it was initiated by the Spirit; as we shall see, these were languages known somewhere in the world, but not by the speaker)*" (Acts 2:4).

The Bible teaches that the Baptism with the Spirit is an experience received after Salvation, and is always, and without exception, accompanied by speaking with other Tongues as the Spirit of God gives the utterance.

THE CROSS OF CHRIST

It is the Cross of Christ that made it possible for the Holy Spirit to come into the hearts and lives of Believers and there to abide forever. Jesus said:

"And I will pray the Father, and He shall give you another Comforter *('Parakletos,' which means 'One called to the side of another to help')*, that He may abide with you forever *(before the Cross, the Holy Spirit could only help a few individuals, and then only for a period of time; since the Cross, He lives in the hearts and lives of Believers, and does so forever)*" (Jn. 14:16).

Paul said that the blood of bulls and goats could not take

away sins; therefore, the Law under the Old Covenant stipulated by animal blood, was woefully insufficient. So, the sin debt remained, making it impossible for the Holy Spirit to come into the hearts and lives of Believers to abide permanently. As we stated in the above notes, He did come into the hearts and lives of some people such as the Prophets, etc., to help them carry out the task assigned them, and then the evidence is He would then leave. As far as the sanctifying process was concerned, there is no record that the Holy Spirit helped in this at all. But when Jesus died on the Cross, thereby atoning for all sin, past, present, and future, at least for all who will believe (Jn. 3:16), all sin was then taken away. That's why John the Baptist said to Christ, *"Behold the Lamb of God, Who takes away the sin of the world"* (Jn. 1:29).

So, it is the Cross of Christ that made it possible for the Holy Spirit to come in a brand-new dimension, in effect, taking up His Abode in the hearts and lives of all Believers. Paul said:

> **"Know you not that you are the Temple of God** *(where the Holy Spirit abides)***, and** *that* **the Spirit of God dwells in you?"** (I Cor. 3:16).

WHAT IS THE DIFFERENCE IN BEING BORN OF THE SPIRIT AND BEING BAPTIZED WITH THE SPIRIT?

• Being *"born of the Spirit,"* is that which happens to every single person who comes to Christ. It is the Work of Regeneration that's carried out by the Holy Spirit in the heart and life of the believing sinner, and does so at the moment of conversion. At that time, the Holy Spirit most definitely does come into the life of the Believer and, as stated, there to abide permanently (Jn. 3:1-8; 16:7-15).

• The Baptism with the Spirit is an experience that follows Salvation, and is always accompanied by the speaking with other Tongues. It is for the purpose of giving the Believer Power (Acts 1:8). The Baptism with the Spirit gives the Holy Spirit access to the Believer (Jn. 14:16-18), and the Believer access to the Spirit (Jn. 16:13-15; Acts 2:4; 10:44-46; 19:1-7).

THREE IMPORTANT FACTORS

There are many important things about the Holy Spirit that we ought to know, but to make it easy to understand, I have narrowed it down to three. They are:

1. When Jesus entered His public Ministry, he was first of all baptized with the Holy Spirit. Luke wrote:

"And the Holy Spirit descended in a bodily shape like a Dove upon Him *(the Holy Spirit is a Person, the Third Person of the Godhead, separate from the Father and the Son)*, and a Voice came from Heaven, which said *(the Voice of God the Father)*, You are My Beloved Son *(literally, 'as for You,' in contradistinction to all others)*; in You I am well pleased *(God is pleased with us, only as long as we are in Christ)*" (Lk. 3:22).

The statement is, if Jesus, Who was and is the Son of the Living God, in effect, God manifest in the flesh, One, and the only One Who is Perfect, if He needed the Holy Spirit to carry forth His Work and Ministry, where does that leave us?

The truth is, without being baptized with the Holy Spirit, with the evidence of speaking with other Tongues, precious little is going to be done for the Lord. I didn't say that nothing would be done, but I am saying precious little will be done.

2. Just before His Ascension, which, in effect, was His last Message to His personal Disciples and, in fact, all His followers, the Scripture says:

"And, being assembled together with *them* *(speaks of the time He ascended back to the Father; this was probably the time of the 'above five hundred' [I Cor. 15:6])*,

Commanded them *(not a suggestion)* **that they should not depart from Jerusalem** *(the site of the Temple where the Holy Spirit would descend)*, **but wait for the Promise of the Father** *(spoke of the Holy Spirit, which had been promised by the Father [Lk. 24:49; Joel, Chpt. 2])*, **which, said** *He,* **you have heard of Me** *(you have also heard Me say these things [Jn. 7:37-39; 14:12-17, 26; 15:26; 16:7-15])*.

"**For John truly baptized with water** *(merely symbolized the very best Baptism Believers could receive before the Day of Pentecost)*; **but you shall be baptized with the Holy Spirit not many days hence** *(spoke of the coming Day of Pentecost, although Jesus did not use that term at that time)*" **(Acts 1:4-5).**

If it is to be noticed, our Lord, as stated, did not suggest to them that they be filled with the Spirit, but rather *"Commanded them,"* which was the same as a military charge.

Actually He was saying to them, *"Don't go witness for Me, don't go try to further My Work, actually, don't say anything about Me, until you are first baptized with the Spirit."* This is how important that was.

As well, it must be understood, that these people to whom He spoke, were already Born-Again. They were not to enter Jerusalem in order to be Saved, but rather to be baptized with the Spirit.

3. Unless the Church has the earmarks of the Book of Acts Church, then whatever it is, in the Eyes of God, it's not constituted as *"Church."* It is the Holy Spirit, and not man, who put together the Early Church; therefore, the earmarks should be in our modern Churches as well. Those earmarks are:

• **Salvation by the Blood (Eph. 2:13).**

• **The Baptism with the Holy Spirit, with the evidence of** speaking with other Tongues (Acts 2:4; 10:44-46; 19:1-7).

• **Divine Healing (James 5:14-15).**

• **A victorious, overcoming Christian Life, victorious over** the world, the flesh, and the Devil (Rom. 6:1-14; 8:1-2, 11).

• The eminent return of our Lord to this Earth to rule and reign for 1,000 years (Rev. 20:4-6).

THE BAPTISM WITH THE HOLY SPIRIT IS AN EXPERIENCE SEPARATE AND APART FROM SALVATION

The Believer cannot be baptized with the Spirit until he or she has first been Born-Again (Jn. 14:17). This experience, however, does not make one more Saved. The moment the person comes to Christ, they are just as Saved as they will ever be, because there is no such thing as a partial Justification. The Baptism with the Holy Spirit is an experience that follows Salvation, at least if the Believer asks for it, and is meant, as stated, to provide power in order that the Work of the Lord may be carried out. While one may be baptized with the Holy Spirit immediately after conversion, or any time after conversion, it is never simultaneous with conversion.

There are five accounts in the Book of Acts of Believers being baptized with the Spirit. These five accounts prove that the Baptism with the Spirit is an experience separate, distinct, and apart from Salvation. They are:

1. The Day of Pentecost: As it should be understood, all of these who were baptized on the Day of Pentecost were already Saved. The number included the original Twelve minus Judas, plus over a hundred others (Acts, Chpt. 2).

2. The Samaritans who were baptized with the Spirit: Philip had preached a Revival in *"a city of Samaria,"* where many had been Saved, but yet none were baptized with the Spirit. A short time later, Peter and John went to this area and preached to these people, *"that they might receive the Holy Spirit"* (Acts 8:15). Now, if all Believers are baptized with the Holy Spirit simultaneous at conversion, then what was it that Peter and John were doing?

3. Acts, Chapter 9 records the conversion of Paul and his subsequent baptism. Paul was Saved on the Road to Damascus,

and three days later, Ananias, at the behest of the Lord, went and prayed for Paul that he might *"be filled with the Holy Spirit"* (Acts 9:17). Once again, this took place three days after his conversion.

4. The experience of Cornelius and his household: The experience of Cornelius and those with him was a little different. As Peter preached to them, they were Saved, and then moments later baptized with the Spirit (Acts 10:44-46).

5. The Ephesian Disciples: The Scripture says these men were *"Disciples."* Whenever the word *"Disciples"* is used in the Book of Acts, always and without exception, it refers to one who has accepted Christ. Paul said, *"Have you received the Holy Spirit since you believed?"*

In the Greek, this is literally, *"having believed, did you receive?"*

These individuals answered Paul and said, *"We have not so much as heard whether there be any Holy Spirit."* This didn't mean that they did not know the existence of the Holy Spirit, but that they were not aware that the age of the Spirit had come.

Paul prayed for them, actually laying his hands upon them, and the Scripture says that all of them were baptized with the Spirit (Acts 19:2).

The proof is inescapable in these five experiences, that the Baptism with the Spirit is not received automatically with conversion as many teach, but is always subsequent to Salvation.

SPEAKING WITH OTHER TONGUES

In these five accounts just given, we find overwhelming evidence that speaking with other Tongues is the initial physical evidence that one has been baptized with the Spirit. And, if one has not spoken with other Tongues, then one has not been baptized with the Spirit.

• In Acts, Chapter 2 it says, *"And they were all filled with the Holy Spirit, and began to speak with other Tongues, as the Spirit gave them utterance"* (Acts 2:4).

• In Acts, Chapter 8, as previously stated, we are given the account of Peter and John going to Samaria and preaching to those Samaritans that had been Saved under the preaching of Philip. The Scripture says that they *"prayed for them that they might receive the Holy Spirit"* (Acts 8:15).

While it doesn't mention anything about Tongues, it does say this, even as Peter rebuked Simon the Sorcerer, by saying to him, *"You have neither part nor lot in this matter"* (Acts 8:21).

The word *"matter"* in the Greek, as it is used here, is *"logos,"* and means *"a word or speech."* So actually Peter said, *"You have neither part nor lot in this utterance."* It is clear here that he was speaking of *"tongues."*

• Acts, Chapter 9 gives us the account of the conversion of the Apostle Paul, plus him being *"filled with the Holy Spirit."* In fact, the Scripture doesn't give us any information as it regards what happened. It only says the following:

"And Ananias went his way, and entered into the house; and putting his hands on him said, Brother Saul, the Lord, even Jesus Who appeared unto you in the way as you came, has sent me, that you might receive your sight, and be filled with the Holy Spirit" (Acts 9:17).

It doesn't tell us anything, as stated, about what happened, but we know that Paul spoke with other Tongues, for he said himself, concerning his life and living, *"I thank my God, I speak with Tongues more than you all"* (I Cor. 14:18).

As well, Paul was not speaking of his ability at being linguistic, which refers to being able to speak several languages, which he, no doubt, did. He was rather referring to speaking with other Tongues, when it is to be used, and when it is not to be used, which information is given to us by the Apostle in the Fourteenth Chapter of I Corinthians.

• The Tenth Chapter of Acts tells us, as previously stated, of Cornelius and his household being filled with the Spirit. The Scripture says: *"While Peter yet spoke these words, the Holy Spirit fell on all them which heard the Word.*

"And they of the Circumcision which believed were astonished,

as many as came with Peter, because that on the Gentiles also was poured out the Gift of the Holy Spirit.

"For they heard them speak with Tongues, and magnify God" (Acts 10:44-46).

• In Acts, Chapter 19 we have the record of Paul praying for the Ephesian Believers, and them being filled with the Spirit. The Scripture says:

"And when Paul had laid his hands upon them, the Holy Spirit came on them; and they spoke with Tongues, and prophesied" (Acts 19:6).

• And then we find in the Fourteenth Chapter of I Corinthians, Paul giving implicit instructions as to how Tongues are to be used. I hardly think he would have gone to all of that explanation, if speaking with other Tongues wasn't a viable part of the Christian experience.

As stated, being baptized with the Holy Spirit, and speaking with other Tongues, does not make one more Saved. That is not its purpose. It is a result of Salvation, certainly not the cause. One will find that presently, and throughout Church history, when Believers who are not Spirit-filled get hungry for the Lord, invariably they will be led to the Baptism with the Holy Spirit.

WHAT ARE TONGUES?

The Word of God is replete with information as to what Tongues are. They are always and without exception, a language, spoken somewhere in the world, but not known or understood by the speaker. The Scripture gives us the following information. It says, and I continue to quote from THE EXPOSITOR'S STUDY BIBLE:

"And there were dwelling at Jerusalem Jews, devout men, out of every nation under Heaven *(Jews were then scattered all over the Roman World, with thousands coming in from every nation to keep the Feast).*

"**Now when this was noised abroad** *(multitudes who were in the Temple heard and saw the proceedings and, as well, began to tell others)*, **the multitude came together** *(what was happening attracted a multitude)*, **and was confounded, because that every man heard them speak in his own language** *(means that these on-looking Jews heard these people speaking in many different languages, in fact, languages of the nations of their residence, wherever that might have been, proving that this was not gibberish or babble as some claim)*.

"**And they were all amazed and marveled** *(mostly centered upon this speaking with other Tongues)*, **saying one to another, Behold, are not all these which speak Galilaeans?** *(This means that the Galilaean accent was peculiar and well-known [Mk. 14:70; Lk. 22:59].)*

"**And how hear we every man in our own tongue, wherein we were born?** *(This proves once again that this was not babble, mere chatter, or gibberish, but rather a language known somewhere in the world, but not by the speaker.)*

DIFFERENT NATIONALITIES

"**Parthians, and Medes, and Elamites, and the dwellers in Mesopotamia, and in Judaea, and Cappadocia, in Pontus, and Asia,**

"**Phrygia, and Pamphylia, in Egypt, and in the parts of Libya about Cyrene, and strangers of Rome, Jews and proselytes,**

"**Cretes and Arabians, we do hear them speak in our tongues the wonderful Works of God** *(this tells us what speaking in tongues actually is, a recitation of the 'Wonderful Works of God')*.

"**And they were all amazed, and were in doubt** *(should have been translated, 'and were perplexed'; they had no rational answer to their perplexity)*, **saying one to another,**

What does this mean? *(This was asking more in wonder than demanding an answer.)*

"**Others mocking said** *(they scoffed; whether by gesture or word, they jeered at the Testimony of this given by the Holy Spirit)*, **These men are full of new wine** *(was actually an accusation that they were drunk, i.e., 'intoxicated'; some were amazed and some 'mocked,' which continues to be done even unto this hour)*.

THE WORD GIVEN BY PETER

"**But Peter, standing up with the Eleven, lifted up his voice, and said unto them** *(Peter will now preach the inaugural Message of the Church on that Day of Pentecost)*, **You men of Judaea, and all you who dwell at Jerusalem, be this known unto you, and hearken to my words** *(the Message was probably delivered on Solomon's Porch, a part of the Court of the Gentiles; it was where debates and such like were commonly conducted)*:

"**For these are not drunken, as you suppose** *(in effect, says they are drunk, but not in the common manner)*, **seeing it is *but* the third hour of the day** *(9 a.m.)*.

"**But this is that which was spoken by the Prophet Joel** *(please notice that Peter did not say, 'this fulfills that spoken by the Prophet Joel,' but rather, 'this is that . . .' meaning that it will continue)*;

"**And it shall come to pass in the Last Days, says God** *(proclaims these 'Last Days' as beginning on the Day of Pentecost, and continuing through the coming Great Tribulation)*, **I will pour out of My Spirit upon all flesh** *(speaks of all people everywhere and, therefore, not limited to some particular geographical location; as well, it is not limited respecting race, color, or creed)*: **and your sons and your daughters shall Prophesy** *(includes both genders)*, **and your young men shall see Visions, and your old men shall dream Dreams** *(all given by the Holy Spirit;*

the Hebrew language insinuates, 'both your young men and old men shall see visions, and both your old men and young men shall dream dreams'; it applies to both genders as well)*:

"And on My servants and on My hand-maidens I will pour out in those days of My Spirit *(is meant purposely to address two classes of people who had been given very little status in the past, slaves and women)*; **and they shall Prophesy** *(pertains to one of the 'Gifts of the Spirit' [I Cor. 12:8-10])*" **(Acts 2:5-18).**

All of this proves beyond the shadow of a doubt that *"Tongues"* are a language known somewhere in the world, but not by the speaker.

WHAT GOOD ARE TONGUES?

Many have asked the question, *"What good does it do you?"* Most of the time such questions are asked in sarcasm. Let's see what the Bible says about the value of speaking with other Tongues.

• It says, *"And began to speak with other Tongues, as the Spirit gave them utterance"* (Acts 2:4). I should think it should be understood that anything that the Holy Spirit would give, is good and, in fact, very good.

• *"The Wonderful Works of God."* When these Believers on the Day of Pentecost were baptized with the Spirit, all of the people seeing and hearing them speak, said, *"We do hear them speak in our tongues the Wonderful Works of God."* I should think it should be obvious as to the good of relating such!

• The Scripture says, *"For he who speaks in an unknown Tongue speaks not unto men, but unto God"* (I Cor. 14:2). Again, one would have to deem something as wonderful that speaks unto God.

• *"He who speaks in an unknown tongue edifies himself"* (I Cor. 14:4). All of us need edification and, in fact, we need it constantly. Speaking with other Tongues carries out this needy work within our hearts and lives.

• When one speaks and prays in Tongues, the Scripture says, *"My spirit prays"* (I Cor. 14:14). Whenever our spirit prays, one can be certain that what is said to the Lord is correct!

• Nearly 800 years before the Day of Pentecost, the great Prophet Isaiah said, *"For with stammering lips and another tongue will He speak to this people.*

"To whom He said, This is the rest wherewith you may cause the weary to rest; and this is the refreshing: yet they would not hear" (Isa. 28:11-12).

The two Verses here quoted tell us that speaking with other Tongues brings about a *"rest"* from the tiredness of the journey of life. As well, worshipping with other Tongues brings about a *"refreshing,"* which rejuvenates the person. This mentioned by Isaiah presents two Blessings as it regards speaking and worshipping with Tongues, of which there are many. Regrettably, despite this tremendous Gift given to the People of God, at least to those who will believe, like Judah of old, most *"will not hear,"* even as Paul quoted Isaiah (I Cor. 14:21).

I think from the Scripture, even what we have just quoted regarding Isaiah, one can say that speaking with other Tongues is at least one of the Lord's Provisions for this high pressured life in which we now live. We are told by medical doctors that stress is a cause of many problems in our physical bodies. This is, as stated, at least one of the answers given by the Lord for *"stress."* Worshipping the Lord in Tongues, helps us, as stated, to rest from the tiredness of the journey, while at the same time it is a *"refreshing,"* which gives us strength to go forward.

To say the least, I think it would be very unwise to speak disparagingly of that which the Lord does.

Since the great Latter Rain outpouring of the Spirit at the turn of the Twentieth Century, we are told that over 500 million people have been baptized with the Holy Spirit with the evidence of speaking with other Tongues. Truly the Prophecy of Joel has been fulfilled, and is being fulfilled, where he said, and was quoted by Peter, *"And it shall come to pass in the Last Days, says God, I will pour out of My Spirit upon all flesh"* (Acts 2:16-17).

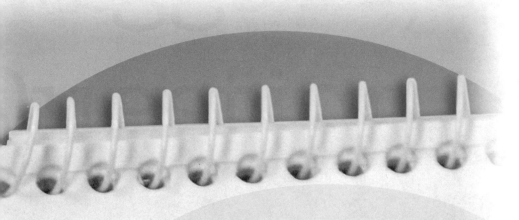

CHAPTER 15

The Doctrine Of The Church

THE DOCTRINE OF THE CHURCH

The Greek word for Church is *"Ekklesia,"* and means *"A Called-out Assembly,"* or *"A Ceremonial Assembly of God's Covenant people."* *"Synagogue"* is the Hebrew word used in Old Testament Times, which had to do with the Sabbath meeting, which probably began at about the time of Ezra or Nehemiah, about 400 years before Christ, but that is only speculation. By the Early Church referring to itself as an *"Ekklesia,"* this means that it broke entirely with its Jewish roots, and did so by rejecting the term *"Synagogue."*

While the word *"Church"* means different things to different people, the accepted meaning is that it is *"a universal body of all Believers in all places, in other words, all who are born-again."* It actually has nothing to do with a denomination, or a building, or even an institution. It refers simply to all who are truly Born-Again.

The Early Church, of which we read about in the Book of Acts and the Epistles had no Church buildings per se, as we have today. They met in homes, in caves, even out in the woods. They could not have buildings simply because Rome would not allow such. In fact, Rome looked at Christians as a part of the Jewish religion. So, in their thinking, the Synagogues of the Jews, sufficed for all, which they did allow. But of course, the Christians were not welcome in the Synagogues, and really had no desire to be there. So their meeting place was wherever it could be.

JESUS, THE BUILDER OF THE CHURCH

Concerning this, Matthew writes. He said:

"When Jesus came into the coasts *(borders)* of Caesarea Philippi *(about thirty miles north of the Sea of Galilee)*, He asked His Disciples, saying, Whom do men say that I the Son of Man am? *(The third form of unbelief manifested itself in popular indifference, indolence, or mere curiosity respecting the Messiah Himself. Upon the answer to this all-important question, hinges the Salvation of man.)*

"**And they said, Some** *say that you are* **John the Baptist: some, Elijah; and others, Jeremiah, or one of the Prophets** *(this form of unbelief manifests itself in the frivolity of the natural heart).*

"**He said unto them, But whom say you that I am?** *(Addressed personally to the Twelve.)*

"**And Simon Peter answered and said, You are the Christ, the Son of the Living God** *(the Great Confession).*

"**And Jesus answered and said unto him, Blessed are you, Simon Bar–jona** *(Peter is the son of Jonah, as Jesus is the Son of God)***: for flesh and blood have not revealed** *it* **unto you** *(mere human ingenuity)***, but My Father Who is in Heaven** *(all Spiritual Knowledge must be by Revelation).*

THE ROCK, CHRIST JESUS

"**And I say also unto you, That you are Peter** *(the Lord changed his name from Simon to Peter, which means 'a fragment of a rock')***, and upon this rock** *(immovable mass; Jesus is the Living Rock on which the Redeemed as living stones are built; for other foundation can no man lay [I Cor. 3:11])* **I will build My Church** *(the Church belongs to Christ, and He is the Head [Col. 1:18])***; and the gates of Hell shall not prevail against it** *(the power of death caused by sin, shall not prevail against it, which victory was won at the Cross [Vss. 21, 24]).*

"**And I will give unto you** *('you' refers to all Believers)* **the keys of the Kingdom of Heaven** *(refers to symbols of authority, the privilege of preaching or proclaiming the Gospel, which is the privilege of every Believer)***: and whatsoever you shall bind on earth shall be bound in Heaven** *(Christ has given the authority and power to* *every Believer to bind Satan and his minions of darkness, and to do so by using the Name of Jesus [Mk. 16:17-18; Lk. 10:19])*: **and whatsoever you shall loose on earth shall be loosed in Heaven** *(looses the Power of God according to the usage of the Name of Jesus; this is the authority of the Believer).*

"Then charged He *(Commanded)* **His Disciples that they should tell no man that He was Jesus the Christ** *(the Name as used here, is a proclamation of Messiahship; by this time, it is painfully obvious that Israel has rejected her Messiah and, therefore, any further proclamation is pointless!)*" **(Mat. 16:13-20).**

PAUL AS THE MASTER BUILDER
OF THE CHURCH UNDER CHRIST

It was to Paul that the meaning of the New Covenant was given, which, in essence, was and is the meaning of the Cross. Concerning this he said:

"But I certify you, Brethren *(make known)*, **that the Gospel which was preached of me** *(the Message of the Cross)* **is not after man.** *(Any message other than the Cross is definitely devised by man.)*

"For I neither received it of man *(Paul had not learned this great Truth from human teachers)*, **neither was I taught** *it (he denies instruction from other men)*, **but by the Revelation of Jesus Christ.** *(Revelation is the mighty Act of God whereby the Holy Spirit discloses to the human mind that which could not be understood without Divine Intervention)*" **(Gal. 1:11-12).**

Concerning this *"Gospel"* which meaning was given to him, he also said:

"But though we *(Paul and his associates)*, **or an Angel**

from Heaven, preach any other gospel unto you than
that which we have preached unto you *(Jesus Christ
and Him Crucified)*, **let him be accursed** *(eternally condemned; the Holy Spirit speaks this through Paul, making
this very serious)*.

"As we said before, so say I now again *(at sometime
past, he had said the same thing to them, making their
defection even more serious)*, If any *man* preach any other
gospel unto you *(anything other than the Cross)* than that
you have received *(which Saved your souls)*, let him be
accursed *('eternally condemned,' which means the loss of
the soul)*.

"For do I now persuade men, or God? *(In essence,
Paul is saying, 'do I preach man's doctrine, or God's?')* or
do I seek to please men? *(This is what false apostles do.)*
for if I yet pleased men, I should not be the Servant of
Christ *(one cannot please both men and God at the same
time)*" (Gal. 1:8-10).

THE MASTER BUILDER

Concerning the Church, Paul said as well:

"Who then is Paul, and who *is* Apollos *(the idea is these
men, though used greatly by God, were still mere men)*, but
Ministers by whom you believed *(better translated, 'Though
whom you believed')*, even as the Lord gave to every man?
*(Whatever Gifts each Preacher had came from the Lord,
and was not due to their own, abilities or merit.)*

"I have planted *(refers to Paul being the founder
of the Church per se under Christ)*, Apollos watered
(the strengthening of the Faith of wavering Churches);
but God gave the increase *(pertains to souls and their
Spiritual Growth)*.

"So then neither is he who plants any thing, neither
he who waters *(the Planter and the Waterer are nothing by*

comparison to the Lord); **but God Who gives the increase.** *(Man by his own ability cannot bring about the increase, no matter how much he plants or waters, spiritually speaking.)*

LABOURERS TOGETHER WITH GOD

"**Now he who plants and he who waters are one** *(literally means in the Greek, 'one thing')*: **and every man shall receive his own reward according to his own labour.** *(Paul did not say, 'according to his own success,' but rather 'labor.' God hasn't called us to be successful, but He has called us to be faithful.)*

"**For we are labourers together with God** *(pertains to Labor in the harvest)*: **you are God's husbandry** *(God's field, God's tilled land)*, **you are God's building** *(Vineyard)*.

"**According to the Grace of God which is given unto me, as a wise masterbuilder** *(in essence, Paul, under Christ, founded the Church)*, **I have laid the foundation** *(Jesus Christ and Him Crucified)*, **and another builds thereon** *(speaks of all Preachers who followed thereafter, even unto this very moment, and have built upon this Foundation)*. **But let every man take heed how he builds thereupon.** *(All must preach the same Doctrine Paul preached, in essence, 'Jesus Christ and Him Crucified.')*

"**For other foundation can no man lay than that is laid** *(anything other than the Cross is another foundation and, therefore, unacceptable to the Lord)*, **which is Jesus Christ** *(Who He is, God manifest in the flesh, and What He did, Redemption through the Cross)*.

"**Now if any man build upon this foundation gold, silver, precious stones** *(presents Paul using symbols; the first three are materials which will stand the test of fire, symbolic of the Word of God which is the Standard)*, **wood, hay, stubble** *(will not stand the test of fire)*;

EVERY MAN'S WORK

"**Every man's work shall be made manifest** *(at the Judgment Seat of Christ)*: **for the day shall declare it** *(the time of the Judgment Seat of Christ)*, **because it shall be revealed by fire** *(the fire of God's Word)*; **and the fire shall try every man's work of what sort it is.** *('Fire' in the Greek is 'puri,' and speaks of the ability of Christ, Who will be the Judge and Who sees through everything we do [Rev. 2:18]. He Alone knows our very motives!)*
"**If any man's work abide which he has built thereupon** *(assuming it to be true)*, **he shall receive a reward** *(pertains to that which will be eternal, although we aren't told what it will be)*.
"**If any man's work shall be burned, he shall suffer loss** *(refers to the loss of reward, but not Salvation)*: **but he himself shall be Saved; yet so as by fire.** *(Actually, this means the person is Saved 'despite the fire.' While the fire of the Word of God will definitely burn up improper works, it will not touch our Salvation, that being in Christ and the Cross)*" **(I Cor. 3:5-15).**

JESUS CHRIST IS THE HEAD OF THE CHURCH

And we must quickly add He is an active Head, not merely a passive Head, as some claim. The Scripture says of Him in this particular:

"**In Whom we have Redemption through His Blood** *(proclaims the price that was paid for our Salvation)*, **even the forgiveness of sins** *(at the Cross, the Lord broke the power of sin, and took away its guilt [Rom. 6:6])*:
"**Who is the Image of the invisible God** *(the Son is the exact reproduction of the Father; a derived Image)*, **the Firstborn of every creature** *(actually means Jesus is the Creator of all things)*:

"For by Him were all things created *(presents the Justification of the title given Christ in the preceding Verse)*, that are in Heaven, and that are in earth, visible and invisible *(things seen and not seen)*, whether *they be* thrones, or dominions, or principalities, or powers *(refers to both Holy and fallen Angels)*: all things were created by Him, and for Him *(Christ is the Creator of all [Jn. 1:3])*:

"And He is before all things *(preexistence)*, and by Him all things consist. *(All things come to pass within this sphere of His Personality, and are dependent upon it.)*

"And He is the Head of the Body, the Church *(the Creator of the world is also Head of the Church)*: Who is the Beginning *(refers to Christ as the Origin or Beginning of the Church)*, the firstborn from the dead *(does not refer to Jesus being Born-Again as some teach, but rather that He was the first to be raised from the dead as it regards the Resurrection, never to die again)*; that in all *things* He might have the preeminence. *(He is the First and Foremost as it relates to the Church.)*

"For it pleased *the Father* that in Him should all fulness dwell *(this 'fullness' denotes the sum total of the Divine Powers and Attributes)*;

"And, having made Peace *(justifying Peace)* through the Blood of His Cross *(presents His Blood as being that which satisfied the just demands of the broken Law)*, by Him to reconcile all things unto Himself *(speaks of the result of Faith in the Cross)*; by Him, *I say,* whether *they be* things in earth, or things in Heaven. *(The Cross not only addressed the Fall of man, but, as well, the Fall of Lucifer)*" (Col. 1:14-20).

CHURCH GOVERNMENT

That which governs the Church, is given to us in the Epistles. In other words, the Word of God as it regards the Epistles, is the Government of God intended for His Church.

Satan probably gains a greater foothold through Church Government than anything else. The problem is, men attempting to usurp authority over the Government of God, by inserting their own government, whatever it might be. The major task of the Church is to ever remain true to the Word of God, and as it pertains to all of its actions and efforts.

A Pastor friend of mine was questioning the leader of a large Pentecostal denomination as it regards a certain practice. My friend asked for a Chapter and Verse as it regarded the situation. The man could not give him such, because the practice was not Scriptural. This is the bane of the Church, the adopting of principles and rudiments which are devised by men. This is where Church denominations get off track more than anything else. The Word of God ceases to be the criteria for all things as it regards their efforts.

WRONG DIRECTION

Perhaps the greatest example in the Early Church is found in Paul confronting Peter. It must be remembered, that Peter was older than Paul and, as well, he was looked at by the Church in those days as the Prince of the Apostles. But yet, Paul called him to task over a certain issue, because it was wrong direction. The Scripture says:

"**But when Peter was come to Antioch** *(Antioch Syria, the city used by God to spearhead world Evangelism)*, **I withstood him to the face** *(means Paul openly opposed and reproved him, even though Peter was the eldest)*, **because he was to be blamed** *(for abandoning the Cross and resorting to Law)*.

"**For before that certain came from James** *(gives us all too well another example as to why Apostles, or anyone else for that matter, are not to be the final word, but rather the Word of God itself)*, **he** *(Peter)* **did eat with the Gentiles** *(Peter knew the Gospel of Grace)*: **but when they**

were come *(those from James in Jerusalem)*, **he withdrew and separated himself, fearing them which were of the Circumcision.** *(The problem was 'man fear.' Some of the Jewish Christians were still trying to hold to the Law of Moses, which means they accepted Jesus as the Messiah, but gave no credence to the Cross whatsoever. This ultimately occasioned the necessity of Paul writing the Epistle to the Hebrews.)*

"And the other Jews *(in the Church at Antioch)* **dissembled likewise with him** *(with Peter)*; **insomuch that Barnabas also was carried away with their dissimulation** *(hypocrisy)*.

"But when I saw that they walked not uprightly according to the Truth of the Gospel *(they were forsaking the Cross)*, **I said unto Peter before *them* all** *(Paul's rebuke was in the presence of everybody, the whole Antioch Church)*, **If you, being a Jew, live after the manner of Gentiles, and not as do the Jews, why do you compel the Gentiles to live as do the Jews?** *(Hypocrisy!)*" **(Gal. 2:11-14).**

THE CALL OF GOD

The Ministry is not an avocation, a vocation, or a career. It is a Calling from God. In fact, if a man or woman has a true Call of God on their lives as it regards one of the Five-fold Callings, they would have to step down to be the President of the United States. That's how high this Calling is. There is nothing in the world that remotely equals such.

Concerning this Calling, the Holy Spirit through the Apostle Paul said, and I continue to quote from THE EXPOSITOR'S STUDY BIBLE:

"**And He gave** *(our Lord does the Calling)* **some, Apostles** *(has reference to the fact that not all who are called to be Ministers will be called to be Apostles; this applies to the other designations as well; 'Apostles' serve* *as the de facto leaders of the Church, and do so through the particular Message given to them by the Lord for the Church)*; **and some, Prophets** *(who stand in the Office of the Prophet, thereby, foretelling and forthtelling)*; **and some, Evangelists** *(to gather the harvest)*; **and some, Pastors** *(Shepherds)* **and Teachers** *(those with a special Ministry to teach the Word to the Body of Christ; 'Apostles' can and do function in all of the Callings)*;

THE PURPOSE OF THE GIFTS

The Scripture continues:

"**For the perfecting of the Saints** *(to 'equip for service'),* **for the work of the Ministry** *(to proclaim the Message of Redemption to the entirety of the world),* **for the edifying of the Body of Christ** *(for the spiritual building up of the Church)*:

"**Till we all come in the unity of the Faith** *(to bring all Believers to a proper knowledge of Christ and the Cross),* **and of the knowledge of the Son of God** *(which again refers to what He did for us at the Cross),* **unto a perfect man** *(the Believer who functions in maturity),* **unto the measure of the stature of the fulness of Christ** *(the 'measure' is the 'fullness of Christ,' which can only be attained by a proper Faith in the Cross)*:

"**That we *henceforth* be no more children** *(presents the opposite of maturity, and speaks of those whose faith is in that other than the Cross),* **tossed to and fro, and carried about with every wind of doctrine, by the sleight of men** *(Satan uses preachers),* ***and* cunning craftiness** *(they make a way, other than the Cross, which seems to be right),* **whereby they lie in wait to deceive** *(refers to a deliberate planning or system)*;

"**But speaking the Truth in Love** *(powerfully proclaiming the Truth of the Cross, but always with Love),* **may**

grow up into Him in all things *(proper Spiritual Growth can take place only according to proper Faith in the Cross [I Cor. 1:21, 23; 2:2])*, **which is the Head,** *even* **Christ** *(Christ is the Head of the Church, and is such by virtue of the Cross)*" **(Eph. 4:11-15).**

THE MESSAGE

The Church has a distinct Message that is if it operates in Truth. That Message is, *"Jesus Christ and Him Crucified"* (I Cor. 1:23). Any other message is spurious, and will serve no positive purpose. In fact, any other message will bring about harm.

Man is lost not so much because of what he does, but rather because of what He is. He is a sinner, and he must have a Saviour, and that Saviour is the Lord Jesus Christ, and the Lord Jesus Christ Alone. But it's not only Who He is, but, as well, what He has done. We speak of the Cross. We must preach the Cross, because it was there that all sin was atoned, all victory was won, and where Satan and every power of darkness were totally defeated. If the Church, in fact, preaches anything else other than the Cross, whatever it is they are preaching, and ever how good it may seem to be on the surface, if the truth be known, it's not the Gospel. If souls are to be Saved, if lives are to be changed, if light is to replace darkness, if Heaven is to replace Hell, it is the Cross of Christ Alone, and our proclamation of that Finished Work, which will accomplish the task. Nothing else will!

SELF-IMPROVEMENT

This is the age of self-improvement; however, the one glaring problem with that effort is, *"self cannot improve self."* But yet, the message of self-improvement is the message of the hour, because it appeals greatly to the flesh, it is widely accepted. Man loves to think that he is able to solve his problem, get himself out of his dilemma, make himself anew, but what does the Word of God say about that?

"Can the Ethiopian change his skin, or the leopard his spots? Then may you also do good, who are accustomed to do evil" (Jer. 13:23).

To be blunt, that's the reason that humanistic psychology is a crock. That's the reason that all of man's efforts in this capacity are no more than a waste.

While it is definitely true that self needs to be improved, and greatly so, the truth is, that man, as stated, cannot improve self by the means or method of self. But yet, self can most definitely be improved. It is the Holy Spirit Who can bring about this change, and the Holy Spirit Alone Who can bring about this change.

THE HOLY SPIRIT

Paul said:

"There **is therefore now no condemnation** *(guilt)* **to them who are in Christ Jesus** *(refers back to Rom. 6:3-5 and our being baptized into His Death, which speaks of the Crucifixion)*, **who walk not after the flesh** *(depending on one's personal strength and ability or great religious efforts in order to overcome sin)*, **but after the Spirit** *(the Holy Spirit works exclusively within the legal confines of the Finished Work of Christ; our Faith in that Finished Work, i.e., 'the Cross,' guarantees the help of the Holy Spirit, which guarantees Victory).*

"For the Law *(that which we are about to give is a Law of God, devised by the Godhead in eternity past [I Pet. 1:18-20]; this Law, in fact, is 'God's Prescribed Order of Victory')* **of the Spirit** *(Holy Spirit, i.e., 'the way the Spirit works')* **of Life** *(all life comes from Christ, but through the Holy Spirit [Jn. 16:13-14])* **in Christ Jesus** *(any time Paul uses this term or one of its derivatives, he is, without fail, referring to what Christ did at the Cross,* *which makes this 'life' possible)* **has made me free** *(given me total Victory)* **from the Law of Sin and Death** *(these are the two most powerful Laws in the Universe; the 'Law of the Spirit of Life in Christ Jesus' alone is stronger than the 'Law of Sin and Death'; this means that if the Believer attempts to live for God by any manner other than Faith in Christ and the Cross, he is doomed to failure)*.

WHAT THE LAW COULD NOT DO

"For what the Law could not do, in that it was weak through the flesh *(those under Law had only their willpower, which is woefully insufficient; so despite how hard they tried, they were unable to keep the Law then, and the same inability persists presently; any person who tries to live for God by a system of laws is doomed to failure, because the Holy Spirit will not function in that capacity)*, **God sending His Own Son** *(refers to man's helpless condition, unable to save himself and unable to keep even a simple Law and, therefore, in dire need of a Saviour)* **in the likeness of sinful flesh** *(this means that Christ was really human, conformed in appearance to flesh which is characterized by sin, but yet sinless)*, **and for sin** *(to atone for sin, to destroy its power, and to save and Sanctify its victims)*, **condemned sin in the flesh** *(destroyed the power of sin by giving His Perfect Body as a Sacrifice for sin, which made it possible for sin to be defeated in our flesh; it was all through the Cross)*:

"That the Righteousness of the Law might be fulfilled in us *(the Law finding its full accomplishment in us can only be done by Faith in Christ, and what Christ has done for us at the Cross)*, **who walk not after the flesh** *(not after our own strength and ability)*, **but after the Spirit** *(the word 'walk' refers to the manner in which we order our life; when we place our Faith in Christ and the Cross, understanding that all things come from God to us by means* *of the Cross, ever making it the Object of our Faith, the Holy Spirit can then work mightily within us, bringing about the Fruit of the Spirit; that is what 'walking after the Spirit' actually means!).*

"For they who are after the flesh do mind the things of the flesh *(refers to Believers trying to live for the Lord by means other than Faith in the Cross of Christ)***; but they who are after the Spirit the things of the Spirit** *(those who place their Faith in Christ and the Cross, do so exclusively; they are doing what the Spirit desires, which alone can bring Victory)***" (Rom. 8:1-5).**

Paul plainly and clearly tells us the Message that will bring about the Work of the Holy Spirit within our lives, Who Alone can improve self. Even though the following has already been given in this Volume, still, because of the great significance of that which we address, please allow the repetition.

The following is a short diagram which tells us how to live for God, how to order our behavior, how that the Holy Spirit can work within our lives. It is simple and to the point but yet easily understood.

FOCUS: The Lord Jesus Christ (Jn. 14:6).

OBJECT OF FAITH: The Cross of Christ (Rom. 6:1-14; I Cor. 1:17-18, 23; 2:2).

POWER SOURCE: The Holy Spirit (Rom. 8:1-2, 11).

RESULTS: Victory (Rom. 6:14).

Now let's turn it around using the same formula, but yet the way of the flesh, which is regrettably, the method of most of the modern church.

FOCUS: Works

OBJECT OF FAITH: One's performance

POWER SOURCE: Self

RESULTS: Defeat!

The following, as stated, now tells us the Message that will bring about Victory within our lives, and in every capacity and, in fact, that alone which can bring Victory.

THE TRUE MESSAGE OF THE CHURCH

I quote from THE EXPOSITOR'S STUDY BIBLE:

"**For Christ sent me not to baptize** *(presents to us a Cardinal Truth)*, **but to preach the Gospel** *(the manner in which one may be Saved from sin)*: **not with wisdom of words** *(intellectualism is not the Gospel)*, **lest the Cross of Christ should be made of none effect.** *(This tells us in no uncertain terms that the Cross of Christ must always be the emphasis of the Message.)*

"**For the preaching** *(Word)* **of the Cross is to them who perish foolishness** *(Spiritual things cannot be discerned by unredeemed people, but that doesn't matter; the Cross must be preached just the same, even as we shall see)*; **but unto us which are Saved it is the Power of God.** *(The Cross is the Power of God simply because it was there that the total sin debt was paid, giving the Holy Spirit, in Whom the Power resides, latitude to work mightily within our lives.)*

"**For it is written** *(Isa. 29:14)*, **I will destroy the wisdom of the wise, and will bring to nothing the understanding of the prudent** *(speaks to those who are wise in their own eyes, in effect, having forsaken the Ways of the Lord)*.

"**Where** *is* **the wise?** *(This presents the first of three classes of learned people who lived in that day.)* **where** *is* **the Scribe?** *(This pertained to the Jewish Theologians of that day.)* **where** *is* **the disputer of this world?** *(This speaks of the Greeks, who were seekers of mystical and metaphysical interpretations.)* **has not God made foolish the wisdom of this world?** *(This pertains to what God did in sending His Son to Redeem humanity, which He did by the Cross. All the wisdom of the world couldn't do this!)*

THE WORLD BY WISDOM KNEW NOT GOD

"**For after that in the Wisdom of God the world**

by wisdom knew not God *(man's puny wisdom, even the best he has to offer, cannot come to know God in any manner)*, it pleased God by the foolishness of preaching *(preaching the Cross)* to save them who believe. *(Paul is not dealing with the art of preaching here, but with what is preached.)*

"For the Jews require a sign *(the sign of the Messiah taking the Throne and making Israel a great Nation once again)*, and the Greeks seek after wisdom *(they thought that such solved the human problem; however, if it did, why were they ever seeking after more wisdom?)*:

"But we preach Christ Crucified *(this is the Foundation of the Word of God and, thereby, of Salvation)*, unto the Jews a stumblingblock *(the Cross was the stumblingblock)*, and unto the Greeks foolishness *(both found it difficult to accept as God a dead Man hanging on a Cross, for such Christ was to them)*;

"But unto them who are called *(refers to those who accept the Call, for the entirety of mankind is invited [Jn. 3:16; Rev. 22:17])*, both Jews and Greeks *(actually stands for both 'Jews and Gentiles')*, Christ the Power of God *(what He did at the Cross atoned for all sin, thereby, making it possible for the Holy Spirit to exhibit His Power within our lives)*, and the Wisdom of God. *(This Wisdom devised a Plan of Salvation which pardoned guilty men and at the same time vindicated and glorified the Justice of God, which stands out as the wisest and most remarkable Plan of all time.)*

GOD IS WISER THAN MEN

"Because the foolishness of God is wiser than men *(God achieves the mightiest ends by the humblest means)*; and the weakness of God is stronger than men *(refers to that which men take to be weak, but actually is not — the Cross)*.

"For you see your Calling, Brethren *(refers to the nature and method of their Heavenly Calling)*, how that not many wise men after the flesh, not many mighty, not many noble, *are Called (are Called and accept)*:

"But God has chosen the foolish things of the world to confound the wise *(the preaching of the Cross confounds the wise because it falls out to changed lives, which nothing man has can do)*; and God has chosen the weak things of the world to confound the things which are mighty *(the Cross is looked at as weakness, but it brings about great strength and power, regarding those who accept the Finished Work of Christ)*;

"And base things of the world, and things which are despised, has God chosen *(it is God working in the base things and the despised things which brings about miraculous things)*, *yes,* and things which are not, to bring to nought things that are *(God can use that which is nothing within itself, but with Him all things become possible)*:

"That no flesh *(human effort)* should glory in His Presence.

"But of Him are you in Christ Jesus *(pertains to this great Plan of God which is far beyond all wisdom of the world; we are 'in Christ Jesus,' by virtue of the Cross — what He did there)*, Who of God is made unto us Wisdom, and Righteousness, and Sanctification, and Redemption *(we have all of this by the Holy Spirit, through Christ and what He did at the Cross; this means the Cross must ever be the Object of our Faith)*:

"That, according as it is written *(Jer. 9:23)*, he who glories, let him glory in the Lord. *(He who boasts, let him boast in the Lord, and not in particular preachers.)*

"And I, Brethren, when I came to you, came not with excellency of speech or of wisdom *(means that he depended not on oratorical abilities, nor did he delve into philosophy, which was all the rage of that particular day)*, declaring unto you the Testimony of God *(which is Christ and Him Crucified).*

"**For I determined not to know anything among you** *(with purpose and design, Paul did not resort to the knowledge or philosophy of the world regarding the preaching of the Gospel)*, **save Jesus Christ, and Him Crucified** *(that and that alone is the Message which will save the sinner, set the captive free, and give the Believer perpetual victory)*" **(I Cor. 1:17-31; 2:1-2).**

THE GREAT COMMISSION

It is incumbent upon the Church to take this great and glorious Gospel of Jesus Christ and His Power to save, to a hurting, dying and lost world. God has already done everything that Heaven can do in order that this be made possible. He sent His Only Son to serve as a Sacrifice for sin, at least for all who will believe. He then sent us the Holy Spirit in a completely new dimension, to give us power that we might do that which we need to do. Concerning the Holy Spirit and His Work, Jesus said:

THE HOLY SPIRIT AND
THE GREAT COMMISSION

"**And, being assembled together with** *them (speaks of the time He ascended back to the Father; this was probably the time of the 'above five hundred' [I Cor. 15:6]),* **Commanded them** *(not a suggestion)* **that they should not depart from Jerusalem** *(the site of the Temple where the Holy Spirit would descend)*, **but wait for the Promise of the Father** *(spoke of the Holy Spirit which had been promised by the Father [Lk. 24:49; Joel, Chpt. 2])*, **which, said** *He,* **you have heard of Me** *(you have also heard Me say these things [Jn. 7:37-39; 14:12-17, 26; 15:26; 16:7-15]).*

"**For John truly baptized with water** *(merely symbolized the very best Baptism Believers could receive before the Day of Pentecost)*; **but you shall be baptized with the**

Holy Spirit not many days hence *(spoke of the coming Day of Pentecost, although Jesus did not use that term at that time)*" **(Acts 1:4-5).**

And then He tells them, and which, as well, refers to all followers:

"**But you shall receive power** *(Miracle-working Power)*, **after that the Holy Spirit is come upon you** *(specifically states that this 'Power' is inherent in the Holy Spirit, and solely in His Domain)*: **and you shall be witnesses** *(doesn't mean witnessing to souls, but rather to one giving one's all in every capacity for Christ, even to the laying down of one's life)* **unto Me** *(without the Baptism with the Holy Spirit, one cannot really know Jesus as one should)* **both in Jerusalem, and in all Judaea, and in Samaria, and unto the uttermost part of the Earth** *(proclaims the Work of God as being worldwide)*" **(Acts 1:8).**

THREE THINGS THAT MUST CHARACTERIZE THE CHURCH

1. Before Jesus began His public Ministry, He was first baptized with the Holy Spirit (Mat. 3:16-17). If Jesus, the Son of the Living God, in fact, God manifested in the flesh, needed the Holy Spirit, doesn't it stand to reason that we do as well?!

2. According to the Passages we have just quoted, the last Word that Jesus gave to His Followers was the Command that first of all, before they testified for Him, before they planted Churches, before they did anything, they must first be *"baptized with the Holy Spirit."* As we stated in the notes above, it was not a suggestion, but rather a Command! To be sure, that Command is just as incumbent upon us presently as it was then. The Truth is, without the Baptism with the Holy Spirit, which is always and without exception accompanied by the speaking with other Tongues (Acts 2:4) precious little is going to be done

for Christ. As we've already stated in this Volume, the Bible teaches that the Baptism with the Holy Spirit is an experience separate and apart from Salvation, in fact, always subsequent to Salvation (Acts 8:14-17; 9:17-18; 11:16-18; 19:1-7).

3. If the modern Church doesn't carry the earmarks of the Book of Acts Church, then in the Eyes of God, Whose Eyes Alone matter, it's really not Church. Those earmarks are:

• Salvation by the Blood of Jesus (I Jn. 1:7).

• The Baptism with the Holy Spirit, with the evidence of speaking with other Tongues (Acts 2:1-18).

• Power to live an overcoming life according to our Faith in Christ and what He did for us at the Cross, which then gives the Holy Spirit latitude to work within our lives (Rom. 6:1-14; 8:1-2, 11; Gal. 2:20-21).

• The Power of the Lord to heal the sick (James 5:14-18).

• That we preach the Rapture of the Church (I Thess. 4:13-18).

• That we preach the Second Coming of our Lord, to rule and reign on this Earth for 1,000 years, along with all the Glorified Saints (Rev., Chpt. 19).

Those are the salient earmarks of the Church, at least what it ought to be, and what it ought to preach.

TAKING THE GOSPEL TO THE WORLD

As we have stated, there is only one Message that will set the captive free, and that is, *"Jesus Christ and Him Crucified"* (I Cor. 1:23). Concerning this, which concerns the Great Commission, the Scripture says:

"And Jesus came and spoke unto them *(the same meeting on the mountain, and constitutes the Great Commission)*, saying, All power is given unto Me in Heaven and in Earth *(this is not given to Him as Son of God; for, as God nothing can be added to Him or taken from Him; it is rather a power, which He has merited by His Incarnation and His*

Death at Calvary on the Cross [Phil. 2:8-10]; this authority extends not only over men, so that He governs and protects the Church, disposes human events, controls hearts and opinions; but the forces of Heaven also are at His Command; the Holy Spirit is bestowed by Him, and the Angels are in His employ as ministering to the members of His Body. When He said, 'all power,' He meant, 'all power!').

"Go ye therefore *(applies to any and all who follow Christ, and in all ages)*, **and teach all nations** *(should have been translated, 'and preach to all nations', for the word 'teach' here refers to a proclamation of truth)*, **baptizing them in the Name of the Father, and of the Son, and of the Holy Spirit** *(presents the only formula for Water Baptism given in the Word of God)***:**

"Teaching them *(means to give instruction)* **to observe all things** *(the whole Gospel for the whole man)* **whatsoever I have commanded you** *(not a suggestion)***: and, lo, I am with you always** *(It is I, Myself, God, and Man, Who am — not 'will be'— hence, forever present among you, and with you as Companion, Friend, Guide, Saviour, God)*, *even* **unto the end of the world** *(should have been translated 'age')***. Amen** *(it is the guarantee of My Promise)*" **(Mat. 28:18-20).**

MARK

Mark added the following concerning the Great Commission and I quote:

"And He said unto them, Go ye into all the world *(the Gospel of Christ is not merely a western Gospel, as some claim, but is for the entirety of the world)*, **and preach the Gospel to every creature** *('preaching' is God's method, as is here plainly obvious; as well, it is imperative that every single person have the opportunity to hear; this is the responsibility of every Believer).*

"**He who believes** *(believes in Christ and what He did for us at the Cross)* **and is baptized** *(baptized into Christ [Rom. 6:3-5] not Water Baptism)* **shall be Saved; but he who believes not shall be damned** *(Jn. 3:16)*.

"**And these signs shall follow them who believe** *(not these 'sins' shall follow them who believe)*; **In My Name shall they cast out devils** *(demons — Jesus defeated Satan, fallen Angels, and all demon spirits at the Cross [Col. 2:14-15])*; **they shall speak with new Tongues** *(baptism with the Holy Spirit with the evidence of speaking with other Tongues [Acts 2:4])*;

"**They shall take up serpents** *(put away demon spirits [Lk. 10:19] has nothing to do with reptiles)*; **and if they drink any deadly thing, it shall not hurt them** *(speaks of protection; in no way does it speak of purposely drinking poison, etc., in order to prove one's faith; the word, 'if,' speaks of accidental ingestion)*; **they shall lay hands on the sick, and they shall recover** *(means to do so 'in the Name of Jesus' [Acts 5:12; 13:3; 14:3; 19:11; 28:8; I Tim. 4:14; II Tim. 1:6; Heb. 6:2; James 5:14])*" **(Mk. 16:15-18).**

ST. LUKE

The following is that given by Luke concerning the Great Commission:

"**And He said unto them, These** *are* **the words which I spoke unto you, while I was yet with you, that all things must be fulfilled, which were written in the Law of Moses, and** *in* **the Prophets, and** *in* **the Psalms, concerning Me** *(the Jews divided the Old Testament into three parts — the Law of Moses, the Prophets, and the Psalms, which consisted of the Wisdom Books; the entire Story of the Old Testament is the Story of Jesus and the Cross, and what the Cross affords; in fact, if we do not understand that, we cannot fully understand the Word of God; as is made* *plainly obvious here, 'Christ and Him Crucified' is the key to all understanding).*

"Then opened He their understanding, that they might understand the Scriptures *(he who doesn't understand the Scriptures, understands little or nothing; let us say it again: 'Jesus Christ and Him Crucified,' is the Story of the Bible; every Doctrine must be built upon that Foundation, which constitutes the house built upon the Rock; otherwise, it's a house built upon sand),*

"And said unto them, Thus it is written *(proves what I have just stated concerning Christ and the Cross),* **and thus it behoved Christ to suffer, and to rise from the dead the third day** *(let us say it again, this is the Story of the Bible)***:**

REPENTANCE

"And that Repentance and Remission of sins should be preached in His Name *(presents God's method of proclaiming His Word, and carrying out His Work; any other method is unscriptural)* **among all nations, beginning at Jerusalem** *(God's Plan of Salvation is identical for all regarding race, color, or culture; it is for the whole world).*

"And you are witnesses of these things *(Christianity was not begun as the result of an enlightened philosophy, as with all religions; it was begun by men and women who literally witnessed the Incarnate Son of God in all His earthly Ministry, as well as His Death and Resurrection; consequently, they could say, 'we have seen, and do testify').*

"And, behold, I send the Promise of My Father upon you *(the Baptism with the Holy Spirit, which would come on the Day of Pentecost [Acts 1:4-5])***: but tarry you in the city of Jerusalem** *(this was where the Temple was located, and where the Day of Pentecost was always celebrated, which would occasion the outpouring of the Spirit; this was only for the initial outpouring; since then, Jesus*

baptizes with the Holy Spirit wherever the person might be
[Acts, Chpts. 8-10, 19]), **until you be endued with power
from on high** *(this is the Baptism with the Holy Spirit,
which is always accompanied by the speaking with other
Tongues [Acts 2:4]; without being thus endued, the Believer
and the Church are of little worth to the Kingdom of God)"*
(Lk. 24:44-49).

As Christians, what kind of Gospel are we taking to the
world?

The following is a Chapter from a book given to me, but
without the name of the book. Only the Chapter was provided.
Consequently, I have no way of knowing who wrote it, but I do
know this, the Word given is that which desperately needs to
be heeded. I regret that I cannot give credit to the man who
wrote it, but I definitely believe it is a Message that desperately
needs to be heard. I quote:

"NEEDED: A REFORMATION WITHIN THE CHURCH"

*"The first look is toward Christ, Who is her Head, her Lord
and her All.*

*"After that she must be self-regarding and world-regarding,
with a proper balance between the two.*

*"By self-regarding I do not mean self-centered. I mean that
the Church must examine herself constantly to see if she be in
the faith; she must engage in severe self-criticism, with a cheerful
readiness to make amends; she must live in a state of perpetual
penitence, seeking God with her whole heart; she must constantly
check her life and conduct against the Holy Scriptures and bring
her life into line with the Will of God.*

*"By world-regarding I mean that the Church must know why
she is here on Earth; that she must acknowledge her indebtedness
to all mankind (Rom. 1:14-15); that she must take seriously the
Words of her Lord, 'Go into all the world and preach the good
news to all creation,' and 'you will be My witnesses in Jerusalem,*

and in all Judea and Samaria, and to the ends of the Earth.'

THE TASK OF THE CHURCH

"The task of the Church is twofold:
"1. To spread Christianity throughout the world.
"2. To make sure that the Christianity that she spreads is the pure New Testament kind.

THOSE WHO SPREAD THE WORD

"Theoretically the Seed being the Word of God, should produce the same kind of fruit regardless of the spiritual condition of those who scatter it; but it does not work that way. The identical message preached to the heathen by men of differing degrees of Godliness will produce different kinds of converts and result in a quality of Christianity varying according to the purity and power of those who preach it.

AFTER ITS KIND

"Christianity will always reproduce itself after its kind. A worldly-minded, unspiritual Church, when she crosses the ocean to give her witness to peoples of other tongues and other cultures, is sure to bring forth on other shores a Christianity much like her own.

"Not the naked Word only but the character of the witness determines the quality of the convert. The Church can do no more than transplant herself. What she is in one land she will be in another. A crab apple does not become a Grimes Golden by being carried from one country to another. God has written His Law deep into all life; everything must bring forth after its kind.

THE FOREMOST OBLIGATION

"The popular notion that the first obligation of the Church

is to spread the Gospel to the uttermost parts of the Earth is false. Her first obligation is to be spiritually worthy to spread it. Our Lord said 'Go,' but He also said 'Wait,' and the waiting had to come before the going. Had the Disciples gone forth as Missionaries before the Day of Pentecost, it would have been an overwhelming spiritual disaster, for they could have done no more than make converts after their own likeness, and this would have altered for the worse the whole history of the western world and had consequences throughout the ages to come.

A DEGENERATE BRAND OF CHRISTIANITY

"To spread an effete, degenerate brand of Christianity to pagan lands is not to fulfill the Commandment of Christ or to discharge our obligation to the heathen. These terrible words of Jesus haunt my soul: 'You travel over land and sea to win a single convert, and when he becomes one, you make him twice as much a son of Hell as you are' (Mat. 23:15).

"To win men to Judaism from among the Gentile nations was altogether a good and right thing to do. Thousands of happy converts were won to the Gospel of Moses during the years of Israel's spiritual ascendancy; but at the time of Christ Judaism had sunk so low that her missionary effort wrought actual harm instead of good.

A SUBNORMAL, POWERLESS CHURCH

"It would appear logical that a subnormal, powerless Church would not engage in missionary activity, but again the facts contradict the theory. Christian groups that have long ago lost every trace of moral fire, nevertheless continue to grow at home and reproduce themselves in other lands. Indeed there is scarcely a fringe sect or heretical cult these days but is enjoying amazing success among the backward people of the world.

"The evangelical wing of the Church has in recent years become world-regarding to a remarkable degree. Within the last

twenty years evangelical missionary activity on foreign fields has been stepped up tremendously. But there is in the whole thing one dangerous weakness. That weakness is the naïve assumption that we have only to reach the last tribe with our brand of Christianity and the world has been evangelized. This is an assumption that we dare not make.

BELOW THE NEW TESTAMENT STANDARD

"Evangelical Christianity, at least in the United States, is now tragically below the New Testament standard. Worldliness is an accepted part of our way of life. Our religious mood is social instead of spiritual. We have lost the art of worship. We are not producing Saints. Our models are successful businessmen, celebrated athletes and theatrical personalities. We carry on our religious activities after the methods of the modern advertiser. Our homes have been turned into theaters. Our literature is shallow and our hymnody borders on sacrilege. And scarcely anyone appears to care.

"We must have a better kind of Christian soon or within another half century we may have no true Christianity at all. Increased numbers of demi-Christians are not enough. We must have a reformation."

THE VISION

If I remember the date correctly it was July 1, 1985. As I usually did every morning, I would drive to a secluded spot, which was by a railroad track that was not too very far from our home. I would park there and study the Word for a period of time, and then walk down the track and spend time in prayer. This particular morning was no exception, but yet something tremendous would take place.

I had studied the Word for a period of time, and now got out of the car, and began to walk down the track seeking the Lord. As stated, there were no houses nearby, so it afforded a place of privacy, and I always enjoyed very much this time spent with the Lord each morning.

I had not been praying very long, perhaps only a few minutes, when all of a sudden everything changed all around me. As far as the eye could see in every direction, the landscape was filled with cotton, and I might say ready to be harvested. The stalks were heavily laden, in other words, a good crop.

Off in the distance I could see two mechanical cotton pickers that were attempting to gather the harvest. They were woefully few for the gigantic task that lay ahead.

THE STORM

And then I looked to my left, and I saw a terrible storm that was coming down upon this vast array of cotton. I've never seen the clouds so black, as the lightning played in jagged forks through the heavens. It was obvious that if the harvest wasn't gathered soon, this storm would totally and completely destroy it all. Incidentally, that storm came from the east.

THE LORD SPOKE TO ME

It was at that moment that the Lord spoke to my heart respecting what I was seeing. He told me that the fields of cotton were typical of the harvest. Actually He had said in His earthly Ministry, *"Say not ye, There are yet four months, then comes harvest? behold, I say unto you, Lift up your eyes, look on the fields, for they are white already to harvest"* (Jn. 4:35).

Then He said something to me Personally as it regards this Ministry, which I do not feel at liberty to repeat.

DELAY?

The Lord addressed Himself to the gathering storm, and then said, *"I will delay the storm for a period of time, until the harvest can be gathered."* He then said to me: *"Put the Telecast in every country of the world that will open its doors to you."* And then, *"Don't fail Me."* He again related something personally about our Ministry, which I do not feel at liberty to relate.

As stated, that was in 1985, and to be sure that Vision has never really left my mind.

THE EVENTS THAT FOLLOWED

The events that followed almost killed me! Countless times I wondered, how that the Command of my Lord could be carried out regarding the Telecast and the harvest. But now (2009), once again the Telecast is being aired in over 100 countries in the world. I do not know exactly how long the Lord will delay the storm. I do not know exactly what He will do with this Ministry. I just know what the Lord spoke to me in 1985. And to the best of my strength and ability, I must endeavor to carry out what He told me to do that day those years ago.

In the meantime, He has opened up to me the Message of the Cross, actually that which was originally given to the Apostle Paul. Now the Message is complete! It is now a completed Gospel which we are attempting to take to the world. That is the business of the Church, actually the business of every single Born-Again Believer.

THAT WHICH YOU SUPPORT

As we quoted our dear Brother's Message concerning the type of Christianity that's being taken to the world, how timely and how appropriate were his words. You the reader should take them to heart. You must make certain that what you are supporting is actually the Gospel of the New Testament. It must be the Message of the Cross, simply because there is no other!

Jesus said: *"And this Gospel of the Kingdom shall be preached in all the world for a witness unto all nations; and then shall the end come"* (Mat. 24:14).

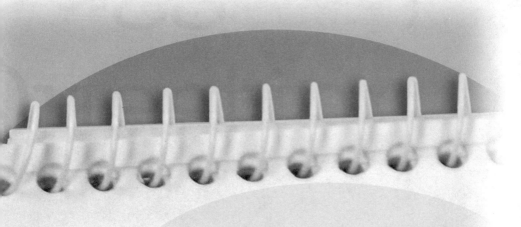

CHAPTER 16

The Doctrine Of The Cross

THE DOCTRINE OF THE CROSS

The material that we hope to bring you in this Chapter is the most important that you as a Believer will ever know or have presented to you. I realize that's quite a statement, but I know it to be true. I am not speaking of my ability or the lack thereof as it regards the subject matter, but rather the subject matter itself. Unless the Believer understands this which the Apostle Paul gave to us, even as the Lord gave it to him (Gal. 1:12), while he can be a Christian, and can even make Heaven his home, the fact is, he cannot live a victorious, overcoming, Christian life.

Considering that our Lord paid an awful price for our Redemption, I should think it would be obvious that He wants us to have all that is possible to have at this time. But unfortunately, most Christians are living far beneath the Spiritual Privileges they could have.

I do not say this from an academic perspective, but rather from experience, even bitter experience. If by the Grace of God, we can impart Truth to you that will enable you to live a victorious life; your Victory will be my reward.

THE GOSPEL OF JESUS CHRIST

Paul said:

"**For Christ sent me not to baptize** *(presents to us a Cardinal Truth)*, **but to preach the Gospel** *(the manner in which one may be Saved from sin)*: **not with wisdom of words** *(intellectualism is not the Gospel)*, **lest the Cross of Christ should be made of none effect.** *(This tells us in no uncertain terms that the Cross of Christ must always be the emphasis of the Message)*" **(I Cor. 1:17).**

In this one Verse, the Apostle tells us what the Gospel of Jesus Christ actually is. It is the Message of the Cross.

This means, if the preacher is not preaching the Cross, then whatever it is he is preaching, in its own way it may be good, but it's not the Gospel, and it will not help anyone. In fact, the only Message that will save, help, heal, bless, instruct, lead, guide, empower, is the Message of the Cross. In our next Chapter we will address the means by which all of this comes about.

Unfortunately, the modern Church is little preaching the Cross anymore. As a result, whatever is being preached is not the Gospel, at least for the most part, and will do precious little, if any, good.

The message that is being preached presently is one of *"morality"* and *"ethics."* Now those two words sound very good to most, because most everyone wants better morals, and most everyone wants that which is ethical. But to treat this subject in the way that it is presently being treated, one is really only treating the symptoms. Man's real problem is not a lack of ethics or immorality; even those things are the end results of his state. Man's problem is sin, and there is only one answer for sin, and that is the Cross of Christ.

But modern man, at least according to most preachers, is not really a sinner, he's just not properly motivated, or else he really doesn't know how wonderful and good he actually is. So he needs a preacher to tell him these things, which will solve his problems; however, the sad truth is, no problems are solved at all by this means.

The Gospel of Jesus Christ, and we are speaking of the Message of the Cross, is not a Gospel of diplomacy. It is rather an ultimatum! We do the thing God's Way or else it's not done at all.

AN ILLUSTRATION

Some time back I saw a cartoon that explains the modern Ministry to the proverbial *"T."*

Two men were standing and looking at a huge machine that was working away. Smoke was coming out of its stacks, and pulleys were turning and wheels were churning. It was one great beehive of motion.

One man asked the other one, *"What does it do?"*

The one to whom the question was asked, looked somewhat blank and answered, *"Do?"*

The truth is the machine did not do anything. It did not manufacture anything, it did not repair anything, it was just a machine of motion.

That's basically the same thing the modern church is doing. It's just one vast beehive of motion, with nothing being done for the Lord. In other words, no souls are Saved, no Believers are baptized with the Holy Spirit, no lives are changed, no sick are healed, no bondages broken, etc. — despite all the motion!

Let us say it again, if the preacher is not preaching the Cross, he's not preaching the Gospel, and if he's not preaching the Gospel, whatever it is he is preaching, is of no consequence!

THE MESSAGE OF THE CROSS
IS THE POWER OF GOD

Paul said:

"For the preaching *(Word)* of the Cross is to them who perish foolishness *(Spiritual things cannot be discerned by unredeemed people, but that doesn't matter; the Cross must be preached just the same, even as we shall see)*; but unto us who are Saved it is the Power of God. *(The Cross is the Power of God simply because it was there that the total sin debt was paid, giving the Holy Spirit, in Whom the Power resides, latitude to work mightily within our lives)*" (I Cor. 1:18).

First of all, the word translated *"preaching,"* in the above Scripture, in the Greek is *"logos."* It either means *"word"* or *"message,"* and should have been translated that way. It would then read, *"For the Message of the Cross. . . ."*

How is the Message of the Cross the Power of God?

There was no power in that wooden beam on which Jesus died! In fact, if the actual Cross on which Jesus died had been preserved all these centuries, and was now found, there would be no more power in that piece of wood than in any other piece of wood. As well, there was no power in the death of Christ per se. In fact, the Scripture says, *"He was crucified through weakness"* (II Cor. 13:4).

This does not mean that He was personally weak, but that it was a contrived weakness. In other words, he could have called down any number of Angels if He had desired to have done so. So, how is the Message of the Cross the Power of God?

The Power is in the Holy Spirit (Acts 1:8). The idea is, when Jesus died on the Cross, He atoned for all sin, past, present, and future, at least for all who will believe (Jn. 3:16). Now that the sin debt is forever paid, this made it possible for the Holy Spirit to come into the heart and life of the Believer, there to abide permanently (Jn. 14:16-17).

The Cross of Christ was a legal work. It satisfied a legal debt that man legally owed God, but could not pay. When the Law was satisfied, which it was by the Death of Christ, then the Holy Spirit could come into the heart and life of the Believer to reside permanently (I Cor. 3:16). As stated, He is the One Who has the Power. But it is the Cross of Christ that has made it all possible.

Unfortunately, most in the modern church don't know this. In other words, they don't know how the Holy Spirit works. In fact, this which we are bringing to you is so much a legal entity, that the Holy Spirit calls it a *"Law."* He said:

THE LAW OF THE SPIRIT OF LIFE IN CHRIST JESUS

And I quote from THE EXPOSITOR'S STUDY BIBLE:

"**For the Law** *(that which we are about to give is a Law of God, devised by the Godhead in eternity past [I Pet. 1:18-20]; this Law, in fact, is 'God's Prescribed Order of*

Victory') **of the Spirit** *(Holy Spirit, i.e., 'the way the Spirit works')* **of Life** *(all life comes from Christ, but through the Holy Spirit [Jn. 16:13-14])* **in Christ Jesus** *(any time Paul uses this term or one of its derivatives, he is, without fail, referring to what Christ did at the Cross, which makes this 'life' possible)* **has made me free** *(given me total Victory)* **from the Law of Sin and Death** *(these are the two most powerful Laws in the Universe; the 'Law of the Spirit of Life in Christ Jesus' alone is stronger than the 'Law of Sin and Death'; this means that if the Believer attempts to live for God by any manner other than Faith in Christ and the Cross, he is doomed to failure)*" **(Rom. 8:2).**

To show how close the Sacrifice of Christ and the Holy Spirit are, please note carefully the following:

THE SLAIN LAMB AND THE SPIRIT OF GOD

The following is the Scripture and the notes concerning this subject, taken directly from THE EXPOSITOR'S STUDY BIBLE. John the Beloved wrote:

> **"And one of the Elders said unto me, Weep not** *(states that man's dilemma has been solved)***: behold, the Lion of the Tribe of Judah, the Root of David, has prevailed to open the Book, and to loose the Seven Seals thereof** *(presents Jesus Christ).*
> **"And I beheld, and, lo, in the midst of the Throne and of the four Beasts, and in the midst of the Elders, stood a Lamb as it had been slain** *(the Crucifixion of Christ is represented here by the word 'Lamb,' which refers to the fact that it was the Cross which Redeemed mankind; the slain Lamb Alone has Redeemed all things)***, having seven horns** *(horns denote dominion, and 'seven' denotes total dominion; all of this was done for you and me, meaning that we can have total dominion over the powers of darkness,*

and in every capacity; so there is no excuse for a lack of victory) **and seven eyes** *(denotes total, perfect, pure, and complete illumination of all things spiritual, which is again made possible for you and me by the Cross; if the Believer makes the Cross the Object of his Faith, he will never be drawn away by false doctrine)*, **which are the Seven Spirits of God sent forth into all the Earth** *(signifying that the Holy Spirit, in all His Perfection and universality, functions entirely within the parameters of the Finished Work of Christ; in other words, it is required that we ever make the Cross the Object of our Faith, which gives the Holy Spirit latitude, and guarantees the 'dominion,' and the 'illumination' [Isa. 11:2; Rom. 8:2])*.

"**And He** *(the Lord Jesus Christ)* **came and took the Book out of the Right Hand of Him** *(God the Father)* **Who sat upon the Throne.** *(All of Heaven stands in awe as the Lamb steps forward to take the Book)*" **(Rev. 5:5-7).**

THE MANNER IN WHICH THE HOLY SPIRIT WORKS

Most so-called Christians ignore the Holy Spirit altogether. Even Pentecostals and Charismatics, at least for the most part, have little idea as to how the Holy Spirit Works. They think that whatever He does is automatic. Consider the following:

If the Holy Spirit, without our cooperation, automatically did whatever it is that needed to be done, this would mean that there would never again be another failure on the part of the Believer, never again a sin committed, etc. But we all know that's not the case, don't we?!

The truth is, if the Believer doesn't place his faith exclusively in Christ and the Cross, and maintain it exclusively in Christ and the Cross, the Holy Spirit will be greatly limited as to what He can do in us, by us, or for us. As we have stated, He Works strictly within the parameters of the Finished Work, i.e., "the Cross of Christ," which demands that our Faith be exclusively in the Cross of Christ. The reason is simple, that's where the

price was paid, and the Victory was forever won (Rom. 6:1-14; I Cor. 2:2; Gal., Chpt. 5; 6:14; Eph. 2:13-18; Col. 2:14-15).

The Holy Spirit doesn't require much of us, but He does require one thing, and without reservation. Our Faith must exclusively be in Christ and the Cross, understanding that this is God's Prescribed Order of Victory.

THE CROSS OF CHRIST IS THE FOUNDATION OF ALL DOCTRINE

The heading means that every doctrine in the Bible must be built on the Foundation of the Cross, or else in some way it will be spurious. An erroneous understanding of the Cross of Christ, or ignoring the Cross of Christ, or denying the Cross of Christ, presents the seedbed of all false doctrine. This is where we go astray, that is if we do not have a correct interpretation of the Cross of Christ. If our faith is in something other than the Cross of Christ, whatever is produced will be false.

As we have stated, the Cross of Christ is the Foundation on which all doctrine must be constructed.

How do we know that?

Peter said:

"Forasmuch as you know that you were not redeemed with corruptible things, *as* silver and gold *(presents the fact that the most precious commodities [silver and gold] could not redeem fallen man)*, from your vain conversation *(vain lifestyle) received* by tradition from your fathers *(speaks of original sin that is passed on from father to child at conception)*;

"But with the Precious Blood of Christ *(presents the payment, which proclaims the poured out Life of Christ on behalf of sinners)*, as of a Lamb without blemish and without spot *(speaks of the lambs offered as substitutes in the Old Jewish economy; the Death of Christ was not an execution or assassination, but rather a Sacrifice; the*

424 Brother Swaggart, How Can I Understand The Bible?

Offering of Himself presented a Perfect Sacrifice, for He was Perfect in every respect [Ex. 12:5]):

"**Who verily was foreordained before the foundation of the world** *(refers to the fact that God, in His Omniscience, knew He would create man, man would Fall, and man would be redeemed by Christ going to the Cross; this was all done before the Universe was created; this means the Cross of Christ is the Foundation Doctrine of all Doctrine, referring to the fact that all Doctrine must be built upon that Foundation, or else it is specious)*, **but was manifest in these last times for you** *(refers to the invisible God Who, in the Person of the Son, was made visible to human eyesight by assuming a human body and human limitations)*" **(I Pet. 1:18-20).**

The Cross of Christ is the Foundation of all doctrine, meaning that all doctrine must be built on this Foundation, simply because it was the first Doctrine formulated in the Mind of the Godhead, even before man was created, or even the world was created.

This means many things, of which the following two are a beginning:

1. The Cross of Christ is the dividing line between the Church and the Apostate Church. In fact, it has always been that way. We find the first account given to us in the Fourth Chapter of Genesis, as it regards Cain and Abel. Because we are nearing the end, however, I believe this dividing line of the Cross is more prominent than ever.

2. The Cross of Christ is the only answer for sin. There is no other, because there need be no other. The Message is ageless. It will never have to be amended in any form, simply because it is perfect (Heb. 13:20).

THE CROSS OF CHRIST IS THE STORY OF THE BIBLE

One might say that *"Jesus Christ and Him Crucified,"* is the

Story of the Word of God, even as the Word of God is the Story
of *"Jesus Christ and Him Crucified."*

The very first example of the Cross is found immediately
after the Fall. At that time, the Scripture says as it regards
Adam and Eve:

> "And the eyes of them both were opened *(refers to
> the consciousness of guilt as a result of their sin)*, and they
> knew that they were naked *(refers to the fact that they
> had lost the enswathing light of purity, which previously
> had clothed their bodies)*; and they sewed fig leaves
> together, and made themselves aprons *(sinners clothe
> themselves with morality, sacraments, and religious
> ceremonies; they are as worthless as Adam's apron of fig
> leaves)*" (Gen. 3:7).

Concerning their nakedness, the Scripture says:

> "Unto Adam also and to his wife did the LORD God
> make coats of skins, and clothed them *(in the making of
> coats of skins, God, in effect, was telling Adam and Eve that
> their fig leaves were insufficient; as well, He was teaching
> them that without the shedding of blood, which pertained
> to the animals that gave their lives, which were Types of
> Christ, is no remission of sin; in this first sacrifice was
> laid the foundation of the entirety of the Plan of God as
> it regards Redemption; also, it must be noticed that it is
> the 'LORD God' Who furnished these coats, and not man
> himself; this tells us that Salvation is altogether of God
> and not at all of man; the Life of Christ given on the Cross,
> and given as our Substitute, provides the only covering for
> sin; everything else must be rejected)*" (Gen. 3:21).

The Fourth Chapter of Genesis proclaims in vivid detail
the Substitute. The Lord had related to the First Family even
though fallen, that they could have forgiveness of sin and

fellowship with Him, and He gave the manner in which this could be done.

They were to build an Altar, which was a Type of the Cross, and they were to kill a lamb, which was a Type of Christ, burn its little body on the Altar, a Type of the Judgment of God, which came upon our Lord, instead of upon us, with the blood poured out at the base of the Altar. The blood signified Him giving His Life. Hence, the principle of Redemption is spelled out, in the offering up of the slain lamb. Thus was the Sacrificial System introduced on the first page of human history, and continued through the centuries. When the Law of Moses was given, the Sacrificial System was the very heart of the Law. In fact, had it not been for the Sacrificial System, Israel would have been doomed, just as man is doomed now unless he takes hold of the Christ of the Cross.

All of this was a stopgap measure until Jesus would come, Who would be the literal Sacrifice.

His very purpose of coming to this Earth, of God becoming Man, the Man Christ Jesus, was to be a Sacrifice. The Apostle John outlines it perfectly in the great Gospel that bears his name. He said:

THE INCARNATION

"In the beginning *(does not infer that Christ as God had a beginning, because as God He had no beginning, but rather refers to the time of Creation [Gen. 1:1])* was the Word *(the Holy Spirit through John describes Jesus as 'the Eternal Logos')*, and the Word was with God *('was in relationship with God,' and expresses the idea of the Trinity)*, and the Word was God *(meaning that He did not cease to be God during the Incarnation; He 'was' and 'is' God from eternity past to eternity future)*.

"The same was in the beginning with God *(this very Person was in eternity with God; there's only one God, but manifested in Three Persons — God the Father, God the*

Son, God the Holy Spirit).

"**All things were made by Him** *(all things came into being through Him; it refers to every item of Creation one by one, rather than all things regarded in totality)*; **and without Him was not any thing made that was made** *(nothing, not even one single thing, was made independently of His cooperation and volition).*

"**In Him was Life** *(presents Jesus, the Eternal Logos, as the first cause)*; **and the Life was the Light of men** *(He Alone is the Life Source of Light; if one doesn't know Christ, one is in darkness).*

"**And the Light shines in darkness** *(speaks of the Incarnation of Christ, and His coming into this world; His 'Light,' because it is derived from His Life, drives out 'darkness')*; **and the darkness comprehended it not** *(should have been translated, 'apprehended it not'; it means that Satan, even though he tried with all his might, could not stop 'the Light'; today it shines all over the world, and one day soon, there will be nothing left but that 'Light')*" **(Jn. 1:1-5).**

JOHN THE BELOVED

Then John the Beloved said:

"**And the Word was made flesh** *(refers to the Incarnation, 'God becoming man')*, **and dwelt among us** *(refers to Jesus, although Perfect, not holding Himself aloft from all others, but rather lived as all men, even a peasant)*, **(and we beheld His Glory, the Glory as of the Only Begotten of the Father,)** *(speaks of His Deity, although hidden from the eyes of the merely curious; while Christ laid aside the expression of His Deity, He never lost the possession of His Deity)* **full of Grace and Truth** *(as 'flesh,' proclaimed His Humanity, 'Grace and Truth' His Deity)*" **(Jn. 1:14).**

And now John gives the reason for the Word being made

flesh. He records the statement about Christ given by John the Baptist. He said:

"**The next day** *(refers to the day after John had been questioned by the emissaries from the Sanhedrin)* **John sees Jesus coming unto him** *(is, no doubt, after the baptism of Jesus, and the temptation in the wilderness)*, **and said, Behold the Lamb of God** *(proclaims Jesus as the Sacrifice for sin, in fact, the Sin-Offering, Whom all the multiple millions of offered lambs had represented)*, **which takes away the sin of the world** *(animal blood could only cover sin, it could not take it away; but Jesus offering Himself as the Perfect Sacrifice took away the sin of the world; He not only cleansed acts of sin but, as well, addressed the root cause [Col. 2:14-15])*" **(Jn. 1:29).**

GOD'S PRESCRIBED ORDER OF VICTORY

When we say *"victory"* we are speaking of Victory in every capacity, be it spiritual, financial, domestical, physical, etc. God's Prescribed Order for this Victory is *"the Cross of Christ."*

Of course, the primary victory of which the Bible addresses itself is Victory over sin. That properly handled and addressed, everything else will fall into place.

Paul said:

"**But this Man** *(this Priest, Christ Jesus)*, **after He had offered One Sacrifice for sins forever** *(speaks of the Cross)*, **sat down on the Right Hand of God** *(refers to the great contrast with the Priests under the Levitical system, who never sat down because their work was never completed; the Work of Christ was a 'Finished Work,' and needed no repetition)*;

"**From henceforth expecting till His enemies be made His footstool.** *(These enemies are Satan and all the fallen Angels and demon spirits, plus all who follow Satan.)*

"For by one Offering He has perfected forever them who are Sanctified. *(Everything one needs is found in the Cross [Gal. 6:14])*" **(Heb. 10:12-14)**.

The first five Verses of Romans, Chapter 6 proclaim to us God's Prescribed Order. Of course, the entirety of the Sixth Chapter of Romans opens up to us this great truth, and in every capacity; however, the first five Verses tell us what the Prescribed Order actually is.

THE PROBLEM IS SIN

More particularly as it regards the Believer, the problem is the sin nature.

The sin nature is that which happened to Adam and Eve at the Fall, and which passed down to all thereafter. It means that their very nature became one of sin, transgression, iniquity, disobedience, etc. It is the cause of all the difficulties, war, crime, man's inhumanity to man, that's in the world presently and, in fact, ever has been the cause. Every unbeliever is ruled by the sin nature 24 hours a day, 7 days a week. When the believing sinner comes to Christ, at that moment, the sin nature, although not removed, is made dormant. But unfortunately, every single believing sinner, after coming to Christ, fails the Lord in some way. It happens to every one of us. Now, sin is abhorrent to the Believer. Now knowing God's Prescribed Order of Victory, the Believer sets about to try not to commit the same sin again. Every time, he will place his Faith in something other than the Cross. While many other things may be very helpful in their own right, and very legitimate, still, the answer for sin, and the only answer, is the Cross of Christ. But inevitably, the flesh gravitates toward works, i.e., *"law."*

Now, the Believer doesn't understand that he is placing his faith in that which God cannot bless, and it will be some time before he fully understands this. Regrettably, and because of a lack of teaching on this all-important subject, most Believers never come to a place of proper understanding; therefore, they remain in the Seventh Chapter of Romans all of their spiritual existence. That's the reason the teaching of the Cross as it regards both Salvation and Sanctification is so very, very important. In fact, it is the single most important body of understanding that the Believer could have. The tragedy is, irrespective of its great significance, most Christians, even preachers, have no idea as to the part the Cross plays as it regards our Sanctification, i.e., *"How we live for God on a daily basis."*

The only way to have victory over the sin nature, and we speak of perpetual Victory, even on a daily basis, is for the Believer to place his faith exclusively in Christ and the Cross, and maintain his Faith in Christ and the Cross. Then and only then can the Holy Spirit work within our lives, thereby bringing about the Fruit of the Spirit and, thereby, helping us to be what we ought to be in Christ. That is God's Prescribed Order. Concerning this, Paul said:

THE SIN NATURE

"**What shall we say then?** *(This is meant to direct attention to Rom. 5:20.)* **Shall we continue in sin, that Grace may abound?** *(Just because Grace is greater than sin doesn't mean that the Believer has a license to sin.)*

"**God forbid** *(presents Paul's answer to the question, 'Away with the thought, let not such a thing occur').* **How shall we, who are dead to sin** *(dead to the sin nature)*, **live any longer therein?** *(This portrays what the Believer is now in Christ)*" **(Rom. 6:1-2).**

THE CROSS OF CHRIST

Now the Apostle tells us the answer to the sin nature and, in fact, the only answer. He said:

"Know you not, that so many of us as were baptized

into Jesus Christ *(plainly says that this Baptism is into Christ and not water [I Cor. 1:17; 12:13; Gal. 3:27; Eph. 4:5; Col. 2:11-13])* **were baptized into His Death?** *(When Christ died on the Cross, in the Mind of God, we died with Him; in other words, He became our Substitute, and our identification with Him in His Death gives us all the benefits for which He died; the idea is that He did it all for us!)*

"**Therefore we are buried with Him by baptism into death** *(not only did we die with Him, but we were buried with Him as well, which means that all the sin and trans-gression of the past were buried; when they put Him in the Tomb, they put all of our sins into that Tomb as well)*: **that like as Christ was raised up from the dead by the Glory of the Father, even so we also should walk in Newness of Life** *(we died with Him, we were buried with Him, and His Resurrection was our Resurrection to a 'Newness of Life')*.

"**For if we have been planted together** *(with Christ)* **in the likeness of His Death** *(Paul proclaims the Cross as the instrument through which all Blessings come; consequently, the Cross must ever be the Object of our Faith, which gives the Holy Spirit latitude to work within our lives)*, **we shall be also** *in the likeness* **of** *His* **Resurrection** *(we can have the 'likeness of His Resurrection,' i.e., 'live this Resurrec-tion Life,' only as long as we understand the 'likeness of His Death,' which refers to the Cross as the means by which all of this is done)*" **(Rom. 6:3-5).**

Perhaps the following formula, as simple as it is, will help us to understand this all-important subject to a greater degree.

THE WAY OF THE SPIRIT

FOCUS: The Lord Jesus Christ (Jn. 14:6).
OBJECT OF FAITH: The Cross of Christ (Rom. 6:1-14).
POWER SOURCE: The Holy Spirit (Rom. 8:1-2, 11).

RESULTS: Victory (Rom. 6:14).

Now let's use the same formula, but the manner in which it is being used by most Believers.

MAN'S WAY

FOCUS: Works.
OBJECT OF FAITH: Performance.
POWER SOURCE: Self.
RESULTS: Defeat!

Regrettably and sadly, the latter formula is the manner in which most Believers are attempting to live this life for the Lord. They aren't doing it God's Way, but rather man's way, with the latter always leading to continued failure.

WHAT DOES IT MEAN TO PREACH THE CROSS?

Paul said:

"For the preaching *(Word)* of the Cross is to them who perish foolishness *(Spiritual things cannot be discerned by unredeemed people, but that doesn't matter; the Cross must be preached just the same, even as we shall see)*; but unto us who are Saved it is the Power of God. *(The Cross is the Power of God simply because it was there that the total sin debt was paid, giving the Holy Spirit, in Whom the Power resides, latitude to work mightily within our lives)*" (I Cor. 1:18).

Most preachers, at least those who claim to preach the Bible, preach the Cross of Christ for Salvation, and rightly so! However, most preachers have no idea whatsoever as to the part the Cross plays in our life and living as it regards Sanctification. That's the reason that the church is constantly putting forth one scheme, one fad after the other, trying to address the problem of sin, in other words, failure in the lives of Believers. There is only one answer, and that is the Cross of Christ.

If the Preacher is truly preaching the Cross, this means that he understands that the Cross of Christ pertains not only to our Salvation, where all sin was atoned, but, as well, to our daily life and living, in other words, our Sanctification.

And how does the Cross apply to our Sanctification?

When the Believing sinner comes to Christ, the truth is, he knows nothing about the Lord, and he certainly knows nothing about the Cross. He just simply calls on the Name of the Lord, means it in his heart, and he is Saved (Rom. 10:9-10, 13).

But after the believing sinner comes to Christ, is made a new creation, with old things passing away, and all things becoming new, in other words, he is truly Born-Again, he is to understand, that as his Salvation is in the Cross, his Sanctification is in the Cross also. This means that we are to place our Faith unreservedly in the Cross of Christ, in fact, ever making the Cross the Object of our Faith. This is to be done constantly, ever understanding, that all that we need, is found in what Jesus did at the Cross.

And please understand, when we speak of the Cross, we aren't speaking of a wooden beam, but more particularly, the benefits of what Jesus did for us there. These benefits, upon Faith, will continue to come to us forever and forever.

The idea is this:

THE HOLY SPIRIT AND THE BELIEVER

What we need to be in Christ, we cannot bring it about by our own machinations, strength, or power. This is what Jesus was talking about when He said, that if we were to come after Him, that we had to *"deny ourselves"* (Lk. 9:23). To be sure, He wasn't speaking of asceticism, which refers to denying ourselves all things that were comfortable or pleasurable, but rather, denying our own ability, talent, education, motivation, strength, power, in other words, everything that is indicative of the human being. No matter how strong we are, no matter how much education we have, what we need to be in Christ, we cannot by our own machinations bring it about ourselves. And this is where the great problem begins. Now that we are Saved and even Spirit-filled, somehow, we think that whatever it takes we can do it. We can't!

It is the Holy Spirit Alone, Who lives within our hearts and lives, and does so permanently, Who can bring about that which we need to have and need to be. And He works exclusively within the parameters of the Finished Work of Christ.

In other words, it is the Cross of Christ that has given the Holy Spirit the latitude, i.e., *"the legal right,"* to carry forth His Work within our lives. It is the Cross that has made it all possible. In fact the Scripture says: *"The Law of the Spirit of Life in Christ Jesus, has made me free from the Law of Sin and Death"* (Rom. 8:2).

Because this is so important, please allow me again to quote this Scripture from THE EXPOSITOR'S STUDY BIBLE:

THE LAW OF THE SPIRIT OF LIFE
IN CHRIST JESUS

    "For the Law *(that which we are about to give is a Law of God, devised by the Godhead in eternity past [I Pet. 1:18-20]; this Law, in fact, is 'God's Prescribed Order of Victory')* **of the Spirit** *(Holy Spirit, i.e., 'the way the Spirit works')* **of Life** *(all life comes from Christ, but through the Holy Spirit [Jn. 16:13-14])* **in Christ Jesus** *(any time Paul uses this term or one of its derivatives, he is, without fail, referring to what Christ did at the Cross, which makes this 'life' possible)* **has made me free** *(given me total Victory)* **from the Law of Sin and Death** *(these are the two most powerful Laws in the Universe; the 'Law of the Spirit of Life in Christ Jesus' alone is stronger than the 'Law of Sin and Death'; this means that if the Believer attempts to live for God by any manner other than Faith in Christ and the Cross, he is doomed to failure)*" **(Rom. 8:2).**

While the Bible, as stated, does not teach sinless perfection, it most definitely does teach that *"sin* (i.e., the sin nature) *is not to have dominion over us"* (Rom. 6:14).

The only way this can be achieved, the only way it can be brought about, which is God's Way, is that we ever make the Cross of Christ the Object of our Faith. That and that alone, is the way of the Spirit.

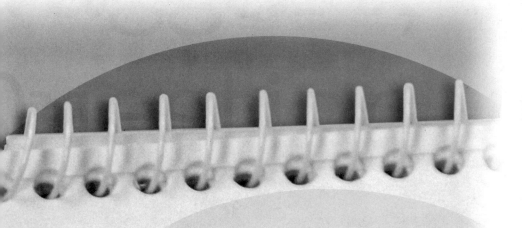

CHAPTER 17

The Doctrine Of The Kingdom Age

THE DOCTRINE OF THE KINGDOM AGE

The Kingdom Age, sometimes referred to as the Millennial Reign, will last for 1,000 years. Jesus Christ will rule Personally and, in fact, He, in essence, will be the Government of the world. It will be a time of peace and prosperity like the world has never known in all of its history. In fact, Satan and all his demon spirits and fallen Angels will be locked away in the bottomless pit at this particular time. So, the one who steals, kills, and destroys, will have no access to this world per se. There will be no war at this time, and a world without war, is something that it has never seen previously, except for one short particular time frame, which we will address momentarily. As well, there will be no more sickness, and death will take a vacation, except in most stringent circumstances. As well, one might say, there will be two classes of people on the Earth at this time, which we will explain later.

THE BEGINNING OF THE KINGDOM AGE

Actually, the beginning of the Kingdom Age will commence at the conclusion of the Battle of Armageddon, which will also be the conclusion of the Great Tribulation. Jesus said concerning the particular time of the Great Tribulation:

> "For then shall be great tribulation *(the last three and one half years)*, such as was not since the beginning of the world to this time, no, nor ever shall be *(the worst the world has ever known, and will be so bad that it will never be repeated)*.
> "And except those days should be shortened, there should no flesh be saved *(refers to Israel coming close to extinction)*: but for the elect's *(Israel's)* sake those days shall be shortened *(by the Second Coming)*" (Mat. 24:21-22).

At the most crucial time of the Battle of Armageddon, when

it looks like Israel will be totally and completely destroyed, in other words, totally annihilated, Jesus Christ will come back. To be sure, His Coming will be the most cataclysmic event, the most earth shaking event, the most traumatic event that the world will have ever known in all of its history. In fact, there is absolutely nothing that can even remotely describe what it will be like. Concerning this time, Jesus Himself said:

THE SECOND COMING

"**Immediately after the tribulation of those days** *(speaks of the time immediately preceding the Second Coming)* **shall the sun be darkened, and the moon shall not give her light** *(the light of these orbs will be dim by comparison to the Light of the Son of God),* **and the stars shall fall from Heaven** *(a display of Heavenly fireworks at the Second Coming),* **and the powers of the Heavens shall be shaken** *(will work with the Son of God against the Antichrist, at the Second Coming)*:

"**And then shall appear the sign of the Son of Man in Heaven** *(pertains to the Second Coming, which will take place in the midst of these Earth and Heaven shaking events)*: **and then shall all the tribes of the Earth mourn** *(concerns all the nations of the world which possibly will see this phenomenon by television),* **and they shall see the Son of Man** *(denotes Christ and His human, Glorified Body)* **coming in the clouds of Heaven with power and great glory** *(lends credence to the thought that much of the world will see Him by television as He makes His descent)*" (Mat. 24:29-30).

THE DESCRIPTION OF THE SECOND COMING AS GIVEN BY THE PROPHET ZECHARIAH

"**In that day, says the LORD, I will smite every horse with astonishment, and his rider with madness: and I** will open My Eyes upon the house of Judah, and will smite every horse of the people with blindness *('In that day, says the LORD,' refers to the Battle of Armageddon. 'I will smite every horse with astonishment, and his rider with madness,' pertains to a frenzy inspired by terror. In fact, the last phrase is the same as the first, but repeated to emphasize its certitude.)*

"And the governors of Judah shall say in their heart, The inhabitants of Jerusalem shall be my strength and the LORD of Hosts their God. *(This Verse portrays, possibly, the very first collective faith of the leaders and people of Israel and the Lord their God since the days of Josiah, if even then. This will, no doubt, be at the instant of the Lord's return, with Israel in the process of repenting at that very time.)*

THE GOVERNORS OF JUDAH

"In that day will I make the governors of Judah like an hearth of fire among the wood, and like a torch of fire in a sheaf; and they shall devour all the people round about, on the right hand and on the left: and Jerusalem shall be inhabited again in her own place, even in Jerusalem. *(Concerning the first phrase, the idea is: the Lord, upon His return, will give the 'governors of Judah' wisdom and strength respecting the closing hours of the battle to a degree possibly that man has never known. The phrase, 'And Jerusalem shall be inhabited again in her own place, even in Jerusalem,' refers to the city being saved from the onslaught of the man of sin. It being 'inhabited again' concerns the rebuilding by the Messiah. It will, no doubt, be the most beautiful city on the face of the Earth.)*

THE RESCUE OF JUDAH

"The LORD also shall save the tents of Judah first,

that the glory of the House of David and the Glory of the inhabitants of Jerusalem do not magnify themselves against Judah. *(The idea of this Verse is: Judah recognizes and confesses as a source of strength the Faith of Jerusalem; the Messiah will reward this humility by rescuing Judah first; thus will there be equality of glory to both. 'Judah' refers to the entirety of the area given to the Tribe of Judah during the time of Joshua. The reason for this is because Jesus came from the Tribe of Judah [Gen. 49:10]).*

POWERFUL WARRIORS

"In that day shall the LORD defend the inhabitants of Jerusalem; and he who is feeble among them at that day shall be as David; and the House of David shall be as God, as the Angel of the LORD before them. *(This refers to the coming Battle of Armageddon. 'And he who is feeble among them at that day shall be as David,' refers back to Verse 6. David was Israel's greatest warrior and was that because of the Anointing of the Holy Spirit upon him for this purpose. Likewise, the Holy Spirit tells us here that, at that coming day, the most 'feeble among them' will have the strength of a 'mighty David.'*

" 'And the house of David shall be as God,' has to do with the Tribe of Judah. 'As the Angel of the LORD before them,' pertains to Jehovah, Who led Israel through the wilderness after their deliverance from Egypt.)

"And it shall come to pass in that day, that I will seek to destroy all the nations that come against Jerusalem. *(Once again, this is the Battle of Armageddon)*" (Zech. 12:4-9).

THE MESSIAH REVEALED TO ISRAEL

"And I will pour upon the house of David and upon the inhabitants of Jerusalem, the Spirit of Grace and of supplications: and they shall look upon Me Whom

they have pierced, and they shall mourn for Him, as one mourns for his only son, and shall be in bitterness for Him, as one that is in bitterness for his firstborn. *(The phrase, 'And I will pour . . .,' refers to the Lord pouring out fire upon Zion's adversaries, but the Holy Spirit upon her inhabitants [II Thess., Chpt. 1]. If one is to notice, the Messiah Himself is speaking in the entirety of this Chapter as far as the word 'pierced'; then the Holy Spirit points to the moral effect produced by the revelation.*

"'Upon the House of David,' proclaims the Promise originally given to David concerning his seed upon the Throne of Israel [II Sam. 7:12-16].

"The phrase, 'I will pour upon them the Spirit of Grace,' concerns the goodness of God and means they are no longer trusting in their Law, but instead the 'Grace of God,' which is found only in the Lord Jesus Christ.

"'And I will pour upon them the Spirit of Supplications,' speaks of Israel supplicating the Lord, and the Lord supplicating the Father on their behalf. The word means 'to ask humbly and earnestly.'

"'And they shall look upon Me Whom they have pierced,' identifies who and what they are and Who He is.

"'And they shall mourn for Him, as one mourns for his only son,' now proclaims the moral effect produced by this Revelation, as given by the Holy Spirit. They will then make their supplications to Him for Mercy and Forgiveness. 'And shall be in bitterness for Him,' means 'a sense of intense shame.' It speaks of True Repentance.

"The last phrase, 'As one who is in bitterness for his firstborn,' refers to the loss of an only son, the firstborn. In effect, they killed their own son, and the firstborn at that, which meant that the family line could not continue; it was, in fact, destroyed, at least as far as the Covenant was concerned; however, this 'Son,' or 'Firstborn,' rose from the dead. Even though they would not accept it then, they will accept it now — and because He lives, they shall live

also!)" **(Zech. 12:10).**

THE CRUCIFIED MESSIAH REVEALED

When Jesus comes back, thereby, gloriously defeating the Antichrist in the Battle of Armageddon, at that time, as stated, He will lock Satan away along with all of his demon forces in the bottomless pit. Jesus will then be revealed to Israel and the world. Concerning this moment, the Scripture says:

"And one shall say unto Him, What are these wounds in Your Hand? Then He shall answer, Those with which I was wounded in the house of My friends. *(In these Passages, the false prophets are placed beside the True Prophet, the Lord Jesus Christ. They, before the Coming of the Lord, too oftentimes were rewarded, while He, as each True Prophet, was greatly opposed, even crucified. The false prophets thrust themselves forward and claimed reverence and position; He Himself, the greatest of the Prophets, did not claim to be a professional Prophet — that was not His Mission in coming to Earth — but became a Bond-servant and a Shepherd; made and appointed such in the Divine Purpose of Redemption. For man having sold himself into slavery, it was necessary that Christ should take that position in order to redeem him.*

" 'And one shall say unto Him,' refers to the moment of recognition, as outlined in 12:10, where it says, 'And they shall look upon Me Whom they have pierced, and they shall mourn for Him.' This will be immediately after the Second Coming, with the Antichrist now defeated and Christ standing before Israel. They will then know, beyond the shadow of a doubt, that He is the Messiah; then will they ask, 'What are these wounds in Your Hands?'

"These wounds, which He will ever carry, will be an instant and constant of Who He is and what was done to Him, which presents Him as the Sin-bearer of the world.

Even though He was the Redeemer of all mankind, still, this shows how He was treated by man, especially by His Own.

" 'Then He shall answer,' will be an answer that will cause their terrible 'mourning' of 12:10-14. It will also be the cause of the 'Fountain opened to the House of David and to the inhabitants of Jerusalem for sin and for uncleanness' [13:1].

" 'Those with which I was wounded in the house of My friends,' proclaims His Crucifixion and those who did it to Him. The words, 'My friends,' are said in irony)" **(Zech. 13:6).**

THE EXTENT OF THE DOMINION OF CHRIST

"And the LORD shall be King over all the Earth; in that day there shall be one LORD, and His Name One. *(The first phrase refers to the Lord Jesus Christ and His total dominion over all nations. 'In that day there shall be one LORD,' rather says, 'Jehovah shall be One.' He shall be universally acknowledged as 'the blessed and only Potentate' [I Tim. 6:15])"* **(Zech. 14:9).**

THE WORDS OF THE PROPHET ISAIAH CONCERNING THE REIGN OF CHRIST IN THE KINGDOM AGE

"The word that Isaiah the son of Amoz saw concerning Judah and Jerusalem. *(The word 'saw,' as used here by Isaiah, basically means the same thing as 'Vision.')*

"And it shall come to pass in the last days, that the mountain of the LORD's House shall be established in the top of the mountains, and shall be exalted above the hills; and all nations shall flow into it. *(Verses 2-4 in this Chapter correspond to Micah 4:1-3. Micah's Prophecy was seventeen years later than Isaiah's. Some wonder if the latter Prophet borrowed from the former, but this shows* *a want of intelligence. When God repeats a message, the repetition emphasizes its preciousness to Him and its importance to man.*

"In both of the Prophecies, Isaiah and Micah, the Lord reveals the character of the Kingdom He proposed to set up on the Earth; in the latter, it is repeated to the nations. All of this will take place in the coming Kingdom Age.)

"And many people shall go and say, Come ye, and let us go up to the mountain of the LORD, to the House of the God of Jacob; and He will teach us of His Ways, and we will walk in His Paths: for out of Zion shall go forth the Law, and the Word of the LORD from Jerusalem. *(The 'Law,' as referred to here, has no reference to the Law of Moses, but rather to instruction, direction, and teaching. Again, this is the coming Kingdom Age, when the Messiah, 'The Greater than Solomon,' will rule the world by Wisdom, Grace, and Love.)*

MESSIAH'S COURT

"And He shall judge among the nations, and shall rebuke many people: and they shall beat their swords into plowshares, and their spears into pruninghooks: nation shall not lift up sword against nation, neither shall they learn war anymore. *(The words, 'Judge among,' should read 'arbitrate between', and 'rebuke' would have been better translated 'decide the disputes of.' Man's courts of arbitration are doomed to failure, but, to Messiah's Court, success is promised here)"* **(Isa. 2:1-4).**

NO MORE WAR

In 1980 the nations of the world were spending some three million dollars a minute on weapons. What it is at the time of this writing (2009), I do not know; however, I seriously doubt that it has decreased.

Think what that amount of money would do as it regards the building of the infrastructure of nations! But despite all the peace treaties and agreements, so-called, wars never end. Actually, there have been only 33 years of peace in this world since the beginning of time. Let me explain!

When Jesus was born, Rome ruled the world of that day.

The year Jesus was born, which has been surmised at being somewhere between 14 B.C. and A.D. 5, the great war gates of Janus in Rome were closed. This meant that there was no major conflict going on anywhere in the Roman Empire. In fact, those gates stayed closed for some 33 years, the exact time of Jesus' Life and Ministry.

While Rome, of course, had no idea as to the reason for this time of peace, the Word of God is very clear. It says:

THE REJOICING OF THE ANGELS

"And there were in the same country *(referred to the area around Bethlehem)* shepherds abiding in the field *(pertained to the lowest caste in society at that time)*, keeping watch over their flock by night *(gives indication that December 25th was not the day on which Jesus was born; it was the custom to send flocks out after the Passover, which was in April, to stay until the first rain in October or November)*.

"And, lo, the Angel of the Lord came upon them *(proclaims the fact that the Birth of the Lord was not announced to the notables of Israel, but rather to obscure shepherds)*, and the Glory of the Lord shone round about them: and they were sore afraid *(this was the visible token of the Presence of the Eternal, which appeared first in the bush before Moses, and then in the pillar of fire and cloud, which guided the desert wanderings, and then in the Tabernacle and the Temple)*.

"And the Angel said unto them, Fear not: for, behold, I bring you good tidings of great joy, which shall be to

all people *(includes all races).*

"**For unto you is born this day in the city of David a Saviour, Who is Christ the Lord** *(this Baby was not to become a King and a Saviour — He was born both).*

"**And this *shall be* a sign unto you; You shall find the Baby wrapped in swaddling clothes, lying in a manger.**

"**And suddenly there was with the Angel a multitude of the Heavenly Host praising God, and saying** *(many other Angels had been with the Angel who spoke to the shepherds, but now the shepherds can see them as well; this presents sinless Angels praising God for sending the Redeemer; if they did so, certainly we should as well),*

"**Glory to God in the highest, and on Earth peace, good will toward men** *(Jesus is that 'peace'; during His approximate 33 years of life on this Earth, the Roman Empire was relatively at peace; it was because the Prince of Peace was here; peace will not return until Jesus returns)*" **(Lk. 2:8-14).**

In fact, He said the following concerning this very thing:

WARS AND RUMORS OF WARS

When Jesus came the first time, as stated, born as a baby in a manger in Bethlehem, when He began His public Ministry, His basic Message was:

"**Repent: for the Kingdom of Heaven is at hand** *(the Kingdom from Heaven, headed up by Christ, for the purpose of reestablishing the Kingdom of God over the Earth; the Kingdom was rejected by Israel)*" **(Mat. 4:17).**

Inasmuch as the Kingdom was rejected, for it was not possible to have the Kingdom without the King, and that King was the Lord Jesus Christ, this submitted the entirety of the world to continued war and bloodshed, which has now lasted for some 2,000 years. In fact, His Disciples asked Him the question:

"Tell us, when shall these things be? *(Has to do here with the utterance He had just given concerning the destruction of the Temple.)* and what *shall be* the sign of Your Coming *(refers to the Second Coming)*, and of the end of the world? *(Should have been translated 'age.')*

"And Jesus answered and said unto them *(will now give the future of Israel, and how it will effect the entirety of the world)*, Take heed that no man deceive you *(places deception as Satan's greatest weapon)*.

"For many shall come in My Name *(concerns itself primarily with the time immediately before the coming Great Tribulation, and especially its first half)*, saying, I am Christ; and shall deceive many *(the greatest of these will be the Antichrist, who will claim to be the Messiah)*.

"And you shall hear of wars and rumours of wars *(has abounded from the beginning, but will accelerate during the first half of the Great Tribulation)*: see that you be not troubled *(concerns true Believers)*: for all *these things* must come to pass *(we are very near presently to the beginning of fulfillment of what Jesus said)*, but the end is not yet *(the end will be at the Second Coming)*.

"For nation shall rise against nation, and kingdom against kingdom: and there shall be famines, and pestilences, and earthquakes, in divers places *(few places in the world, if any, will be exempt from these judgments)*.

"All these *are* the beginning of sorrows *(first half of the Great Tribulation)*" (Mat. 24:3-8).

The Second Coming, however, will usher in the greatest era of peace the world has ever known, in fact, *"peace"* which will last for some 1,000 years. That being the case, all the money now spent for war, can then be devoted to peaceful means, which within itself, will bring phenomenal prosperity.

JESUS CHRIST, THE POTENTATE OF THE WORLD

Concerning this, the great Prophet Isaiah also stated:

"And there shall come forth a Rod out of the stem of Jesse, and a Branch shall grow out of his roots *(this Verse has to do with the Incarnation, with the balance of the Chapter referring to the glorious reign of Christ during the Millennium. The word 'Rod,' in this instance, refers to a 'tender branch,' which means a tender shoot sprouting out of the root of a dead, fallen tree, referring both to humanity in general and Israel in particular. Jesse was David's father, and through this family the Messiah would come; and so He did!)*

"And the Spirit of the LORD shall rest upon Him *(upon Christ)***, the Spirit of Wisdom and Understanding, the Spirit of Counsel and Might, the Spirit of Knowledge and of the Fear of the LORD** *(this proclaims the Perfection of the Holy Spirit in all His Attributes listed here resting upon the Messiah)***;**

"And shall make Him of quick understanding in the Fear of the LORD: and He shall not judge after the sight of His Eyes, neither reprove after the hearing of His Ears *(the words, 'quick understanding,' would probably have been better translated 'the breath of His Nostrils shall be in the Fear of the LORD.' It suggests a disposition instinct with delight in God and fragrant with God [Gen. 8:21]. As a result, His Judgment of all things will be perfect)***:**

"But with Righteousness shall He judge the poor, and reprove with equity for the meek of the Earth: and He shall smite the Earth with the rod of His Mouth, and with the breath of His Lips shall He slay the wicked. *(The 'smiting of the Earth' might be better stated 'the oppressor of the land,' referring to the Antichrist. The word 'reprove' means 'to set right with equity' or 'to administer justice on behalf of the meek.')*

"And Righteousness shall be the girdle of His Loins, and Faithfulness the girdle of His Reins. *(This Verse presents Immanuel as Priest. The 'loins' speak of the physical, with the 'reins' speaking of the heart and, therefore, the spiritual. For the first time, the human family in Christ will witness perfection. In fact, the Man Christ Jesus will be girdled with Perfection)*" **(Isa. 11:1-5).**

CONDITIONS DURING THE MILLENNIUM

When Adam fell, it affected not only the human race to come, but also the entirety of creation. Concerning this, the Scripture says:

"For the earnest expectation of the creature *(should have been translated, 'for the earnest expectation of the Creation')* waits for the manifestation of the sons of God *(pertains to the coming Resurrection of Life).*

"For the creature *(Creation)* was made subject to vanity *(Adam's Fall signaled the Fall of Creation)*, not willingly *(the Creation did not sin, even as such cannot sin, but became subject to the result of sin which is death)*, but by reason of Him Who has subjected *the same* in Hope *(speaks of God as the One Who passed sentence because of Adam's Fall, but at the same time gave us a 'Hope'; that 'Hope' is Christ, Who will rectify all things),*

"Because the creature *(Creation)* itself also shall be delivered *(presents this 'Hope' as effecting that Deliverance, which He did by the Cross)* from the bondage of corruption *(speaks of mortality, i.e., 'death')* into the glorious liberty of the Children of God *(when man fell, Creation fell! when man shall be delivered, Creation will be delivered as well, and is expressed in the word 'also').*

"For we know that the whole Creation *(everything has been affected by Satan's rebellion and Adam's Fall)* groans and travails in pain together until now *(refers to the common longing of the elements of the Creation to be brought back to their original perfection)"* **(Rom. 8:19-22).**

When Jesus comes back, the Creation will return to its original design. Concerning that, the Prophet Isaiah also said:

THE GREAT CHANGE

"The wolf also shall dwell with the lamb, and the leopard shall lie down with the kid; and the calf and the young lion and the fatling together; and a little child shall lead them. *(The character and nature of the Planet, including its occupants and even the animal creation, will revert to their posture as before the Fall.)*
"And the cow and the bear shall feed *(feed together)***; their young ones shall lie down together: and the lion shall eat straw like the ox.** *(This Passage plainly tells us that the carnivorous nature of the animal kingdom will be totally and eternally changed.)*
"And the sucking child shall play on the hole of the asp, and the weaned child shall put his hand on the cockatrice' den. *(Even though some of the curse will remain on the serpent in the Millennium, in that he continues to writhe in the dust, still, the deadly part will be removed [Gen. 3:14].)*
"They shall not hurt nor destroy in all My Holy Mountain: for the Earth shall be full of the knowledge of the LORD, as the waters cover the sea. *(The 'Holy Mountain' refers to the Dwelling-place of Christ during the Kingdom Age, which will be Jerusalem. And from that vantage point shall go out the 'knowledge of the LORD,' which will cover the entirety of the Earth.)*
"And in that day there shall be a root of Jesse, which shall stand for an ensign of the people; to it shall the Gentiles seek: and His Rest shall be glorious. *(The words 'in that day,' as in most cases, refer to the Great Tribulation,*

the Battle of Armageddon, the Second Coming of the Lord, and the coming Kingdom Age.

"The 'root of Jesse' refers to David and the Promise made by the Lord to David in II Sam., Chpt. 7. Hence, Christ is really the 'root of Jesse,' 'the Son of David')" **(Isa. 11:6-10).**

THE PLACE OF ISRAEL IN
THE COMING KINGDOM AGE

Actually, Israel will be the leading nation in the world of that day. In other words, that which the Lord originally planned for these people shall then be realized. In fact, Israel was formed out of the loins of Abraham, and the womb of Sarah, for the express purpose that was threefold. Those purposes were:
  1. **To give the world the Word of God.**
  2. **To serve as the Womb of the Messiah.**
  3. **To evangelize the world.**

They succeeded with the first two, although with great difficulty, but failed miserably with the third. They will yet serve this purpose of world evangelism in the coming Kingdom Age.

The horror of the Fall of Israel knows no bounds. Paul tells us why:

THE FALL OF ISRAEL

"For they being ignorant of God's Righteousness *(spells the story not only of ancient Israel, but almost the entirety of the world, and for all time; 'God's Righteousness' is that which is afforded by Christ, and received by exercising Faith in Him and what He did at the Cross, all on our behalf; Israel's ignorance was willful!)***, and going about to establish their own righteousness** *(the case of anyone who attempts to establish Righteousness by any method other than Faith in Christ and the Cross)***, have not submitted themselves unto the Righteousness of God**

(God's Righteousness is ensconced in Christ and what He did at the Cross).

"For Christ *is* the end of the Law for Righteousness *(Christ fulfilled the totality of the Law)* to everyone who believes *(Faith in Christ guarantees the Righteousness which the Law had, but could not give)*" (Rom. 10:3-4).

Israel failed to recognize her Messiah when He came, and then above that, crucified Him. They stated:

"We have no king but Caesar" (St. Jn. 19:15). They were to find to their terrible dismay that Caesar was a hard taskmaster!

They then said, *"His Blood be on us, and on our children"* (Mat. 27:25). They invoked a malediction upon themselves and upon their children at that time. It rests upon them still, and was, and is, a malediction of appalling horror and suffering.

They took themselves out from under the Hand of God, and did so intentionally and, as a result they have wandered the world as vagabonds for nearly 2,000 years, only becoming a viable State in 1948. Sadly and regrettably, even though they have seen some horrible times in the past, with the Holocaust being but one, their worst time is yet to come (Mat. 24:21).

However, the Prophets of old, and the Apostles of the New Testament, have predicted their restoration. The great Paul said:

ISRAEL'S RESTORATION

"And they also *(Israel)*, if they abide not still in unbelief, shall be grafted in *(Israel's unbelief will end at the Second Coming)*: for God is able to graft them in again *(and that He will do!)*" (Rom. 11:23).

The great Apostle then said:

"For I would not, Brethren, that you should be ignorant of this mystery *(what has happened to Israel)*, lest you should be wise in your own conceits *(the Gentiles were not pulled in because of any merit or Righteousness on their part, but strictly because of the Grace of God)*; **that blindness in part is happened to Israel** *(is the 'mystery' of which Paul speaks)*, **until the fullness of the Gentiles be come in** *(refers to the Church; in fact, the Church Age is even now coming to a close).*

"**And so all Israel shall be Saved** *(when the Church Age ends, and the Second Coming commences; then Israel will accept Christ and be Saved)*: **as it is written** *(Isa. 27:9; 59:20-21)*, **There shall come out of Sion the Deliverer** *(Jesus Christ will be the Deliverer)*, **and shall turn away ungodliness from Jacob** *(Christ will deliver Israel from the Antichrist, and more importantly will deliver them from their sins)*:

"**For this** *is* **My Covenant unto them** *(a Promise)*, **when I shall take away their sins** *(as stated, it will be done at the Second Coming [Zech. 13:1])*" **(Rom. 11:25-27).**

ISRAEL IN THE COMING KINGDOM AGE, THE PRIESTLY NATION OF THE WORLD

The last nine Chapters of Ezekiel proclaim to us the manner in which Israel will serve the Lord in the coming Kingdom Age and, as well, serve the entirety of the world. They will finally be what the Lord all along intended that they be.

The little piece of land in the Middle East called *"Israel,"* is the only area on the face of the Earth, to which the Lord has laid special claim. To be sure, He is the Creator of the entirety of the Planet and, in essence, it all belongs to Him; however, His claim regarding Israel is special to say the least. The Muslim world will destroy themselves on that rock.

The scepter of world leadership referred to by Christ as, *"The time of the Gentiles,"* has passed to the hands of the United States. Great responsibilities go with this privilege, not the least of them being the protection of Israel. If we do our duty in this respect, somehow, our problems of this nation will be solved.

God help us if we do otherwise!

In fact, that scepter of world power passed from the faltering hands of the kings of Judah some 500 years before Christ. It first went to Babylon, then to Medo-Persia, then to Greece, and finally to Rome. Under Rome, Israel was totally and completely destroyed, and scattered all over the world, where they wandered as vagabonds for nearly 2,000 years.

Israel must accept Christ, which they will do at the Second Coming. Then virtually every Jew on the face of the Earth will come to Israel, and gladly so. As stated, they will then serve as originally intended. In fact, the great Prophet Ezekiel closed out his great Book with the words concerning Jerusalem stating, *"The LORD is there"* (Ezek. 48:35).

The phrase *"The LORD is there,"* means in Hebrew, *"Adonai-Shammah"* or *"Jehovah-Shammah,"* meaning literally what it says. For the Messiah will be there reigning visibly and eternally in Israel.

Of this time, Isaiah said: *"Of the increase of His Government and peace there shall be no end, upon the throne of David, and upon His Kingdom, to order it, and to establish it with judgment and with justice from henceforth even for ever. The zeal of the LORD of Hosts will perform this"* (Isa. 9:7).

TWO CLASSES OF PEOPLE

During the coming Kingdom Age, there will be two groups, or one might say, two classes of people on the Earth at that time. They are:

1. The Glorified Saints.

2. The natural people, some who will give their hearts to Christ, and some who won't.

THE GLORIFIED SAINTS

The Glorified Saints are those who will have part in the First Resurrection of Life. This will include every Saint of God who has ever lived, all the way from the beginning. John the Beloved wrote as it regards this:

"And I saw Thrones, and they sat upon them, and judgment was given unto them *(refers to the 24 Elders who represent the entire Plan of God, which pertains to the Redeemed of all Ages; we aren't told who these men are)*: and *I saw* the souls of them who were beheaded for the witness of Jesus, and for the Word of God, and which had not worshipped the Beast, neither his image, neither had received *his* mark upon their foreheads, or in their hands *(categorizes the Tribulation Saints who gave their lives for the cause of Christ; the idea is that these will be included in the first Resurrection of Life, and will enjoy all its privileges)*; and they lived and reigned with Christ a thousand years. *(This is the Kingdom Age.)*

"But the rest of the dead lived not again until the thousand years were finished. *(This pertains to all the unsaved, in fact, all those who lived and died since the dawn of time. The souls and spirits of these people are now in Hell [Lk. 16:19-31].)* This *is* the First Resurrection *(proclaims the fact that these two Resurrections, the Resurrection of the Just and the Resurrection of the Unjust, will be separated by 1,000 years)*.

"Blessed and Holy *is* he who has part in the First Resurrection *(this is the Resurrection of Life, which will include every Saint of God who has ever lived from Abel to the last Tribulation Saint; all will be given Glorified Bodies)*: on such the second death has no power *(the 'second death' is to be cast into the Lake of Fire, and to be there forever and forever [Rev. 2:8]; all who are washed in the Blood of the Lamb need not fear the second death)*, but they shall be Priests of God and of Christ, and shall reign with Him a thousand years. *(All Believers who have part in the First Resurrection will at the same time serve as mediators, so to speak, between the population of the world and God*

and Christ. The 'thousand years' portrays the Kingdom
Age, when Christ will reign supreme over the entire Earth)"
(Rev. 20:4-6).

GLORIFIED

All of these Believers will be given Glorified Bodies. And
what will they be like?
John the Beloved gives us some information. He said:

"**Beloved, now are we the sons of God** *(we are just as
much a 'son of God' now as we will be after the Resurrection)*,
and it does not yet appear what we shall be *(our present
state as a 'son of God' is not at all like that we shall be in
the coming Resurrection)*: **but we know that, when He
shall appear** *(the Rapture)*, **we shall be like Him** *(speaks of
being glorified)*; **for we shall see Him as He is.** *(Physical
eyes in a mortal body could not look upon that glory, only
eyes in Glorified Bodies)*" **(I Jn. 3:2).**

If we are going to have Glorified Bodies as did Jesus, exactly
what was He like after His Resurrection?
He said of Himself as He spoke to His Disciples:

"**Behold My Hands and My Feet, that it is I Myself:
handle Me, and see** *(they will now understand what His
Resurrection really was)*; **for a spirit has not flesh and
bones, as you see Me have** *(in other words, Jesus was
telling them that He was not a disembodied spirit; He,
in fact, had a physical body of flesh and bones; no blood
is mentioned because the Glorified Body has no blood;
whereas now the life of the flesh is in the blood, then, when
our bodies are Glorified, the life will be in the Spirit, i.e.,
'Holy Spirit')*" **(Lk. 24:39).**

We also know the Glorified Body has the capabilities of

simply vanishing. As it regards the two Disciples who had Christ join them, but they knew Him not, after He spoke with them a good while, and even had supper with them, then the Scripture says, *"And He vanished out of their sight"* (Lk. 24:31).

Not only could He vanish, but it also seems that He could suddenly appear. Concerning this, the Scripture also says:

THE APPEARANCE OF CHRIST

"Then the same day at evening, being the first *day* of the week *(proclaims the first gathering on a Sunday)*, when the doors were shut where the Disciples were assembled for fear of the Jews *(the 'fear' expressed here pertained to the idea or thought that the religious authorities having now murdered Jesus, may very well seek to do the same to His closest Followers; the Day of Pentecost would remove this 'fear')*, came Jesus and stood in the midst *(gives us no information as to how this was done; He just seems to have suddenly appeared)*, and said unto them, Peace *be* unto you *(presents a common salutation, but coming from Him, and especially at this time, it spoke Volumes)*" (Jn. 20:19).

We know also that the Glorified Body will not have a sin nature, and not having a sin nature, it will never die. Concerning this, Paul wrote:

INCORRUPTIBLE!

"In a moment, in the twinkling of an eye *(proclaims how long it will take for this change to take place)*, at the last trump *(does not denote by the use of the word 'last' that there will be successive trumpet blasts, but rather denotes that this is the close of things, referring to the Church Age)*: for the trumpet shall sound *(it is the 'Trump of God' [I Thess. 4:16])*, and the dead shall be raised incorruptible *(the Sainted Dead, with no sin nature)*, and we shall be changed *(put on the Glorified Body)*.

"For this corruptible *(sin nature)* must put on incorruption *(a Glorified Body with no sin nature)*, and this mortal *(subject to death)* **must** put on immortality *(will never die)*.

"So when this corruptible *(sin nature)* shall have put on incorruption *(the Divine Nature in total control by the Holy Spirit)*, and this mortal *(subject to death)* shall have put on immortality *(will never die)*, then shall be brought to pass the saying that is written, Death is swallowed up in victory *([Isa. 25:8], the full benefits of the Cross will then be ours, of which we now have only the Firstfruits [Rom. 8:23])*" **(I Cor. 15:52-54).**

THE NATURAL PEOPLE

These will be the people on Earth during the Kingdom Age who came over from the Great Tribulation, meaning they did not give their hearts to Christ at that time and, as well, those who will be born during the 1,000 year reign of Christ. Many of these people during this time will give their hearts to Christ, and will live forever by virtue of the Tree of Life; however, they will not have Glorified Bodies. That's the reason that John said: *"Blessed and Holy is he who has part in the First Resurrection"* (Rev. 20:6).

These people will conduct themselves then as they do now, meaning that there will be families and children born to these families, etc. As it regards all who have Glorified Bodies, there will be no marriage among them and, as well, no children born, etc.

WHAT WILL HAPPEN TO THOSE DURING THAT TIME WHO DO NOT ACCEPT CHRIST?

It is true that there will be many during the Kingdom

Age who have come over from the Great Tribulation and, as well, many who will be born during that time, who will not accept Christ.

Concerning that time, John also wrote:

"**And when the thousand years are expired** *(should have been translated, 'finished')*, **Satan shall be loosed out of his prison** *(is not meant to infer a mere arbitrary act on the part of God; He has a very valid reason for doing this)*,

"**And shall go out to deceive the nations which are in the four quarters of the Earth, Gog and Magog** *(the main reason the Lord allows Satan this latitude is, it seems, to rid the Earth of all who oppose Christ; George Williams says: 'The Creation Sabbath witnessed the first seduction, and the Millennial Sabbath will witness the last'; the 'Gog and Magog' spoken of by John is a Hebrew term expressive of multitude and magnitude; here it embraces all nations, 'the four quarters of the Earth')*, **to gather them together to battle: the number of whom** *is* **as the sand of the sea** *(proclaims the fact that virtually all of the population at that particular time, which did not accept Christ during the Kingdom Age, will throw in their lot with Satan)*.

"**And they went up on the breadth of the earth, and compassed the camp of the Saints about, and the beloved city** *(pictures Satan coming against Jerusalem with his army, which will be the last attack against that city)*: **and fire came down from God out of Heaven, and devoured them.** *(Stipulates that the Lord will make short work of this insurrection. In fact, very little information is given regarding this event, as is obvious.)*

"**And the Devil who deceived them was cast into the Lake of Fire and brimstone** *(marks the end of Satan regarding his influence in the world, and, in fact, in any part of the Creation of God)*, **where the Beast and the False Prophet** *are* *(proclaims the fact that these two were placed* in *'the Lake of Fire and Brimstone' some one thousand years earlier [Rev. 19:20]*)**, and shall be tormented day and night forever and ever.** *(This signifies the Eternity of this place. It is a matter of interest to note that Satan's first act is recorded in Gen., Chpt. 3 [the Third Chapter from the beginning], whereas his last act on a worldwide scale is mentioned in Rev., Chpt. 20 [the Third Chapter from the end])*" **(Rev. 20:7-10).**

As stated, it seems that all the unsaved at that time will throw in their lot with Satan, which portrays to us the incurable evil of the human heart. When this episode is ended, there will be no one left on Earth who is not a follower of Christ.

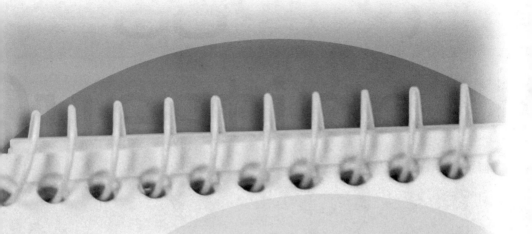

CHAPTER 18

The Doctrine Of The Rapture

THE DOCTRINE OF THE RAPTURE

"But I would not have you to be ignorant, Brethren, concerning them which are asleep *(refers to Believers who have died)*, that you sorrow not, even as others which have no hope. *(This concerns those who do not know the Lord who will have no part in the First Resurrection of Life and, therefore, no hope for Heaven.)*

"For if we believe that Jesus died and rose again *(the very Foundation of Christianity is the Death and Resurrection of Christ; it is the proof of life after death in a glorified state for all Saints in that life, which, incidentally, will never end)*, even so them also which sleep in Jesus will God bring with Him. *(This refers to the Rapture of the Church, or the Resurrection of all Believers, with both phrases meaning the same thing, even as Paul describes in I Cor., Chpt. 15. At death, the soul and the spirit of the Child of God instantly go to be with Jesus [Phil. 1:23], while the physical body goes back to dust. At the Rapture, God will replace what was the physical body with a Glorified Body, united with the soul and the spirit. In fact, the soul and the spirit of each individual will accompany the Lord down close to this Earth to be united with a Glorified Body, which will then make the Believer whole.)*

THE WORD OF THE LORD

"For this we say unto you by the Word of the Lord *(presents the Doctrine of the Rapture of the Church as the 'Word of the Lord')*, that we who are alive *and* remain unto the coming of the Lord *(all Believers who are alive at the Rapture)* shall not prevent them which are asleep. *(This refers to the fact that the living Saints will not precede or go before the dead Saints.)*

"For the Lord Himself shall descend from Heaven with a shout *(refers to 'the same Jesus' which the Angels proclaimed in Acts 1:11)*, **with the voice of the Archangel** *(refers to Michael, the only one referred to as such [Jude, Vs. 9])*, **and with the Trump of God** *(doesn't exactly say God will personally blow this Trumpet, but that it definitely does belong to Him, whoever does signal the blast)*: **and the dead in Christ shall rise first** *(the criteria for being ready for the Rapture is to be 'in Christ,' which means that all who are truly Born-Again will definitely go in the Rapture)*:

"**Then we who are alive** *and* **remain shall be caught up** *(Raptured)* **together with them** *(the Resurrected dead)* **in the clouds** *(clouds of Saints, not clouds as we normally think of such)*, **to meet the Lord in the air** *(the Greek word for 'air' is 'aer,' and refers to the lower atmosphere, or from about 6,000 feet down; so, the Lord will come at least within 6,000 feet of the Earth, perhaps even lower, with all the Saints meeting Him there; but He, at that time, will not come all the way to the Earth, that awaiting the Second Coming, which will be seven or more years later)*: **and so shall we ever be with the Lord.** *(This presents the greatest meeting humanity will have ever known.)*

"**Wherefore comfort one another with these words.** *(This pertains to the future of the Child of God, which is Glorious indeed!)*" **(I Thess. 4:13-18).**

WHAT IS THE DOCTRINE OF THE RAPTURE OF THE CHURCH?

The word *"Rapture"* means ecstasy or joy, which will characterize all Believers at the moment of this experience.

As is obvious, the word *"Rapture"* is not found in the Bible, but most definitely that which Rapture represents is plainly Scriptural, even as we have just quoted from I Thessalonians 4:13-18. Actually, *"Rapture"* and *"Resurrection,"* are two different words for the same event. One may argue the timing of this event, but they most definitely cannot successfully argue the fact of this event. I Thessalonians, Chapter 4 tells us that the Rapture will take place, while I Corinthians, Chapter 15 tells us what will happen when it takes place. Paul said to the Church at Corinth and, as well, to all Believers:

"Behold, I show you a mystery *(a new Revelation given by the Holy Spirit to Paul concerning the Resurrection, i.e., Rapture)*; We shall not all sleep *(at the time of the Resurrection [Rapture], many Christians will be alive)*, but we shall all be changed *(both those who are dead and those who are alive)*,

"In a moment, in the twinkling of an eye *(proclaims how long it will take for this change to take place)*, at the last trump *(does not denote by the use of the word 'last' that there will be successive trumpet blasts, but rather denotes that this is the close of things, referring to the Church Age)*: for the trumpet shall sound *(it is the 'Trump of God' [I Thess. 4:16])*, and the dead shall be raised incorruptible *(the Sainted Dead, with no sin nature)*, and we shall be changed *(put on the Glorified Body)*.

"For this corruptible *(sin nature)* must put on incorruption *(a Glorified Body with no sin nature)*, and this mortal *(subject to death)* **must** put on immortality *(will never die)*.

NO MORE SIN NATURE

"So when this corruptible *(sin nature)* shall have put on incorruption *(the Divine Nature in total control by the Holy Spirit)*, and this mortal *(subject to death)* shall have put on immortality *(will never die)*, then shall be brought to pass the saying that is written, Death is swallowed up in victory *([Isa. 25:8], the full benefits of the Cross will then be ours, of which we now have only the Firstfruits [Rom. 8:23])*.

"O death, where *is* your sting? *(This presents the*

Apostle looking ahead, and exulting in this great coming victory. Sin was forever Atoned at the Cross, which took away the sting of death.) **O grave, where *is* your victory?** *(Due to death being conquered, the 'grave' is no more and, once again, all because of what Christ did at the Cross [Col. 2:14-15].)*

"The sting of death *is* sin *(actually says, 'The sting of the death is the sin'; the words 'the sin' refer to the sin nature, which came about at the Fall, and results in death [Rom. 6:23])*; **and the strength of sin *is* the Law.** *(This is the Law of Moses. It defined sin and stressed its penalty, which is death [Col. 2:14-15].)*

"But thanks *be* to God, which gives us the victory through our Lord Jesus Christ. *(This victory was won exclusively at the Cross, with the Resurrection ratifying what had been done)*" **(I Cor. 15:51-57).**

Again we state, the Rapture and the Resurrection are two different words for the same event. This means that while one may argue the time of the Rapture, one cannot Scripturally argue the fact of the Rapture, i.e., *"Resurrection."* So, for Believers who claim they don't believe in the Rapture, they should be asked if they believe in the Resurrection.

WHAT ARE THE QUALIFICATIONS FOR GOING IN THE RAPTURE?

Actually, there is only one qualification, and that is to be *"born again."* If a person is Born-Again, they are totally and completely justified, and because there is no such thing as a partial Justification. So, while their spiritual state may not be what it ought to be, their Spiritual Standing in Christ doesn't change.

Some have claimed that one has to be baptized with the Holy Spirit and speak with other Tongues in order to be ready for the Rapture. While we strongly believe in the Baptism with the Holy Spirit, and speaking with other Tongues, still, the only

qualification is to be Born-Again.

This means that when the Rapture takes place, every Born-Again person on the face of the globe will instantly be changed, and will go *"to meet the Lord in the air"* (I Thess. 4:17).

There are millions of people in Churches, however, who think they are Saved, when in reality they aren't. They are religious but lost! Despite being religious, those people will not go in the Rapture. In fact, immediately after the Rapture, there will, no doubt, be millions who will accept Christ at that time as their Saviour. Concerning this group the Scripture says:

"**After this I beheld, and, lo, a great multitude** *(pertains to martyrs who gave their lives for the Lord Jesus Christ in the Great Tribulation)*, **which no man could number** *(represents the many, possibly millions, who will be Saved in the Great Tribulation)*, **of all nations, and kindreds, and people, and tongues, stood before the Throne, and before the Lamb** *(by use of the word 'Lamb,' we know and realize that their sin-stained garments have been washed in the Blood of the Lamb)*, **clothed with white robes, and palms in their hands** *(could be paraphrased, 'dressed in richest wedding garments of purest, dazzling, white'; these are God's Blood-bought; the palms represent joy [Neh. 8:17])*;

"**And cried with a loud voice** *(proclaims great joy)*, **saying, Salvation to our God who sits upon the Throne, and unto the Lamb.** *(Once again, we are told here how God has brought about Salvation. It is through what Jesus did at the Cross, and through that means alone.)*

"**And one of the Elders answered, saying unto me** *(proclaims one of the 24 addressing questions that are in John's mind, but have not been asked)*, **What are these which are arrayed in white robes?** *(This would be better translated, 'Who are these?')* **and whence came they?** *(Where do they come from?)*

"**And I said unto him, Sir, you know** *(presents reverent* *regard, but definitely not worship).* **And he said to me, These are they which came out of great tribulation** *(refers to a specific group),* **and have washed their robes, and made them white in the Blood of the Lamb.** *(They were Saved by trusting Christ and what He did at the Cross. In the Book of Revelation, the emphasis placed on the Cross is overwhelming)"* **(Rev. 7:9-10, 13-14).**

THE MANNER OF THE RAPTURE

The Rapture, one might say, will cover a span of time from the general Rapture to the conclusion of the Great Tribulation, which will be several years. While it's all one Rapture, one might say that it will take place in four parts. They are:

1. The General Rapture: This is the Rapture outlined in I Thessalonians 4:13-18. It will include all the Sainted Dead who have ever lived, all the way from the very dawn of time. Actually, they will be the first ones to arise. And then every Born-Again person in the world alive at that time will also be included.

2. The second group will be the *"Tribulation Saints,"* which we have just briefly addressed. This will include all who come to Christ from the time of the general Rapture and will extend to the conclusion of the Great Tribulation, which will be a time frame of from seven to ten or more years. In other words, all of these will be included in the First Resurrection of Life.

3. The third group will be the 144,000 Jews who will come to Christ during the Great Tribulation. The Scripture says of them:

"**And she** *(Israel)* **brought forth a manchild** *(as stated, this is the 144,000 Jews who will come to Christ during the first half of the Great Tribulation [Chpt. 7]; we aren't told exactly how this will be done),* **who was to rule all nations with a rod of iron** *(Israel, under Christ, will definitely fill this role in the coming Millennial Reign):* **and her child was caught up unto God, and** *to* **His Throne.** *(This refers*

*to the Rapture of the 144,000, which will take place at about
the midpoint of the Great Tribulation)"* **(Rev. 12:5).**

4. **The two witnesses: These are addressed in Revelation
11:1-12. These two witnesses will be Elijah, and most probably
Enoch. These two men have never died, having been translated,
and as it is appointed unto all once to die, their two deaths will
fulfill the Scripture (Heb. 9:27). These two men will be greatly
used of God throughout the last half of the Great Tribulation;
however, the Lord will allow them to be killed at the conclusion
of that terrible time, but after three and a half days the Lord
will raise them from the dead and rapture them to Glory
(Rev. 11:1-13).**

**All of this beginning with the general Rapture unto the
Rapture of the two witnesses, is referred to as** *"The First Resurrection."* **Then John said:**

"Blessed and Holy *is* **he who has part in the First
Resurrection** *(this is the Resurrection of Life, which will
include every Saint of God who has ever lived from Abel
to the last Tribulation Saint; all will be given Glorified
Bodies):* **on such the second death has no power** *(the
'second death' is to be cast into the Lake of Fire, and to be
there forever and forever [Rev. 2:8]; all who are washed
in the Blood of the Lamb need not fear the second death)*,
**but they shall be Priests of God and of Christ, and shall
reign with Him a thousand years.** *(All Believers who have
part in the First Resurrection will at the same time serve
as mediators, so to speak, between the population of the
world and God and Christ. The 'thousand years' portrays
the Kingdom Age, when Christ will reign supreme over the
entire Earth)"* **(Rev. 20:6).**

WHEN WILL THE RAPTURE OCCUR?

The exact time is not known; however, we are given some

clues in the Word of God as to the general time frame of the Rapture.

Revelation, Chapters 3 and 4 constitute the Church Age. The last message was to the Church at Laodicea. I think that most agree that we are now living in the Laodicean Age regarding the Church.

John then wrote:

"After this I looked *(represents the time after the Churches, or in other words after the Rapture)*, and, behold, a door *was* opened in Heaven *(gives John the ability to see what is taking place there)*: and the first voice which I heard *was* as it were of a trumpet talking with me *(is actually the Voice of Jesus, harking back to Rev. 1:10)*; which said, Come up hither, and I will show you things which must be hereafter *(after the Rapture of the Church)*" (Rev. 4:1).

The Rapture of the Church will signal the end of the Church Age. We are now living in the closing days of the Church Age, which has lasted now approximately 2,000 years. So, the Rapture must be near.

The Apostle Paul gave us another clue. He said:

"And now you know what withholds *(speaks of the Church)* that he might be revealed in his time. *(This speaks of the Antichrist who will be revealed or made known after the Rapture of the Church.)*

"For the mystery of iniquity does already work *(concerns false teaching by false teachers)*: only he *(the Church)* who now lets *(who now hinders evil)* *will let* *(will continue to hinder)*, until he *(the Church)* be taken out of the way. *(The pronoun 'he' confuses some people. In Verses 4 and 6, the pronoun 'he' refers to the Antichrist, while in Verse 7 'he' refers to the Church.)*

"And then *(after the Rapture of the Church)* shall that

Wicked *(the Antichrist)* **be revealed** *(proving conclusively that the Rapture takes place before the Great Tribulation [Mat. 24:21]),* **whom the Lord shall consume with the spirit of His Mouth** *(should have been translated, 'the Breath of His Mouth' [Isa. 11:4]),* **and shall destroy with the brightness of His Coming** *(both phrases refer to the Second Coming)"* **(II Thess. 2:6-8).**

So, we are told in these Passages, that the Rapture of the Church will take place before the advent of the Antichrist.

Actually, while these two clues are prominent, there is one more clue that is even more prominent, the most prominent of all. It is Israel!

ISRAEL, GOD'S PROPHETIC TIME CLOCK

As it has been said, if we desire to know what time frame we are in as it regards Bible Prophecy concerning the Endtime, we only need look at Israel.

Jesus gave us some clues in the following parable.

THE PARABLE OF THE FIG TREE

"Now learn a Parable of the fig tree *(the Bible presents three trees, the fig, the olive, and the vine, as representing the Nation of Israel, nationally, spiritually, and dispensationally)*; **When his branch is yet tender, and putteth forth leaves** *(is meant to serve as the illustration of Israel nationally)*, **you know that summer** *is* **near** *(refers to Israel as the greatest Prophetic Sign of all, telling us that we are now living in the last of the Last Days)*:

"So likewise you *(points to the modern Church)*, **when you shall see all these things** *(which we are now seeing as it regards Israel)*, **know that it is near,** *even* **at the doors** *(the fulfillment of Endtime Prophecies)"* **(Mat. 24:32-33).**

THE SECOND TIME

Israel was totally destroyed in A.D. 70 and, in fact, scattered all over the world of that day. In fact, for nearly 2,000 years they lived scattered virtually all over the Planet. And then in 1948, they once again became a nation. In fact, no other nation has ever remotely done such a thing. I refer to a certain people scattered all over the world, and then coming together and once again becoming a nation as did Israel. This shows that it was God all the time.

The great Prophet Isaiah said and concerning this very time:

"And it shall come to pass in that day, that the Lord shall set His Hand again the second time to recover the remnant of His People, which shall be left, from Assyria, and from Egypt, and from Pathros, and from Cush, and from Elam, and from Shinar, and from Hamath, and from the islands of the sea. *(Once again, 'in that day,' refers to Christ reigning Personally in Jerusalem. The first gathering of the 'remnant,' as it refers to Israel, took place when Israel was gathered out of the Medo-Persian Empire and brought back to the Promised Land, which took place approximately 400 years before Christ. In a sense, the second gathering began in 1948. It will be fulfilled in totality at the beginning of the Kingdom Age, when Jews all over the world will recognize Christ as their Messiah and, thereby, desire to come to Israel and to live near Him.)*

"And He shall set up an ensign for the nations, and shall assemble the outcasts of Israel, and gather together the dispersed of Judah from the four corners of the Earth. *(Here, Israel is called 'outcasts,' and they have been such ever since their rejection of Christ and the destruction of Jerusalem by Titus in A.D. 70.*

"The central theme of this Verse is Christ. Israel will now [during the Kingdom Age] recognize Him, and Him Alone, as their True Messiah. Jerusalem, the place of His

Crucifixion, will now be the place of His Glory. The Jews will come to this Glory from 'the four corners of the Earth')" **(Isa. 11:11-12).**

Knowing that it is the Lord Who has formed Israel into a nation again, and that against overwhelming odds, and knowing that Israel plays a heavy part, actually the greatest part of all, in Endtime Prophecies, we know that the time of the Rapture must be very near.

THE BLESSED HOPE

John the Beloved wrote and said:

"Beloved, now are we the sons of God *(we are just as much a 'son of God' now as we will be after the Resurrection)*, and it does not yet appear what we shall be *(our present state as a 'son of God' is not at all like that we shall be in the coming Resurrection)*: but we know that, when He shall appear *(the Rapture)*, we shall be like Him *(speaks of being Glorified)*; for we shall see Him as He is. *(Physical eyes in a mortal body could not look upon that Glory, only eyes in Glorified Bodies.)*
"And every man who has this hope in Him *(the Resurrection)* purifies himself *(takes advantage of what Christ did for us at the Cross, which is the only way one can be pure)*, even as He *(Christ)* is pure *(places Christ as our example)*" **(I Jn. 3:2-3).**

CHAPTER 19

The Doctrine Of The Second Coming Of The Lord

THE DOCTRINE OF THE SECOND COMING OF THE LORD

As someone has rightly said, *"While the Rapture will save the Church, likewise the Second Coming will save the world."*

This means that apostasy will be so rampant in these Last Days that if the Rapture is delayed much longer, there will be precious few who are truly Born-Again. Likewise, if the Second Coming doesn't take place, in all likelihood the world would be completely destroyed; however, the Second Coming will stop that.

Both the Church, and we speak of those who are truly Born-Again, and this world, belong to God. He created this world, and He died for the Church. And yet, the battle has raged from the very beginning as Satan has done everything within his power to destroy the Church, i.e., Israel and the Church and, as well, to try to take possession of the Earth. While he most definitely has caused tremendous damage, he will not take best in the end. The Second Coming will see his defeat in totality.

WHAT IS THE SECOND COMING?

The Second Coming is Christ Personally coming back to this Earth to set up a Government and a Kingdom that will last for 1,000 years, and then forever.

The Second Coming of the Lord is one of the most often quoted predictions in the entirety of the Word of God. The first record of such was by Enoch, who lived about 1,000 years before the flood. Jude, the half brother of our Lord, commenting on the apostasy of the Last Days said the following, which includes the prediction by Enoch:

"But these *(false teachers)* speak evil of those things which they know not *(the adage here applies, 'fools rush in where Angels fear to tread')*: but what they

know naturally, as brute beasts *(Jude refers to these false teachers as being in the class of unreasoning animals)*, **in those things they corrupt themselves** *(could have been translated, 'by these things are being brought to ruin')*.

"**Woe unto them!** *(Concerning apostasy and apostates, the Holy Spirit says to them, 'Woe!')* **for they have gone in the way of Cain** *(the type of a religious man who believes in God and 'religion,' but after his own will, and who rejects Redemption by blood)*, **and ran greedily after the error of Balaam for reward** *(the error of Balaam was that he was blind to the higher morality of the Cross, through which God maintains and enforces the authority and awful sanctions of His Law, so that He can be Just and the Justifier of the believing sinner; he loved the wages of unrighteousness in coveting the gifts of Balak [Num. 22:7, 17, 37; 24:11; II Pet. 2:15])*, **and perished in the gainsaying of Core** *(the gainsaying of this man was his rebellion against Aaron as God's appointed Priest; this was, in principle, a denial of the High Priesthood of Christ [Num., Chpt. 16])*.

"**These are spots** *(rocks)* **in your feasts of charity, when they feast with you** *(these false teachers participated in the Lord's Supper, thereby, claiming to be godly)*, **feeding themselves without fear** *(furthering their own schemes and lusts instead of tending the flock of God)*: **clouds they are without water** *(such disappoints the ground that needs rain; likewise, these false teachers look good outwardly, but inwardly there is no substance)*, **carried about of winds** *(they seek Believers with itching ears; they have no true course of the Word of God)*; **trees whose fruit withers, without fruit** *(there is no proper fruit, simply because good fruit cannot come from a bad tree)*, **twice dead** *(they were dead in trespasses and sins before being Saved, and now they have gone back on God and are dead again, i.e., 'twice dead')*, **plucked up by the roots** *(they are not like the true tree planted by the waters)*;

FALSE DOCTRINE

"**Raging waves of the sea** *(refers to the destruction caused by false doctrine)*, **foaming out their own shame** *(false doctrine is like the foam or scum at the seashore)*; **wandering stars** *(an unpredictable star which provides no guidance for navigation)*, **to whom is reserved the blackness of darkness forever** *(refers to their eternal doom [II Pet. 2:4])*.

"**And Enoch also, the seventh from Adam** *(the Old Testament person of that name, the man who 'walked with God' [Gen. 5:18-24])*, **Prophesied of these** *(the translation should read, 'Prophesied with respect to these false teachers of these Last Days')*, **saying, Behold, the Lord comes with ten thousands of His Saints** *(is actually, 'His Holy ten thousands,' which literally means 'an unlimited number'; this quotation is taken from the Book of Enoch, which was lost for many centuries with the exception of a few fragments, but was found in its entirety in a copy of the Ethiopia Bible in 1773)*,

JUDGMENT

"**To execute Judgment upon all** *(refers to Christ Judging the nations of the world, which will commence at the beginning of the Millennial Reign)*, **and to convince all who are ungodly among them of all their ungodly deeds which they have ungodly committed** *(the word 'ungodly' is used four times in this Verse, telling us that the ungodliness is total; as well, 'all' is used four times, which means that none will escape this Judgment)*, **and of all their hard** *speeches* **which ungodly sinners have spoken against Him** *(every ungodly statement against Christ will be addressed at that time)*.

"**These are murmurers, complainers, walking after their own lusts** *(Jude has in mind men who cannot get* *enough to satisfy their lusts, and thus complain)*; **and their mouth speaks great swelling** *words,* **having men's persons in admiration because of advantage** *(refers to showing 'respect of person'; they use flattery for the sake of profit)*" (Jude, Vss. 10-16).

THE LAST ACCOUNT GIVEN IN THE BIBLE

The last account of the Second Coming portrays the actual happening. It was given by John the Beloved. He said, and I continue to quote from THE EXPOSITOR'S STUDY BIBLE:

"**And I saw Heaven opened** *(records the final Prophetic hour regarding the Second Coming, without a doubt the greatest moment in human history)*, **and behold a white horse** *(in effect, proclaims a war horse [Zech. 14:3])*; **and He Who sat upon him** *was* **called Faithful and True** *(faithful to His Promises and True to His Judgments; He contrasts with the false Messiah of Rev. 6:2, who was neither faithful nor true)*, **and in Righteousness He does Judge and make war** *(refers to the manner of His Second Coming)*.

"**His eyes** *were* **as a flame of fire** *(represents Judgment)*, **and on His Head** *were* **many crowns** *(represents the fact that He will not be Lord of just one realm; He will be Lord of all realms)*; **and He had a Name written, that no man knew, but He Himself** *(not meaning that it is unknown, but rather it is definitely unknowable; it will remain unreachable to man, meaning that its depths can never be fully plumbed)*.

"**And He** *was* **clothed with a vesture dipped in Blood** *(speaks of the Cross where He shed His Life's Blood, which gives Him the right to Judge the world)*: **and His Name is called The Word of God.** *(His revealed Name is the Word of God, for He revealed God in His Grace and Power to make Him known, so the Believer can say, 'I know Him.')*

"**And the armies** *which were* **in Heaven followed**

Him upon white horses *(these 'armies' are the Saints of God, in fact, all the Saints who have ever lived, meaning we will be with Him at the Second Coming)*, **clothed in fine linen, white and clean.** *(Harks back to Verse 8. It is the Righteousness of the Saints, all made possible by the Cross)*" **(Rev. 19:11-14).**

Of course, there are scores of Passages between the first mention given by Enoch and the last given by John the Beloved (Isa. 9:7; 24:23; 34:1-8; Ezek., Chpts. 38-39; Dan. 2:44-45; Zech. 14:1-7; Mat. 24:37-44; II Thess. 2:1-12; etc.).

WHEN WILL THE SECOND COMING OCCUR?

It will occur during the Battle of Armageddon.

Concerning that time, John the Beloved wrote, and portrays the manner of His Coming. He said:

"**And out of His Mouth goes a sharp sword** *(represents Christ functioning totally and completely in the realm of the Word of God)*, **that with it He should smite the nations** *(refers to all the nations that will join the Antichrist in his efforts to destroy Israel; it is the Battle of Armageddon)*: **and He shall rule them with a rod of iron** *(refers to the fact that the Lord of Glory will not allow or tolerate in any shape, form, or fashion that which 'steals, kills, and destroys')*: **and He treads the winepress of the fierceness and wrath of Almighty God** *(refers to the Battle of Armageddon)*.

"**And He has on** *His* **Vesture and on His Thigh a name written, KING OF KINGS, AND LORD OF LORDS** *(proclaims the fact that there will be no doubt as to Who He actually is)*.

"**And I saw an Angel standing in the sun** *(proclaims the fact that Faith believes what is written, even if the mind cannot comprehend what is written)*; **and he cried with a** loud voice, saying to all the fowls who fly in the midst of Heaven *(denotes, as is obvious, supremacy over the Creation)*, Come and gather yourselves together unto the supper of the Great God *(this is symbolic, but it is spoken in this way to proclaim the magnitude of that coming time [Ezek. 39:2, 11-12])*;

THE BATTLE OF ARMAGEDDON

"That you may eat the flesh of kings, and the flesh of captains, and the flesh of mighty men, and the flesh of horses, and of them who sit on them, and the flesh of all *men, both* free and bond, both small and great. *(This proclaims the fact that the Power of Almighty God doesn't blink at those on this Earth who consider themselves to be 'great.' The Judgment will be identical for all [Ezek. 39:18-20].)*

"And I saw the beast *(John saw the Antichrist leading this mighty army; this is the 'man of sin' mentioned by Paul in II Thess., Chpt. 2)*, and the kings of the earth, and their armies *(refers to all the Antichrist could get to join him; it includes the 'kings of the East' of Rev. 16:12)*, gathered together to make war against Him Who sat on the horse, and against His Army *(refers to Christ and the great army of Heaven which is with Him; as stated, this is the Battle of Armageddon [Ezek., Chpts. 38-39])*.

"And the beast was taken, and with him the false prophet who wrought miracles before him *(refers to both of them falling in the Battle of Armageddon)*, with which he deceived them who had received the mark of the beast, and them who worshipped his image *(pertains to Satan's chief weapon, which is deception)*. These both were cast alive into a Lake of Fire burning with brimstone *(thus is the destiny of the Antichrist and the False Prophet, and all who follow them)*.

"And the remnant were slain with the sword of Him

Who sat upon the horse, which *sword* proceeded out of His Mouth *(the Lord Jesus will speak the Word in the Battle of Armageddon, and whatever He speaks will take place)*: and all the fowls were filled with their flesh. *(This proclaims the end of this conflict. The Antichrist and his hoards will announce to the world what they are going to do regarding Israel, but the end result will be buzzards gorging on their flesh)*" **(Rev. 19:15-21).**

THE PURPOSE OF THE SECOND COMING

The purpose will be severalfold. They are:
• To save Israel, who will be at the point of destruction and, therefore, annihilation.
• To defeat the Antichrist and his army.
• To cast Satan into the bottomless pit.
• To set up a Government on Earth, which will usher in the greatest freedom and prosperity the world has ever known. It will last for 1,000 years, and then forever.

The following is the entirety of Chapters 38 and 39 from the great Book of Ezekiel. To properly describe the purpose of the Second Coming, one has to capture the flavor of what will happen at that time, with such being given to us in these two Chapters in Ezekiel. Even though it is quite lengthy, I feel the notes given with the Text make it intensely interesting. The great Prophet said:

"And the Word of the LORD came unto me saying,
"Son of man, set your face against Gog, the land of Magog, the chief prince of Meshech and Tubal, and prophesy against him *('Gog' is another name for the Antichrist)*,
"And say, Thus says the Lord GOD; Behold, I am against you, O Gog, the chief prince of Meshech and Tubal *(for many years, Bible teachers have thought that these Passages referred to Russia, but a closer investigation*

of the statements prove otherwise; therefore, the phrase 'Behold, I am against you, O Gog,' is not referring to Russia, but instead to the Antichrist):

"And I will turn you back, and put hooks into your jaws, and I will bring you forth, and all your army, horses and horsemen, all of them clothed with all sorts of armour, even a great company with bucklers and shields, all of them handling swords *(this Prophecy refers to the Battle of Armageddon, which will be the second invasion by the Antichrist of Israel, in which he will be totally destroyed. The first invasion will take place in the midst of the Great Tribulation, when the Antichrist will then show his true colors)*:

DIFFERENT NATIONS

"Persia, Ethiopia, and Libya with them; all of them with shield and helmet:

"Gomer, and all his bands; the house of Togarmah of the north quarters, and all his bands: and many people with you. *(These Passages merely reinforce the statements previously made, that the army of the Antichrist will consist of people from many countries, including Russia.)*

"Be thou prepared, and prepare for yourself, you, and all your company that are assembled unto you, and be thou a guard unto them. *('Be thou prepared,' merely refers to a taunt given by the Holy Spirit to the Antichrist. In other words, 'prepare yourself to the very best of your ability, and still it will avail you nothing, as you will be totally defeated.')*

"After many days you shall be visited: in the latter years you shall come into the land that is brought back from the sword, and is gathered out of many people, against the mountains of Israel, which have been always waste: but it is brought forth out of the nations, and they shall dwell safely all of them. *(The two phrases, 'After many days' and 'in the latter years,' refer to this present time and the immediate future, therefore, any claims that this Chapter has already been fulfilled are spurious.*

" 'The land that is brought back from the sword,' refers to the many conflicts Israel has had since becoming a nation in 1948.

" 'And is gathered out of many people,' refers to the various nations, such as Egypt, Syria, Iraq, etc., which did not desire Israel to become a nation, and which, therefore, greatly opposed her.

ISRAEL BECOMING A STATE

" 'But it is brought forth out of the nations,' pertains to the United Nations voting that Israel would become a State, with even Russia voting her approval.

" 'And they shall dwell safely all of them,' refers to the terrible horror of the Holocaust in World War II, with some 6,000,000 Jews being slaughtered by Hitler, and Israel then demanding a homeland instead of being scattered all over the world. Their feeling was that if this could be obtained, then they would be 'safe.')

THE ANTICHRIST

"You shall ascend and come like a storm, you shall be like a cloud to cover the land, you, and all your bands, and many people with you. *(As stated, this is the Battle of Armageddon.)*

"Thus says the Lord GOD; It shall also come to pass, that at the same time shall things come into your mind, and you shall think an evil thought *(the 'evil thought' will consist of the plans of the Antichrist, inspired of Satan, to destroy Israel and the Jews. That plan is the Battle of Armageddon!)***:**

"And you shall say, I will go up to the land of unwalled

villages; I will go to them who are at rest, who dwell safely, all of them dwelling without walls, and having neither bars nor gates *(the phrases, 'the land of unwalled villages,' 'dwelling without walls,' and 'having neither bars nor gates,' refer to Israel's efforts at mobilization to be rather weak, at least in the mind of the Antichrist),*

"To take a spoil, and to take a prey; to turn your hand upon the desolate places that are now inhabited, and upon the people that are gathered out of the nations, which have gotten cattle and goods, who dwell in the midst of the land. *(This is the invasion of Israel by the Antichrist, called the 'Battle of Armageddon,' which will precipitate the Second Coming of the Lord.)*

"Sheba, and Dedan, and the merchants of Tarshish, with all the young lions thereof, shall say unto you, Are you come to take a spoil? have you gathered your company to take a prey? to carry away silver and gold, to take away cattle and goods, to take a great spoil? *(The questions asked by these particular nations are not meant to proclaim an adversarial position; in fact, they will probably throw in their lot with the Antichrist, hoping to get a part of the 'great spoil')*

THE BATTLE OF ARMAGEDDON

"Therefore, son of man, prophesy and say unto Gog, Thus says the Lord GOD; In that day when My People of Israel dwell safely, shall you not know it? *(The idea of this Verse is: despite the Antichrist invading Israel and defeating her at the midpoint of the Great Tribulation, thereby breaking his seven-year pact, still, due to him having pressing business elsewhere [Dan. 11:44], Israel will then filter back into the land, reoccupying it, and seemingly will dwell safely. This will, no doubt, infuriate the 'man of sin,' and he will set about to handle the situation once and for all!)*

"**And you shall come from your place out of the north parts, you, and many people with you, all of them riding upon horses, a great company, and a mighty army** *(the 'north parts' do not refer to Russia, as some think, but rather to Syria. In fact, the Antichrist [Gog] will come from Syria; however, the Syria of Daniel's Prophesies, of which this speaks, included modern Syria, Iraq, and Iran)***:**

"**And you shall come up against My People of Israel, as a cloud to cover the land; it shall be in the latter days, and I will bring you against My Land, that the heathen may know Me, when I shall be sanctified in you, O Gog, before their eyes.** *('In the latter days,' refers to the last of the Last Days, which pertain to the present and near future. In other words, these Prophecies have already begun to come to pass, and, with each passing day, will accelerate their fulfillment.)*

"**Thus says the Lord GOD; Are you he of whom I have spoken in old time by My Servants the Prophets of Israel, which prophesied in those days many years that I would bring you against them?** *(The Lord is actually speaking here of the Prophecies given to Ezekiel of which this is one, as well as those of Isaiah, Daniel, Zechariah, and others!)*

THE WRATH OF GOD

"**And it shall come to pass at the same time when Gog shall come against the land of Israel, says the Lord GOD, that my fury shall come up in My Face.** *(Once again, this is the Battle of Armageddon. 'My fury shall come up in My Face,' corresponds to the statement of Zechariah [Zech. 14:3].)*

"**For in My Jealousy and in the fire of My Wrath have I spoken, Surely in that day there shall be a great shaking in the land of Israel** *(the 'great shaking in the Land* *of Israel' can only transpire in the Battle of Armageddon, and only by the Hand of the Lord)*;

"So that the fishes of the sea, and the fowls of the Heaven, and the beasts of the field, and all creeping things that creep upon the Earth, and all the men who are upon the face of the Earth, shall shake at My Presence, and the mountains shall be thrown down, and the steep places shall fall, and every wall shall fall to the ground. *(This Verse pertains to the Second Coming, which will be the most cataclysmic event in human history.)*

"And I will call for a sword against him throughout all My Mountains, says the Lord GOD; every man's sword shall be against his brother. *(This portrays the fact that the Lord has control over all things!)*

"And I will plead against him with pestilence and with blood; and I will rain upon him, and upon his bands, and upon the many people who are with him, an overflowing rain, and great hailstones, fire, and brimstone. *(This Verse proclaims the fact that the Lord will use the elements, over which neither the Antichrist nor any other man has any control.)*

"Thus will I magnify Myself, and sanctify Myself; and I will be known in the eyes of many nations, and they shall know that I am the LORD. *('Thus will I magnify Myself,' has reference to anger held in check for a long time, and then exploding with a fury that defies description.)*

EZEKIEL, CHAPTER 39

"Therefore, thou son of man, prophesy against Gog, and say, Thus says the Lord GOD, Behold, I am against you, O Gog, the chief prince of Meshech and Tubal *(this Chapter proclaims Gog's defeat by the Lord Jesus Christ. As stated, it is the Battle of Armageddon, as described in Rev. 16:16)*:

"And I will turn you back, and leave but the sixth

part of you, and will cause you to come up from the north parts, and will bring you upon the mountains of Israel *(five-sixths of the army of the Antichrist will be killed by the Second Coming of the Lord. 'And will cause you to come up from the north parts,' does not, as previously stated, refer to Russia. It instead refers to the invasion route being the same as it was for the Assyrians, Babylonians, Grecians, and others in the past)*:

THE DEFEAT OF THE ANTICHRIST

"And I will smite your bow out of your left hand, and will cause your arrows to fall out of your right hand. *(The Antichrist, called 'Gog,' will think he is fighting Israel only, when, in Truth, he is fighting the Lord, a battle he cannot hope to win.)*

"You shall fall upon the mountains of Israel, you, and all your bands, and the people that is with you: I will give you unto the ravenous birds of every sort, and to the beasts of the field to be devoured. *(The idea is that the defeat of the Antichrist and his armies will be so severe that vultures and beasts will feed upon the multitudes of dead bodies littering the 'mountains of Israel.'*

" 'You shall fall,' signifies not only the defeat of the 'man of sin,' but also the collapse of corrupt human society, which includes corrupt human government.)

"You shall fall upon the open field: for I have spoken it, says the Lord GOD. *('Open field,' refers to the time of the defeat of the Antichrist. It will be in the very midst of the Battle, with the Antichrist bearing down on Jerusalem, thinking that victory is within his grasp [Zech. 14:1-3].)*

"And I will send a fire on Magog, and among them who dwell carelessly in the isles: and they shall know that I am the LORD. *('Send a fire on Magog,' simply means that the Lord will personally use the elements of the heavens to destroy the vast Gentile armies following the Antichrist.*

"'And among them who dwell carelessly in the isles,' pertains to other nations of the world, which, in their minds, are neutral and are simply turning a blind eye to this wholesale slaughter against Israel by the Antichrist.)

THE HOLY NAME!

"So will I make My Holy Name known in the midst of My People Israel; and I will not let them pollute My Holy Name any more: and the heathen shall know that I am the LORD, the Holy One in Israel.** *(This Verse captures all the Promises made by the Lord to the Patriarchs and Prophets of old!)*

"Behold, it is come, and it is done, says the Lord GOD; this is the day whereof I have spoken.** *(This Verse pertains to the coming Great Tribulation, and more especially to these events at the very conclusion of that particular time, including the Battle of Armageddon [Zech. 14:7].)*

"And they who dwell in the cities of Israel shall go forth, and shall set on fire and burn the weapons, both the shields and the bucklers, the bows and the arrows, and the handstaves, and the spears, and they shall burn them with fire seven years** *(to think of something being burned 'with fire seven years' allows us to know the extent of the destruction)*:

"So that they shall take no wood out of the field, neither cut down any out of the forests; for they shall burn the weapons with fire: and they shall spoil those who spoiled them, and rob those who robbed them, says the Lord GOD.**

SEVEN MONTHS TO BURY THE DEAD

"And it shall come to pass in that day, that I will give

unto Gog a place there of graves in Israel, the valley of the passengers on the east of the sea: and it shall stop the noses of the passengers: and there shall they bury Gog and all his multitude: and they shall call it The valley of Hamon-gog. *(No doubt, several millions of men are going to be killed in that which is known as 'the Battle of Armageddon.' Even employing modern equipment to hasten the burial of so many human bodies, still, the stench will 'stop the noses of the passengers.')*

"And seven months shall the House of Israel be burying of them, that they may cleanse the land.

"Yes, all the people of the land shall bury them; and it shall be to them a renown the day that I shall be glorified, says the Lord GOD. *(The Lord links this spectacle to the sanctifying of His Name.)*

"And they shall sever out men of continual employment, passing through the land to bury with the passengers those who remain upon the face of the Earth, to cleanse it: after the end of seven months shall they search. *(The Executive Government of Israel will employ and pay the men described in this Verse to collect the human bones, wherever found, and bury them in the huge trench or area of Verse 11. This project, as stated, will require seven months.)*

"And the passengers who pass through the land, when any sees a man's bone, then shall he set up a sign by it, till the buriers have buried it in the valley of Hamon-gog. *(It seems that all the bones will be collected and taken to 'the valley of Hamon-gog,' and there buried. If this is the case, it will be done for a reason, the portraying of such as a monument to Satan's defeat, and the victory; even the great victory, of the Lord Jesus Christ.)*

"And also the name of the city shall be Hamonah. Thus shall they cleanse the land. *(The name 'Hamonah' means 'multitude.' No doubt, it will be a 'city' of graves, housing the silent dead, and not a city of the living.)*

BIRDS AND ANIMALS GATHERED
FOR A SACRIFICIAL FEAST

"And, thou son of man, thus says the Lord GOD; Speak unto every feathered fowl, and to every beast of the field, Assemble yourselves, and come; gather your- selves on every side to My sacrifice that I do sacrifice for you, even a great sacrifice upon the mountains of Israel, that you may eat flesh, and drink blood. *(This is the same command as Rev. 19:17-18, 20).*

"You shall eat the flesh of the mighty, and drink the blood of the princes of the Earth, of rams, of lambs, and of goats, of bullocks, all of them fatlings of Bashan. *(The words, 'the mighty' and 'princes,' signify the military and political elite of the army of the Antichrist. As well, the 'rams, lambs, goats, and bullocks' signify the same!)*

"And you shall eat fat till you be full, and drink blood till you be drunken, of My Sacrifice which I have sacrificed for you. *(The idea is that if they would not accept the Sacrifice of Christ at Calvary, then they would be made a sacrifice, which they were, but which would not save their souls, but would serve as a part of the Salvation of the world.)*

"Thus you shall be filled at My Table with horses and chariots, with mighty men, and with all men of war, says the Lord GOD. *(The Antichrist will think to set a 'table' portraying the defeat of Israel, but instead he and his army will be the 'table,' i.e., 'My Table,' i.e., the Table of the Lord.)*

THE PURPOSE OF GOD

"And I will set My Glory among the heathen, and all the heathen shall see My Judgment that I have executed, and My Hand that I have laid upon them. *(The Bible regards as 'the heathen' all who do not accept the Lord Jesus*

Christ as their Saviour. Therefore, that includes almost all the world.)

"So the House of Israel shall know that I am the LORD their God from that day and forward. *(Along with 'the heathen' seeing this glorious spectacle, likewise, 'the House of Israel' will now 'know' exactly Who the Messiah is. They will know that the One they rejected and crucified is actually 'the LORD their God.' They will know it 'from that very day and forward.')*

"And the heathen shall know that the House of Israel went into captivity for their iniquity: because they trespassed against Me, therefore hid I My Face from them, and gave them into the hand of their enemies: so fell they all by the sword. *(The dispersions under the Assyrians and the Romans having been effected by the sword, as well as all who have been exiled through the centuries, and more particularly the terrible Holocaust of World War II, it can justly be stated: 'they all fell by the sword.'*

" 'They trespassed against Me,' refers to Israel's rebellion from the very beginning, which finally necessitated their destruction and dispersion; however, the crowning 'trespass' of all was their rejection of Christ and His Crucifixion. As a result, they were given over 'into the hand of their enemies,' where they remained for nearly 2,000 years.)

"According to their uncleanness and according to their transgressions have I done unto them, and hid My Face from them. *(As they did not desire Him, He 'hid His Face from them.' This was all He could do! Regrettably, this scenario has not yet ended. Continuing to reject Him, Israel will instead accept 'another' as their Messiah [Jn. 5:43]. This will happen in the very near future, and will bring Israel yet another Holocaust [Mat. 24:21-22].*

"However, and finally, Israel will come out of the darkness into the light, and will accept Christ as their Saviour and Messiah. The following Passages tell us how!)

ISRAEL TO BE REGATHERED AND CONVERTED

"Therefore thus says the Lord GOD; Now will I bring again the captivity of Jacob, and have mercy upon the whole House of Israel, and will be jealous for My Holy Name *(He will have 'Mercy' because of their Repentance, which will take place at the Second Coming. The phrase 'And will be jealous for My Holy Name,' is a fearsome statement. 'His Holy Name,' stands behind His Word. He is 'Jealous' that His Honor be protected and that every single Prophecy be fulfilled)*;

"After that they have borne their shame, and all their trespasses whereby they have trespassed against Me, when they dwelt safely in their land, and none made them afraid. *(The idea of this and succeeding Verses is the explanation of the word 'now' in the previous Verse. The 'shame' resulting from the 'trespasses' is now over. 'Now' they can 'dwell safely in their land, and none shall make them afraid.')*

"When I have brought them again from the people, and gathered them out of their enemies' lands, and am sanctified in them in the sight of many nations *(this great gathering will take place after the Second Coming of Christ, and will include every Jew from every country in the world, who will be brought, and gladly, to Israel. 'And am sanctified in them in the sight of many nations,' refers to His Plan for them finally being realized)*;

"Then shall they know that I am the LORD their God, which caused them to be led into captivity among the heathen: but I have gathered them unto their own land, and have left none of them any more there. *(So certain is the future Restoration of Israel that the past tense is used here in predicting it.)*

"Neither will I hide My Face any more from them: for I have poured out My Spirit upon the House of Israel, says the Lord GOD. *(This Passage and many others emphatically state that Israel will never again go astray because of the 'poured out Spirit of God' upon them. This Vision opens and closes with a valley of dry bones. The first Vision saw the resurrection of those bones [Chpt. 37]; in the second part of the Vision, nothing but bones will remain, signifying the catastrophic end of the armies of the Antichrist.*

"So these two valleys contrast the one with the other — the one, a testimony to God's Faithfulness and Love; the other, to His Fidelity and Judgment)" **(Ezek., Chpts. 38-39)**

A MODERN PICTURE OF THE SECOND COMING

As we have already stated, the Second Coming of Christ will be without a doubt, the most stupendous, even the most cataclysmic event the world has ever known in all of its history. In fact, there is absolutely nothing by which it can be compared.

Satan through the Antichrist will make his great attempt, actually his last one, to destroy these ancient people called the Jews. This time he will not make the mistake of being insufficiently armed and, thereby, being weak. In fact, his army will have the very latest of technological advancement and, as well, millions of men, no doubt, to carry out his wishes.

His wishes will be not only to defeat Israel, but, he proposes to do what Haman, Herod, and Hitler could not do, to annihilate them down to the last man, woman, and child. He will show no mercy! And if he can do this, this means that all the predictions of Israel's Restoration in the Bible will count for nothing. That being the case, Satan after this long, long night of conflict, will win the day. He will now be the Lord of the Universe and this world, as well, will be his for a possession.

SUCCESS?

And it looks like that he will succeed. His army has swept all of northern Israel, and he is now bearing down on the city of Jerusalem, with half of it already fallen. Even though the Jewish soldiers are fighting like maniacs, actually giving no ground until they die, still, their opposition is fruitless.

Without a doubt, thousands of television cameras and photographers will be there recording this event, with it being sent all over in the world, portraying the success of the Antichrist. He will want the whole world to see the spectacle, to hear the roar and the scream of his jets, the bursting of the bombs, the screams of the dying and the wounded regarding the Jews, it is all being recorded for posterity. As stated, he will do what Haman, Herod, and Hitler were not able to do. As television cameramen are given every latitude in order that they may portray this great victory to the world, he reasons that success is now his. In another few hours it will all be over. He will be the master of the world!

ISRAEL'S TRAVAIL!

Israel with her back to the wall, and with half of Jerusalem now fallen, with already two thirds of her population slaughtered, and with the balance looking as though they will die as well, they now begin to call on the Lord.

The United States who stood behind Israel for so long, will be absent at this time. Not wanting to offend the Antichrist, they will remain neutral. So, there is no help coming from that source. In fact, there is no other nation in the world that will help, Israel is alone! If there is any help to receive, it must come from the Lord and no other.

In fact, the great Prophet Isaiah, some 2,750 years ago, prophesied of this event, actually even predicting in Prophecy the prayer that Israel would pray. It will be a prayer of Repentance, of finally confessing what they really are, as well as a plea for merciful help! The following is basically what they will say at that tragic hour.

"But we are all as an unclean thing, and all our

righteousness are as filthy rags; and we all do fade as a leaf; and our iniquities, like the wind, have taken us away. *(Here Israel confesses the reason for their desperate condition. At long last, they own up as to exactly what it is, 'our iniquities.'*

"'But we are all as an unclean thing,' is actually saying before God that they are a spiritual leper. They now recognize that their self-righteousness is no more than 'filthy rags,' which refer to the menstrual flux of a woman regarding her monthly period.

"It is very difficult for men, and especially religious men, to admit to such! Hence, not many religious men are Saved!)

"And there is none who calls upon Your Name, who stirs up himself to take hold of You: for You have hid Your Face from us, and have consumed us, because of our iniquities. *(Once again, Israel admits that it is her 'iniquities,' which have brought about the Judgment of God upon her. She has only herself to blame!)*

"But now, O LORD, you are our Father; we are the clay, and You our Potter; and we all are the work of Your Hand. *(In this Passage is the gist of the great Salvation Message of Christianity. Only God can change the shape of the clay, thereby molding the vessel into the shape and design that is desired, thereby mending the flaws and weaknesses.)*

PLEASE LORD, DO NOT REMEMBER INIQUITY

"Be not wroth very sore, O LORD, neither remember iniquity for ever: behold, see, we beseech You, we are all Your People. *(The appeal here is for God to begin all over again, like the potter with the clay. The idea of the phrase, 'Be not wroth very sore,' refers to the fact that God had become very angry with His People. The reason for that anger was sin on the part of Israel. God cannot abide sin in the lives of His Own People any more than He can in* *the wicked.)*

"Your holy cities are a wilderness, Zion is a wilderness, Jerusalem a desolation. *(As we have stated, the entirety of this prayer of Repentance, which began in the Fifteenth Verse of the previous Chapter, will be prayed by Israel at the end of the Great Tribulation — at the Second Advent of Christ.)*

"Our holy and our beautiful house, where our fathers praised You, is burned up with fire: and all our pleasant things are laid waste. *(This speaks of the Temple that is yet to be built in Jerusalem. In fact, when the Antichrist turns on Israel, he will make their Temple his religious headquarters, committing every act of vileness that one could think.)*

"Will You refrain Yourself for these things, O LORD? will You hold Your Peace, and afflict us very sore? *(Israel first repents of her terrible sins, pleading God's Mercy, Grace, and Love. They then bring to His attention the terrible plight of the 'holy cities,' and of 'Jerusalem.' Last of all, they proclaim to Him the destruction of the Temple.*

"They then ask, 'Will You refrain Yourself for these things, O LORD?'

"The answer is certain. He will not refrain Himself! He will not hold His Peace!)" **(Isa. 64:6-12).**

THE LORD WILL HEAR AND HEED THAT PRAYER

It has been so long in coming, nearly 2,000 years. The words, *"Let His Blood be upon us and upon our children,"* and, *"We have no king but Caesar,"* (Mat. 27:25; Jn. 19:15), have brought upon them a sorrow of unprecedented proportions. They have found that Caesar was a hard taskmaster.

But most definitely, the Lord will now hear their prayer and their plea. In fact, the whole of this Great Tribulation, the opposition by the Antichrist, their near annihilation, have all been for but one purpose, and that's to bring them to this place — the place of Repentance.

TELEVISION

In answer to their prayer, the Lord will show Himself as never before. In fact, He will have with Him, every Saint of God, every Believer who has ever lived, all the way back to the very dawn of time. They will be multiplicities of millions, all riding horses, with Christ as the leading One.

As this mighty army, a thousand times, even a million times, even a billion times more powerful than the armies of the Antichrist, bear down closer to the Earth, what is taking place in the heavens finally becomes visible. At first, the thousands of television cameramen and directors will, no doubt, think that this is possibly another weapon by the Antichrist; however, the dazzling glory of the appearance of the Son of God will cause them to turn their cameras toward the heavens, to try to explain what is taking place. The truth is, they will be speechless, allowing the cameras to do their work for them. Jesus Himself said of this coming time:

THE COMING OF THE SON OF MAN

"For as the lightning cometh out of the east, and shineth even unto the west *(is meant to proclaim the most cataclysmic event the world has ever known)*; so shall also the coming of the Son of Man be *(no one will have to ask, is this really Christ; it will be overly obvious!)*.

"For wheresoever the carcass is *(speaks of the Battle of Armageddon)*, there will the eagles be gathered together *(should have been translated, 'there will the vultures be gathered together' [refers to Ezek. 39:17])*.

"Immediately after the tribulation of those days *(speaks of the time immediately preceding the Second Coming)* shall the sun be darkened, and the moon shall not give her light *(the light of these orbs will be dim by comparison to the Light of the Son of God)*, and the stars shall fall from Heaven *(a display of Heavenly fireworks at the Second Coming)*, **and the powers of the Heavens shall be shaken** *(will work with the Son of God against the Antichrist, at the Second Coming)*:

"**And then shall appear the sign of the Son of Man in Heaven** *(pertains to the Second Coming, which will take place in the midst of these Earth and Heaven shaking events)*: **and then shall all the tribes of the Earth mourn** *(concerns all the nations of the world which possibly will see this phenomenon by Television)*, **and they shall see the Son of Man** *(denotes Christ and His human, Glorified Body)* **coming in the clouds of Heaven with Power and great glory** *(lends credence to the thought that much of the world will see Him by television as He makes His Descent)*" (Mat. 24:27-30).

The destruction of the army of the Antichrist will be the most complete destruction the world has ever known of any army.

Ever how large that army will be, as we quoted to you from the Thirty-ninth Chapter of Ezekiel, five sixths of the millions of men and women in this army will be slaughtered (Ezek. 39:2). To do all of this, the Lord will use the elements of the heavens, using great hail stones to serve as artillery and, as well, meteorites, no doubt, by the tens of thousands (Ezek. 38:22).

Along with all of this, the heavens themselves, knowing their Creator is coming to take control, will put on a display of glory such as the heavens have never seen before (Mat. 24:29), all recorded by television for the entirety of the world to see. So, instead of seeing the victory of the Antichrist and the annihilation of the Jews, the world will see the defeat of the Antichrist, and the victory of the Jews, a victory, in fact, so complete, as to defy all description.

THE REVELATION OF CHRIST TO ISRAEL

When Jesus comes back, Israel in the midst of her great victory, because of what the Lord has done, will still not recognize

Him as the One they crucified. Concerning this, the Scripture says:

"And one shall say unto Him, What are these wounds in Your Hands? Then He shall answer, Those with which I was wounded in the house of My friends" (Zech. 13:6).

The notes in THE EXPOSITOR'S STUDY BIBLE pertaining to this Scripture are as follows:

"*In these Passages, the false prophets are placed beside the True Prophet, the Lord Jesus Christ. They, before the Coming of the Lord, too oftentimes were rewarded, while He, as each True Prophet, was greatly opposed, even crucified. The false prophets thrust themselves forward and claimed reverence and position; He Himself, the greatest of the Prophets, did not claim to be a professional Prophet — that was not His Mission in coming to Earth but became a Bond-servant and a Shepherd; made and appointed such in Divine Purpose of Redemption. For man having sold himself into slavery, it was necessary that Christ should take that position in order to redeem him.*

"*'And one shall say unto Him,' refers to the moment of recognition, as outlined in 12:10, where it says, 'And they shall look upon Me Whom they have pierced, and they shall mourn for Him.' This will be immediately after the Second Coming, with the Antichrist now defeated and Christ standing before Israel. They will then know, beyond the shadow of a doubt, that He is the Messiah; then will they ask, 'What are these wounds in Your Hands?'*

"*These wounds, which He will ever carry, will be an instant and constant reminder of Who He is and what was done to Him, which presents Him as the Sin-Bearer of the world. Even though He was the Redeemer of all mankind, still, this shows how He was treated by man, especially by His Own.*

"*'Then He shall answer,' will be an answer that will cause their terrible 'mourning' of 12:10-14. It will also be the cause of the 'Fountain opened to the House of David and to the inhabitants of Jerusalem for sin and for uncleanness' [13:1].*

"*'Those with which I was wounded in the house of My friends,' proclaims His Crucifixion and those who did it to Him. The words, 'My friends,' are said in irony.*"

ISRAEL'S REDEMPTION THROUGH THE SUFFERING OF THE MESSIAH

Immediately after answering Israel's question as to the wounds in His Hands, the Lord even more graphically, takes Israel back to the Cross. And with that, we will close this Chapter on the Second Coming of our Lord. He said:

"Awake, O sword, against My Shepherd, and against the Man Who is My fellow, says the LORD of Hosts: smite the shepherd, and the sheep shall be scattered: and I will turn My Hand upon the little ones" (Zech. 13:7).

The notes from THE EXPOSITOR'S STUDY BIBLE regarding this Scripture inform us:

"*'Awake, O sword, against My Shepherd,' concerns the Crucifixion of Christ, because Christ was the 'Good Shepherd' [Jn. 10:11], in effect, 'God's Shepherd.' 'And against the Man Who is My fellow, says the LORD of Hosts,' refers to Christ as the 'Fellow' of Jehovah.*

"*'Smite the Shepherd,' pertains to the fact that not only was sin upon the sinless Substitute at Calvary, but the Substitute Himself, Jehovah's equal. He Himself must die in order that man might live; for the curse that rested upon man was the doom of death [separation from God] because of sin. Christ's Death was, therefore, necessary to satisfy that claim and to vindicate and magnify Divine Righteousness.*

"*'And the sheep shall be scattered,' pertains to them 'scattered' as a nation, but not finally lost, for His Hand, pierced by the flock shall cause the 'little ones' to return to Zion, which these Passages and many others proclaim! 'And I will turn My Hand upon the little ones,' pertains to the Coming of the Lord and the Restoration of Israel, which will bring 'the little ones' back.*

"*In astronomy, a near Planet and a distant fixed star may appear side-by-side in the heavens, though the one is millions of miles more distant than the others; so, in the Scriptures, often two Prophecies may be side-by-side in the Text but, as here, be separated by many hundreds, sometimes thousands of years.)*"

So we say with John the Beloved, "*Amen. Even so, come, Lord Jesus*" (Rev. 22:20).

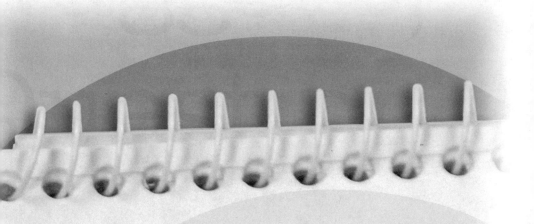

CHAPTER 20

The Doctrine Of Water Baptism And The Lord's Supper

THE DOCTRINE OF WATER BAPTISM AND THE LORD'S SUPPER

First of all, *"Water Baptism,"* or *"The Lord's Supper,"* should not be looked at as *"Sacraments."* They should be looked at rather as *"Ordinances."*

The word *"Sacraments"* in the minds of many, refer to the act of Salvation, meaning that if these ceremonies are engaged, the participants experience Salvation. That is totally unscriptural.

While the word *"Sacraments,"* which really refers to that which is *"sacred,"* can be used without it referring to Salvation, nevertheless, in the minds of most, when using the word as it pertains to Water Baptism or the Lord's Supper, it is equated with Salvation. So, it is best, as stated, to use the word *"Ordinances,"* which means a practice or ceremony ordained or decreed by Deity.

IMMERSION OR SPRINKLING?

The Bible teaches immersion. The Scripture says:

"And Jesus, when He was baptized *(this was the beginning of His earthly Ministry)*, went up straightway *(immediately)* out of the water *(refers to Baptism by immersion and not by sprinkling)*" (Mat. 3:16).

Water Baptism typifies the Death, Burial, and Resurrection of Christ, and is the same for the Believer.

When Christ was standing in the water in the River Jordan, this typified His Death. When He was laid back, and totally immersed under the water, this typified His Burial. Being brought up out of the water, typified His Resurrection. As stated, it is the same for the Believer.

There is no way that sprinkling can carry out this Type, as should be obvious.

BUT WHAT IF A RIVER OR BODY OF WATER IS NOT AVAILABLE?

If such would be the case and, no doubt, it has been in times past, to obey the injunction of our Lord, sprinkling for the immediate time would be sufficient; however, if a Believer was caught in such a dilemma, when a body of water did become available, he should then be baptized by immersion.

There is no saving grace in Water Baptism or the Lord's Supper. All Saving Grace is in Faith registered in Christ and what He has done for us at the Cross (Eph. 2:8-9).

BAPTISMAL REGENERATION AND INFANT BAPTISM

Neither one is Scriptural!

Both, baptismal regeneration and infant baptism, claim as a result of the ceremony, that one is Saved. There is nothing in the Word of God to substantiate such thinking. In fact, untold millions have died eternally lost because they believed that lie, and a lie it is! Once again, people are Saved, irrespective as to whom they might be, not by joining a Church, not by giving so much money, not by a particular ceremony, as wonderful as that ceremony might be in its own right, but simply by evidencing Faith in Christ and what Christ did for us at the Cross.

Paul said:

"**For by Grace** *(the Goodness of God)* **are you Saved through Faith** *(Faith in Christ, with the Cross ever as its Object)*; **and that not of yourselves** *(none of this is of us, but all is of Him)*: *it is* **the Gift of God** *(anytime the word 'Gift' is used, God is speaking of His Son and His Substitutionary Work on the Cross, which makes all of this possible)*:

"**Not of works** *(man cannot merit Salvation, irrespective what he does)*, **lest any man should boast** *(boast in his own ability and strength; we are allowed to boast only in the Cross [Gal. 6:14])*.

"**For we are His workmanship** *(if we are God's work-manship, our Salvation cannot be of ourselves)*, **created in Christ Jesus unto good works** *(speaks of the results of Salvation, and never the cause)*, **which God has before ordained that we should walk in them.** *(The 'good works' the Apostle speaks of has to do with Faith in Christ and the Cross, which enables the Believer to live a Holy life)*" **(Eph. 2:8-10).**

THE HISTORY OF INFANT BAPTISM

Infant baptism appeared in Church history about the year A.D. 370. It came about as a result of the doctrine of baptismal regeneration — the teaching that baptism is essential to Salvation; or if you want to turn it around, that Water Baptism saves the soul (or at least is a part of a person's Salvation). So, consequently, as the teaching of baptismal regeneration began to be propagated, it was natural for those holding to this doctrine to believe that everyone should be baptized as soon as possible. Thus, the baptism of infants still in the innocent state (and as yet unaccountable for their actions) came into vogue among many of the Churches. Once again I state: these two grievous errors (baptismal regeneration, which teaches that Water Baptism saves, and infant baptism) have probably caused more people to go to Hell than any other doctrine.

THE EARLY CHURCH

Incidentally, the Church that we read about in the Book of Acts, and referred to as the Early Church, was that which was founded, so to speak, by the Holy Spirit. In fact, the Lord used the Apostle Paul to serve as the master builder of the Church (I Cor. 3:10). Even though Satan tried repeatedly to insert false doctrine into the New Covenant, which meaning was given to the Apostle Paul (Gal. 1:12), still, Satan little succeeded. In fact, this particular Church touched much of the Roman world of its day.

It basically stayed true to the Lord, which means it stayed true to the Word of God, throughout the lifetime of the original Apostles, and even those who followed them; however, about 100 years after the founding of the Church, incidentally by the Holy Spirit, the Church began to apostatize. Gradually it began to adopt false doctrine, and finally emerged into what is presently known as the Catholic Church. If I remember correctly, it was the year 607 that the title *"Pope"* was first given to the Bishop of Rome. So that means that the Catholic Church was not begun by Simon Peter as our Catholic friends claim! To be blunt, that particular Church is the result of apostasy.

MORE HISTORY

The professed conversion of Emperor Constantine in A.D. 313 was looked upon by many persons as a great triumph for Christianity; however, it more than likely was the greatest tragedy in Church history, because it resulted in the union of Church and State and the establishment of a hierarchy that ultimately developed into the Roman Catholic system. There is great question whether Constantine was ever truly converted. At the time of his supposed vision of the sign of the Cross, he promised to become a Christian. But he was not baptized in water until near death, having postponed the act in the belief that Baptism washed away all past sins, and he wanted all his sins to be in the past tense before he died. In other words, he wanted the freedom to sin as much as he wanted; and then when he was too old or too sick to care, he would have them all washed away by the act of Baptism.

In A.D. 416 infant baptism was made compulsory through-out the Roman Empire. Naturally this filled the Churches with unconverted members who had only been *"baptized into favor."* So, whatever power the Church had in the past relative to actual conversions was now null and void. The world consequently was plunged into the gloom of the Dark Ages, which endured for more than twelve centuries, actually until the Reformation.

During this time God had a remnant who remained faithful to Him; they never consented to the union of Church and State, or to baptismal regeneration, or to infant baptism. These people were called by various names, but probably could better be summed up by their generic name, *"Anabaptists,"* meaning, rebaptizers. These people ignored infant baptism and rebaptized those who had truly been Saved through personal Faith. They also had a generic name for themselves, *"Anapedobaptists,"* meaning *"against infant baptism."*

THE STRANGE THING

The strange thing about these two diabolical doctrines of baptismal regeneration and infant baptism is that the great reformers (Martin Luther, for one) brought with them out of Rome, these two dreaded errors: the union of Church and State and infant baptism. Strangely enough, in those days, not only did the Roman Catholic Church persecute those who were not conformed to its ways, but after the Lutheran Church became the established Church of Germany, it persecuted the nonconformists as well — of course, not as stringently so, and not in such numbers as those before them.

John Calvin, as well as Cromwell in England and John Knox in Scotland, all stuck to the union of Church and State and infant baptism and used their power, when they had power, to seek to force others to conform to their own views.

Unaware to a lot of people, this thing came to the Americas as well in the early days of this republic. Before the Massachusetts Bay Colony was twenty years old, it was decreed by statute that *"If any person or persons within this jurisdiction shall either openly condemn or oppose the baptizing of infants, or go about secretly to seduce others from the approbation or use thereof, or shall purposely depart from the congregation at the administration of the ordinance — after due time and means of conviction — every such person or persons shall be subject to banishment."*

Religious persecution existed even in the early days of the United States of America. Roger Williams and others were banished (when banishment meant to go and live with the Indians) because they would not submit to the doctrine of baptismal regeneration or the baptizing of infants.

However, it was the constitution of the Rhode Island Colony (founded by Roger Williams, John Clark, and others) that established religious liberty by law for the first time in 1,300 years (over the world). Thus it was that Rhode Island, founded by a small group of Believers, was the first spot on Earth where religious liberty became the law of the land. The settlement was made in 1638, and the colony was legally established in 1663. Virginia followed, to be the second, in 1786.

As you can see, the doctrine of infant baptism has a long and bloody history, and it has been one of Satan's chief weapons to condemn untold millions of people to Hell.

FURTHER EXPLANATION

What does the above have to do with us today? A great deal!

You see, the union of Church and State continues today in many countries of the world. In these State Churches Pastors and leaders christen babies, which means they make them *"Christians"* by baptizing them; thus, the person having been christened as a baby believes he is on his way to Heaven simply because he was christened (or baptized) in infancy. Having been taught all his life that this saved him, he naturally considers himself saved by the act of infant baptism. The Roman Catholic Church teaches baptismal regeneration and practices infant baptism. Its statement of doctrine says, *"The Sacrament of Baptism is administered on adults by the pouring of water and the pronouncement of the proper words, and cleanses from original sin."*

The Reformed Church says, *"Children are baptized as heirs of the Kingdom of God and of His Covenant."*

The Lutheran Church teaches that Baptism, whether of

infants or adults, is a means of regeneration.

Because of the following declaration I believe the Episcopal Church teaches that Salvation comes through infant baptism. In his confirmation the Catechist answers a question about his baptism in infancy by saying: *"In my Baptism . . . I was made a member of Christ, a Child of God, and an inheritor of the Kingdom of God."* (This is printed in the prayer book and can be read there by anyone interested enough to look for it.)

Most people who practice infant baptism believe the ceremony has something to do with the Salvation of the child. These are traditions of men, so we can follow the Commandments of God, or follow after the traditions of men; it is up to us.

CLEAR BIBLE TEACHING

The Word of God is clear regarding the matter of Salvation. Jesus said, *"He who believes on the Son has Everlasting Life: and he who believes not the Son shall not see life; but the wrath of God abides on him"* (Jn. 3:36). *"He who believes on Him is not condemned: but he who believes not is condemned already, because he has not believed in the Name of the Only Begotten Son of God"* (Jn. 3:18).

Basically there are two groups of people in the world today: those who believe on the Son and those who do not. Those who believe are not condemned; they have Everlasting Life (whatever Church they may belong to, or no Church at all). Those who believe not on the Son are condemned already, and they shall not see life, but the Wrath of God abides on them.

This is clear, unmistakable teaching and language of the Bible.

If you will notice, the Word of God never says simply believe and be saved, but rather believe *"on the Lord Jesus Christ"* and be Saved. The Word of God always identifies the Object of Faith, which is the Lord Jesus Christ Himself. *"For God so loved the world, that He gave His Only Begotten Son, that whosoever believes in Him shall not perish, but have Everlasting*

Life" (Jn. 3:16). It is not enough just to believe; a person must believe *"in Him."*

When the Philippian jailer asked, *"Sirs, what must I do to be Saved?"* Paul answered, *"Believe on the Lord Jesus Christ, and you shall be Saved"* (Acts 16:30-31). It was not enough simply to believe; such belief, such trust, such dependence had to be *"in Him."*

TRUST IN THE LORD

If a person is trusting in Baptism for Salvation, he cannot be trusting *"in Him."* Christ is not one Way of Salvation; He is the Only Way of Salvation (Jn. 14:6; 10:1, 7, 9). There is no promise in the Word of God to those who believe partially in Christ. In other words, a person cannot trust the Lord Jesus Christ ninety percent and Water Baptism ten percent, or Jesus fifty percent and Baptism fifty percent, or Jesus ninety-five percent and a Church five percent, etc. As a matter of fact, there is no such thing as partially trusting Christ, which means there is no such thing as a partial Justification. The man who is partially trusting is not trusting at all. Yet, the sad fact is that the majority of people in Churches in the United States and the world today are not trusting Christ at all — because they are trusting Him partially.

It is even sadder to realize that more people are going to Hell through religious organizations than any other way. That is a shocking and startling statement, but it is true. Jesus said, *"Many shall say to Me in that day, Lord, Lord, have we not prophesied in Your Name? and in Your Name have cast out devils? and in Your Name done many wonderful works? And then will I profess unto them, I never knew you: depart from Me, you who work iniquity"* (Mat. 7:22-23).

You see, any works offered to Christ for Salvation are called by Jesus Himself, *"works of iniquity."*

There is an old song that expresses my feelings totally. It says:

"My hope is built on nothing less,
"Than Jesus' Blood and Righteousness;
"I dare not trust the sweetest frame,
"But wholly lean on Jesus' Name.
"On Christ the solid Rock I stand;
"All other ground is sinking sand,
"All other ground is sinking sand."

(Portions of the source material on infant baptism were derived from a message by the late Dr. William Pettingill, entitled *"Infant Baptism".*)

THE SCRIPTURAL FORMULA FOR WATER BAPTISM

Trinitarians baptize according to Matthew 28:19, using the words of the Lord Jesus Christ where He said that we should baptize in the Name of the Father, and of the Son, and of the Holy Spirit. We do this for many reasons, and I will go into some of the details concerning the differences between the Matthew 28:19 formula, and those who claim that individuals should be baptized in the Name of Jesus only.

Jesus said: *"Go ye therefore, and teach all nations, baptizing them in the Name of the Father, and of the Son, and of the Holy Spirit"* (Mat. 28:19).

The Jesus Only people are firm that the Matthew 28:19 method is not once found in the Book of Acts, and was unknown in the Early Church, but was introduced centuries later by apostates in total disregard of apostolic practice. Trinitarians are, therefore, they say, admonished to conform to the Scriptural pattern, and to follow the example of those who have the true *"Revelation"* of the Name. This is taken to mean that unless one is baptized in the Name of Jesus Christ, they cannot be forgiven their sins, which is a form of baptismal regeneration. What we have given in abbreviated form is, I believe, the sum total of the Jesus Only doctrine concerning the method of Water Baptism.

NAMES

The Jesus Only people claim that the words *"Father"* and *"Son"* do not constitute names. We maintain they do. We believe that Matthew 28:19 definitely confirms that *"Father"* is a Name, that *"Son,"* is a Name, that *"Holy Spirit"* is a Name, simply because we are not generalizing just any father or just any son. We are talking about God the Father and God the Son; and most anyone in Christendom today would readily recognize and know Who is being spoken of.

In Isaiah 9:6, the Bible says, *"His Name shall be called Wonderful, Counselor, the Mighty God, The Everlasting Father, The Prince of Peace."* Each one of these appellations would be labeled a title by Jesus Only interpreters, but Isaiah's Text calls each one a *"Name."* This is also the one Verse of Scripture in the entirety of God's Word, where Jesus Christ is called the *"Father,"* even which we have already addressed; and still, somehow, these people are blinded to the fact that this Verse actually disproves their theory concerning titles and names, simply because it gives the name of *"Father"* to Jesus.

So I simply ask the question, according to Isaiah, isn't *"Wonderful"* a name? Isn't *"Prince of Peace"* a Name? Isaiah used five different names here and yet, under Divine Inspiration, he specifically chose the singular when he said, *"And His 'Name' shall be called. . . ."* So what more needs to be said in answer to this strange insistence that if *"Father, Son, and Holy Spirit"* are names (plural), then Matthew 28:19 should read, they say, *"In the names of?"* The writers, under Divine Inspiration, however, used the singular instead of the plural. They did it for a Divine reason.

THE BOOK OF ACTS AND
THE BAPTISMAL FORMULA

There's not a single incident in the Book of Acts where any particular baptismal method is given. There is no record of the dialogue of the baptizer while standing in the water with the convert. You will look in vain for any Scripture which would state, *"I baptize you in the Name of Jesus Christ"* (or any other variation of the Precious Name of our Lord). If one would produce such an explicit procedure, I would be thrilled to admit that we have a Scriptural right to baptize thus, but it cannot be produced. It doesn't exist.

On a personal basis, I really have no preference as to what the Bible teaches. I only want to know what it teaches, and then do my best to obey what is given to us.

The Jesus Only people read into the record that which is not there. They have taken the words of Peter, assumed that they were the properly expressed formula, and they place them onto the lips of those who baptize in water — without a shred of evidence to support their action. The Jesus Only proponents proclaim that Acts 2:38 is the baptismal formula. *"Then Peter said unto them, Repent, and be baptized every one of you in the Name of Jesus Christ for the Remission of sins, and you shall receive the Gift of the Holy Spirit"* (Acts 2:38).

And yet Acts 8:16 and Acts 19:5 simply state they were baptized in the Name of the Lord Jesus.

"For as yet He was fallen upon none of them: only they were baptized in the Name of the Lord Jesus" (Acts 8:16).

And then: *"When they heard this, they were baptized in the Name of the Lord Jesus"* (Acts 19:5). And if you will notice, in these two latter Verses, the word *"Christ"* was omitted altogether.

PETER

If Peter, on the Day of Pentecost, received a Baptism *"Revelation,"* which the Jesus Only proponents proclaim is *"in the Name of Jesus Christ,"* why, we ask, is the later variation produced, which we have just quoted? You see, there is no fixed wording to follow, and there is no regular or prescribed usage of certain words. So the question has to be asked, *"Should we baptize in the Name of Jesus Christ, or in Christ Jesus, or in the Lord, or in the Lord Jesus, or in the Lord Jesus Christ?"* Who would be correct? Was Peter right? or Phillip? or Paul?

Jesus Only exponents say they are sticklers (fanatics) for the exact Words of Scripture and that they use the identical words of the Apostles; yet their demands are not accompanied by quotations from God's Word, or the Words themselves. Even in those Passages where their purported words are found, their full formula is lacking. One of their chief proponents some years ago stated that the following formula should be used: *"I baptize you in the Name of the Lord Jesus Christ, which is the Name of the Father, and of the Son, and of the Holy Spirit."* When this particular brother was asked to cite Chapter and Verse for this formula, he was speechless. Apparently, it had not ever occurred to him that the formula he had conjured up had no Scriptural connotation whatsoever.

BAPTISMAL FORMULA?

So the question still must be asked, *"Which is the right way to baptize and what was the meaning of Peter's or Paul's words in the Book of Acts?"*

There is no way one can take the Passages in the Book of Acts to be intended as a Baptismal formula. The words should be regarded as a compendious description of the entire rite. In Acts 2:38, 8:16, and 10:48, the details of the Baptismal ceremony are not set forth. What is set forth is a condensed, brief, abridged reference to the sacred experience. The words describe the sphere, the foundation or ground of Baptism, rather than the prescribed words of the formula.

Every Trinitarian using the Matthew 28:19 formula refers to Water Baptism as *"Christian Baptism"* and this is as it should be, for Christ is assuredly the central figure in Water Baptism. Jesus Christ is the One Who died and rose again; not the Father and not the Holy Spirit. It is into His Death that we are symbolically buried, and in the likeness of His Resurrection we are symbolically raised to walk in Newness of Life; therefore, belief in and confession of the Lord Jesus Christ, and what He did for us at the Cross, is a central part of our Baptismal ceremony.

THE REASON WE ACCEPT THE MATTHEW 28:19 BAPTISMAL FORMULA

• Both the Minister and the Believer render obedience to the Master's own explicit Command whenever the words are used, *"In the Name of the Father, and of the Son, and of the Holy Spirit."*

• Matthew 28:19 fits the definition of a formula. It is an orderly statement of Faith and Doctrine. It is the prescribed words of a ceremony or rite. The words of the Lord Himself are all contained in one concise declaration. It is not necessary, as in the Jesus Only formula, to combine it with other Scriptures in order to get the complete name. It is complete within itself.

• Matthew 28:19 incorporates an orderly statement of Faith. It summarizes the scattered and unsystemized thought and language of the entire New Testament concerning the nature of the Godhead. He Who spoke these Words desired their use as the formula, for they were purposely designed to set forth a Doctrine of the Trinity in this initiatory Christian Rite. The Master's Own Baptism by John was a vivid precedent for associating the Trinity with Baptism. Jesus was there in Person, God spoke from Heaven, and the Holy Spirit descended like a Dove upon Him (Mat. 4:16-17).

• Matthew 28:19 is the only Command in the entire Bible given specifically to those performing the Rite of Baptism. If you will examine all the Passages in Acts dealing with Baptism, you will discover that the commands there are to the Believers themselves and not to the Baptizer, or the Minister. Matthew 28:19 is a direct Order to those who administer the ordinance informing them to baptize *"in the Name of the Father, and of the Son, and of the Holy Spirit."*

• It is unthinkable that the Disciples disobeyed the express

Command of their Lord. The only logical and Scriptural conclusion is that the Apostles and other leaders not only obeyed His Command to baptize but also obeyed His Command to *"baptize in the Name of the Father, and of the Son, and of the Holy Spirit."*

• The Matthew 28:19 baptismal formula is abundantly confirmed by the earliest Christian writings while the Jesus Only formula has no historical support at all. Justin's first apology was written in A.D. 153 — about 90 years after the death of Peter and Paul. It was about 60 years after the death of John the Apostle. Justin was a contemporary of Polycarp, who was a Disciple of John himself, and he stated that Matthew 28:19 was the correct formula.

THE DIDACHE

There is another book called *"The Teaching Of The Twelve Apostles"* and it is the oldest book outside the New Testament. It is also known as the *"Didache"* and is dated by most authorities between A.D. 70 and A.D. 100. Although the author of the book is unknown, it is a compilation of the teachings of the Apostles, which he had apparently learned either by personal instruction, oral tradition, or through their (the Apostle's) own writings or other New Testament writings then in circulation. While it does not possess the inspiration of the Scriptures, the *"Didache"* is an authentic record of primitive Christianity. It includes instructions for baptizing that we ought to baptize in the Name of the Father, and of the Son, and of the Holy Spirit, and also that we ought to baptize in running or living water. There again, the Matthew 28:19 formula is used. And, lest we forget, I would remind you that there is not a single recorded incident in the Bible or any other genuine First Century book where any other formula was ever used in the first 100 years of the Christian Era.

• Matthew 28:19 can be used as the formula and the Baptism still be in the Name of Jesus Christ because the Son is Jesus

Christ. Jesus Christ is the sphere, the foundation, and the ground for Trinitarian Baptism. Belief in, and confession of Christ is the very heart of our Baptism. Consequently, the word spoken by most Ministers of the Gospel, baptizing according to Matthew 28:19, follow this pattern: *"On the confession of your Faith in the Lord Jesus Christ, I baptize you in the Name of the Father, and of the Son, and of the Holy Spirit."*

DOES THE WATER SAVE?

The Jesus Only proponents basically teach, as we have previously stated, baptismal regeneration. In other words, the water saves. This teaching, plus the implication that if one is not baptized in the Name of Jesus Only (or similar expressions), such is a most effective means of frightening people into accepting the Jesus Only doctrine. The people are taught that if they are not baptized in this manner, their sins cannot be forgiven and they will be lost and will burn in Hell eternally. In fact, fear is the motivating factor in this particular doctrine.

Most Trinitarians believe Water Baptism to be a simple step of obedience to the Lord. We believe in immersion, seeing that the meaning of the word *"baptize"* as being a Symbol of the Death, Burial, and the Resurrection of Jesus Christ. We believe that Water Baptism is not so much as some would make it, nor so little as others would make it. The Lord Himself defined its purpose: to fulfill all Righteousness.

It is our Christian duty to be baptized. It is also our joyous privilege to testify publicly by the act of Baptism that Jesus Christ is our Saviour and Lord; nevertheless, we can not attach the same importance to Water Baptism as some legalists such as the Jesus Only advocates do.

SAVED?

We would not attempt to exclude from the Kingdom all those who have not been baptized in the precise manner in which we deem Scriptural. The pages of Church history are filled with the names of men whose Baptism in water we may regard as incorrect, but whose lives and Ministries testify to an unquestionable experience with God. Yet, many Jesus Only adherents state and believe that if individuals have not been baptized according to the Jesus Only formula, they are not even considered saved. Some would make the statement that they are not *"fully saved."* Of course it is difficult to understand at all how a person can be partially saved, i.e., *"partially justified."* We maintain apart from the definite Spiritual and Scriptural relationship with the Lord, there is no virtue in the waters of Baptism; or in the bread and wine, for that matter, of the Lord's Supper. In Acts 22:16, if when Paul used the word *"wash away your sins"* and this means the water would actually save a person; it would seem strange that Paul would also say . . .

"I thank God that I baptized none of you, but Crispus and Gaius" (I Cor. 1:14).

Actually, when Paul used the term, *"Arise, and be baptized, and wash away your sins"* (Acts 22:16), it could be translated, *"Arise, and be baptized, and because your sins have been washed away."*

The statement refers to a present action being done because of a past action; he was being baptized in water because his sins had already been washed away by the Blood of Jesus.

No, Baptism is a symbol of what it represents namely the Death, Burial, and Resurrection of our Lord.

THE BLOOD OF JESUS CHRIST

What is it that washes away sins? *"The Blood of Jesus Christ, His Son, cleanses us from all sin"* (I Jn. 1:7). Sin is, basically, an inner state which may or may not express itself outwardly. It stands to reason that mere outward work like Water Baptism can remove that which is inward. Also, water is a Scriptural Symbol for the Word used in Ephesians 5:26; Psalms 119:9; John 15:3. As well, when Jesus spoke to Nicodemus saying:

"Verily, verily, I say unto you, Except a man be born of water and of the Spirit, he cannot enter into the Kingdom of God" (Jn. 3:5), by using the phrase *"born of water,"* he was not speaking of Water Baptism, but rather the natural birth of a baby, which is proven in Verse 6.

As well, if water saves, what type of water should be used — tap water, running water, still water, deep water, shallow water, river water, or what type of water? What would happen if there was no water in which to administer the sacred Rite? Would that mean a person would be consigned to Hell forever, even though he had believed in and on the Lord Jesus Christ, if there was no water in which Baptism could be applied, and the individual is dying?

THE THIEF ON THE CROSS

What happened to the thief on the Cross when Jesus turned to him and said, *"This day you shall be with Me in Paradise"*? There was no way for him to be baptized. Did he die and go to Hell? Certainly not. Water has never begotten anyone. Water is water, whether it's flowing water, still water, Baptismal water, or so-called holy water. Only believing in the Lord Jesus Christ makes one born of God.

"For by Grace are you Saved through Faith . . ." it is *"not of works, lest any man should boast"* (Eph. 2:8).

Incidentally, there are three Baptisms in which the Believer should engage.

THREE BAPTISMS

1. The Baptism into Christ, which is done by Faith, and speaks of the Crucifixion of Christ, and us symbolically being crucified with Him, buried with Him, and raised with Him in Newness of Life. It has nothing to do with water (Rom. 6:3-5).

2. Water Baptism (Mat. 28:19).

3. Baptism with the Holy Spirit (Mat. 3:11; Acts 2:4).

THE LORD'S SUPPER

As Water Baptism does not save anyone, likewise, neither does the rite or ceremony regarding the Lord's Supper save anyone.

As Water Baptism is a Symbol of the Death, Burial, and Resurrection of Christ, likewise, the Lord's Supper is similar, with this emphasis, however, being totally on the Crucifixion of Christ. Regrettably, there are millions of people who have based and are basing the entirety of their Salvation on the ceremony of the Lord's Supper. In other words, they think by participating in this Church Ordinance, that such constitutes Salvation. It doesn't, and is not meant to in any capacity. The following is what Paul said regarding this very important subject:

THE REVELATION GIVEN TO PAUL

"For I have received of the Lord that which also I delivered unto you *(refers to the instructions he is about to give concerning the Lord's Supper)*, That the Lord Jesus the *same* night in which He was betrayed took bread *(recalls the sacred occasion)*:

"And when He had given thanks, He broke *it,* and said, Take, eat *(the remarkable thing about this is the interpretation our Lord gives)*: this is My Body, which is broken for you *(is meant to symbolize the Death of Christ on the Cross)*: this do in remembrance of Me. *(This pertains to the Believer actually partaking of that Sacrifice by Faith. In brief, this is the meaning of the New Covenant.)*

"After the same manner also *He took* the cup, when He had supped, saying, This cup is the New Testament in My Blood *(the New Covenant would be ratified by the shedding of Jesus' Own Blood, which forever satisfied the sin debt)*: this do you, as oft as you drink *it,* in remembrance of Me *(never forgetting what He has done for us, speaking of the Cross)*.

"For as often as you eat this bread, and drink this

cup *(symbolic gestures)*, **you do show the Lord's Death till He come.** *(This is meant to proclaim not only the Atoning Sacrifice necessary for our Salvation, but, as well, as an ongoing cause of our continued victory in life.)*

UNWORTHILY

"Wherefore whosoever shall eat this bread, and drink *this* cup of the Lord, unworthily *(tells us emphatically that this can be done, and is done constantly, I'm afraid)*, **shall be guilty of the Body and Blood of the Lord** *(in danger of Judgment, subject to Judgment).*

"But let a man examine himself *(examine his Faith as to what is its real object)*, **and so let him eat of *that* bread, and drink of *that* cup** *(after careful examination).*

"For he who eats and drinks unworthily, eats and drinks damnation to himself *(does not necessarily mean the loss of one's soul, but rather temporal penalties, which can become much more serious)*, **not discerning the Lord's Body.** *(Not properly discerning the Cross refers to a lack of understanding regarding the Cross. All of this tells us that every single thing we have from the Lord, comes to us exclusively by means of the Cross of Christ. If we do not understand that, we are not properly 'discerning the Lord's Body.')*

"For this cause *(not properly discerning the Lord's Body)* **many** *(a considerable number)* ***are* weak and sickly among you** *(the cause of much sickness among Christians)*, **and many sleep.** *(This means that many Christians die prematurely. They don't lose their souls, but they do cut their lives short. This shows us, I seriously think, how important properly understanding the Cross is.).*

"For if we would judge ourselves *(we should examine ourselves constantly, as to whether our Faith is properly placed in the Cross of Christ), we should not be judged (with sickness, and even premature death)*" **(I Cor. 11:23-31).**

WHAT THE HOLY SPIRIT IS TELLING US

• Emphatically, the Holy Spirit through Paul is telling us that before we partake of the Lord's Supper, that we should *"examine ourselves."*

• To eat or drink unworthily means that we have our faith in something other than Christ and Him Crucified.

• The Lord does not require sinless perfection in order for us to partake of this Ordinance. But He does require, and unequivocally so, that our Faith be exclusively in Christ and what He did for us at the Cross.

• Failing to do this, can cause Believers to be sickly in a physical sense, and can even bring on premature death. As stated in the notes, such will not cause one to lose one's soul, but it will cut one's life short.

The Lord's Supper is a beautiful Ordinance, typifying the death of our Saviour in the giving of Himself as a Sacrifice which brings to us Eternal Life, at least to those who will believe. It must never be altered, changed, or ignored. That's why Paul said and emphatically so, *"We preach Christ Crucified . . ."* (I Cor. 1:23).